T0329832

Thinking Clearly with Data

Thinking Clearly with Data

A Guide to Quantitative Reasoning
and Analysis

ETHAN BUENO DE MESQUITA
ANTHONY FOWLER

PRINCETON UNIVERSITY PRESS
Princeton and Oxford

Published by Princeton University Press
41 William Street, Princeton, New Jersey 08540
6 Oxford Street, Woodstock, Oxfordshire OX20 1TR

press.princeton.edu

Library of Congress Cataloging-in-Publication Data

Names: Bueno de Mesquita, Ethan, 1974– author. | Fowler, Anthony, author.
Title: Thinking clearly with data : a guide to quantitative reasoning and analysis / Ethan Bueno de Mesquita and Anthony Fowler.
Description: 1st. edition. | Princeton : Princeton University Press, 2021. | Includes index.
Identifiers: LCCN 2021011897 (print) | LCCN 2021011898 (ebook) | ISBN 9780691214368 (hardback) | ISBN 9780691214351 (paperback) | ISBN 9780691215013 (epub)
Subjects: LCSH: Sociology–Statistical methods. | Sociology–Methodology.
Classification: LCC HM535 .B84 2021 (print) | LCC HM535 (ebook) | DDC 302.01/5195–dc23
LC record available at https://lccn.loc.gov/2021011897
LC ebook record available at https://lccn.loc.gov/2021011898

British Library Cataloging-in-Publication Data is available

Editorial: Bridget Flannery-McCoy, Alena Chekanov
Jacket/Cover Design: Wanda España
Production: Erin Suydam
Publicity: Kate Hensley
Copyeditor: Elizabeth J. Asborno

Cover image: Igor Kisselev / Alamy Stock Vector

This book has been composed in Minion Pro

10 9 8 7 6 5 4 3 2 1

Ethan: for Abe and Hannah

Anthony: for Gloria

Short Contents

Contents

Preface

The world has changed in transformative ways. Data and evidence are ubiquitous. Quantitative information suffuses our talk of everything from policy to health care to job searches to politics to sports to education to dating to national security.

As a result, statistics and quantitative reasoning must no longer be the purview of only those who have a knack for mathematics or are headed for technical careers. Acquiring competence in foundational quantitative reasoning is now a fundamental responsibility of every educated human being and citizen. And this necessitates new ways of teaching and learning.

It was with that goal in mind that we decided to write *Thinking Clearly with Data*. But we didn't start with the book. Much of the material and ideas that ultimately found their way into the coming chapters were first developed for courses aimed at providing to students with little technical background the tools needed to be serious, thoughtful, and skeptical consumers of quantitative information. These courses include traditional university offerings, like introductions to quantitative reasoning taught to both undergraduate and graduate students at the University of Chicago. But they also include executive education courses offered to policy makers, military officers, national security experts, intelligence professionals, and journalists.

We learned a lot of lessons along the way that inform the choices we made in writing and organizing this book. Perhaps the most important was to create a shared language.

We knew we didn't want to teach a traditional statistics course. Such courses, in our view, are often too technical for many students and don't get to the most important and interesting issues, the ones that really matter for using quantitative information to make our lives and the world better. So, it was tempting to jump as quickly as possible to the exciting topics, like why correlation doesn't imply causation. But that would have been a mistake. A person can't understand why correlation doesn't imply causation until they understand what correlation and causation are.

For that reason, part 1 of this book is all about establishing a shared language. We define, conceptually and technically (but still accessibly), what we mean when we talk about correlation and causation—not in the sense of how to calculate a correlation coefficient or how to write down a causal effect in potential outcomes notation (though both will be covered), but in the sense of the questions, What do the words, properly understood and digested, mean in plain English? What's hard about correlation and causation? Why are they usefully separated? What are these two kinds of things, correlations and causal relationships, good for?

But what about the problem of motivation? If you don't put the good stuff up front, how do you keep people engaged? Well, first, who says a conceptual understanding of what causality does and does not mean isn't the good stuff? It is great stuff. But, more to the point, our approach is this: if you want people to be engaged, make the material engaging. To us, this means several things.

The first is to tell stories. Throughout, you will find every conceptual discussion augmented by at least one extended, genuine, real-world example. Some of those examples will be about scientific studies. Many will be about personal experiences of ours where thinking clearly about quantitative evidence made a difference in the decisions we made. Others will involve reflections on the use of data and evidence in news, sports, policy, health care, and culture. This stuff really matters for how lives are lived and decisions are made in every realm of human endeavor. We want to keep that fact in the foreground. That is also why, despite the fact that this is a book by two political scientists, many of the examples are not drawn from politics.

The second way to engage readers is to emphasize ideas first and technicalities second. We love technicalities. But technicality can often be the enemy of understanding. When things get technical, lots of people stop thinking and start memorizing. We fervently wish to avoid that. So we always talk about the ideas and why they matter first. We treat things graphically whenever we can. And we do as little math as possible. But as little as possible isn't zero, for at least two reasons.

Familiarity with some technical matters is part of being a clear thinker. You can't understand mean reversion if you don't know what a mean or noise is. You can't understand publication bias and the replication crisis if you don't know what *statistical significance* means or what a *p*-value is. And it is hard to understand the problem of confounding or the answers offered by different research designs without being able to interpret a regression.

Moreover, sometimes being clear and precise requires a bit of math. We spend lots of time talking conceptually about counterfactuals and causality. But counterfactual talk can get a bit mystical. There is an extra degree of clarity that comes from writing down some potential outcomes and a proper definition of an effect that we think is indispensable. So we do not dispense with it. But, always, our emphasis is on clear thinking.

A third lesson for engaging writing is that it isn't enough for each chapter or lesson to tell a story. The whole course (or book) must do so. For us, the story is that making good decisions and doing good in our data-driven age requires clear thinking from each and every one of us. We can't just leave it to the experts, for many experts were never taught to think clearly about quantitative information. So we have to do it for ourselves or we will be frequently misled and may well make terrible mistakes.

Organization

That story informs the organization of the book. As we already noted, we open in part 1 by creating a shared language, focusing on the ideas of correlation and causation as the cornerstones of quantitative analysis.

With those ideas in hand, part 2 focuses on how we use data and evidence to figure out whether a correlation, causal or not, exists between features of the world. One of our goals in this part of the book is to convince everyone that there is plenty of good stuff, even before causal inference. Chapter 4 gets us motivated by explaining the incredibly common mistake of selecting on the dependent variable, by showing how trying to establish correlation without variation is impossible, and by illustrating the staggering number of instances when this mistake really matters. Chapter 5 turns to measuring correlations, focusing on a graphical explanation of regression. Chapter 6 introduces statistical significance and hypothesis testing, framing everything in terms of a device we call our favorite equation, which recurs throughout the book:

$$\text{Estimate} = \text{Estimand} + \text{Bias} + \text{Noise}$$

If chapter 4 didn't already achieve this goal, chapter 7 makes it clear that there is plenty at stake in thinking clearly about what it means to establish a relationship in data by discussing the problems of p-hacking, publication bias, and related issues. Finally, chapter 8 covers the under-discussed topic of reversion to the mean and then uses it in conjunction with our prior discussion of publication bias to reflect on the replication crisis and the common phenomenon of scientific estimates shrinking over time.

Part 3 turns to causal inference, reminding readers of how important knowledge of causality is for making decisions about how to intervene in the world. Chapter 9 explains why correlation need not imply causation, discussing both confounders and reverse causality. Chapter 10 addresses the issue of statistical controls and provides some graphical explanations in the context of regression. Chapters 11–13 provide an overview of how scholars use research designs to try to learn about causality. Chapter 11 covers both randomized and natural experiments, introducing instrumental variables as a method for dealing with issues of noncompliance. Chapters 12 and 13 cover regression discontinuity and difference-in-differences designs, respectively. Chapter 14 closes this part of the book with a discussion of the challenges of learning about causal mechanisms.

Part 4 points out that we are not done once we've tackled causality. Even reliable knowledge of causal effects is not, on its own, sufficient to ensure that we are thinking clearly about how to use quantitative information to make good decisions. Chapter 15 points out how easy it is to fool yourself into thinking that a piece of quantitative information that answers one question in fact answers an entirely different one, encouraging readers to avoid this mistake by translating information presented technically into substance. In the course of so doing, we introduce Bayes' rule. Chapter 16 turns to issues of measurement, external validity, and extrapolation, which also leads us into a discussion of sample selection bias. And, finally, chapter 17 confronts some of the fundamental limits that quantitative analysis, no matter how clearly thought about, faces in informing decision making.

At the end of each chapter, there are exercises that readers can work through on their own to make sure they are grasping the material. Some of these exercises involve analyzing data, which can be tackled by readers and students who have learned (or are learning) how to use statistical software like Stata or R. The end of each chapter also has a "Readings and References" section that will allow curious readers to find the sources that are mentioned in the main text and dive more deeply into a particular topic.

Who Is This Book For?

We hope this book is for everybody interested in learning to think clearly about data, evidence, and quantitative reasoning. As we've mentioned, we have used these materials for a wide range of audiences, from undergraduates to highly accomplished professionals.

In our view, to prepare for living in our data-driven age, every undergraduate should meet material like this, ideally in their first couple of years of college. So we wrote the book in the hope that it would be helpful to instructors in many different disciplines who teach quantitative reasoning, whether in general education courses or in an introductory course inside a department. We believe this will be especially true for instructors who want to take an approach that is more conceptual than the traditional statistics- or methods-based approach, while still covering some fundamental technical content.

We think the book works equally well for professional students. We have taught it to graduate students earning master's degrees in public policy. Some go on to take more technical courses in econometrics or program evaluation. But, for many, the essential skill is to learn to think critically and clearly about quantitative information. Our approach fits the needs of these students while, at the same time, providing the conceptual foundations that more technically inclined students will need in future courses.

Colleagues at other universities have also employed these materials in more advanced courses for social science majors who, for instance, must learn quantitative methods in preparation for writing a thesis. In that setting, our book may benefit from being coupled with another text that is somewhat more technical or places more emphasis on issues of statistical computing. In all of these settings, we hope the exercises at the end of each chapter will be helpful. These include applied data analyses, for which data are available to download online.

Finally, we also believe this book will be useful to many doctoral students. Often, in doctoral training, statistical material is taught quickly and at a high level of technicality. This can be productive; mastering advanced techniques is both challenging and important. But, in our experience, even the best doctoral students can lose sight of what really matters—how we learn about the world from data—as they focus on proving theorems and programming estimators. We very much hope that this book might serve as a guide to such students, helping to keep the big picture in clear view even as they work hard on the technical details.

Acknowledgments

As we mentioned, some of the materials in this book were developed as a joint effort for an undergraduate class of Anthony's and for an executive education class that Jake Shapiro, Liam Collins, Cathy Fetell, and Ethan designed together. Jake, Liam, and Cathy are due lots of credit and have our deep appreciation.

We'd like to thank Scott Ashworth, Chris Berry, Chris Blattman, Matt Brems, Bruce Bueno de Mesquita, Kerwin Charles, Devin Chesney, Lindsey Cormack, Andy Eggers, Nathan Favero, Alex Fouirnaies, Matt Gabel, Jeff Grogger, Andy Hall, Kosuke Imai, Renan Levine, Andrew Little, Jens Ludwig, Mordecai Magencey, Andrew Means, Pablo Montagnes, Emily Ritter, Steve Schwab, Mike Spagat, Dustin Tingley, Stephane Wolton, and Austin Wright for their incredibly helpful feedback.

Tom Budescu, Gautam Nair, Tom Naset, Jeff Ruff, Vanitha Virudachalam, Becky Wang, and Xingyu Yin provided terrific research assistance at the early stages of putting this project together. It was great fun to work with them and we are grateful for their contributions.

We'd like to thank our students for catching numerous mistakes and errors in previous drafts. AK Alilonu, Denise Azadeh, Ellie Rutkey, and Al Shah found a truly embarrassing number of them. Thank you!

The team at Princeton University Press was terrific. We are especially appreciative of Bridget Flannery-McCoy for believing in the project and for her guidance and to Alena Chekanov for overseeing so much of the process. And we owe a debt of gratitude to

Danna Lockwood for her incredible work helping us improve the writing, presentation, and organization of the book. We also very much appreciate Melody Negron's terrific oversight of production and David Luljak's always excellent indexing.

Ethan would like to thank his colleagues at the Harris School and his many collaborators, coauthors, and students, all of whom are an intellectual inspiration and have improved the clarity of his own thinking with years of heroic effort. He is deeply grateful to his wife, Rebecca, who put up with the grumpiness that inevitably accompanies finishing a book with the support, love, and patience with which she meets all the joys of life with Ethan. This one is dedicated to his kids, Hannah and Abe, who are a joy and a pleasure. His fondest hope is that this book will find its way into enough classrooms that, one day, they might have the mortifying experience of being assigned to read a book dedicated to themselves. That would be quantifiable success.

Anthony would like to thank his advisors, coauthors, and colleagues who make him a clearer thinker with every interaction. He is grateful to his parents, who have have encouraged and supported him throughout his life, even though he currently has no plans to go to law school or medical school. And most importantly, he thanks Gloria, his wife and best friend, who has read countless drafts of academic papers, endured far too many conversations about regressions, dabbled in data entry, vetted every idea, contributed a disproportionate share of her own, and enriched his life in ways that defy quantification.

CHAPTER 1

Thinking Clearly in a Data-Driven Age

What You'll Learn

- Learning to think clearly and conceptually about quantitative information is important for lots of reasons, even if you have no interest in a career as a data analyst.
- Even well-trained people often make crucial errors with data.
- Thinking and data are complements, not substitutes.
- The skills you learn in this book will help you use evidence to make better decisions in your personal and professional life and be a more thoughtful and well-informed citizen.

Introduction

We live in a data-driven age. According to former Google CEO Eric Schmidt, the contemporary world creates as much new data every two days as had been created from the beginning of time through the year 2003. All this information is supposed to have the power to improve our lives, but to harness this power we must learn to think clearly about our data-driven world. Clear thinking is hard—especially when mixed up with all the technical details that typically surround data and data analysis.

Thinking clearly in a data-driven age is, first and foremost, about staying focused on ideas and questions. Technicality, though important, should serve those ideas and questions. Unfortunately, the statistics and quantitative reasoning classes in which most people learn about data do exactly the opposite—that is, they focus on technical details. Students learn mathematical formulas, memorize the names of statistical procedures, and start crunching numbers without ever having been asked to think clearly and conceptually about what they are doing or why they are doing it. Such an approach can work for people to whom thinking mathematically comes naturally. But we believe it is counterproductive for the vast majority of us. When technicality pushes students to stop thinking and start memorizing, they miss the forest for the trees. And it's also no fun.

Our focus, by contrast, is on conceptual understanding. What features of the world are you comparing when you analyze data? What questions can different kinds of comparisons answer? Do you have the right question and comparison for the problem you are trying to solve? Why might an answer that sounds convincing actually be misleading? How might you use creative approaches to provide a more informative answer?

It isn't that we don't think the technical details are important. Rather, we believe that technique without conceptual understanding or clear thinking is a recipe for disaster. In our view, once you can think clearly about quantitative analysis, and once you understand why asking careful and precise questions is so important, technique will follow naturally. Moreover, this way is more fun.

In this spirit, we've written this book to require no prior exposure to data analysis, statistics, or quantitative methods. Because we believe conceptual thinking is more important, we've minimized (though certainly not eliminated) technical material in favor of plain-English explanations wherever possible. Our hope is that this book will be used as an introduction and a guide to how to think about and do quantitative analysis. We believe anyone can become a sophisticated consumer (and even producer) of quantitative information. It just takes some patience, perseverance, hard work, and a firm resolve to never allow technicality to be a substitute for clear thinking.

Most people don't become professional quantitative analysts. But whether you do or do not, we are confident you will use the skills you learn in this book in a variety of ways. Many of you will have quantitative analysts working for or with you. And all of you will read studies, news reports, and briefings in which someone tries to convince you of a conclusion using quantitative analyses. This book will equip you with the clear thinking skills necessary to ask the right questions, be skeptical when appropriate, and distinguish between useful and misleading evidence.

Cautionary Tales

To whet your appetite for the hard work ahead, let's start with a few cautionary tales that highlight the importance of thinking clearly in a data-driven age.

Abe's Hasty Diagnosis

Ethan's first child, Abe, was born in July 2006. As a baby, he screamed and cried almost non-stop at night for five months. Abe was otherwise happy and healthy, though a bit on the small side. When he was one year old the family moved to Chicago, without which move, you'd not be reading this book. (That last sentence contains a special kind of claim called a *counterfactual*. Counterfactuals are really important, and you are going to learn all about them in chapter 3.) After noticing that Abe was small for his age and growing more slowly than expected, his pediatrician decided to run some tests.

After some lab work, the doctors were pretty sure Abe had celiac disease—a digestive disease characterized by gluten intolerance. The good news: celiac disease is not life threatening or even terribly serious if properly managed through diet. The bad news: in 2007, the gluten-free dietary options for kids were pretty miserable.

It turns out that Abe actually had two celiac-related blood tests. One came back positive (indicating that he had the disease), the other negative (indicating that he did not have the disease). According to the doctors, the positive test was over 80 percent accurate. "This is a strong diagnosis," they said. The suggested course of action was to put Abe on a gluten-free diet for a couple of months to see if his weight increased. If it did, they could either do a more definitive biopsy or simply keep Abe gluten-free for the rest of his life.

Ethan asked for a look at the report on Abe's bloodwork. The doctors indicated they didn't think that would be useful since Ethan isn't a doctor. This response was neither surprising nor hard to understand. People, especially experts and authority figures, often don't like acknowledging the limits of their knowledge. But Ethan wanted to make the right decision for his son, so he pushed hard for the information. One of the goals of this book is to give you some of the skills and confidence to be your own advocate in this way when using information to make decisions in your life.

Two numbers characterize the effectiveness of any diagnostic test. The first is its false negative rate, which is how frequently the test says a sick person is healthy. The second is its false positive rate, which is how frequently the test says a healthy person is sick. You need to know *both* the false positive rate and the false negative rate to interpret a diagnostic test's results. So Abe's doctors' statement that the positive blood test was 80 percent accurate wasn't very informative. Did that mean it had a 20 percent false negative rate? A 20 percent false positive rate? Do 80 percent of people who test positive have celiac disease?

Fortunately, a quick Google search turned up both the false positive and false negative rates for both of Abe's tests. Here's what Ethan learned. The test on which Abe came up positive for celiac disease has a false negative rate of about 20 percent. That is, if 100 people with celiac disease took the test, about 80 of them would correctly test positive and the other 20 would incorrectly test negative. This fact, we assume, is where the claim of 80 percent accuracy came from. The test, however, has a false positive rate of 50 percent! People who don't have celiac disease are just as likely to test positive as they are to test negative. (This test, it is worth noting, is no longer recommended for diagnosing celiac disease.) In contrast, the test on which Abe came up negative for celiac disease had much lower false negative and false positive rates.

Before getting the test results, a reasonable estimate of the probability of Abe having celiac disease, given his small size, was around 1 in 100. That is, about 1 out of every 100 small kids has celiac disease. Armed with the lab reports and the false positive and false negative rates, Ethan was able to calculate how likely Abe was to have celiac disease given his small size and the test results. Amazingly, the combination of testing positive on an inaccurate test and testing negative on an accurate test actually meant that the evidence suggested that Abe was much *less* likely than 1 in 100 to have celiac disease. In fact, as we will show you in chapter 15, the best estimate of the likelihood of Abe having celiac, given the test results, was about 1 in 1,000. The blood tests that Abe's doctors were sure supported the celiac diagnosis actually strongly supported the opposite conclusion. Abe was almost certain not to have celiac disease.

Ethan called the doctors to explain what he'd learned and to suggest that moving his pasta-obsessed son to a gluten-free diet, perhaps for life, was not the prudent next step. Their response: "A diagnosis like this can be hard to hear." Ethan found a new pediatrician.

Here's the upshot. Abe did not have celiac disease. The kid was just a bit small. Today he is a normal-sized kid with a ravenous appetite. But if his father didn't know how to think about quantitative evidence or lacked the confidence to challenge a mistaken expert, he'd have spent his childhood eating rice cakes. Rice cakes are gross, so he might still be small.

Civil Resistance

As many around the world have experienced, citizens often find themselves in deep disagreement with their government. When things get bad enough, they sometimes decide to organize protests. If you ever find yourself doing such organizing, you will face many important decisions. Perhaps none is more important than whether to build a movement with a non-violent strategy or one open to a strategy involving more vio-lent forms of confrontation. In thinking through this quandry, you will surely want to consult your personal ethics. But you might also want to know what the evidence says about the costs and benefits of each approach. Which kind of organization is most likely to succeed in changing government behavior? Is one or the other approach more likely to land you in prison, the hospital, or the morgue?

There is some quantitative evidence that you might use to inform your decisions. First, comparing anti-government movements across the globe and over time, govern-ments more often make concessions to fully non-violent groups than to groups that use violence. And even comparing across groups that do use violence, governments more frequently make concessions to those groups that engage in violence against military and government targets rather than against civilians. Second, the personal risks asso-ciated with violent protest are greater than those associated with non-violent protest. Governments repress violent uprisings more often than they do non-violent protests, making concerns about prison, the hospital, and the morgue more acute.

This evidence sounds quite convincing. A non-violent strategy seems the obvi-ous choice. It is apparently both more effective and less risky. And, indeed, on the basis of this kind of data, political scientists Erica Chenoweth and Evan Perkoski con-clude that "planning, training, and preparation to maintain nonviolent discipline is key—especially (and paradoxically) when confronting brutal regimes."

But let's reconsider the evidence. Start by asking yourself, In what kind of a setting is a group likely to engage in non-violent rather than violent protest? A few thoughts occur to us. Perhaps people are more likely to engage in non-violent protest when they face a government that they think is particularly likely to heed the demands of its citizens. Or perhaps people are more likely to engage in non-violent protest when they have broad-based support among their fellow citizens, represent a group in society that can attract media attention, or face a less brutal government.

If any of these things are true, we should worry about the claim that maintaining non-violent discipline is key to building a successful anti-government movement. (Which isn't to say that we are advocating violence.) Let's see why.

Empirical studies find that, on average, governments more frequently make con-cessions in places that had non-violent, rather than violent, protests. The claimed implication rests on a particular interpretation of that difference—namely, that the higher frequency of government concessions in non-violent places is *caused* by the use of non-violent tactics. Put differently, all else held equal, if a given movement using vio-lent methods had switched to using non-violent methods, the government would have been more likely to grant concessions. But is this causal interpretation really justified by the evidence?

Suppose it's the case that protest movements are more likely to turn to violence when they do not have broad-based support among their fellow citizens. Then, when we com-pare places that had violent protests to places that had non-violent protests, all else (other than protest tactics) is not held equal. Those places differ in at least two ways. First, they differ in terms of whether they had violent or non-violent protests. Second, they differ in terms of how supportive the public was of the protest movement.

This second difference is a problem for the causal interpretation. You might imagine that public opinion has an independent effect on the government's willingness to grant concessions. That is, all else held equal (including protest tactics), governments might be more willing to grant concessions to protest movements with broad-based public support. If this is the case, then we can't really know whether the fact that governments grant concessions more often to non-violent protest movements than to violent protest movements is because of the difference in protest tactics or because the non-violent movements also happen to be the movements with broad-based public support. This is the classic problem of mistaking correlation for causation.

It is worth noting a few things. First, if government concessions are in fact due to public opinion, then it could be the case that, were we actually able to hold all else equal in our comparison of violent and non-violent protests, we would find the opposite relationship—that is, that non-violence is not more effective than violence (it could even be less effective). Given this kind of evidence, we just can't know.

Second, in this example, the conclusion that appears to follow if you don't force yourself to think clearly is one we would all like to be true. Who among us would not like to live in a world where non-violence is always preferred to violence? But the whole point of using evidence to help us make decisions is to force us to confront the possibility that the world may not be as we believe or hope it is. Indeed, it is in precisely those situations where the evidence seems to say exactly what you would like it to say that it is particularly important to force yourself to think clearly.

Third, we've pointed to one challenge in assessing the effects of peaceful versus violent protest, but there are others. For instance, think about the other empirical claim we discussed: that violent protests are more likely to provoke the government into repressive crack-downs than are non-violent protests. Recall, we suggested that people might be more likely to engage in non-violent protest when they are less angry at their government, perhaps because the government is less brutal. Ask yourself why, if this is true, we have a similar problem of interpretation. Why might the fact that there are more government crack-downs following violent protests than non-violent protests *not* mean that switching from violence to non-violence will reduce the risk of crack-downs? The argument follows a similar logic to the one we just made regarding concessions. If you don't see how the argument works yet, that's okay. You will by the end of chapter 9.

Broken-Windows Policing

In 1982, the criminologist George L. Kelling and the sociologist James Q. Wilson published an article in *The Atlantic* proposing a new theory of crime and policing that had enormous and long-lasting effects on crime policy in the United States and beyond.

Kelling and Wilson's theory is called *broken windows*. It was inspired by a program in Newark, New Jersey, that got police out of their cars and walking a beat. According to Kelling and Wilson, the program reduced crime by elevating "the level of public order." Public order is important, they argue, because its absence sets in motion a vicious cycle:

> A piece of property is abandoned, weeds grow up, a window is smashed. Adults stop scolding rowdy children…Families move out, unattached adults move in. Teenagers gather in front of the corner store. The merchant asks them to move; they refuse. Fights occur. Litter accumulates. People start drinking in front of the grocery…
>
> Residents will think that crime, especially violent crime, is on the rise…They will use the streets less often…Such an area is vulnerable to criminal invasion.

This idea that policing focused on minimizing disorder can reduce violent crime had a big impact on police tactics. Most prominently, the broken-windows theory was the guiding philosophy in New York City in the 1990s. In a 1998 speech, then New York mayor Rudy Giuliani said,

> We have made the "Broken Windows" theory an integral part of our law enforcement strategy...
>
> You concentrate on the little things, and send the clear message that this City cares about maintaining a sense of law and order...then the City as a whole will begin to become safer.

And, indeed, crime in New York city did decline when the police started focusing "on the little things." According to a study by Hope Corman and H. Naci Mocan, misdemeanor arrests increased 70 percent during the 1990s and violent crime decreased by more than 56 percent, double the national average.

To assess the extent to which broken-windows policing was responsible for this fall in crime, Kelling and William Sousa studied the relationship between violent crime and broken-windows approaches across New York City's precincts. If minimizing disorder causes a reduction in violent crime, they argued, then we should expect the largest reductions in crime to have occurred in neighborhoods where the police were most focused on the broken-windows approach. And this is just what they found. In precincts where misdemeanor arrests (the "little things") were higher, violent crime decreased more. They calculated that "the average NYPD precinct...could expect to suffer one less violent crime for approximately every 28 additional misdemeanor arrests."

This sounds pretty convincing. But let's not be too quick to conclude that arresting people for misdemeanors is the answer to ending violent crime. Two other scholars, Bernard Harcourt and Jens Ludwig, encourage us to think a little more clearly about what might be going on in the data.

The issue that Harcourt and Ludwig point out is something called *reversion to the mean* (which we'll talk about a lot more in chapter 8). Here's the basic concern. In any given year, the amount of crime in a precinct is determined by lots of factors, including policing, drugs, the economy, the weather, and so on. Many of those factors are unknown to us. Some of them are fleeting; they come and go across precincts from year to year. As such, in any given precinct, we can think of there being some "baseline" level of crime, with some years randomly having more crime and some years randomly having less (relative to that precinct-specific baseline).

In any given year, if a precinct had a high level of crime (relative to its baseline), then it had bad luck on the unknown and fleeting factors that help cause crime. Probably next year its luck won't be as bad (that's what *fleeting* means), so that precinct will likely have less crime. And if a precinct had a low level of crime (relative to its baseline) this year, then it had good luck on the unknown and fleeting factors, and it will probably have worse luck next year (crime will go back up). Thus, year to year, the crime level in a precinct tends to revert toward the *mean* (i.e., the precinct's baseline level of crime).

Now, imagine a precinct that had a really high level of violent crime in the late 1980s. Two things are likely to be true of that precinct. First, it is probably a precinct with a high baseline of violent crime. Second, it is also probably a precinct that had a bad year or two—that is, for idiosyncratic and fleeting reasons, the level of crime in the late 1980s was high relative to that precinct's baseline. The same, of course, is true in reverse for precincts that had a low level of crime in the late 1980s. They probably have a low baseline of crime, and they also probably had a particularly good couple of years.

Why is this a problem for Kelling and Sousa's conclusions? Because of reversion to the mean, we would expect the most violent precincts in the late 1980s to show a reduction in violent crime on average, even with no change in policing. And unsurprisingly, given the police's objectives, but unfortunately for the study, it was precisely those high-crime precincts in the 1980s that were most likely to get broken-windows policing in the early 1990s. So, when we see a reduction in violent crime in the precincts that had the most broken-windows policing, we don't know if it's the policing strategy or reversion to the mean that's at work.

Harcourt and Ludwig go a step further to try to find more compelling evidence. Roughly speaking, they look at how changes in misdemeanor arrests relate to changes in violent crime in precincts that had similar levels of violent crime in the late 1980s. By comparing precincts with similar starting levels of violent crime, they go some way toward eliminating the problem of reversion to the mean. Surprisingly, this simple change actually flips the relationship! Rather than confirming Kelling and Sousa's finding that misdemeanor arrests are associated with a reduction in violent crime, Harcourt and Ludwig find that precincts that focused more on misdemeanor arrests actually appear to have experienced an *increase* in violent crime. Exactly the opposite of what we would expect if the broken-windows theory is correct.

Now, this reversal doesn't settle the matter on the efficacy of broken-windows policing. The relationship between misdemeanor arrests and violent crime that Harcourt and Ludwig find could be there for lots of reasons other than misdemeanor arrests causing an increase in violent crime. For instance, perhaps the neighborhoods with increasing misdemeanors are becoming less safe in general and would have experienced more violent crime regardless of policing strategies. What these results do show is that the data, properly considered, certainly don't offer the kind of unequivocal confirmation of the broken-windows ideas that you might have thought from Kelling and Sousa's finding. And you can only see this if you have the ability to think clearly about some subtle issues.

This flawed thinking was important. Evidence-based arguments like Kelling and Sousa's played a role in convincing politicians and policy makers that broken-windows policing was the right path forward when, in fact, it might have diverted resources away from preventing and investigating violent crime and may have created a more adversarial and unjust relationship between the police and the disproportionately poor and minority populations who were frequently cited for "the small stuff."

Thinking and Data Are Complements, Not Substitutes

Our quantitative world is full of lots of exciting new data and analytic tools to analyze that data with fancy names like machine learning algorithms, artificial intelligence, random forests, and neural networks. Increasingly, we are even told that this new technology will make it possible for the machines to do the thinking for us. But that isn't right. As our cautionary tales highlight, no data analysis, no matter how futuristic its name, will work if we aren't asking the right questions, if we aren't making the right comparisons, if the underlying assumptions aren't sound, or if the data used aren't appropriate. Just because an argument contains seemingly sophisticated quantitative data analysis, that doesn't mean the argument is rigorous or right. To harness the power of data to make better decisions, we must combine quantitative analysis with clear thinking.

Our stories also illustrate how our intuitions can lead us astray. It takes lots of care and practice to train ourselves to think clearly about evidence. The doctors' intuition that Abe had celiac disease because of a test with 80 percent accuracy and the researchers' intuition that broken-windows policing works because crime decreased in places where it was deployed seem sensible. But both intuitions were wrong, suggesting that we should be skeptical of our initial hunches. The good news is that clear thinking can become intuitive if you work at it.

Data and quantitative tools are not a substitute for clear thinking. In fact, quantitative skills without clear thinking are quite dangerous. We suspect, as you read the coming chapters, you will be jarred by the extent to which unclear thinking affects even the most important decisions people make. Through the course of this book, we will see how misinterpreted information distorts life-and-death medical choices, national and international counterterrorism policies, business and philanthropic decisions made by some of the world's wealthiest people, how we set priorities for our children's education, and a host of other issues from the banal to the profound. Essentially, no aspect of life is immune from critical mistakes in understanding and interpreting quantitative information.

In our experience, this is because unclear thinking about evidence is deeply ingrained in human psychology. Certainly our own intuitions, left unchecked, are frequently subject to basic errors. Our guess is that yours are too. Most disturbingly, the experts on whose advice you depend—be they doctors, business consultants, journalists, teachers, financial advisors, scientists, or what have you—are often just as prone to making such errors as the rest of us. All too often, because they are experts, we trust their judgment without question, and so do they. That is why it is so important to learn to think clearly about quantitative evidence for yourself. That is the only way to know how to ask the right questions that lead you, and those on whose advice you depend, to the most reliable and productive conclusions possible.

How could experts in so many fields make important errors so often? Expertise, in any area, comes from training, practice, and experience. No one expects to become an expert in engineering, finance, plumbing, or medicine without instruction and years of work. But, despite its fundamental and increasing importance for so much of life in our quantitative age, almost no one invests this kind of effort into learning to think clearly with data. And, as we've said, even when they do, they tend to be taught in a way that over-emphasizes the technical and under-emphasizes the conceptual, even though the fundamental problems are almost always about conceptual mistakes in thinking rather than technical mistakes in calculation.

The lack of expertise in thinking presents us with two challenges. First, if so much expert advice and analysis is unreliable, how do you know what to believe? Second, how can you identify those expert opinions that do in fact reflect clear thinking?

This book provides a framework for addressing these challenges. Each of the coming chapters explains and illustrates, through a variety of examples, fundamental principles of clear thinking in a data-driven world. Part 1 establishes some shared language—clarifying what we mean by correlation and causation and what each is useful for. Part 2 discusses how we can tell whether a statistical relationship is genuine. Part 3 discusses how we can tell if that relationship reflects a causal phenomenon or not. And part 4 discusses how we should and shouldn't incorporate quantitative information into our decision making.

Our hope is that reading this book will help you internalize the principles of clear thinking in a deep enough way that they start to become second nature. You will know you are on the right path when you find yourself noticing basic mistakes in how people think and talk about the meaning of evidence everywhere you turn—as you watch the news, peruse magazines, talk to business associates, visit the doctor, listen to the color commentary during athletic competitions, read scientific studies, or participate in school, church, or other communal activities. You will, we suspect, find it difficult to believe how much nonsense you're regularly told by all kinds of experts. When this starts to happen, try to remain humble and constructive in your criticisms. But do feel free to share your copy of this book with those whose arguments you find are in particular need of it. Or better yet, encourage them to buy their own copy!

Readings and References

The essay on non-violent protest by Erica Chenoweth and Evan Perkoski that we quote can be found at https://politicalviolenceataglance.org/2018/05/08/states-are-far-less-likely-to-engage-in-mass-violence-against-nonviolent-uprisings-than-violent-uprisings/.

The following book contains more research on the relationship between non-violence and efficacy:

Erica Chenoweth and Maria J. Stephan. 2011. *Why Civil Resistance Works: The Strategic Logic of Nonviolent Conflict*. Columbia University Press.

The following articles were discussed in this order on the topic of broken windows policing:

George L. Kelling and James Q. Wilson. 1982. "Broken Windows: The Police and Neighborhood Safety." *The Atlantic*. March https://www.theatlantic.com/magazine/archive/1982/03/broken-windows/304465/.

Archives of Rudolph W. Giuliani. 1998. "The Next Phase of Quality of Life: Creating a More Civil City." February 24. http://www.nyc.gov/html/rwg/html/98a/quality.html.

Hope Corman and H. Naci Mocan. 2005. "Carrots, Sticks, and Broken Windows." *Journal of Law and Economics* 48(1):235–66.

George L. Kelling and William H. Sousa, Jr. 2001. Do Police Matter? An Analysis of the Impact of New York City's Police Reforms. Civic Report for the Center for Civic Innovation at the Manhattan Institute.

Bernard E. Harcourt and Jens Ludwig. 2006. "Broken Windows: New Evidence from New York City and a Five-City Social Experiment." *University of Chicago Law Review* 73:271–320. *The published version has a misprinted sign in the key table. For the correction, see Errata, 74* U. Chi. L. Rev. 407 (2007).

PART I

Establishing a Common Language

CHAPTER 2

Correlation: What Is It and What Is It Good For?

What You'll Learn

- Correlations tell us about the extent to which two features of the world tend to occur together.
- In order to measure correlations, we must have data with variation in both features of the world.
- Correlations *can* be potentially useful for description, forecasting, and causal inference. But we have to think clearly about when they're appropriate for each of these tasks.
- Correlations are about linear relationships, but that's not as limiting as you might think.

Introduction

Correlation doesn't imply causation. That's a good adage. However, in our experience, it's less useful than it might be because, while many people know that correlation doesn't imply causation, hardly anyone knows what correlation and causation are.

In part 1, we are going to spend some time establishing a shared vocabulary. Making sure that we are all using these and a few other key terms to mean the same thing is absolutely critical if we are to think clearly about them in the chapters to come.

This chapter is about correlation: what it is and what it's good for. Correlation is the primary tool through which quantitative analysts describe the world, forecast future events, and answer scientific questions. Careful analysts do not avoid or disregard correlations. But they must think clearly about which kinds of questions correlations can and cannot answer in different situations.

What Is a Correlation?

The *correlation* between two features of the world is the extent to which they tend to occur together. This definition tells us that a correlation is a relationship between two things (which we call *features of the world* or *variables*). If two features of the world tend to occur together, they are *positively correlated*. If the occurrence of one feature of the world is unrelated to the occurrence of another feature of the world, they are *uncorrelated*. And if when one feature of the world occurs the other tends not to occur, they are *negatively correlated*.

Table 2.1. Oil production and type of government.

	Not Major Oil Producer	Major Oil Producer	Total
Democracy	118	9	127
Autocracy	29	11	40
Total	147	20	167

What does it mean for two features of the world to tend to occur together? Let's start with an example of the simplest kind. Suppose we want to assess the correlation between two features of the world, and there are only two possible values for each one (we call these *binary* variables). For instance, whether it is after noon or before noon is a binary variable (by contrast, the time measured in hours, minutes, and seconds is not binary; it can take many more than two values).

Political scientists and economists sometimes talk about the *resource curse* or the *paradox of plenty*. The idea is that countries with an abundance of natural resources are often less economically developed and less democratic than those with fewer natural resources. Natural resources might make a country less likely to invest in other forms of development, or they might make a country more subject to violence and autocracy.

To assess the extent of this resource curse, we might want to know the correlation between natural resources and some feature of the economic or political system. That process starts with collecting some data, which we've done. To measure natural resources we looked at which countries are major oil producers. We classify a country as a major oil producer if it exports more than forty thousand barrels per day per million people. And for the political system we looked at which countries are considered autocracies versus democracies by the Polity IV Project. Table 2.1 indicates how many countries fit into each of the four possible categories: democracy and major oil producer, democracy and not major oil producer, autocracy and major oil producer, and autocracy and not major oil producer.

We can figure out if these two binary variables—being a major oil producer or not and autocracy versus democracy—are correlated by making a comparison. For instance, we could ask whether major oil producers are more likely to be autocracies than countries that aren't major oil producers. Or, similarly, we could ask whether autocracies are more likely to be major oil producers than democracies. If one of these statements is true, the other must be true as well. And these comparisons tell us whether these two features of the world—being a major oil producer and being an autocracy—tend to occur together.

In table 2.1, oil production and autocracy are indeed positively correlated. Fifty-five percent of major oil producers are autocracies ($\frac{11}{20} = .55$) while only about 20 percent of countries that aren't major oil producers are autocracies ($\frac{29}{147} \approx .20$). Equivalently, 27.5 percent of autocracies are major oil producers ($\frac{11}{40} = .275$), while only about 7 percent of democracies are ($\frac{9}{127} \approx .07$). In other words, major oil producers are more likely to be autocracies than are countries that aren't major oil producers, and then, necessarily, autocracies are more likely to be major oil producers than democracies.

As a descriptive matter, we find this positive correlation interesting. It is also potentially useful for prediction. Suppose there were some other countries outside our data

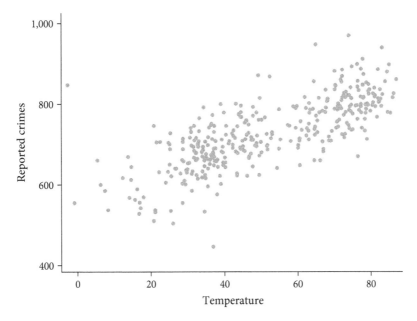

Figure 2.1. Crime and temperature (in degrees Fahrenheit) in Chicago across days in 2018.

whose system of government we were uncertain of. Knowing whether or not they were major oil producers would be helpful in predicting which kind of government they likely have.

Such knowledge could even potentially be useful for causal inference. Perhaps new oil reserves are discovered in a country and the State Department wants to know what effect this is likely to have on the country's political system. This kind of data might be informative about that causal question as well. Though, as we'll discuss in great detail in chapter 9, we must be very careful when giving correlations this sort of causal interpretation.

We can assess correlations even when our data are such that it is hard to make a table of all the possible combinations like we did above. Suppose, for example, that we want to assess the relationship between crime and temperature in Chicago. We could assemble a spreadsheet in which each row corresponds to a day and each column corresponds to a feature of each day. We often call the rows *observations* and the features listed in the columns *variables*. In this case, the observations are different days. One variable could be the average temperature on that day as measured at Midway Airport. Another could be the number of crimes reported in the entire city of Chicago on that day. Another still could indicate whether the *Chicago Tribune* ran a story about crime on its front page on that day. As you can see, variables can take values that are binary (front page story or not), discrete but not binary (number of crimes), or continuous (average temperature).

We collected data like this for Chicago in 2018, and we'd like to assess the correlation between crime and temperature. But how can we assess the correlation between two non-binary variables?

One starting point is to make a simple graph, called a *scatter plot*. Figure 2.1 shows one for our 2018 Chicago data. In it, each point corresponds to an observation in our data—here, that means each point is a day in Chicago in 2018. The horizontal axis of our figure is the average temperature at Midway Airport on that day. The vertical axis

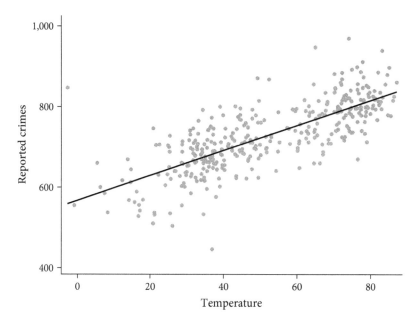

Figure 2.2. A line of best fit summarizing the relationship between crime and temperature (in degrees Fahrenheit) in Chicago across days in 2018.

is the number of crimes reported in the city on that day. So the location of each point shows the average temperature and the amount of crime on a given day.

Just by looking at the figure, you can see that it appears that there is a positive correlation between temperature and crime. Points to the left of the graph on the horizontal axis (colder days) tend to also be pretty low on the vertical axis (lower crime days), and days to right of the graph on the horizontal axis (warmer days) tend to also be pretty high on the vertical axis (higher crime days).

But how can we quantify this visual first impression? There are actually many different statistics that we can use to do so. One such statistic is called the *slope*. Suppose we found *the line of best fit* for the data. By *best fit*, we mean, roughly, the line that minimizes how far the data points are from the line on average. (We will be more precise about this in chapter 5.) The slope of the line of best fit is one way of describing the correlation between these two continuous variables.

Figure 2.2 shows the scatter plot with that line added. The slope of the line tells us something about the relationship between those two variables. If the slope is negative, the correlation is negative. If the slope is zero, temperature and crime are uncorrelated. If the slope is positive, the correlation is positive. And the steepness of the slope tells us about the strength of the correlation between these two variables. Here we see that they are positively correlated—there tends to be more crime on warmer days. In particular, the slope is 3.1, so on average for every additional degree of temperature (in Fahrenheit), there are 3.1 more crimes.

Notice that how you interpret the slope depends on which variable is on the vertical axis and which one is on the horizontal axis. Had we drawn the graph the other way around (as in figure 2.3), we would be describing the relationship between the same two variables. But this time, we would have learned that for every additional

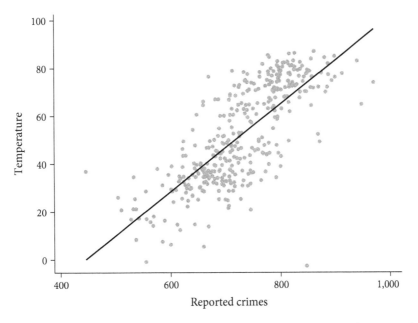

Figure 2.3. A line of best fit summarizing the relationship between temperature and crime in Chicago across days in 2018.

reported crime, on average, the temperature is 0.18 degrees higher. The sign of the slope (positive or negative) is the same regardless of which variable is on the horizontal or vertical axis because changing which variable is on which axis does not change whether they are positively or negatively correlated. But the actual number describing the slope and its substantive interpretation—that is, what it says about the world—has changed.

Fact or Correlation?

In order to establish whether a correlation exists, you must always make a comparison of some kind. For example, to learn about the correlation between temperature and crime, we need to compare hot and cold days and see whether the levels of crime differ, or alternatively, we can compare high- and low-crime days to see if their temperatures differ. This means that to assess the correlation between two variables, we need to have variation in both variables. For example, if we collected data only on days when the average temperature was 0 degrees, we would have no way of assessing the correlation between temperature and crime. And the same is true if we only examined days with five hundred reported crimes.

With this in mind, let's pause to check how clearly you are thinking about what a correlation is and how we learn about one. Don't worry if you aren't all the way there yet. Understanding whether a correlation exists turns out to be tricky. We are going to spend all of chapter 4 on this topic. Nonetheless, it is helpful to do a preliminary check now. So let's give it a try.

Think about the following statements. Which ones describe a correlation, and which ones do not?

1. People who live to be 100 years old typically take vitamins.
2. Cities with more crime tend to hire more police officers.
3. Successful people have spent at least ten thousand hours honing their craft.
4. Most politicians facing a scandal win reelection.
5. Older people vote more than younger people.

While each of these statements reports a fact, not all of those facts describe a correlation—that is, evidence on whether two features of the world tend to occur together. In particular, statements 1, 3, and 4 do not describe correlations, while statements 2 and 5 do. Let's unpack this.

Statements 1, 3, and 4 are facts. They come from data. They sound scientific. And if we added specific numbers to these statements, we could call them *statistics*. But not all facts or statistics describe correlations. The key issue is that these statements do not describe whether or not two features of the world tend to occur together—that is, they do not compare across different values of both features of the world.

To get a sense of this, focus on statement 4:

Most politicians facing a scandal win reelection.

Two features of the world are discussed. The first is whether a politician is facing a scandal. The second is whether the politician successfully wins reelection. The correlation being hinted at is a positive correlation between facing a scandal and winning reelection. But we don't actually learn from this statement of fact whether those two features of the world tend to occur together—that is, we have not compared the rate of reelection for those facing scandal to the rate of reelection for those not facing scandal.

We can assess this correlation, but not with the data described in statement 4. To assess the correlation, we'd need variation in both variables—facing a scandal and winning reelection. Just for fun, let's examine this correlation in some real data on incumbent members of the U.S. House of Representatives seeking reelection between 2006 and 2012. Scott Basinger from the University of Houston has systematically collected data on congressional scandals. Utilizing his data, let's see how many cases fall into four relevant cases: members facing a scandal who were reelected, members facing a scandal who were not reelected, scandal-free members who were reelected, and scandal-free members who were not reelected.

In table 2.2, we see that statement 4 is indeed a fact: 62 out of 70 (about 89%) members of Congress facing a scandal who sought reelection won. But we also see that most members of Congress not facing a scandal won reelection. In fact, 1,192 out of 1,293 (about 92%) of these scandal-free members won reelection. By comparing the scandal-plagued members to the scandal-free members, we now see that there is actually a slight negative correlation between facing a scandal and winning reelection.

Table 2.2. Most members of Congress facing a scandal are reelected, but scandal and reelection are negatively correlated.

	No Scandal	Scandal	Total
Not Reelected	101	8	109
Reelected	1,192	62	1,254
Total	1,293	70	1,363

We hope it is now clear why statement 4 does not convey enough information to know whether or not there is a correlation between scandal and reelection. The problem is that the statement is only about politicians facing scandal. It tells us that more of those politicians win reelection than lose. But to figure out if there is a correlation between scandal and winning reelection, we need to compare the share of politicians facing a scandal who win reelection to the share of scandal-free politicians who win. Had only 85 percent of the scandal-free members of Congress won reelection, there would be a positive correlation between scandal and reelection. Had 89 percent of them won, there would have been no correlation. But since we now know the true rate of reelection for scandal-free members was 92 percent, we see that there is a negative correlation. A similar analysis would show that statements 1 and 3 also don't convey enough information, on their own, to assess a correlation.

Statements 2 and 5 do describe correlations. Both statements make a comparison. Statement 2 tells us that cities with more crime have, on average, larger police forces than cities with less crime. And statement 5 tells us that older people tend to vote at higher rates than younger people. In both cases, we are comparing differences in one variable (police force size or voting rates) across differences in the other variable (crime rates or age). This is the kind of information you need to establish a correlation.

As we said at the outset, don't worry if you feel confused. Thinking clearly about what kind of information is necessary to establish a correlation, as opposed to just a fact, is tricky. We are going to spend chapter 4 making sure you really get it.

What Is a Correlation Good For?

Now that we have a shared understanding of what a correlation is, let's talk about what a correlation is good for. We've noted that correlations are perhaps the most important tool of quantitative analysts. But why? Broadly speaking, it's because correlations tell us what we should predict about some feature of the world given what we know about other features of the world.

There are at least three uses for this kind of knowledge: (1) description, (2) forecasting, and (3) causal inference. Any time we make use of a correlation, we want to think clearly about which of these three tasks we're attempting and what has to be true about the world for a correlation to be useful for that task in our particular setting.

Description

Describing the relationships between features of the world is the most straightforward use for correlations.

Why might we want to describe the relationship between features of the world? Suppose you were interested in whether younger people are underrepresented at the polls in a particular election, relative to their size in the population. A description of the relationship between age and voting might be helpful. Figure 2.4 shows a scatter plot of data on age and average voter turnout for the 2014 U.S. congressional election. In this figure, an observation is an age cohort. For each year of age, the figure shows the proportion of eligible voters who turned out to vote.

The figure also plots the line that best fits the data. This line has a slope of 0.006. In other words, on average, for every additional year of age, the chances that an individual turned out to vote in 2014 increases by 0.6 percentage points. So younger people do indeed appear to be underrepresented, as they turn out at lower rates than older people.

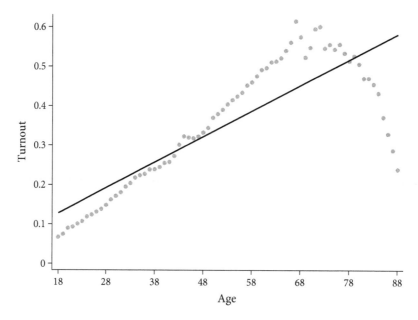

Figure 2.4. Voter turnout and age in the 2014 election.

This kind of descriptive analysis may be interesting in and of itself. It's important to know that younger people were less likely than older people to vote in 2014 and were therefore underrepresented in the electoral process. That relationship may inform how you think about the outcome of that election. Moreover, knowledge of this correlation might motivate you to further investigate the causes and consequences of the phenomenon of younger people turning out at low rates.

Of course, this descriptive relationship need not imply that these younger people will continue to vote at lower rates in future elections. So you can't necessarily use this knowledge to forecast future voter turnout. And it also doesn't mean that these younger people will necessarily become more likely to vote as they age. So you probably can't interpret this relationship causally. This descriptive analysis just tells us that older people were more likely to vote than younger people, on average, in the 2014 election. To push the interpretation further, you'd need to be willing to make stronger assumptions about the world, which we will now explore.

Forecasting

Another motivation for looking at correlations is *forecasting* or *prediction*—two terms that we will use interchangeably. Forecasting involves using information from some sample population to make predictions about a different population.

For instance, you might be using data on voters from past elections to make predictions about voters in future elections. Or you might be using the voters in one state to make predictions about voters in another state. Suppose you're running an electoral campaign, you have limited resources, and you're trying to figure out which of your supporters you should target with a knock on the door reminding them to turn out to vote. If you were already highly confident that an individual was going to vote in the absence of your intervention, you wouldn't want to waste your volunteers' time by knocking on that door. So accurate forecasting of voter turnout rates could improve the efficiency of your campaign.

Correlations like the one above regarding age and voter turnout could be useful for this kind of forecasting. Since age is strongly correlated with turnout, it might be a useful variable for forecasting who is and is not already likely to vote. For instance, if you were able to predict, on the basis of age, that some group of voters is virtually certain to turn out even without your campaign efforts, you might want to focus your mobilization resources on other voters.

To use the correlation between age and voter turnout for forecasting in this way, you don't need to know why they are correlated. But, unlike if you just want to *describe* the relationship between age and voter turnout in the 2014 election, if you want to *forecast*, you need to be willing to make some additional assumptions about the world.

This raises two important concerns that you must think clearly about in order to use correlation for forecasting responsibly. The first is whether the relationship you found in your sample is indicative of a broader phenomenon or whether it is the result of chance variation in your data. Answering this question requires *statistical inference*, which is the topic of chapter 6. Second, even if you are convinced that you've found a real relationship in your sample, you'll want to think about whether your sample is representative of the population about which you are trying to make predictions. We will explore representativeness in greater detail in our discussion of samples and external validity in chapters 6 and 16.

Let's go back to using age and voter turnout from one election to make predictions about another election. Doing so only makes sense if it is reasonable to assume that the relationship between these two variables isn't changing too quickly. That is, the correlation between age and voter turnout in, for example, the 2014 election would only be useful for figuring out which voters to target in the 2016 election if it seems likely that the relationship between age and turnout in 2016 will be more or less the same as the relationship between age and turnout in 2014. Similarly, if you only had data on age and voter turnout in the 2014 election for twenty-five states, you might use the correlation between age and turnout in those states to inform a strategy in the other twenty-five states. But this would only be sensible if you had reason to believe that the relationship between age and turnout was likely to be similar in the states on which you did and did not have data.

You'd also want to take care in making predictions beyond the range of available data. Our data tell us voter turnout rates for voters ages 18–88. Lines, however, go on forever. So the line of best fit gives us predictions for any age. But we should be careful extrapolating our predictions about voter turnout to, say, 100-year-olds, since we don't have any data for them, so we can't know whether the relationship described by the line is likely to hold for them or not, even for the 2014 election. And we can be sure the line's predictions for turnout by 10-year-olds won't be accurate—they aren't even allowed to vote.

Relatedly, when using some statistic, like the slope of a line of best fit, to do prediction, we need to think about whether the relationship is actually linear. If not, a linear summary of the relationship might be misleading. We'll discuss this in greater detail below.

It is worth noting that, in practical applications, it would be unusual to try to do forecasting simply using the correlation between two variables. One might, instead, try to predict voter turnout using its relationship with a host of variables like gender, race, income, education, and previous voter turnout. We'll discuss such multivariable and conditional correlations in chapter 5.

Using data for forecasting and prediction is a rapidly growing area for analysts in policy, business, policing, sports, government, intelligence, and many other fields. For instance, suppose you're running your city's public health department. Every time you send a health inspector to a restaurant, it costs time and money. But restaurant violations of the health code do harm to your city's residents. Therefore, you would very much like to send inspectors to those restaurants that are most likely to be in violation of the health codes, so as not to waste time and money on inspections that don't end up improving public safety. The more accurately you can forecast which restaurants are in violation, the more effectively you can deploy your inspectors. You could imagine using data on restaurants that did and did not violate health codes in the past to try to predict such violations on the basis of their correlation with other observable features of a restaurant. Plausibly useful restaurant features might include Yelp reviews, information about hospital visits for food poisoning, location, prices, and so on. Then, with these correlations in hand, you could use future Yelp reviews and other information to predict which restaurants are likely in violation of the health codes and target those restaurants for inspection.

This example points to another tricky issue. The very act of using correlations for prediction can sometimes make correlations that held in the past cease to hold in the future. For instance, suppose the health department observes a strong correlation between restaurants that are open twenty-four hours a day and health code violations. On the basis of that correlation, they might start sending health inspectors disproportionately to twenty-four-hour restaurants. A savvy restaurant owner who becomes aware of the new policy might adapt to fool the health department, say closing from 2:00 to 3:00 a.m. every night. This small change in operating hours would presumably do nothing to clean up the restaurant. But the manager would have gamed the system, rendering predictions based on past data inaccurate for the future. We'll discuss this general problem of adaptation in greater detail in chapter 16.

Forecasting would also be useful to a policy maker who would like to know the expected length of an economic downturn for budgetary purposes, a banker who wants to know the credit worthiness of potential borrowers, or an insurance company that wants to know how many car accidents a potential client is likely to get in this year. The managers of our beloved Chicago Bears would love to predict which college football players could be drafted to increase the team's chances of winning a Super Bowl. But given their past track record, we don't hold out much hope. Data can't work miracles.

It is also worth thinking about the potential ethical implications of using predictions to guide behavior. For instance, research finds that consumer complaints about cleanliness in online restaurant reviews are positively correlated with health code violations. This is potentially useful predictive information—governments could use data collected from review sites to figure out where to send restaurant inspectors. In response to such findings, an article in *The Atlantic* declared, "Yelp might clean up the restaurant industry." But a study by Kristen Altenburger and Daniel Ho shows that online reviewers are biased against Asian restaurants—comparing restaurants that received the same score from food-safety inspectors, they find that reviewers were more likely to complain about cleanliness in the Asian restaurants. This means that if governments make use of the helpful predictive correlation between online reviews and health code violations, it will inadvertently discriminate against Asian restaurants by disproportionately targeting them for inspection. Do you want your government to make use of such information? Or are there ethical or social costs of targeting restaurants for inspection in an ethnically biased way that outweigh the benefits of more accurate predictions? We will return to some of these ethical issues at the end of the book.

Causal Inference

Another reason we might be interested in correlations is to learn about causal relationships. Many of the most interesting questions that quantitative analysts face are inherently causal. That is, they are about how changing some feature of the world would cause a change in some other feature of the world. Would lowering the cost of college improve income inequality? Would implementing a universal basic income reduce homelessness? Would a new marketing strategy boost profits? These are all causal questions. As we'll see throughout the book, using correlations to make inferences about causal relationships is common. But it is also fraught with opportunities for unclear thinking. (Understanding causality will be the subject of the next chapter.)

Using correlation for causal inference has all the potential issues we just discussed when thinking about using correlation for prediction and there are new issues. The key one is that correlation need not imply causation. That is, a correlation between two features of the world doesn't mean one of them causes the other.

Suppose you want to know the effect of high school math training on subsequent success in college. This is an important question if you're a high school student, a parent or counselor of a high school student, or a policy maker setting educational standards. Will high school students be more likely to attend and complete college if they take advanced math in high school?

As it turns out, the correlation between taking advanced math and completing college is positive and quite strong—for instance, people who take calculus in high school are much more likely to graduate from college than people who do not. And the correlation is even stronger for algebra 2, trigonometry, and pre-calculus. But that doesn't mean that taking calculus causes students to complete college.

Of course, one possible source of this correlation is that calculus prepares students for college and causes them to become more likely to graduate. But that isn't the only possible source of this correlation. For instance, maybe, on average, kids who take calculus are more academically motivated than kids who don't. And maybe motivated kids are more likely to complete college regardless of whether or not they take calculus in high school. If that is the case, we would see a positive correlation between taking calculus and completing college even if calculus itself has no effect on college completion. Rather, whether a student took calculus would simply be an indirect measure of motivation, which is correlated with completing college.

What's at stake here? Well, if the causal story is right, then requiring a student to take calculus who otherwise wouldn't will help that student complete college by offering better preparation. But if the motivation story is right, then requiring that student to take calculus will not help with college completion. In that story, calculus is just an indicator of motivation. Requiring a student to take calculus does not magically make that student more motivated. It could even turn out that requiring that student to take calculus might impose real costs—in terms of self-esteem, motivation, or time spent on other activities—without any offsetting benefits.

The exact mistake we just described was made in a peer-reviewed scientific article. The researchers compared the college performance of people who did and did not take a variety of intensive high school math courses. On the basis of a positive correlation, they suggested that high school counselors "use the results of this study to inform students and their parents and guardians of the important role that high school math courses play with regard to subsequent bachelor's degree completion." That is, they mistook correlation for causation. On the basis of these correlations, they recommended that students who were not otherwise planning to do so should enroll in intensive math courses to increase their chances of graduating from college.

We'll return to the problem of mistaking correlation for causation in part 3. For now, you should note that, although purported experts do it all the time, in general, it is wrong to infer causality from correlations.

Measuring Correlations

There are several common statistics that can be used to describe and measure the correlation between variables. Here we discuss three of them: the *covariance*, the *correlation coefficient*, and the *slope of the regression line*. But before going through these three different ways of measuring correlations, we need to talk about means, variances, and standard deviations—statistics that help us summarize and understand variables.

Mean, Variance, and Standard Deviation

Let's focus on our Chicago crime and temperature data. Recall that in this data set, each observation is a day in 2018. And for each day we observe two variables, the number of reported crimes and the average temperature as measured in degrees Fahrenheit at Midway Airport. We aren't going to reproduce the entire data set here, since it has 365 rows (one for each day of 2018). Table 2.3 shows what the data looks like for the month of January. For the remainder of this discussion, we will treat the days of January 2018 as our population of interest.

For any observation i, call the value of the crime variable $crime_i$ and the value of the temperature variable $temperature_i$. In our data table, i can take any value from 1 through 31, corresponding to the thirty-one days of January 2018. So, for instance, the temperature on January 13 was $temperature_{13} = 12.3$, and the number of crimes reported on January 24 was $crime_{24} = 610$.

A variable has a *distribution*—a description of the frequency with which it takes different values. We often want to be able to summarize a variable's distribution with a few key statistics. Here we talk about three of them.

It will help to have a little bit of notation. The symbol $\sum$ (the upper-case Greek letter *sigma*) denotes summation. For example, $\sum_{i=1}^{31} crime_i$ is the sum of all the values of the crime variable from day 1 through day 31. To find it, you take the values of crime for day 1, day 2, day 3, and so on through 31 and sum (add) them together. That is, you add up $crime_1 = 847$ and $crime_2 = 555$ and $crime_3 = 568$ and so on through $crime_{31} = 708$. You find these specific values for the crime variable on each day by referring back to the data in table 2.3.

Now we can calculate the *mean* of each variable's distribution. (Sometimes this is just called the *mean of the variable*, leaving reference to the distribution implicit). The mean is denoted by μ (the Greek letter *mu*). The mean is just the average. We find it by summing the values of the observations (which we now have convenient notation for) and dividing by the number of observations. For January 2018, the means of our two variables are

Table 2.3. Average temperature at Chicago Midway Airport and number of crimes reported in Chicago for each day of January 2018.

Day	Temperature (°F)	Crimes
1	−2.7	847
2	−0.9	555
3	14.2	568
4	6.3	600
5	5.4	660
6	7.5	585
7	25.4	535
8	33.9	618
9	30.1	653
10	44.9	709
11	51.7	698
12	21.6	705
13	12.3	617
14	15.7	563
15	16.8	528
16	14.6	612
17	14.7	644
18	25.6	621
19	34.8	707
20	40.4	724
21	42.9	716
22	48.9	722
23	32.3	716
24	29.2	610
25	35.5	640
26	46.0	759
27	45.6	754
28	35.0	668
29	25.2	650
30	24.7	632
31	37.6	708
Mean	26.3	655.6
Variance	220.3	5183.0
Standard deviation	14.8	72.0

$$\mu_{\text{crime}} = \frac{\sum_{i=1}^{31} \text{crime}_i}{31} = \frac{847 + 555 + \cdots + 708}{31} = 655.6$$

and

$$\mu_{\text{temperature}} = \frac{\sum_{i=1}^{31} \text{temperature}_i}{31} = \frac{-2.7 + -0.9 + \cdots + 37.6}{31} = 26.3.$$

A second statistic of interest is the *variance*, which we denote by σ^2 (the lower-case Greek letter *sigma*, squared). We'll see why it is squared in a moment. The variance is a way of measuring how far from the mean the individual values of the variable tend to be. You might even say that the variance measures how variable the variable is. (You can also think of it, roughly, as a measure of how spread out the variable's distribution is.)

Here's how we calculate the variance. Suppose we have some variable X (like crime or temperature). For each observation, calculate the *deviation* of that observation's value of X from the mean of X. So, for observation i, the deviation is the value of X for observation i (X_i) minus the mean value of X across all observations (μ_X)—that is, $X_i - \mu_X$. On January 13, 2018, the temperature was 12.3 degrees Fahrenheit. The mean temperature in January 2018 was 26.3 degrees Fahrenheit. So January 13's deviation from the January mean was $12.3 - 26.3 = -14$. That is, January 13, 2018, was fourteen degrees colder than the average day in January 2018. By contrast, the deviation of January 23, 2018, was $32.3 - 26.3 = 6$. On January 23, it was six degrees warmer than on the average day in January 2018.

Note that these deviations can be positive or negative since observations can be larger or smaller than the mean. But for the purpose of measuring how variable the observations are, it doesn't matter whether any given deviation is positive or negative. We just want to know how far each observation is from the mean in any direction. So we need to transform the deviations into positive numbers that just measure the distance from the mean rather than the sign and distance. To do this, we could look at the absolute value of the deviations. But for reasons we'll discuss later, we typically make the deviations positive by squaring them instead. The variance is the average value of these squared deviations. So, if there are N observations (in our data, $N = 31$) the variance is

$$\sigma_X^2 = \frac{\sum_i^N (X_i - \mu_X)^2}{N}.$$

For the two variables in our data, the variances are

$$\sigma_{\text{crime}}^2 = \frac{\sum_{i=1}^{31} (\text{crime}_i - \mu_{\text{crime}})^2}{31}$$

$$= \frac{(847 - 655.6)^2 + (555 - 655.6)^2 + \cdots + (708 - 655.6)^2}{31} \approx 5183$$

and

$$\sigma_{\text{temperature}}^2 = \frac{\sum_{i=1}^{31} (\text{temperature}_i - \mu_{\text{temperature}})^2}{31}$$

$$= \frac{(-2.7 - 26.3)^2 + (-0.9 - 26.3)^2 + \cdots + (37.6 - 26.3)^2}{31} \approx 220.3.$$

By focusing on the average of the squared deviations rather than on the average of the absolute value of the deviations, the variance is putting more weight on observations that are farther from the mean. If the richest person in society gets richer, this increases the variance in wealth more than if a moderately rich person gets richer by the same amount. For example, suppose the average wealth is 1. If someone with a wealth of 10 gains 1 more unit of wealth, the variance increases by $\frac{10^2 - 9^2}{N} = \frac{19}{N}$. But if someone with a wealth of 100 gains one more unit of wealth, the variance increases by $\frac{100^2 - 99^2}{N} = \frac{199}{N}$.

The variance is a fine measure of how variable a variable is. But since we've squared everything, there is a sense in which it is not measured on the same scale as the variable itself. Sometimes we want a measure of variability that is on that same scale. When that is the case, we use the *standard deviation*, which is just the square root of the variance. We denote the standard deviation by σ (the lower-case Greek letter *sigma*):

$$\sigma_X = \sqrt{\sigma_X^2} = \sqrt{\frac{\sum_i^N (X_i - \mu_X)^2}{N}}.$$

The standard deviation—which is also a measure of how spread out a variable's distribution is—roughly corresponds to how far we expect observations to be from the mean, on average. Though, as we've noted, compared to the average absolute value of the deviations, it puts extra weight on observations that are farther from the mean.

For the two variables in our data, the standard deviations are

$$\sigma_{\text{crime}} = \sqrt{\frac{\sum_{i=1}^{31} (\text{crime}_i - \mu_{\text{crime}})^2}{31}}$$

$$= \sqrt{\frac{(847 - 655.6)^2 + (555 - 655.6)^2 + \cdots + (708 - 655.6)^2}{31}} \approx 72$$

and

$$\sigma_{\text{temperature}} = \sqrt{\frac{\sum_{i=1}^{31} (\text{temperature}_i - \mu_{\text{temperature}})^2}{31}}$$

$$= \sqrt{\frac{(-2.7 - 26.3)^2 + (-0.9 - 26.3)^2 + \cdots + (37.6 - 26.3)^2}{31}} \approx 15.1.$$

Now that we understand what a mean, variance, and standard deviation are, we can discuss three important ways in which we measure correlations: the *covariance*, the *correlation coefficient*, and the *slope of the regression line*.

Covariance

Suppose we have two variables, like crime and temperature, and we want to measure the correlation between them. One way to do this would be to calculate their *covariance* (denoted *cov*). To keep our notation simple, let's call those two variables X and Y. And let's assume we have a population of size N.

Here's how you calculate the covariance. For every observation, calculate the deviations—that is, how far the value of X is from the mean of X and how far the value of Y is from the mean of Y. Now, for each observation, multiply the two deviations together, so you have $(X_i - \mu_X)(Y_i - \mu_Y)$ for each observation i. Call this the *product of the deviations*. Finally, to find the covariance of X and Y, calculate the average value of this product:

$$\text{cov}(X, Y) = \frac{\sum_{i=1}^{N}(X_i - \mu_X)(Y_i - \mu_Y)}{N}$$

Let's see that the covariance is a measure of the correlation. Consider a particularly strong version of positive correlation: suppose whenever X is bigger than average $(X_i - \mu_X > 0)$, Y is also bigger than average $(Y_i - \mu_Y > 0)$, and whenever X is smaller than average $(X_i - \mu_X < 0)$, Y is also smaller than average $(Y_i - \mu_Y < 0)$. In this case, the product of the deviations will be positive for every observation—either both deviations will be positive, or both deviations will be negative. So the covariance will be positive, reflecting the positive correlation. Now consider a particularly strong version of negative correlation: suppose whenever X is bigger than average, Y is smaller than average, and whenever X is smaller than average, Y is bigger than average. In this case, the product of the deviations will be negative for every observation—one deviation is always negative and the other always positive. So the covariance will be negative, reflecting the negative correlation. Of course, neither of these extreme cases has to hold. But if a larger-than-average X usually goes with a larger-than-average Y, then the covariance will be positive, reflecting a positive correlation. If a larger-than-average X usually goes with a smaller-than-average Y, then the covariance will be negative, reflecting a negative correlation. And if the values of X and Y are unrelated to each other, the covariance will be zero, reflecting the fact that the variables are uncorrelated.

Correlation Coefficient

While the meaning of the sign of the covariance is clear, its magnitude can be a bit hard to interpret, since the product of the deviations depends on how variable the variables are. We can get a more easily interpretable statistic that still measures the correlation by accounting for the variance of the variables.

The *correlation coefficient* (denoted *corr*) is simply the covariance divided by the product of the standard deviations:

$$\text{corr}(X, Y) = \frac{\text{cov}(X, Y)}{\sigma_X \sigma_Y}$$

When we divide the covariance by the product of the standard deviations, we are normalizing things. That is, the covariance could, in principle, take any value. But the correlation coefficient always takes a value between -1 and 1. A value of 0 still indicates no correlation. A value of 1 indicates a positive correlation and perfect linear dependence—that is, if you made a scatter plot of the two variables, you could draw a straight, upward-sloping line through all the points. A value of -1 indicates a negative correlation and perfect linear dependence. A value between 0 and 1 indicates positive correlation but not a perfect linear relationship. And a value between -1 and 0 indicates negative correlation but not a perfect linear relationship.

The correlation coefficient is sometimes denoted by the letter r. And we also some-times square the correlation coefficient to compute a statistic called r-squared or r^2. This statistic always lies between 0 and 1.

One potentially attractive feature of the r^2 statistic is that it can be interpreted as a proportion. It's often interpreted as the proportion of the variation in Y *explained* by X or, equivalently, the proportion of X explained by Y. As we'll discuss in later chapters, the word *explained* can be misleading here. It doesn't mean that the variation in X causes the variation in Y or vice versa. It also doesn't account for the possibility that this observed correlation might have arisen by chance rather than reflecting a genuine phenomenon in the world.

Slope of the Regression Line

One potential concern with the correlation coefficient and the r^2 statistic is that they don't tell you anything about the substantive importance or size of the relation-ship between X and Y. Suppose our two variables of interest are crime and temperature in Chicago. A correlation coefficient of .8 tells us that there is a strong, positive relation-ship between the two variables, but it doesn't tell us what that relationship is. It could be that every degree of temperature corresponds with .1 extra crimes, or it could be that every degree of temperature corresponds with 100 extra crimes. Both are possible with a correlation coefficient of .8. But they mean very different things.

For this reason, we don't spend much time thinking about these ways of measuring correlation. We typically focus on the slope of a line of best fit, as we've already shown you. Moreover, we tend to focus on one particular way of defining which line fits best. Remember, a line of best fit minimizes how far the data points are from the line on average. We typically measure how far a data point is from the line with the square of the distance from the data point to the line (so every value is positive, just like with squaring deviations). We focus on the line of best fit that minimizes the sum of these squared distances (or the *sum of squared errors*). This particular line of best fit is called the ordinary least squares (OLS) regression line, and usually, when someone just says *regression line*, they mean *OLS regression line*. All the lines of best fit we drew earlier in this chapter were OLS regression lines.

The slope of the regression line, it turns out, can be calculated from the covariance and variance. The slope of the regression line (also sometimes called the *regression coefficient*) when Y is on the vertical axis and X is on the horizontal axis is

$$\frac{\mathrm{cov}\,(X, Y)}{\sigma_X^2}.$$

This number tells us, descriptively, how much Y changes, on average, as X increases by one unit. Had we divided by σ_Y^2 instead of σ_X^2, then it would tell us how much X changes, on average, as Y increases by one unit. As we've seen, those can be different numbers.

We'll spend a lot more time on regression lines in chapters 5 and 10.

Populations and Samples

Before moving on, there is one last issue that is worth pausing to highlight. We can think about each of the statistics we've talked about—the mean, the variance, the covari-ance, the correlation coefficient, the slope of the regression line—in two ways. There is a value of each of those statistics that corresponds to the whole population we are interested in. And there is a value of those statistics that corresponds to the sample of data we might happen to have. Either value can be of interest, but they can be importantly different. We have avoided that issue here by focusing on a case where our data and our population are the same—we have crime and temperature for every day in January 2018, which we've treated as our population and our sample. But this won't always be the case. For instance, we might have been interested in the relationship between crime and temperature in January over many years but only had a sample of data for the year 2018. This would give rise to all sorts of questions about what we can learn about January 2019 or January 1918 from our 2018 data. We will revisit these issues in chapter 6.

Straight Talk about Linearity

All of the various ways of measuring correlations that we have discussed focus on assessing linear relationships between variables. We will delve into this topic in more detail later on, especially in chapter 5 when we return to the topic of age and voter turnout in the context of our discussion of regression. But for now we will note that linear relationships are often interesting and important, but not all interesting and important relationships are linear. Consider, for example, the two possible relationships between the variables X and Y illustrated in figure 2.5.

As the regression lines make clear, in both these figures, the correlation between X and Y is 0. But these relationships are clearly different, just not in a way that is captured by the regression line.

In the left panel, there is no correlation between X and Y and there also doesn't seem to be any interesting relationship of any kind. You really can't predict the value of Y from X or vice versa. In the right panel, there is also no correlation between X and Y—on average, high values of X don't tend to occur with high values of Y, nor do low values of X tend to occur with low values of Y. But there is certainly a relationship between these two variables. In fact, X is quite useful in predicting Y in the right panel. This teaches us a lesson. Clear thinking about data requires more than just computing correlations. Among other things, it is important to look at your data (e.g., with scatter plots like these), lest you miss interesting nonlinear relationships.

There are lots of statistical approaches for dealing with non-linearity, and we'll discuss some of them in this book. But, as it turns out, linear tools for describing data can still be useful, even when the variables are related in a non-linear way. For instance, in the right panel of figure 2.5, there is a strong negative correlation between X and Y when X is less than 0 and a strong positive correlation between X and Y when X is greater than 0. So one thing we could do with linear tools is draw two lines of best fit, one for when X is less than 0 and one for when it is greater than 0. That would look like figure 2.6.

Another thing we could do is transform one of the variables so that the relationship looks more linear. For instance, in our example, although there is no correlation between Y and X, there is a strong linear relationship between Y and X^2. In figure 2.7 we plot X^2 on the horizontal axis and Y on the vertical axis. When we transform X into X^2, negative values of X become positive values of X^2 (e.g., -1 becomes 1), while the positive values stay positive (e.g., 1 stays 1). So it is as if we are folding the figure in

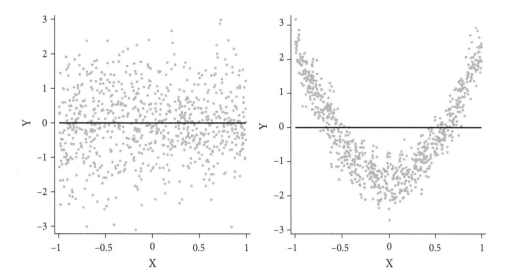

Figure 2.5. Zero correlation can mean many things.

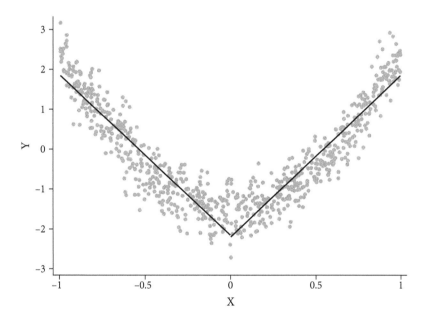

Figure 2.6. Fitting two separate regression lines to a non-linear relationship.

on itself at $X = 0$, and then we're twisting and stretching it a little so that X becomes X^2 (0 stays at 0, 1 stays at 1, .5 becomes $.5^2 = .25$, and so on).

With this transformation, our regression line shows a strong positive relationship between Y and X^2, and we can do a good job describing the relationship between these variables with our linear tools.

It's also worth pointing out that describing the relationship between two variables with a linear function is always appropriate when we're dealing with binary variables.

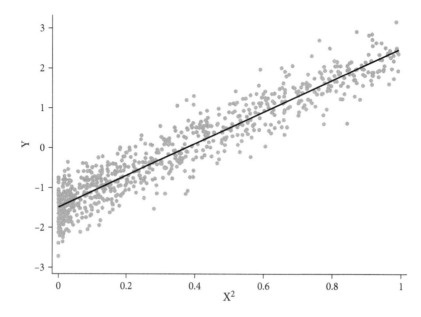

Figure 2.7. Creating a linear relationship by transforming a variable.

For example, let's return to the correlation between oil production and autocracy. Figure 2.8 plots the data. The scatter plot is not very interesting or informative because there are only four possible combinations of our two variables. Accordingly, all of the data points lie on one of those four dots (although we have attempted to make the scatter plot more informative by making the size of the dots proportional to the number of countries at each set of values). However, we can still plot the slope of the regression line. The slope of this line is simply the proportion of major oil-producing countries that are autocracies minus the proportion of non-major oil-producing countries that are autocracies. In other words, we learn the same thing from this picture that we learned from the table at the outset of the chapter.

One reason that we focus so much on linear relationships is that even non-linear relationships tend to look approximately linear if you zoom in enough—that is, if you are interested in a sufficiently small range of values of the variable X. We must be particularly cautious about extrapolating when we zoom in like that. As we move farther from the range of data in which the relationship is approximately linear, our descriptions of the relationship (and, by extension, any predictions we make) will be less and less accurate.

To think more about the dangers of extrapolation, consider an example. Political analysts find that the incumbent party in U.S. presidential elections tends to get about 46 percent of the vote when there is 0 income growth, and an extra 3.5 percentage points of the vote for every percentage point increase in income growth. Of course, they've measured this relationship using data on income growth levels that have actually occurred. Does this mean that we should predict incumbent vote share will be 81 percent if income growth is 10 percent? Probably not. And the incumbent's vote share definitely would not be 116 percent if income growth were 20 percent—that's impossible! But that doesn't mean a linear description of the data isn't useful for the range of income growths that we actually experience.

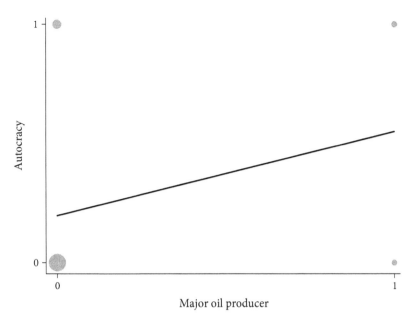

Figure 2.8. A regression line through data with a binary variable gives the difference in means.

Wrapping Up

Correlations form the foundation of data analysis. They are the way we talk about relationships between features of the world. And the various statistics by which we measure correlations—like the covariance, correlation coefficient, or slope of the regression line—are the way we quantify those relationships.

As we've discussed, correlations can be used for a variety of purposes including description, forecasting, and causal inference. In chapter 3, we turn our focus to causality in order to understand what it means and start to get a handle on the aphorism with which we began—correlation need not imply causation. However, a fuller understanding of the relationship between correlation and causation will have to wait until chapter 9.

Key Terms

- **Correlation:** The correlation between two features of the world is the extent to which they tend to occur together.
- **Positively correlated:** When higher (lower) values of one variable tend to occur with higher (lower) values of another variable, we say that the two variables are positively correlated.
- **Negatively correlated:** When higher (lower) values of one variable tend to occur with lower (higher) values of another variable, we say that the two variables are negatively correlated.
- **Uncorrelated:** When there is no correlation between two variables, meaning that higher (lower) values of one variable do not systematically coincide with higher or lower values of the other variable, we say that they are uncorrelated.
- **Line of best fit:** A line that minimizes how far data points are from the line on average, according to some measure of distance from data to the line.

- **Mean (μ):** The average value of a variable.
- **Deviation from the mean:** The distance between an observation's value for some variable and the mean of that variable.
- **Variance (σ^2):** A measure of how variable a variable is. It is the average of the square of the deviations from the mean.
- **Standard deviation (σ):** Another measure of how variable a variable is. The standard deviation is the square root of the variance. It has the advantage of being measured on the same scale as the variable itself and roughly corresponds to how far the typical observation is from the mean (though, like the variance, it puts more weight on observations far from the mean).
- **Covariance (cov):** A measure of the correlation between two variables. It is calculated as the average of the product of the deviations from the mean.
- **Correlation coefficient (r):** Another measure of the correlation between two variables. It is calculated as the covariance divided by the product of the variances. The correlation coefficient takes a value between -1 and 1, with -1 reflecting perfect linear negative dependence, 0 reflecting no correlation, and 1 reflecting perfect linear dependence.
- **r^2:** The square of the correlation coefficient. It takes values between 0 and 1 and is often interpreted as the proportion of the variation in one variable explained by the other variable. But we have to pay careful attention to what we mean by "explained." Importantly, it doesn't mean that variation in one variable causes variation in the other.
- **Sum of squared errors:** The sum of the square of the distance from each data point to a given line of best fit. This gives us one way of measuring how well the line fits/describes/explains the data.
- **OLS regression line:** The line that best fits the data, where *best fits* means that it minimizes the sum of squared error.
- **Slope of a line:** The slope of a line tells you how much the line changes on the vertical axis as you move one unit along the horizontal axis. So a completely horizontal line has a slope of 0. An upward sloping 45-degree line has a slope 1, a downward sloping 45-degree line has a slope of -1, and so on.
- **Slope of the regression line or regression coefficent:** The slope of the regression line describes how the value of one variable changes, on average, when the other variable changes. The slope of the regression line is the covariance of two variables divided by the variance of one of them, sometimes also called the regression coefficient.

Exercises

2.1   Consider the following three statements. Which ones describe a correlation, and which ones do not? Why?

(a) Most professional data analysts took a statistics course in college.

(b) Among Major League Baseball players, pitchers tend to have lower-than-average batting averages. (We'll learn why this is the case in chapter 16.)

(c) Whichever presidential candidate wins Ohio tends to win the Electoral College.

2.2   Consider the last statement about Ohio and presidential elections. Do you think it's useful for description? Forecasting? Causal inference? Why or why not?

2.3   The table below shows some data on which countries are major oil producers and which countries experienced a civil war between 1946 and 2004. Are being a major oil producer and experiencing civil war positively correlated, negatively correlated, or uncorrelated? Explain your answer.

	Civil War	No Civil War
Oil Producer	7	12
Non-Oil Producer	55	94

2.4   The table below provides data about height and income among American men, taken from the National Longitudinal Survey. It is fine to use a calculator for this question, but don't use a spread sheet or statistical software to compute the answers.

Height (in)	Average Income $
60	39,428
61	35,087
62	40,575
63	39,825
64	55,508
65	56,377
66	59,746
67	66,699
68	59,787
69	66,176
70	79,202
71	70,432
72	77,975
73	72,606
74	71,063
75	80,330

(a) Calculate the mean of each of these variables.
(b) Calculate the variance of each of these variables.
(c) Calculate the standard deviation of each of these variables.
(d) Calculate the covariance between these two variables.
(e) Calculate the correlation coefficient for these variables.
(f) Are the two variables positively correlated, negatively correlated, or uncorrelated? Explain your answer.

Readings and References

For more on the corruption data we discussed take a look at

Scott J. Basinger. 2013. "Scandals and Congressional Elections in the Post-Watergate Era." *Political Research Quarterly* 66(2):385–398.

For more information about the Polity IV Project, which classifies countries as democratic or autocratic, see https://www.systemicpeace.org/polity/polity4.htm.

We discussed two articles on using online reviews to predict health code violations:

Emily Badger. 2013. "How Yelp Might Clean Up the Restaurant Industry." *The Atlantic.* July/August.

Kristen M. Altenburger and Daniel E. Ho. 2018. "When Algorithms Import Private Bias into Public Enforcement: The Promise and Limitations of Statistical Debiasing Solutions." *Journal of Institutional and Theoretical Economics* 174(1):98–122.

The study of advanced math and college completion is.

Jerry Trusty and Spencer G. Niles. 2003. "High-School Math Courses and Completion of the Bachelor's Degree." *Professional School Counseling* 7(2):99–107.

If you are interested in examples of the growing use of forecasting and prediction in addressing important policy problems, have a look at

Jon Kleinberg, Jens Ludwig, Sendhil Mullainathan, and Ziad Obermeyer. 2015. "Prediction Policy Problems." *American Economic Review* 105(5):491–95.

CHAPTER 3

Causation: What Is It and What Is It Good For?

What You'll Learn

- A causal effect is a change in some feature of the world that would result from a change to some other feature of the world.
- Assessing causal relationships is crucial for policy and decision making.
- *"What effect did this have on the outcome?"* is a more conceptually clear question than *"What caused the outcome?"*
- Causal relationships are about comparisons of *counterfactual* worlds. As a result, they are fundamentally unobservable. But, in certain situations, we can learn about them from data.

Introduction

As we saw in chapter 2, knowledge of correlations is useful for many purposes. Among the most important, but also most vexing, purposes is learning about causal relationships.

We make claims about causal knowledge all the time. I did poorly on the test because I didn't get enough sleep. Going to college will improve my future job prospects. A political candidate lost an election because of an attack ad. Violent crime is down because of a new policing strategy.

Thinking clearly about whether a causal relationship exists is perhaps the most important conceptual challenge for learning to use information to make better decisions. This is because causal knowledge is the key to understanding how your decisions and actions affect the world around you. If you propose a new tax policy, test-prep strategy, exercise plan, or advertising campaign, you're doing so not because you think it is correlated with better outcomes. Rather, you must believe that enacting your proposal will actually cause better outcomes.

Our goal in this chapter is to clarify exactly what we mean when we talk about causal relationships. Causality is a deep and perplexing topic to which much attention has been paid by scholars from many different fields. We won't be able to resolve all the thorny philosophical questions here. Instead we've set more modest goals. First, we want to make sure we are all on the same page by defining how we will use causal language for the duration of this book. Then we will explain why the notion of causality we adopt is a particularly valuable one. Finally, we will discuss some other approaches to talking about causality and explain why, from our point of view, they are less helpful than the one we adopt.

What Is Causation?

When we talk about causation, we're talking about the effect of one thing on another. In non-technical terms, a *causal effect* is a change in some feature of the world that would result from a change to some other feature of the world. So, for instance, we would say that the tax rate has a causal effect on government revenue if changing the tax rate would lead to a change in government revenue.

We've defined the notion of an effect in non-technical terms, so you might not have noticed that we actually slipped in a bit of philosophy. What do we mean by *would result*? After all, the world is as it is. Where did this change in some other feature of the world come from?

That's a good question. In fact, our definition of a causal effect relies on a thought experiment about which we need to be explicit. Let's start with an example.

The movie star Gwyneth Paltrow runs a company called Goop that promotes stickers, called Body Vibes, that are supposed to promote health, wellness, *and* good skin. Here's what the Goop website says about Body Vibes:

> Human bodies operate at an ideal energetic frequency, but everyday stresses and anxiety can throw off our internal balance, depleting our energy reserves and weakening our immune systems. Body Vibes stickers come pre-programmed to an ideal frequency, allowing them to target imbalances. While you're wearing them—close to your heart, on your left shoulder or arm—they'll fill in the deficiencies in your reserves, creating a calming effect, smoothing out both physical tension and anxiety. The founders, both aestheticians, also say they help clear skin by reducing inflammation and boosting cell turnover.

Suppose you paid the required six dollars per sticker because you really want clear skin. But then your friends started making fun of you for being a sucker. In defending yourself, you'd want to claim that Body Vibes really do have an effect on the clarity of your skin. But what, exactly, would you mean by that claim?

Here's a way of thinking about this. Imagine an alternative world where, at the exact moment you went to stick on your Body Vibes stickers, unbeknownst to you, one of your friends replaced them with identical-looking stickers that cost ten cents instead of six dollars, but which hadn't been "pre-programmed to an ideal frequency." If your skin clarity would be worse in that alternative world, then we would say that Body Vibes have a positive effect on your skin clarity. If your skin clarity would be the same in that alternative world, we'd have to conclude that Body Vibes don't have the claimed effect on skin clarity And if your skin clarity would actually be better in that alternative world, we'd conclude Body Vibes have a negative effect.

We can extend this thought experiment. There's nothing particularly special about the real world. Once we're already thinking about one alternative world, we might as well think about two. For instance, we could think about the effect of ten-cent stickers compared to magical crystals, even if you've never tried either of those approaches to skin care. We just have to compare two make-believe worlds: one where your friends secretly stuck stickers on your upper left shoulder near your heart, and another where they snuck crystals into your pockets. These kinds of comparisons are called *counterfactual* thought experiments because at least one of the worlds we are comparing isn't the real, factual world—it's in our imaginations. The comparison of outcomes in such a thought experiment is a *counterfactual comparison.*

We can now make sense of the phrase *would result* in our definition of a causal effect. It refers to a counterfactual comparison between the outcome in the actual world and the outcome in a counterfactual world that is identical to the actual world up until the point where the feature of the world claimed to have a causal effect is changed.

This idea of counterfactuals is philosophically subtle. So, to help us make sure we are thinking clearly, we are going to introduce a mathematical framework for representing counterfactuals called *potential outcomes.* Using the potential outcomes framework requires some notation, but it isn't too complicated. And once you master the notation, you will have a much deeper understanding of what causality really is. So let's give it a shot.

Potential Outcomes and Counterfactuals

We are interested in the effect of some *treatment* (say, Body Vibes) on some outcome (say, skin health). Let's call the treatment T. It is a binary variable, taking a value of 0 or 1. If $T = 1$ for some person, that means the person received the Body Vibes treatment. If $T = 0$ for some person, that means the person didn't receive the Body Vibes treatment. We sometimes say that a unit (here, a person) with $T = 1$ is *treated* and a unit with $T = 0$ is *untreated*, although it's often arbitrary what we call treated and what we call untreated (e.g., we could just as easily talk about the effect of *not* wearing Body Vibes).

Similarly, let's refer to the outcome we are interested in as Y. In our example, Y describes a person's skin health. In a metaphysical sense, there is some level of skin health that each individual would have had if they'd used Body Vibes and some level of skin health they would have had if they hadn't used Body Vibes. These are that person's *potential outcomes.* However, at any given moment, we only ever get to observe one of these—each person is either using or not using Body Vibes. Nonetheless, thinking about both potential outcomes helps us to think clearly about counterfactuals:

$$Y_{1i} = \text{outcome for unit } i \text{ if } T = 1$$

$$Y_{0i} = \text{outcome for unit } i \text{ if } T = 0$$

The effect of wearing Body Vibes on person i's skin health is just the difference in i's skin health with and without Body Vibes. In our potential outcomes notation, it is

$$\text{Effect of Body Vibes on } i\text{'s Skin Health} = Y_{1i} - Y_{0i}.$$

Table 3.1 makes this more concrete. We observe ten individuals. For each individual, we observe whether they received Body Vibes and whether their skin is clear. If person i received Body Vibes, their treatment status is $T_i = 1$; if they did not, their treatment status is $T_i = 0$. And if person i had treatment status T, we write their outcome as $Y_{Ti} = 1$ if their skin is clear and $Y_{Ti} = 0$ if their skin is not clear.

The actual outcome for each individual is bold in the table. Individuals 1–5 received Body Vibes, so their actual outcome is Y_{1i}. The table also tells us what these individuals' outcomes would have been if they hadn't received Body Vibes, Y_{0i}. However, in

Table 3.1. Potential outcomes for skin health with and without Body Vibes. For each individual, the actual outcome that we can observe is in bold type. The counterfactual outcome that we do not observe is in regular type.

		Skin Health with Body Vibes Y_{1i}	Skin Health without Body Vibes Y_{0i}	Treatment Effect for Individual i $Y_{1i} - Y_{0i}$
Receive Body Vibes	Individual 1	**1**	1	0
	Individual 2	**0**	0	0
	Individual 3	**0**	0	0
	Individual 4	**1**	1	0
	Individual 5	**1**	1	0
Don't Receive Body Vibes	Individual 6	0	**0**	0
	Individual 7	0	**0**	0
	Individual 8	1	**1**	0
	Individual 9	1	**1**	0
	Individual 10	0	**0**	0

the actual world, no one can observe these counterfactual outcomes, since they don't actually occur. Individuals 6–10 do not receive Body Vibes. So their actual outcome is Y_{0i}. Again, although the table tells us what their outcomes would have been if they'd received Body Vibes, Y_{1i}, these counterfactual outcomes are not observed in the actual world.

Because the table tells us the potential outcomes in the actual and counterfactual worlds, we can find the treatment effect of Body Vibes for each individual by calculating $Y_{1i} - Y_{0i}$. Doing so reveals that Body Vibes don't actually have any effect on the skin health of any individual. Individuals 1, 4, 5, 8, and 9 all have clear skin. But for all of these individuals, that would be true whether or not they received Body Vibes. Individuals 2, 3, 6, 7, and 10 all have unclear skin. Again, however, this would be true with or without Body Vibes. Importantly, as we will come back to later, this absence of a causal effect can't actually be observed in the world because we only observe the actual outcome for each individual, not the potential outcome in the counterfactual world where they had a different treatment status.

We say that causality is about counterfactual comparisons because we can only observe, at most, one of the two quantities, Y_{1i} or Y_{0i}, for any individual at any particular point in time. This means that we can't directly measure the effect of wearing Body Vibes on an individual's skin health. We suspect this fact is key to their business model.

What Is Causation Good For?

Knowledge of causation is necessary for understanding the consequences of an action that changes some feature of the world. In particular, to weigh the costs and benefits of a decision, you need to know how your action will affect the outcomes you care about.

For instance, you can't possibly know if it is a good idea to spend money on a drug to treat heart disease without knowing about a causal relationship—whether the drug reduces the risk of heart disease. The same goes for many decisions. When you are deciding whether or not to intervene in the world in some way—with a policy, an exercise plan, a parenting strategy, a new kind of online learning, or what have you—you want to know how the intervention *affects* the outcomes you care about.

While the examples we've discussed are easily understood in terms of counterfactual comparisons, sometimes thinking in terms of counterfactuals can seem vexing or confusing. In the next sections, we explore some of these issues.

The Fundamental Problem of Causal Inference

In our discussion of table 3.1 we nodded toward an important issue—causal effects as we've defined them can never, ever be directly observed. Everyone either receives Body Vibes or doesn't receive Body Vibes. So you only observe one potential outcome for each person. But the causal effect is the difference in a person's potential outcomes. This inherent unobservability of causal effects is called the *fundamental problem of causal inference*. Let's see exactly why we can't observe causal effects and what that implies for our ability to learn about causality.

The effect of going to college on your income is the difference in your income in a world in which you go to college versus a world in which you are the same up until the college decision but you don't go to college. At least one of those worlds is counterfactual. You can't both go to college and not go to college. That is, you have two potential outcomes—$Y_{college}$ and $Y_{no\ college}$. But you have only one *actual* outcome: either you went to college or you didn't. Given this, we can never observe the effect of going to college on your income since we only observe your income in the actual world, not the counterfactual world.

The fundamental problem of causal inference, then, is that, at any given time, we only observe any given unit of analysis (e.g., a person, basketball team, or country) in one state of affairs. So we can't observe the effect on that unit of being in that state of affairs versus some other state of affairs, because all the other states of affairs are counterfactual. We can't know $Y_{college} - Y_{no\ college}$ for you, because we only observe one of the two values. We saw this fact earlier, in table 3.1, where we noticed that we could only observe the actual outcome for each individual; the other potential outcome was counterfactual.

So how do we make progress on answering causal questions if effects are fundamentally unobservable? Fortunately, there are lots of situations where we don't necessarily need to know the effect for every individual unit of analysis. Instead, we want to know the average effect across lots of individuals.

Suppose, for instance, that the Food and Drug Administration (FDA) is deciding whether to approve a new drug. To learn about the health effects of the drug, scientists conduct a randomized trial, assigning some people to take the drug (the treated group) and other people to take a placebo (the untreated group). Because of the fundamental problem of causal inference, the scientists can't observe the effect of taking the drug on any individual. Each person is either taking the drug or not. But by comparing the average health outcomes for people in the untreated group to the average health outcomes for people in the treated group, they can assess the average effect of the drug. (We'll talk a lot more about how this works in parts 2 and 3.) Doing so allows the scientists to answer what turns out to be the key causal question for the FDA's decision: If we approve the new drug, how will health change in the population on average?

Drug approval is one setting in which knowledge about average effects is sufficient to inform the key decisions. But there are some settings where this is not the case and the fundamental problem of causal inference constitutes a real challenge. For instance, assessing legal liability involves what's called the *but-for* test. The test requires answering questions like "Would a harm to Anthony not have happened but for Ethan's actions?" The fundamental problem of causal inference says we can never know for sure, since the world in which Ethan did not take his action is counterfactual, so we don't know what happens to Anthony in that world. Instead, what we've just said, and will cover in much more detail in the rest of the book, is that there are methods for answering a slightly different question like "On average, when people take actions of the sort Ethan took, does it tend to cause harm to other people?" A convincing answer to that latter question may or may not be compelling in a court that wants to answer the former.

Part of clear thinking about causal relationships involves admitting that sometimes we cannot answer certain questions with complete confidence, even when those questions are very important.

Conceptual Issues

Causality is a deep and difficult topic. The counterfactual definition of causality doesn't provide all the answers. But it can help us think more clearly about some thorny conceptual issues. Let's talk through a few of these.

What Is the Cause?

One frustration people sometimes feel with regard to the counterfactual approach is that some of the causal questions that we are accustomed to asking appear incoherent within the counterfactual framework. Think of questions like the following: Why did housing prices tank during the latest financial crisis? Why did the Chicago Blackhawks win the Stanley Cup? What caused World War I? Questions of causal attribution like these are common. But when causation is defined in terms of counterfactual comparisons, they don't make a ton of sense.

Let's think about World War I. A common claim is that World War I was caused by the assassination in 1914 of Archduke Ferdinand, the heir to the throne of Austria-Hungary. The assassins were part of a movement that wanted Serbia to take control over the southern Balkans, including Bosnia and Herzegovina, which Austria-Hungary had annexed in 1908. The government of Austria-Hungary responded to the assassination with the July Ultimatum, a list of demands so onerous they were certain to be rejected by the Serbian government. When the ultimatum was rejected, Austria-Hungary declared war on Serbia, leading Russia to mobilize its army to defend Serbia. In response, Germany (an ally of Austria-Hungary) declared war on Russia, France (an ally of Russia) declared war on Germany, and the whole mess cascaded into World War I. Thus, the claim goes, the assassination of Archduke Ferdinand caused World War I.

Now, there is a sense in which this claim is perfectly simple to think about in our framework. We can ask, In the counterfactual world in which Ferdinand was not assassinated, would World War I still have occurred? If World War I would not have occurred in that counterfactual world, then it seems right to say that the assassination had an effect on war breaking out. But that is a far cry from saying that the assassination of the archduke was *the* cause of the war. Surely, there are many factors that, had they been different, would have prevented World War I from being fought. Sure, had Archduke Ferdinand not been assassinated, maybe the war wouldn't have been fought. But also, had Austria-Hungary not annexed Bosnia and Herzegovina, perhaps Ferdinand would have never been assassinated and the war would have never been fought, so the annexation was just as much a cause as the assassination. Similarly, had the Serbian government complied with the July Ultimatum, perhaps the war would have been avoided, so the noncompliance with the ultimatum was also a cause. And to further illustrate how many such causes there are, had some fish-like creature in the Paleozoic Era swam left instead of right, perhaps the human race as we know it would not exist, and again, World War I would have never been fought. Or, to take an example with some historical gravitas, the seventeenth-century French mathematician Blaise Pascal, reflecting on Mark Antony's attraction to a long proboscis, quipped, "Cleopatra's nose, had it been shorter, the whole face of the world would have been changed."[1] This led James Fearon, in an essay on counterfactual reasoning, to ask, "Does this imply that the gene controlling the length of Cleopatra's nose was a cause of World War I?" As you can see, then, the problem isn't that it is false that the assassination of Archduke Ferdinand caused World War I. Rather, since so many factors appear to have caused World War I, talk of one single cause seems pointless and misguided.

Once we start thinking about counterfactuals, it becomes pretty clear that things have lots of causes. That makes it hard to answer "What is *the* cause" questions. Instead, it pushes us to ask "Was this a cause" or "Did this have an effect" questions. This is perhaps disappointing.

One thought you might have, in response, is that surely some causes of a phenomenon are more important or more proximate than others. If that is true, perhaps we can still talk about the *important* or the *proximate* causes of World War I. How might we do this?

An approach that some philosophers advocate goes something like this. Imagine all the counterfactual worlds in which World War I did not occur. Some of these counterfactual worlds are very different from the actual world—for instance, World War I probably doesn't occur in many counterfactual worlds in which there is no gravity. Others are quite similar to the actual world—perhaps World War I doesn't occur in a world identical to ours through June 27, 1914, but in which Archduke Ferdinand overslept on June 28. We learn about the proximate causes of World War I by comparing the actual world to the counterfactual world in which World War I did not occur that is most similar to the actual world. This kind of analysis may allow us to give reasonable-sounding answers to "What is *the* cause" questions without abandoning our definition of causation based on counterfactual comparisons. For instance, it seems reasonable to think that the assassination of Archduke Ferdinand is a more proximate cause of World War I than is Cleopatra's nose, the laws of gravity, or the whims of Paleozoic fish.

There is certainly something to this approach. But, that said, it is often hard to assess the importance or proximity of one cause versus another in a principled way. If you know a bit of history, you surely can come up with other causes of World War I that seem equally proximate. For instance, many scholars have argued that early-twentieth-

---

[1] Antony and Cleopatra's love affair had major repercussions for world history. For instance, historians generally believe that the end of the Roman Republic and the establishment of the Roman Empire were ensured when Antony and Cleopatra were defeated by Octavian (later, Emperor Augustus) at the Battle of Actium. Had this not occurred, who knows how differently the rest of western history might have played out?

century military doctrines favoring offensive over defensive strategies played a role in causing World War I. Is the world in which a slightly different military doctrine was adopted more proximate to our world than the one in which Archduke Ferdinand was not assassinated? For that matter, is the world in which one Paleozoic fish took a different turn really such a large leap? It's hard to say.

To see the problem in a somewhat less lofty and perhaps more familiar setting, consider an NCAA Division III women's basketball game between the Chicago Maroons (where some of our star students are also star athletes) and the Emory Eagles. Suppose the Maroons are trailing the Eagles by one point, and the Maroons have just enough time left to take one final shot. They make it, winning the game by one point (in basketball, field goals are worth at least two points). The next day, the *Chicago Maroon* newspaper will fixate on that last shot, and the reporter might even write that the last shot was *the* reason the Maroons won.[2] But think about this counterfactually for a moment. Dozens of shots throughout the game were pivotal. Plausibly, every shot the Maroons made was pivotal—in a counterfactual world in which they missed that shot and everything else played out as it did in the actual world, they would have lost instead of won. Similarly, every shot the Eagles missed was pivotal—in a counterfactual world in which they made it and everything else played out as it actually did, they would have won instead. So what's so special about that last shot? One possibility is that everyone knew that the final shot would be pivotal when it was taken. But very few other causes meet this criterion, certainly not the assassination of Archduke Ferdinand. So, in our view, there is no obvious reason to think that the last shot was a more important cause of the Maroons' victory than the other shots. Instead, we think this example illustrates a basic, if frustrating, fact of life: individual events can have many equally important and consequential causes.

Another surprising fact about the counterfactual approach is that, at least in principle, it's possible for some event to have no causes at all. Suppose that the authors of this book concoct the perfect crime. We both shoot and kill our sworn enemy at the same time, knowing that either bullet would be fatal on its own. When questioned, Anthony says, "Clearly, I can't be charged with a crime. My actions had no effect whatsoever. Had I not fired my gun, the victim would still have died." And similarly, Ethan retorts, "I could not have possibly caused the victim's death either. Had I not shot my gun, he would have still died." While the justice system might not be impressed by our defense, the counterfactual logic is sound. Some events may be the result of a confluence of factors whereby no single factor could have changed the outcome. This theoretical possibility is yet another reason that it might not make much sense to ask questions like "What caused World War I?" It could well be that, for all the factors we like to talk about, taking away any one of them would in fact not have sufficed to prevent the war.

Causality and Counterexamples

One common skeptical reaction to evidence showing the existence of an average effect is to point to counterexamples. Perhaps you've had an experience like the following at a family gathering. You read a study showing that, on average, flu shots reduce the risk of contracting the flu. You mention this over Thanksgiving dinner, encouraging

---

[2] We know it's confusing that the basketball players are the Maroons, the newspaper is the *Maroon*, and probably neither sports teams nor newspapers should be named after a color. Our university is typically not known for athletics or branding.

your loved ones to get the vaccine. But your vaccine-skeptic relative says, "I don't know, I got the flu shot last year and I still got the flu." Many people nod and agree, perhaps pointing out that their friend so-and-so also got the flu shot and still got sick.

The intuition behind this kind of objection-by-way-of-counterexample is something like this: "If flu shots really prevent the flu, then no one who got a flu shot would get the flu. Thus, my one counterexample means the vaccine doesn't work."

This argument does not reflect clear thinking. The evidence says that the flu shot caused flu risk to go down, averaging across lots of people, each with their unique biology, level of flu exposure, environment, and so on. It doesn't say that it eliminated flu risk for each and every individual. But to get flu risk to go down on average, the flu shot must have prevented the flu (i.e., had a causal effect) for at least some people. We just don't know exactly which ones experienced the effect.

Let's think about this in our potential outcomes notation. Think of the potential outcomes as whether or not you get the flu. We'll say $Y = 1$ if you stayed healthy and $Y = 0$ if you got the flu. And think of the treatment as whether you got the flu shot, with $T = 1$ meaning you got the shot and $T = 0$ meaning you didn't.

Maybe there are three different kinds of people—call them the *always sick*, the *never sick*, and the *vaccine responders*. The always sick and the never sick have potential outcomes that don't respond to treatment. The always sick get the flu regardless of whether they get the flu shot, and the never sick never get the flu. In our notation,

$$Y_{1,\text{always sick}} = 0 \qquad Y_{0,\text{always sick}} = 0$$

and

$$Y_{1,\text{never sick}} = 1 \qquad Y_{0,\text{never sick}} = 1$$

But the vaccine responders are different; they get the flu if they don't get the shot, and they don't get the flu if they do get the shot:

$$Y_{1,\text{vaccine responder}} = 1 \qquad Y_{0,\text{vaccine responder}} = 0$$

In a population made up of these three groups of people, getting the flu shot reduces the probability you will get the flu. That is, on average, the treatment effect is positive. You don't know which group you are in. There is a chance you are a vaccine responder. So getting a flu shot reduces your probability of getting sick.

Let's see this in an example. Suppose there are 10 individuals. Individuals 1–5 get the flu shot, while individuals 6–10 don't. Individuals 1, 3, 4, 5, and 8 are always-sick types, so they get the flu. Individuals 5, 6, 7, and 10 are never-sick types, so they stay healthy. Individuals 2 and 9 are vaccine responders. Individual 2 gets the flu shot, so she stays healthy. But individual 9 does not get the flu shot, so he gets sick.

Table 3.2 shows potential outcomes and treatment effects. As we can see, not everyone in this population has a positive treatment effect. But the average of the treatment effects across these 10 individuals is $\frac{2}{10}$ because two of the ten are vaccine responders. So, for any individual, not knowing which type of person they are, there is a 20 percent chance that taking the flu shot will prevent them from getting the flu.

Importantly, pointing to one counterexample is neither here nor there with respect to such evidence. Perhaps your unlucky relative was a person, like individual 1, 3, or 4, whose confluence of circumstances were such that the flu shot didn't have an effect (i.e., they were an always sick). That doesn't mean it didn't have an effect for other people.

Table 3.2. Potential outcomes for flu with and without the flu shot. For each individual, the actual outcome that we can observe is in bold type. The counterfactual outcome that we do not observe is in regular type.

		Health with Flu Shot Y_{1i}	Health without Flu Shot Y_{0i}	Treatment Effect for Individual i $Y_{1i} - Y_{0i}$
Flu Shot	**Individual 1** (always sick)	**0**	0	0
	Individual 2 (vaccine responder)	**1**	0	1
	Individual 3 (always sick)	**0**	0	0
	Individual 4 (always sick)	**0**	0	0
	Individual 5 (never sick)	**1**	1	0
No Flu Shot	**Individual 6** (never sick)	1	**1**	0
	Individual 7 (never sick)	1	**1**	0
	Individual 8 (always sick)	0	**0**	0
	Individual 9 (vaccine responder)	1	**0**	1
	Individual 10 (never sick)	1	**1**	0

And it doesn't even mean that the flu shot won't prevent the flu for that same relative next year or that it won't help you. Absent any further information about which group they are in, any individual's best guess is that the flu shot will reduce their chances of contracting the flu since it does so on average. And we haven't even discussed the more complicated issue that outcomes aren't actually binary, so the shot may have a causal effect on the severity of the flu.

Of course, the possibility that effects are different for different people presents another set of important conceptual challenges. We might be able to detect such *heterogeneous treatment effects*, especially if they correspond with observable categories (e.g., men versus women, older versus younger, healthy versus sick). To identify such heterogeneous effects, we could run a separate experiment for each group, which would tell us the average effect for each group rather than for the whole population. But what if effects differ across people for complicated or obscure reasons that might never occur to us? Then, when we go to look at the effect of some intervention, it is very important to keep in mind that we are learning about an average effect. Some people may have effects much larger than the average. Others may have effects much smaller than the average. Indeed, some people may have no effect at all or an effect in the opposite direction from the average. If we don't know the source of this heterogeneity, all we will be able to say is something about the average, which, as we've discussed, may still be valuable.

Causality and the Law

As we briefly mentioned previously, one place where philosophical questions about causality become of serious practical import is in the law. Administering justice requires assigning blame and assessing liability. If we want to know whether, say, Ethan should be held liable for some harm suffered by Anthony, surely we need to know whether Ethan's actions caused that harm. But, as we've just discussed, talking about causes in this way is conceptually fraught. Many things, from the behavior of a Paleozoic fish to Ethan's alleged negligence, may have had a causal effect on the harm Anthony suffered. Is the fish liable too?

The law is aware of the philosophical conundrum. But it must ultimately come up with some pragmatic resolution that allows judges and lawyers to get on with the business of administering justice. Here's, roughly, where it comes down.

In the Common Law, causality is thought of in terms of two conditions that are closely related to things we've talked about. These are referred to as *cause-in-fact* and *proximate causality*.

Cause-in-fact is essentially counterfactual causality. Whether Ethan's actions are a cause-in-fact of Anthony's suffering is determined by whether Anthony wouldn't have suffered *but for* Ethan's actions.

Of course, as you already know, a counterfactual standard like the but-for test isn't very stringent. World War I wouldn't have happened but for a Paleozoic fish turning the wrong direction. Does that mean we should blame the poor fish for World War I?

The law's answer is no. The fish is off the hook, so to speak. This is where proximity comes in. For there to be liability, the law requires that some cause-in-fact be close enough in the causal chain. This thought is also familiar—for instance, from our argument that the assassination of Archduke Ferdinand is a more proximate cause of World War I than is Cleopatra's nose.

So an assessment of legal causality might go something like this. Suppose you order food delivery and the delivery person drives recklessly, crashing into your neighbor's car. Are you liable for your neighbor's suffering? It is plausible that, but for your decision to order delivery, the delivery person wouldn't have been in the area and your neighbor's car wouldn't have been hit. So your actions are probably a cause-in-fact of your neighbor's suffering. But there are many steps in the causal chain between your actions and the car crash, all of which are out of your hands. So the law would not find you liable for the damage to your neighbor's car.

Of course, as we've discussed, knowing exactly how to apply the conditions of cause-in-fact and proximate causality is tricky. To apply the but-for test, we have to know what the right counterfactual world is. And defining how close is close enough for a proximity test is a fraught problem, full of judgment calls. All of which is to say that these questions about causality are vexing and of great practical importance.

Can Causality Run Backward in Time?

One common intuition is that causality must run forward in time. That is, an event that happens now can have an effect on events that happen in the future. But surely, the thought goes, events that happen in the future can't affect events in the past. Indeed, one common strategy for trying to establish a causal relationship is to show that the supposed cause typically occurs prior to the supposed effect.

Let's check this intuition by thinking about birthday cards. Here's a correlation that we hope is true in the world: the number of birthday cards that get mailed to you in a given week is strongly correlated with it being within a week of your birthday. That is, many more birthday cards are mailed to you in the week before your birthday than in any other week of the year.

Now, although correlation need not imply causation, we suspect that there is a causal relationship here but not the one that's implied by thinking of causal relationships as running forward in time. Receiving birthday cards does not cause your birthday to occur. In a counterfactual world in which those cards were sent at a different time, or even in a counterfactual world in which greeting cards cease to exist, your birthday will still occur on the date you were born. Instead, you might say the causal relationship runs backward in time. Your birthday exerts an effect on the sending of birthday cards. In the counterfactual world in which your birthday occurs in a different month, you will be sent fewer birthday cards in the week preceding your birthday in this world. Thus, on our counterfactual definition, your birthday exerts a causal effect on birthday cards. Causality appears to run backward in time.

There are objections to this line of argument. For instance, one might argue that it isn't your future birthday, but anticipation of that birthday, that exerts a causal effect on the sending of birthday cards. If we changed people's beliefs about whether your birthday is coming up, we'd change their card-sending behavior. But if we changed your actual birthday, without a change in their beliefs, the cards would still be sent. On this argument, causality is operating forward in time, in the intuitive way.

Even that need not be the end of the argument. After all, where did the anticipation of your birthday come from? It presumably came from the fact of your actual birthday. If we changed the fact of your actual birthday in the future, we'd change people's anticipation of your birthday now (which would, in turn, change their card-sending behavior). Perhaps we are back to causality running backward in time. Or perhaps not. Is it really the changing of your birthday in the future that affects people's anticipation today? Or is it telling them about the change in your future birthday, in which case we are right back to causality running forward in time.

As you can no doubt tell by this point, we aren't going to solve this issue here. But we do want you to see two things clearly. First, evidence that one thing occurred before another is not, on its own, convincing evidence that the one caused the other. Second, whether or not you think causality can or cannot run backward in time, we can always define the causal effects in terms of a counterfactual.

Does Causality Require a Physical Connection?

Another intuition many people share is that causation necessarily has to do with physical connection—a view that we'll refer to as *physicalism*. One billiard ball affects another by bumping into it. Maybe such physical connections always underlie causal relationships.

While, of course, there are many examples of causal effects that occur through physical connection, there are good arguments to suggest such physical connection is not required. Think of a person who is deterred from robbing a bank by worry about imprisonment. Such a person's behavior is affected by the existence of the police, the courts, the penal code, and the prison system. The criminal justice system affects whether this person commits a crime, even though there is no physical connection between them.

Indeed, think of our previous discussion of the effect of birthdays on the sending of birthday cards. Birthdays aren't a physical thing in the world at all. It is hard to see what it would even mean for the causal relationship between birthdays and the sending of birthdays cards to occur through physical connection.

A defender of physicalism might say that with enough creativity, we can describe the effect of the criminal justice system on crime in purely physical terms. Perhaps the past arrest and conviction of people who committed crimes led reporters to write about this activity in newspapers, which led the person in question to read about these arrests in the newspaper, which, through a complicated sequence of light hitting the person's eyeballs, led to lots of chemical and electrical connections in that person's brain, which deterred them from committing a crime. You could do a similar exercise for birthdays and birthday cards.

Again, we aren't going to provide a definitive answer. There may be reasonable arguments on both sides of the physicalism debate. The important point is that we can think about counterfactually defined causal relationships that do not depend on anything like the simple, commonsense kind of physical connections suggested by the billiard ball example.

Causation Need Not Imply Correlation

We've agreed that correlation need not imply causation. But, perhaps more surprisingly, causation also need not imply correlation and certainly not correlation in the expected direction. There are many situations in which some feature of the world has (say) a *negative* effect on some other feature of the world, but those two features of the world are *positively* correlated (or vice versa).

You'd probably find a strong, positive correlation between the number of firefighters who have recently visited a house and the amount of fire damage to that house. But if we had to guess, we'd suspect that firefighters, on average, reduce fire damage. In other words, if fewer firefighters had visited, we suspect there would be even more fire damage.

So why is the correlation positive? Firefighters tend to visit houses that are on fire. So, although firefighters reduce fire damage to some degree, the houses that have been visited by firefighters tend to have more fire damage. Hence, not only should one not conclude from a correlation that there must be a causal relationship, but one also should not assume that just because a causal relationship exists, the correlations found in the world will correspond to those causal relationships in some straightforward way.

Wrapping Up

Understanding whether a causal relationship exists is one of the fundamental goals of quantitative analysis. But, if we are going to do that, we need to think clearly about what causality means.

We believe that the best way to conceptualize causality is through a thought experiment involving counterfactuals. A treatment has a causal effect on an outcome if the outcome would have been different had the treatment been different. Of course, in the actual world, the treatment was what it was. We can't observe the counterfactual world in which the treatment was different in order to figure out if the outcome would have been different. This is the fundamental problem of causal inference.

The fact that causal effects are unobservable doesn't mean data analysis cannot help us learn about them. In particular, we can learn about the average effect in some population, even though we can't observe any of the individual effects directly.

Doing so involves making careful use of quantitative knowledge about things like correlations. In part 2 we turn to a more detailed discussion of how we establish and quantify correlations. This will set us up to be able to think clearly in part 3 about estimating causal effects.

Key Terms

- **Causal effect:** Informally, the change in some feature of the world that would result from a change to some other feature of the world. Formally, the difference in the potential outcomes for some unit under two different treatment statuses.
- **Body Vibes:** Stickers that a company called Goop claims cause clear skin. The authors of this book do not endorse Body Vibes, mainly because we will be releasing our own competitor: Brain Vibes. One sticker applied to the temple causes clear thinking.
- **Counterfactual comparison:** A comparison of things in two different worlds or states of affairs, at least one of which does not actually exist.
- **Treatment:** Terminology we use to describe any intervention in the world. We usually use this terminology when we are thinking about the causal effect of the treatment, so we want to know what happens with and without the treatment. Importantly, although it sounds like medical terminology, *treatment* as we use it can refer to *anything* that happens in the world that might have an effect on something else.
- **Potential outcomes framework:** A mathematical framework for representing counterfactuals.
- **Potential outcome:** The potential outcome for some unit under some treatment status is the outcome that unit would experience under that (possibly counterfactual) treatment status.
- **Fundamental problem of causal inference:** This refers to the fact that, since we only observe any given unit in one treatment status at any one time, we can never directly observe the causal effect of a treatment.
- **Heterogeneous treatment effects:** When the effect of a treatment is not the same for every unit of observation (as in the case of flu shots and virtually every other interesting example of a causal relationship), we say that the treatment effects are heterogeneous. Sometimes we're still interested in the average effect even though we know the treatment effects are heterogeneous, and sometimes we want to explicitly study the nature of the heterogeneity. (In contrast, when discussing the unlikely possibility that treatment effects are the same for every unit, we would refer to *homogeneous* treatment effects.)

Exercises

3.1   Sarah says that she is hungry. John hands her a piece of pizza. Sarah eats the pizza and then declares that she is no longer hungry.

(a) The fundamental problem of causal inference seems to say that you can't know that Sarah eating the pizza had a causal effect on her no longer being hungry. Is that right? Explain.

    (b) Do you think you nonetheless have good reasons to believe that eating the pizza had an effect on Sarah no longer being hungry? Explain why or why not.

    (c) Do you have good reasons for believing that John handing Sarah the pizza had a causal effect on her no longer being hungry? In your assessment, are the reasons to believe John's actions had a causal effect better or worse than the reasons to believe Sarah eating the piece of pizza had a causal effect?

3.2   A government is considering making alcohol consumption illegal as part of a public health campaign. Let's think of making alcohol illegal as the treatment T. Write $T = 1$ if the government makes alcohol illegal and $T = 0$ if the government leaves alcohol legal.

    We will think of a binary outcome for each person: either they drink alcohol or they do not. If person i drinks at treatment status T, we write her potential outcome as $Y_{Ti} = 1$, and if she doesn't drink, we write it as $Y_{Ti} = 0$.

    Suppose the society is made up of three groups: the always drinkers, the legal drinkers, and the never drinkers. The always drinkers will drink whether or not alcohol is legal. The legal drinkers will drink if and only if alcohol is legal. The never drinkers won't drink whether or not alcohol is legal.

    (a) Write down, in potential outcomes notation and as a number (0 or 1), each of the two potential outcomes for each of the three groups.

    (b) Write down, in both potential outcomes notation and as a number (0 or 1), the causal effect of making alcohol illegal on drinking for each of the three groups.

    (c) Is there an effect, on average, of banning alcohol in this society?

    (d) Suppose you are out to lunch with some friends and one of them says, "My uncle lives in a place where they banned alcohol and all of his friends kept drinking, so I don't think the ban does anything." Explain, in terms of our example, why this isn't a convincing argument.

3.3   The Republican National Committee (RNC) has hired three consultants and asked them to figure out the cause of their loss in the 2020 presidential election. The first consultant says that they didn't do enough television advertising. The second consultant reports that they should have encouraged more of their supporters to vote rather than criticizing voting by mail. The third consultant concludes that Donald Trump should have done a better job responding to the COVID-19 pandemic and should have shown more compassion on the campaign trail. Confused by the apparently conflicting information, the RNC hires you, a quantitative analyst, to adjudicate between these three possibilities. What would you tell them? How would you proceed?

3.4   In the 2016 U.S. Open golf tournament, Dustin Johnson was leading the tournament in the final round, and his ball was resting on the fifth green. While preparing for his upcoming putt, he tapped his putter on the ground next to the ball and the ball moved. The rules at the time stated that if we were highly certain that a player caused his ball to move, even if it was inadvertent, he or she should incur a penalty. Because you're an expert on causation, the rules officials call you in to evaluate the situation. The officials make the following arguments. Please provide your expert response to each one.

(a) Johnson couldn't have possibly caused the ball to move, because he (and his putter) never touched it.

(b) Johnson shouldn't receive a penalty because the true cause of the ball moving was the greenskeeper. Had the greenskeeper not cut and rolled the greens so much that morning, the ball wouldn't have moved.

(c) An empirically minded official went out to the same green, placed a ball down, tapped his putter on the ground next to the ball, and it didn't move. Therefore, Johnson's actions couldn't have caused the ball to move.

(d) One official was watching the incident up close and says he's virtually certain that if Johnson had not tapped his putter next to the ball, it wouldn't have moved. Therefore, he caused it to move and should receive a penalty.

Readings and References

You can read about Body Vibes on the Goop website. We last accessed it on June 15, 2020. http://goop.com/wearable-stickers-that-promote-healing-really/

The quote from Blaise Pascal on Cleopatra's nose is from his seventeenth-century collection entitled *Pensées*.

The essay about counterfactual reasoning discussing the gene controlling the length of Cleopatra's nose is

James D. Fearon. 2011. "Counterfactuals and Hypothesis Testing in Political Science." *World Politics* 43(2):169–195.

If you'd like to read more about the counterfactual definition of causality, potential outcomes, and surrounding discussions and debates, have a look at these:

David Lewis. 1973. "Causation." *Journal of Philosophy* 70:556–67.

Paul W. Holland. 1986. "Statistics and Causal Inference." *Journal of the American Statistical Association* 81(396):945–60.

Stephen Mumford and Rani Lill Anjum. 2014. *Causality: A Very Short Introduction.* Oxford University Press.

There is also a nice entry by Peter Menzies and Helen Beebee in the *Stanford Encyclopedia of Philosophy*: https://plato.stanford.edu/entries/causation-counterfactual/.

PART II

Does a Relationship Exist?

CHAPTER 4

Correlation Requires Variation

What You'll Learn

- You can't learn about a correlation without variation in both variables of interest.
- In many realms of life—from education to medicine to rocket science—people fall into the trap of trying to make claims about correlations without such variation.
- A particularly common way people fall into this mistake is by *selecting on the dependent variable*, examining only instances when some phenomenon occurred rather than comparing cases where it occurred to cases where it did not.
- Many institutional procedures push us to select on the dependent variable without noticing it.

Introduction

In chapter 2 we discussed the idea that the correlation between two features of the world is the extent to which they tend to occur together. We opened our discussion of correlation by thinking about whether oil production and autocracy are correlated. To figure this out we looked at the country-level data represented in table 4.1.

To determine whether there is a correlation between oil production and autocracy we compared the percentage of major oil producers that are autocracies to the percentage of countries that aren't major oil producers that are autocracies. To make this comparison, we needed four pieces of information: the number of autocracies that are major oil producers, the number of democracies that are major oil producers, the number of autocracies that are not major oil producers, and the number of democracies that are not major oil producers. Had we been lacking any of these pieces of information, we would not have been able to figure out whether oil production and autocracy are correlated.

To see why, suppose we didn't know the number of democracies that are major oil producers. (Of course, we'd also have to not know the total number of countries, so we couldn't just back out the 9 by subtracting the number of countries in the other three categories from the total number of countries.) We still know that about 20 percent ($\frac{29}{147}$) of countries that aren't major oil producers are autocracies. But now we can't figure out

Table 4.1. Oil production and type of government.

	Not Major Oil Producer	Major Oil Producer	Total
Democracy	118	9	127
Autocracy	29	11	40
Total	147	20	167

what proportion of the major oil producers are autocracies. It could be anything. If the number of democracies that are major oil producers turned out to be (say) 11, then 50 percent ($\frac{11}{22}$) of major oil producers would be autocracies and there would be a positive correlation. If the number of democracies that are major oil producers turned out to be (say) 99, then only 10 percent ($\frac{11}{110}$) of major oil producers would be autocracies, so there would be a negative correlation. If the number of democracies that are major oil producers turned out to be 44, then 20 percent ($\frac{11}{55}$) of major oil producers would be autocracies—the same as for countries that are not major oil producers—and there would be no correlation at all. So, just as we saw in our discussion of scandals and congressional representatives in chapter 2, we need to observe all four pieces of information to figure out the correlation.

This is what we mean when we say that correlation requires variation: If you want to figure out whether two variables are correlated, you have to observe variation in both of them. You must observe the number of countries that are and are not major oil producers. And you must observe the number of autocracies and democracies in each group. Just observing variation in one or the other variable is not enough. In chapter 2, when we asked which of five factual statements described a correlation, the problem with the three statements that did not was a lack of variation in one of the variables.

While it may seem obvious, on the basis of our simple binary example, that correlation requires variation, in our experience, it is anything but. Indeed, failing to look for variation in one or another variable while trying to establish a correlation is an exceptionally common mistake.

In this chapter, we explore this mistake and try to unpack why it is so common. Broadly, we think there are two closely related reasons that people so frequently try to establish a correlation without variation. The first reason is called *selecting on the dependent variable*. The second reason is that the world is often organized in ways that push us to make this mistake.

This chapter, more than most in the book, is built around examples. We do this for a reason. We've found that, once we explain that correlation requires variation, people tend to nod their head in agreement, appearing to understand. Indeed, because the point seems obvious when put in plain English, many people are skeptical that this could be such a big problem. And yet, they themselves go right back to making the same mistake. We hope that by showing you lots of examples of very smart people making this mistake in high-stakes environments, we will convince you that this is a real problem and that avoiding this error requires clear thinking, genuine effort, and concentration.

Selecting on the Dependent Variable

If you want to forecast or explain some phenomenon, it is a natural impulse to start by examining previous instances of that phenomenon occurring. This is called *selecting on the dependent variable*. But if you look only at instances when the phenomenon occurred, you are trying to assess a correlation without variation, since you have no variation in whether or not the phenomenon occurred. This is like looking for correlates of autocracy without examining any democracies. It won't work.

The phrase *dependent variable* refers to the variable representing the phenomenon you are trying to forecast or explain. This mistake is referred to as *selecting on the dependent variable* because you are selecting which cases to look at based on the value of the dependent variable (e.g., only looking at autocracies) rather than looking at variation in the dependent variable (e.g., comparing autocracies and democracies).

Consider a few examples. Following the financial crisis of 2008, both scholars and journalists who wanted to understand how to predict future financial crises invested enormous time and energy examining the historic record to look for patterns in previous crises. Malcolm Gladwell, in his book *Outliers*, tries to understand the correlates of personal success by recounting the lives of highly accomplished people, looking for similarities. Congress, considering a change to American counterinsurgency strategy in Afghanistan, heard testimony on the correlates of suicide terrorism from an academic expert who had done an exhaustive study of all suicide terrorist campaigns since 1980, looking for shared characteristics.

As natural as it seems to look for commonalities in past instances of events you want to forecast, it really is a mistake. Correlation requires variation. Each of the studies just described would have been far more informative if they'd had variation in the dependent variable.

The claim that we can't learn about the correlates of financial crises or suicide terrorism by looking for commonalities among historic cases of similar events may seem counterintuitive. But, since we know that correlation requires variation, the mistake is actually quite simple to grasp. Put in the terms of our earlier example, each of these examples is analogous to looking for correlates of oil production without any data on non-oil-producing countries!

To see the key conceptual flaw in all of these arguments in another way, let's start by considering the central claim in Gladwell's *Outliers*, the so-called *10,000-hour rule*.

The 10,000-Hour Rule

Gladwell's idea is that it takes about 10,000 hours of serious practice to master any difficult skill. Talent might matter too, but first and foremost, if you are looking for a great achiever, look for someone who put in that 10,000 hours of practice.

Now, of course, Gladwell isn't just interested in forecasting great success. He thinks the 10,000-hour rule might be causal. If true, this would have far-reaching consequences. Given enough practice, perhaps any of us could achieve almost anything.

But talk of causality is premature. Before we can think about causality, we need to figure out whether Gladwell's evidence is even compelling for the claim of a correlation between 10,000 hours of practice and great success. So let's start there.

Gladwell asks, "Is the ten-thousand-hour rule a general rule of success?" The answer, he concludes, is yes. The evidence? "If we scratch below the surface of every great achiever" we see the same pattern (p. 47). "Virtually every success story... involves someone or some group working harder than their peers" (p. 239). In case after case, from Bill Gates to the Beatles, Gladwell shows that great achievers put in their 10,000 hours—overwhelming evidence, he concludes, that practice predicts success.

Let's try to think a little more clearly about Gladwell's evidence. What has Gladwell shown us? Of course, he hasn't actually looked at every great achiever. But he's shown us evidence that lots of great achievers practice at least 10,000 hours. The big problem

Table 4.2. Great achievers practice more than 10,000 hours.

	Great Achiever	Not Great Achiever	Total
10,000 Hours of Practice	Many	?	
Not 10,000 Hours of Practice	Very few	?	
Total			

is that he's told us nothing about all the people who aren't great achievers. A table of evidence for *Outliers* would look something like table 4.2.

Even granting that Gladwell is correct that most great achievers put in 10,000 hours of practice, this doesn't tell us whether 10,000 hours of practice is correlated with great success. Correlation requires variation. Because he has selected on the dependent variable, Gladwell's data lack variation in achievement. If you want to know whether putting in 10,000 hours of practice correlates with success, it is not enough to observe that most great achievers put in 10,000 hours of practice. We need to know about the non-achievers' practice habits as well.

Of course, Gladwell's analysis does provide some information that we didn't previously have. Momentarily, let's suppose that Gladwell didn't cherry pick his stories in order to fit his narrative (although, of course he did: he's a storyteller, not a scientist). In this case, we've learned that most highly successful people put in 10,000 hours of practice before achieving great success.

Although this is not enough information to measure a correlation, Gladwell and his defenders might argue that we already have a rough sense that most members of the general public who are not great achievers have not put in 10,000 hours of practice. In that case, maybe Gladwell's analysis significantly shifts our beliefs about the correlation between practice and great success, even if he didn't explicitly measure the correlation. In these cases where we already have a good sense of the prevalence of something in the general population, perhaps it's useful to show that the prevalence is different for a certain group of interest.

Maybe. But we're still skeptical that Gladwell's analysis teaches us much. That's because most people probably *have* devoted at least 10,000 hours of practice to *something*. Anthony has spent 10,000 hours on the golf course, and he's no Tiger Woods. Ethan has spent 10,000 hours playing guitar, and he's no Jimi Hendrix. If you've worked at something full time for five years but you're not the most successful person in your field, then you're one of the many, many people in the top-right cell of table 4.2 that Gladwell never considered.

We should also remember that Gladwell is a gifted storyteller. In the extremely unlikely scenario in which Anthony wins the Masters, Gladwell might write an inspiring and convincing story about how, despite being a full-time college professor, Anthony's many years of practice, failure, and more practice allowed him to pull off the greatest Cinderella story in sports history (just let us dream for a moment). But far more likely, Anthony will happily continue to be one of millions, if not billions, of people who love something, work hard at it, but never achieve immense success and who are never considered in Gladwell's analysis.

To test your understanding, let's see the problem with claims like Gladwell's in another setting. We are going to repeat his exact argument, but in a fictional example that we hope makes the problem even clearer.

Table 4.3. What sick people drank (made-up data).

	Sick	Not Sick	Total
Drank Beverage	500		
Didn't Drink Beverage	0		
Total	500		

Table 4.4. What sick and healthy people drank (made-up data).

	Sick	Not Sick	Total
Drank Beverage	500	9,500	10,000
Didn't Drink Beverage	0	0	0
Total	500	9,500	10,000

Suppose a town of 10,000 people experiences a surprising spate of illness. In the course of a month, 500 people are taken ill with the same symptoms. Local health officials want to determine the cause of the illness. They take case histories of the 500 sick people, looking for commonalities. In the course of this investigation, they find that all 500 people consumed the same beverage, from the same source, the day before they were hospitalized.

Table 4.3 shows data corresponding to our fictionalized story.

The facts about the beverage and the illness correspond exactly to the facts about practice and success from *Outliers*. Everyone who gets sick (succeeds) drank the same beverage (put in 10,000 hours). Surely, then, drinking that beverage (practicing 10,000 hours) is an important predictor of illness (great success). If we want to know who else is likely to get sick, we should survey the town and find out who else drank the same beverage. Right?

Suppose we tell you that the beverage in question is tap water. The claim that the "pattern" of illness suggests a correlation between the beverage and the disease now seems questionable. Why? Because many people consume tap water every day. Indeed, in our fictional town, all 500 people who got sick consumed tap water, but so too did the 9,500 who didn't get sick. As table 4.4 makes clear, there is in fact no correlation between the beverage and getting sick: 100 percent of sick people and 100 percent of healthy people drank the beverage.

The 10,000-hour rule is similarly unsubstantiated by data of the sort presented by Gladwell. Yes, lots of successful people practice very hard. So too do lots of less successful people. Think of all the bands that practiced countless hours, played countless gigs, and did not become the Beatles.

Corrupting the Youth

American kids who liked rock music in the 1980s (ask your parents) may remember the Parents Music Resource Center (PMRC). The PMRC was a lobbying group whose members opposed what they perceived to be the increasingly inappropriate content of rock music. Most famous among the founders of the PMRC was Tipper Gore, wife of then Senator and later Vice President Al Gore, who started the group after being shocked by the lyrics of a Prince song.

The PMRC claimed that explicit lyrics were corrupting the youth, causing suicide, sexual violence, and even murder. They denounced "porn rock"—a category that included Bruce Springsteen because the song "I'm on Fire" contained a sexual innuendo—and demanded warning labels be placed on albums. In 1985, the Senate Commerce, Science, and Transportation Committee held hearings. Musicians from across the musical spectrum, from the country singer John Denver to Twisted Sister's Dee Snider testified against the PMRC's position. But the PMRC prevailed.

Let's consider a bit of the argument. Here is the testimony of Jeff Ling, a PMRC consultant:

> Many albums today include songs that encourage suicide, violent revenge, sexual violence, and violence just for violence's sake. . . This is Steve Boucher. Steve died while listening to AC/DC's "Shoot to Thrill." Steve fired his father's gun into his mouth. . . A few days ago I was speaking in San Antonio. The day before I arrived, they buried a young high school student. This young man had taken his tape deck to the football field. He hung himself while listening to AC/DC's "Shoot to Thrill." Suicide has become epidemic in our country among teenagers. Some 6,000 will take their lives this year. Many of these young people find encouragement from some rock stars who present death as a positive, almost attractive alternative. . .Of course, AC/DC is no stranger to violent material. . .One of their fans I know you are aware of is the accused Night Stalker.

Ling's argument, which is typical of crusaders against corruption of the youth, amounts to this:

1. Some young people behave regrettably.
2. The youth who behave regrettably all listen to this terrible rock music.
3. The music must be the cause of the regrettable behavior

Of course, talk of causality is again premature. We'll focus on whether such evidence even suggests a correlation.

Thirty years earlier, in 1954, the Senate heard astoundingly similar testimony about that generation's scourge of the youth, comic books. Here is the neurologist and psychiatrist Fredric Wertham testifying before a Senate subcommittee:

> There is a school in a town in New York State where there has been a great deal of stealing. Some time ago some boys attacked another boy and they twisted his arm so viciously that it broke in two places, and, just like in a comic book, the bone came through the skin.
>
> In the same school about 10 days later 7 boys pounced on another boy and pushed his head against the concrete so that the boy was unconscious and had to be taken to the hospital. He had a concussion of the brain.
>
> In this same high school in 1 year 26 girls became pregnant. The score this year, I think, is eight. Maybe it is nine by now.
>
> Now, Mr. Chairman, this is what I call ethical and moral confusion. I don't think that any of these boys or girls individually vary very much. It cannot be explained individually, alone.
>
> Here is a general moral confusion and I think that these girls were seduced mentally long before they were seduced physically, and, of course, all those people

there are very, very great—not all of them, but most of them, are very great comic book readers, have been and are.

This kind of argument persists in the contemporary environment. We have all heard, and perhaps even made, similar claims about the insidious effects of television or video games or social media. For instance, following the horrific shootings at Columbine High School, the U.S. Department of Education and the Secret Service set up a joint task force to determine what factors would allow school officials to anticipate and prevent school violence. The task force studied all thirty-seven incidents of school violence from 1974 through 2000. While concluding that there is no single profile of a school shooter, they also reported the following (among many other things):

1. "Many attackers felt bullied, persecuted, or injured by others prior to the attack."
2. "Most attackers were known to have had difficulty coping with significant losses or personal failures."
3. "Most attackers engaged in some behavior, prior to the incident, that caused others concern or indicated a need for help."
4. "Over half of the attackers demonstrated some interest in violence, through movies, video games, books, and other media."

A similar commission was convened in 2018. While less focused on specific corrupters of the youth, this commission too at times fell into selecting on the dependent variable. For instance, in a chapter recommending increased focus on character education, the commission notes that many school shooters experienced social isolation, without comparing this to levels of social isolation among those who do not engage in violence:

In the aftermath of the Parkland shooting, multiple reports indicated the alleged shooter experienced feelings of isolation and depression in the years leading up to the shooting. . . . Perpetrators of previous school shootings shared that sense of detachment. For example, one Columbine shooter was characterized as depressed and reclusive. . . . Family members and acquaintances of the Virginia Tech shooter said that, as his isolation grew during his senior year, his "attention to schoolwork and class time dropped." . . . The same was true at Sandy Hook.

At times the commission does avoid selecting on the dependent variable. In a chapter on mental health, they write,

Individuals who commit mass shootings may or may not have a serious mental illness (SMI). There is little population-level evidence to support the notion that those diagnosed with mental illness are more likely than anyone else to commit gun crimes.

But not long after, they return to arguments that suggest they are looking for correlation without variation:

A U.S. Department of Education and U.S. Secret Service analysis found that as many as a quarter of individuals who committed mass shootings had been in treatment for mental illnesses. . . Such individuals often feel aggrieved and extremely angry, and nurture fantasies of violent revenge.

These are not the only such government reports; such analyses are seemingly inevitable after acts of youth violence. But, for reasons we've already seen, these findings, like the Senate testimonies above, are misleading. Even if it were true that virtually every young person who behaves in a troubling manner also listens to rock, reads comic books, or plays video games, this would not establish a correlation between such behavior and these supposed corrupters of the youth. Correlation requires variation. Evidence for the proposition that kids who engage in those activities are *more* likely to be violent than kids who do not engage in those activities must involve a comparison of these two types of kids.

If we want to know if there is a relationship between some putative scourge of the youth and violence, we must not select on the dependent variable—that is, we must compare violent kids to non-violent kids and see whether violent kids are more likely to engage in that scourge than non-violent kids. (Again, even then, we can't say the relationship is causal.) The fact that even experts can fail to think clearly about this means that, for all the expert opinion offered on the topic, we know far less than we could about the correlates of youth violence.

High School Dropouts

Let's stick, for the moment, with troubled youth. Early twenty-first-century America has a high school graduation problem. At a time when the economic returns to education are at an all-time high, almost a third of students in the public schools fail to complete high school on time. Over 10 percent never graduate.

In 2006, the Bill and Melinda Gates Foundation decided to put some resources into addressing this issue. As one step in trying to find a solution, they commissioned a study on the correlates of dropping out of high school. The report's main thrust is that high school dropout is not primarily associated with the things you might have guessed— problems at home, lack of academic preparation, or listening to rock music. Rather, the big problem seems to be that kids aren't engaged by the educational environment and find school boring.

As the report states, "nearly half (47 percent) [of dropouts] said a major reason for dropping out was that classes were not interesting." And "nearly 7 in 10 respondents (69 percent) said they were not motivated or inspired to work hard."

Unfortunately, because correlation requires variation, the evidence in this Gates Foundation study, just like the evidence presented by the PMRC and the anti–comic book lobby before it, is pretty uninformative.

The fact that half of high school dropouts report finding school uninteresting does not mean that finding school uninteresting correlates with dropout. Because correlation requires variation, measuring the correlation has to involve comparing dropouts to non-dropouts to see whether dropouts are more likely to find school uninteresting. The Gates Foundation study, because it looks only at high school dropouts, can't make this comparison.

This point isn't just pedantic. Think about it for a second. Both authors of this book went to high school. Neither dropped out. However, both authors recall finding some classes uninteresting. Didn't you?

Now, our personal experiences also don't constitute compelling evidence. So let's see if we can do a little better in figuring out whether finding classes boring is really a key predictor of dropout. Researchers at Indiana University did a nationally representative survey of high school students in 2009. Most of these students are not going to drop out, yet the researchers report that "two out of three respondents (66%) in 2009 are bored at least every day in class." That's even more than the 50 percent of dropouts who find school boring in the Gates Foundation study.

But let's be careful. There are many reasons the Gates Foundation survey and the Indiana University survey can't be compared. They sample different groups of students, ask different questions, and are from different years. So we don't want to leap to conclusions. But at the very least, the Indiana University survey should make you worry that finding school boring is in fact a very common experience for high school students, not just those who drop out.

The future of American education is serious stuff. It is admirable that the Gates Foundation is trying to improve education. But their research ignores a key principle of thinking clearly with data; they are trying to learn about the correlates of educational failure without any variation in failure versus success. This approach cannot work.

Suicide Attacks

In 2009, University of Chicago professor and noted terrorism expert Robert Pape testified to the House of Representatives Armed Services Subcommittee on Terrorism. The topic was General Stanley McChrystal's proposal for a forty-thousand-troop surge to fight the Taliban insurgency in Afghanistan. Here is what Pape had to say:

> The picture is clear, the more Western troops have gone to Afghanistan, the more local residents have viewed themselves as under foreign occupation—and are using suicide and other terrorism to resist it...As my study of suicide terrorism around the world since 1980 shows, what motivates suicide terrorists is not the existence of a terrorist sanctuary, but the presence of foreign forces on land they prize. So, it is little surprise that US troops are producing anti-American suicide attackers.

Pape goes on to recommend a major rethinking of American military strategy in Afghanistan. His argument is based on the claim that suicide attacks are primarily motivated by foreign occupation. His evidence is the data he collected and analyzed in articles and two books on every suicide terrorist campaign in the world since 1980.

The argument sounds plausible. In Afghanistan, U.S. forces were being attacked by suicide bombers who wanted the United States to leave the country. Tamil Tiger suicide bombers attacked a government in Sri Lanka they believed was occupying their homeland. Palestinian suicide bombers attack Israelis, arguing that they are foreign occupiers. It sure seems like occupation is a major correlate of suicide attacks.

Now, the claim that virtually every suicide attack is targeted against a foreign occupier is, we think, debatable. (For instance, while Osama bin Laden claimed the American troops stationed in Saudi Arabia at the invitation of the Saudi government were an occupying force, are we sure we agree with him?) But, for the sake of argument, let's assume that the basic factual claim is correct. Does this mean that there is a correlation between foreign occupation and suicide attacks?

The answer is, of course, no. Correlation requires variation. To understand the correlates of suicide attacks, you can't just study every single instance of a suicide attack and look for commonalities. That is selecting on the dependent variable. You must compare conflicts with suicide attacks to those without.

An easy thing to do in this case is to simply look at every single country and ask: Are foreign-occupied countries more likely to experience suicide attacks than countries that are not foreign occupied? It turns out that a recent study did precisely that comparison and found that the answer was no. In particular, if we compare occupied to non-occupied countries, the difference in likelihood of experiencing suicide violence is less than 1 percentage point!

What is going on? All those examples of suicide bombers that we listed involved attacking foreign occupiers. How could it be that there is almost no correlation between foreign occupation and suicide attacks?

The way to get some intuition is to think about how many foreign occupations there have been that didn't lead to suicide terrorism. The British occupation of Ireland, despite sparking a decades-long campaign of violent resistance, never gave rise to suicide terrorism. Basque separatists in Spain fought a decades-long campaign and never resorted to suicide attacks. At various points during the Cold War (and beyond), the United States stationed troops in Germany, Japan, South Korea, Grenada, Panama, and Haiti (arguably, all as much occupations as the putative occupation of Saudi Arabia) but suffered not even one suicide attack in any of these locations. If occupation predicts suicide violence, what was going on in all these places?

This example has another nice feature. It not only illustrates the mistake of looking for correlation without variation. It shows you how misled you can be by trying to reach conclusions by only looking at cases where the phenomenon of interest (here, suicide attacks) occurs—that is, by selecting on the dependent variable. To see this, it helps to go back in history a little.

Suppose you'd started collecting data on suicide violence in the early 1980s. By 1986 you'd have recorded thirty-three attacks and over one thousand deaths. Essentially every single one of those attacks was carried out by the armed Shi'a militia Hezbollah against American, Israeli, and French targets in Lebanon, including the attack on the U.S. Marines Barracks in Beirut, which killed 320 people.

If you'd looked for commonalities amongst every suicide attack ever committed in 1986, you might have noticed that they were all carried out by Muslims in the Middle East. Using the same logic that led to the conclusion that occupation is a major predictor of suicide attacks, you might have concluded that Islam was the key correlate.

Of course, if you had done a proper comparison, you wouldn't have reached this conclusion. There are a whole lot of Muslim-majority countries in the world. In 1986, almost none of them had experienced suicide violence.

Moreover, if you were trying to forecast where the next suicide attack might occur, this conclusion in 1986 would have led you terribly astray. In 1987, the world saw the first suicide attack by the Liberation Tigers of Tamil Eelam (Tamil Tigers), a group of secular separatists in Sri Lanka with no ties to Islam. The attack marked the beginning of what would become the largest campaign of suicide violence the world had ever seen. When you try to establish correlation without variation, you can get things colossally wrong.

The World Is Organized to Make Us Select on the Dependent Variable

As we've seen, it is incredibly easy to fall into the trap of selecting on the dependent variable simply by failing to think clearly. But matters are even worse than that. The world sometimes seems to be organized in a way that almost forces us to look for correlation without variation. In this section we look at three ways in which that is true:

the organization of certain professions, the practice of post-mortem analyses following disasters, and the way we seek life advice.

Doctors Mostly See Sick People

Anyone who has suffered from significant back pain knows that it is rough. When, inevitably, many of you develop back pain, you will likely go to a doctor, who will send you to get an MRI. Usually, the MRI shows some bulging or herniated discs in the afflicted back. These bulging discs are taken to be the cause, in some not fully understood way, of the back pain (maybe by impinging a nerve).

The recommendations following this diagnosis can vary greatly. Some doctors want to operate. Others will refer you to a pain clinic where yet other doctors might stick you with giant needles with medication that dulls pain and reduces inflammation. Still others will suggest you try physical therapy and take lots of painkillers.

Here's the kicker. As best we can tell, there is precious little evidence that having a bulging disc is correlated with back pain. Here are the facts. People with back pain are quite likely to exhibit disc herniation. Indeed, in a 2011 British study published in the journal *Pain*, about two-thirds of back pain sufferers who were referred for an MRI had nerve compression as a result of a disc bulge or herniation. This seems like evidence that those bulging discs really are a problem.

But remember, correlation requires variation. You should be asking yourself: What about people without back pain? How do their discs look? Good question. The answer is, they look exactly the same as the people's discs who do have back pain! A 1994 study published in the *New England Journal of Medicine* found that about two-thirds of people who do not suffer from back pain also have a disc bulge or herniation. Once you compare both variables of interest, the apparent association between bulging discs and back pain disappears.

It is easy to see how doctors could end up associating bulging discs with back pain. Even if they are thinking clearly, by dint of profession, a doctor is almost doomed not to look at variation. Sick people go to the doctor. Healthy people tend not to. Your typical back doctor just doesn't get much of an opportunity to look at the MRIs of people with well-functioning backs.

Post-Mortems

Another way the world is organized to make us look for correlation without variation is through institutional rules or procedures. A particularly common example is the way organizations respond to both great failures and great successes.

Following a crisis or disaster, organizations want to know what went wrong so they can avoid making similar mistakes in the future. Likewise, following great successes they want to know what went right to establish best practices. Achieving these goals is the role of a post-mortem analysis. Looking closely at an instance of great failure or great success is not, in and of itself, a mistake. Indeed, it is a very sensible starting point. But, if you think clearly, you should already be able to see that, on their own, such post-mortem procedures are not sufficient to establish correlations between what went wrong (or right) and existing practices.

The question you should be trying to answer when assessing lessons learned from a crisis is, Which decisions should have been made differently to avoid the crisis, given what we knew at the time? However, when assessing lessons learned, we often slip

Table 4.5. Rehearsal strategies in the week before competitions where your band performed poorly (made-up data).

	Do Well	Do Poorly	Total
Extra Rehearsals	?	80	?
Take It Easy	?	8	?
Total	?	88	?

into answering a slightly different question: Which decisions should have been made differently to avoid the crisis, given what we know now?

The latter isn't a terribly useful question to answer, for the reasons we've already talked about in this chapter. Suppose you find some decision that, it turns out, seems to have led directly to the disaster. After the fact, it is easy to say, "Had we not taken that action, the disaster wouldn't have happened." But does that mean that you shouldn't take similar such actions in the future? To know the answer to that, you'd want to know whether disasters are more likely to occur in the presence of such actions than in their absence. That is, you want to know whether there is a correlation between taking such actions and disasters occurring. To establish a correlation, you need variation. But a post-mortem, almost by definition, has no variation. You are only looking at an instance of the disaster occurring.

To see what we mean a little more intuitively, let's start with a fictional example. Then we'll turn to some real cases.

Imagine you are a high school band director preparing for a regional competition in a week. You have to decide whether to push the kids hard with a grueling schedule of rehearsals or give them time off so they go into the competition relaxed. You weigh the pros and cons, deciding preparation is more important than mental state. So you schedule a week of extra rehearsals. Unfortunately, the band doesn't play terribly well on the day of the competition, and you are eliminated in the first round.

In your post-mortem analysis you ask the question, What should I have done to avoid the loss? It occurs to you that you've seen a lot of bands lose competitions in this same way (i.e., having rehearsed themselves to death the week before), so you decide to collect some data. You look at the history of all the competitions in which your band was eliminated in the early rounds. Just like in this year's competition, you find that in almost every one of these competitions, you scheduled a heavy rehearsal schedule in the week leading up to the competition.

Let's say you did a week of intensive rehearsing prior to 80 out of 88 losses. The post-mortem conclusion seems clear. In over 90 percent of the cases where your band was eliminated early, it was after a week of exhausting rehearsal. Now you feel even more sure: intensive rehearsal is the wrong strategy. Table 4.5 summarizes what you know so far from your post-mortem analysis.

But this conclusion doesn't necessarily follow from the data you've collected. In fact, from this data alone, there's no way to know whether those rehearsals are associated with performing well or poorly, because you have answered the wrong question.

You don't want to know if bands did extra rehearsals prior to most of the competitions where they performed poorly. You want to know if extra rehearsals are positively or negatively correlated with performing well. The answer to that question will help you know whether those extra rehearsals are a good idea for the next competition.

Table 4.6. Rehearsal strategy in the week before competitions where your band performed well or poorly (made-up data).

	Do Well	Do Poorly	Total
Extra Rehearsals	300	80	380
Take It Easy	12	8	20
Total	312	88	400

To answer that question, you have to look at the correlation between extra rehearsals and performing well in competition. But you can't know the correlation from your post-mortem analysis. Correlation requires variation. Your post-mortem, by focusing only on poor performances, guarantees that you lack the variation needed to establish a correlation.

To do a better job, you could look at the history of all the band competitions you've participated in to see whether you performed well or poorly. Now you have variation in both variables and can fill in all the data, as shown in table 4.6.

From this table it is clear that there is in fact a strong positive correlation between scheduling extra rehearsals and performing well. The probability of your band performing well when you rehearsed hard is about 79 percent ($\frac{300}{380} \approx .79$). By contrast, the probability of your band performing well when you took it easy the week prior to a competition is only 60 percent ($\frac{12}{20} = .60$). The only reason that the post-mortem turned up the finding that almost every poor performance involved intensive rehearsals is that those extra rehearsals are so effective that sensible band directors almost always schedule them.

By finding the variation needed to establish the correlation that is actually relevant to the question at hand, you reach a very different conclusion than you did in your original post-mortem. Following the loss, it seemed like intensive rehearsals were a bad idea. But before the fact, given the information available, rehearsing hard was exactly the right call. Faced with the same situation again, you should probably make the same decision.

This problem is endemic to the process of post-mortems following disasters. We tend to look at the factors that seem like they contributed to the disaster, ask if they were also present in past disasters, and, when they were, conclude that we should eliminate those factors in the future. But, in so doing, we are making the same mistake as the band director. Without variation in whether or not a disaster occurred, we can't actually learn whether the presence of those factors is correlated with the occurrence of a disaster. So we don't know if there are lessons to be learned.

We are going to show you what we mean with two examples of post-mortems that followed major disasters—the *Challenger* space shuttle explosion in 1986 and the financial crisis of 2008. In each case, we will see that, while after the fact it sure looks like some serious and obvious mistakes were made, it is less clear that the decision makers could have known that they were making mistakes before the fact. Moreover, once we've grasped this, we will be able to think more clearly about how to design post-mortems that might be more informative about lessons learned.

The Challenger *disaster*

On January 28, 1986, the space shuttle *Challenger* disintegrated off the coast of Cape Canaveral less than two minutes after launch. Seven crew members were killed. The night before the *Challenger* exploded, a small group of engineers from the NASA contractor responsible for the shuttle's solid rocket boosters predicted that the cold weather would lead to a catastrophic failure that might well compromise the shuttle. The concern was that the critical O-ring seals responsible for containing gases produced by burning rocket fuel were not certified to operate at the low temperatures that preceded this particular launch. If the O-ring seals failed, the engineers argued, hot pressurized gas could burn through the rocket's casing, causing disaster.

These predictions, shunted aside by managers at NASA and the engineers' own firm, proved tragically correct. Many post-mortem analyses focused on NASA's failure to take these concerns seriously. The conclusion most observers reached was that the disaster was caused by organizational and cultural failures at NASA that facilitated group-think and led managers to systematically ignore important objections from experts. For instance, the *Report of the Presidential Commission on the Space Shuttle Challenger Accident* (the Rogers Commission) concluded, "Failures in communication . . . resulted in a decision to launch 51-L based on incomplete and sometimes misleading information, a conflict between engineering data and management judgements, and a NASA management structure that permitted internal flight safety problems to bypass key Shuttle managers."

The *Challenger* case is interesting. No one questions the physics behind the conclusion that the O-rings failed because of cold temperatures. Indeed, the Rogers Commission included the Nobel Prize–winning physicist Richard Feynman precisely so they could say with authority whether the engineers were right on the science. They were. And so, in this sense, launching the shuttle was clearly a mistake.

Because the science is so clear, it seems natural for a post-mortem to ask what it was about the process that led decision makers to ignore engineers making good scientific arguments. Here is where our knowledge of the pitfalls of post-mortems should make us stop and think. We know that, after the fact, the decision to launch was tragically flawed. But we want to evaluate whether it was a bad decision at the time it was made. To do so, we need to know about the correlation between the presence of scientifically valid engineering concerns and the success of shuttle launches. And to know about that correlation, we need variation; we must compare disastrous launches to successful launches.

We aren't engineers, so we aren't going to try to weigh in on whether or not the decision to launch *Challenger* was reasonable at the time it was made. But we can see how, to analyze this, a post-mortem commission would need to ask questions they aren't accustomed to asking. Post-mortem commissions ask what led to the disaster, whether people had raised the relevant objections, and, if so, why those objections weren't listened to. In addition, such commissions need to ask whether engineers also raised scientifically valid concerns prior to lots of successful launches. This doesn't seem implausible. Space shuttle launches are incredibly complex and dangerous undertakings. Perhaps there is almost always a scientifically valid reason for serious concern. If so, then there actually wouldn't be much (if any) correlation between the presence of such concerns and launch success. If this is the case, unless you are prepared to simply shut down the space program, it isn't fair to say that launching following a scientifically plausible objection by an engineer is always a mistake. This is the sort of thing one would want to know from a post-mortem commission before reaching conclusions about changing NASA's organizational culture or management practices.

The financial crisis of 2008

The financial crisis that shook the world economy in 2007 and 2008 began with a crash in the U.S. subprime housing market. This crash had ripple effects across the banking sector that eventually spread throughout the world. Understandably, in the wake of this crisis—at the time, the worst since the Great Depression—policy makers and the public alike were interested in identifying early warning indicators that might help them forecast and forestall future crises.

Perhaps the most important post-mortem analysis attempting to provide such early warning indicators was the book *This Time Is Different* by the economists Carmen M. Reinhart and Kenneth S. Rogoff. Reinhart and Rogoff collected and analyzed data on every major financial crisis of the last eight hundred years. By doing so, they argued, they could identify a few key indicators that almost always precede such a crisis. These include uncommonly large current account deficits (that is, goods and services exported minus imported net of income from abroad), asset price bubbles, and excessive borrowing. For instance, in 2006 the United States had a current account deficit close to 7 percent of GDP, a bubble in the housing market, and ballooning federal debt. Thus, Reinhart and Rogoff conclude, "we've been here before." The implication is that the 2008 U.S. financial crisis could have been predicted by the presence of those same factors that seem to characterize financial crises across time and around the globe. Similar patterns were true before the financial crises in Latin America in the early 2000s, East Asia in the 1990s, Nordic countries in the 1980s, and so on into history.

The problem with this argument is the same as in our earlier examples. Early warning indicators should be correlates of financial crises. Because correlation requires variation, to know if current account deficits, soaring asset prices, and heavy borrowing correlate with financial crises, we need variation in crises. That is, we need to know not only that these factors tend to be present when crises occur but also how frequently they are present when crises do not occur. Without such variation, we cannot establish a correlation.

Reinhart and Rogoff's plan of studying every major financial crisis for eight hundred years cannot answer the question. And there are reasons to be worried about their conclusions. As the MIT political scientist David Andrew Singer points out, one need only look at recent history to cast some doubt on the story. For instance, in the late 1990s the United States had all the early warning signs for a financial crisis. There were large current account deficits as a result of massive foreign investment in dot-coms. Moreover, when the dot-com bubble burst, "it wiped out approximately $5 trillion in market capitalization." Yet no financial crisis occurred. This, of course, is just one anecdote. But it should make you wonder whether the factors Reinhart and Rogoff point to are really good predictors of financial crises or just common features of the world that happen to exist both when financial crises occur and when they don't occur.

Life Advice

We've been arguing that our world is organized in ways that lead us to try to figure out the correlates of success or failure without looking at variation, even though it won't work. It is important to see that this problem isn't confined to big institutional settings. We are all victims of it every day in many small ways.

One simple example is the ways in which we seek life advice, which almost always involves asking successful people how it is that they succeeded. In our business, for instance, graduate students are encouraged to ask senior professors what they did to succeed on the job market. We imagine something similar is true in other professions. There is certainly no shortage of self-help books describing the habits of successful people.

But such wisdom suffers from exactly the problems we've been pointing to. Successful people, reflecting on their lives, are inclined to identify a few decisions they made or a few personal characteristics that seem important and offer them as advice to the next generation. But those successful people typically have no idea whether many other, less successful people made similar decisions or had similar characteristics. That is, their introspection about the correlates of success lacks variation. As such, successful people don't really know whether the lessons they point to in telling their personal stories are correlates of success or not. And so, we leave you with this happy bit of wisdom of our own: Beware life advice. Most of it is probably nonsense.

Wrapping Up

Correlation requires variation. But unclear thinking and organizational mandates often lead us to select on the dependent variable—trying to establish the correlates of some phenomenon by only looking at instances when it occurred. It requires careful attention to make sure you aren't falling into this trap, whether you are doing quantitative analysis or just trying to think informally about evidence. Even just forcing yourself to think about whether you could fill in all four cells of one of our two-by-two tables is a good starting point for avoiding looking for correlation without variation.

You can be even more rigorous by using quantitative techniques to measure correlations. The most important such technique is called regression, the topic of chapter 5.

Key Term

- **Selecting on the dependent variable:** Examining only instances when the phenomenon of interest occurred, rather than comparing cases where it occurred to cases where it did not occur.

Exercises

4.1   In chapter 2 we discussed the differences between statements about correlations and other factual statements that do not convey information about a correlation. Now that you have a deeper understanding that correlation requires variation, consider the following statements. Which ones describe a correlation, and which ones do not?

(a) Most top-performing schools have small student bodies.
(b) Married people are typically happier than unmarried people.
(c) Among professionals, taller basketball players tend to have lower free-throw percentages than shorter players.
(d) The locations in the United States with the highest cancer rates are typically small towns.
(e) Older houses are more likely to have lead paint than newer ones.

(f) Most colds caught in Cook County are caught on cold days. (This one also doubles as a tongue twister.)

4.2 At least twenty billionaires dropped out of college before earning their fortunes, including Bill Gates and Mark Zuckerberg.

(a) Does this mean that dropping out of college is correlated with becoming a billionaire? Why or why not?

(b) Draw the two-by-two table that would allow you to assess whether dropping out of college is correlated with becoming a billionaire. Let's assume that exactly twenty people have dropped out of college and become billionaires, so you know what to put in one of the four cells. Make your best guess for the other cells. At the time of this writing, there are about 7.8 billion people in the world, and about two thousand billionaires. Do you think there is a positive or negative correlation between dropping out of college and becoming a billionaire?

(c) Given your guesses from part (b), what proportion of the non-billionaires would need to be college dropouts in order for the correlation to be negative? What proportion of the non-billionaires would need to be college dropouts in order for the correlation to be positive?

(d) If you're currently a college student deciding whether you want to drop out in the hopes of becoming a billionaire, you may want to restrict attention to people who actually started college. Do you think the correlation between dropping out of college and becoming a billionaire is more or less likely to be positive if we restrict attention to just people who start college?

(e) About 7 percent of the world's population has a college degree. And about a third of people who start college complete it. If we assume that everyone who becomes a billionaire started college, you should now have all the information you need to assess the correlation between becoming a billionaire and dropping out of college among those who start college. Is it positive, negative, or zero?

4.3 Identify one recent case where an analyst made the mistake discussed in this chapter. That is, find a case where someone (at least implicitly) makes a claim about a correlation but they don't have variation in one of their variables. Your example might come from a newspaper article, an academic study, a policy memo, or a statement from a politician or business leader.

(a) Summarize the claim being made (perhaps implicitly) and explain why the evidence does not necessarily support the claim.

(b) Explain what additional data collection and analysis *would* allow the analyst to assess the correlation of interest.

(c) Draw a two-by-two table that illustrates your argument, and discuss what the unknown numbers in the table would have to be in order for the correlation of interest to be positive, negative, or zero.

Readings and References

We extensively discussed

Malcolm Gladwell. 2008. *Outliers: The Story of Success.* Little, Brown.

For more information on Fredric Wertham and his flawed argument about comic books, we recommend

David Hajdu. 2009. *The Ten-Cent Plague: The Great Comic-Book Scare and How It Changed America.* Picador.

And although Wertham's conclusions don't follow from his empirical findings because correlation requires variation, it also turns out that Wertham may have manipulated and fabricated his data. See

Carol L. Tilley. 2012. "Seducing the Innocent: Fredric Wertham and the Falsifications That Helped Condemn Comics." *Information & Culture: A Journal of History* 47(4):383–413.

We discussed two reports by the U.S. Department of Education and the Secret Service on school safety.

- The 2002 report is here: https://www.govinfo.gov/content/pkg/ERIC-ED466024 /pdf/ERIC-ED466024.pdf.
- The 2018 report is here: https://www2.ed.gov/documents/school-safety/school -safety-report.pdf.

The report on the high school dropout problem prepared for the Gates Foundation is

John M. Bridgeland, John J. Dilulio, Jr., and Karen Burke Morison. *The Silent Epidemic: Perspectives of High School Dropouts.* https://docs.gatesfoundation.org/documents/ thesilentepidemic3-06final.pdf.

The survey on boredom in school is called the High School Survey of Student Engagement, and it's administered by the Center for Evaluation and Education Policy at Indiana University. The excerpt is from their 2010 study. For more information, see http://newsinfo.iu.edu/news-archive/14593.html.

For more on suicide attacks, including why we can't learn about the causes or correlates of suicide violence from studying only cases where it occurs, see

Robert A. Pape. 2003. "The Strategic Logic of Suicide Terrorism." *American Political Science Review* 97(3):343–61.

Scott Ashworth, Joshua D. Clinton, Adam Meirowitz, and Kristopher W. Ramsay. 2008. "Design, Inference, and the Strategic Logic of Suicide Terrorism." *American Political Science Review* 102(2):269–73.

Robert A. Pape. 2008. "Methods and Findings in the Study of Suicide Terrorism." *American Political Science Review* 102(2):275–77.

Scott Ashworth, Joshua D. Clinton, Adam Meirowitz, and Kristopher W. Ramsay. 2008. "Design, Inference, and the Strategic Logic of Suicide Terrorism: A Rejoinder." Unpublished note: http://home.uchicago.edu/~sashwort/rejoinder3.pdf.

To read about the high rates of disc bulges and herniation among people with and without back pain (and therefore the lack of correlation between these characteristics and back pain), see

Michael J. DePalma, Jessica M. Ketchum, and Thomas Saullo. 2011. "What Is the Source of Chronic Low Back Pain and Does Age Play a Role?" *Pain Medicine* 12(2):224–33.

Maureen C. Jensen, Michael N. Brant-Zawadzki, Nancy Obuchowski, Michael T. Modic, Dennis Malkasian, and Jeffrey S. Ross. 1994. "Magnetic Resonance Imaging of the Lumbar Spine in People without Back Pain." *New England Journal of Medicine* 331:69–73.

These are the two studies we referenced on the financial crisis of 2008:

Carmen M. Reinhart and Kenneth S. Rogoff. 2009. *This Time Is Different: Eight Centuries of Financial Folly.* Princeton University Press.

David A. Singer. 2010. "Is This Time Different?" *The Political Economist.* Fall, pp. 4–5.

CHAPTER 5

Regression for Describing and Forecasting

What You'll Learn

- Regression involves finding the line of best fit through some data. It is perhaps the most important tool for describing the relationship between two or more variables.
- Under certain conditions, regression can be useful for forecasting.
- Things can go wrong with regression, especially if we have a small amount of data. Among the most important problems that can arise is overfitting.
- Where did regression come from?

Introduction

In chapter 2, we defined *correlation* and discussed its three uses: description, forecasting, and causal inference. We also talked about a variety of ways to quantify correlations, including the slope of the regression line, the covariance, and the correlation coefficient. Regression lines are the most common and useful of these. In this chapter, we are going to take a deeper dive into regression to make sure we are all thinking clearly about this important technique.

Regression Basics

Let's return to the data on crime and temperature in Chicago that we discussed back in chapter 2. Figure 5.1 reminds you what a scatter plot of that data looks like.

As you can see just by looking at the data, generally speaking, warmer days have more crime. But you sometimes want to be more precise about the relationship. If you worked for the Chicago Police Department and your boss asked you to summarize the relationship between temperature and crime, they probably wouldn't be particularly pleased if you just showed up with this graph. They might want a simple summary of the relationship that's easy to understand and communicate to people making policy decisions. This is where linear regression comes in.

A line of best fit provides just the kind of accessible summary of the relationship between temperature and crime that we are looking for. Such a line, if well chosen, will do two things. First, for any given temperature, the line gives us a reasonable approximation (or prediction) of the amount of crime. And second, as we discussed in chapter 2, the slope of the line tells us something about the sign and magnitude of

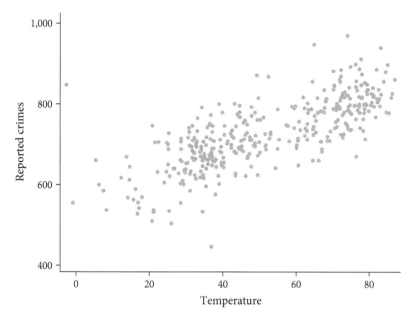

Figure 5.1. Number of reported crimes and the temperature in degrees Fahrenheit in Chicago across days in 2018.

the correlation between the two variables—that is, it tells us approximately how much crime changes as the temperature changes. So let's figure out how we identify the line of best fit, so that we can think clearly about how to interpret and communicate what it has to tell us.

With the exception of completely vertical lines (which wouldn't provide a useful description or forecast anyway), all hypothetical lines that we could draw on the graph of figure 5.1 can be described by what is called a *regression equation* of the following form:

$$\text{Predicted Crime} = \alpha + \beta \cdot \text{Temperature}$$

A regression equation expresses a linear relationship between a *dependent* (or *outcome*) variable on the left-hand side of the equation and an *independent* (or *explanatory*) variable on the right-hand side of the equation. (As we will see later in the chapter, there can be more than one explanatory variable on the right-hand side.) The dependent variable corresponds to the outcome we are trying to describe, predict, or explain. An independent variable corresponds to something we are using to try to describe, predict, or explain the dependent variable.

The regression equation relates the dependent and independent variables linearly through *regression parameters*. The regression parameters define the particular line we are drawing. In our regression equation above, the regression parameters are α and β (the Greek letters *alpha* and *beta*). The regression parameter α is called the *intercept*; it is the predicted number of a crimes on a day when the average temperature is 0 degrees Fahrenheit. The regression parameter β is the *slope*; it is the amount that predicted crime goes up with each degree Fahrenheit. Any possible line on the graph corresponds to one particular combination of α and β. (As we will see later in this chapter, there can be more than two regression parameters if there is more than one independent variable.

And as we will see later in the book, you are free to represent the regression parameters with letters other than α and β when convenient.)

Of course, we don't want to try to describe or predict crime on the basis of temperature using any arbitrary line. The wrong line will yield really bad forecasts. We want to use the line that best fits the data.

In order to find the values of α and β that give us the line that best fits the data, we need to start by defining what the term *best fits* means. We do so quantitatively by choosing a measure of how well any given line does at summarizing or fitting the data. Then we find (or ask our computer to find) the values of α and β that result in the best possible value of that measure. Those values of α and β describe the line of best fit for the data according to the measure we choose.

The measure we choose to evaluate fit is important. As we mentioned briefly in chapter 2, the most commonly used measure (and the one on which we focus) is the *sum of squared errors*. So let's start by being a bit more precise about what this measure means.

For any α and β we choose, our line gives us a prediction of the level of crime on a day with any given temperature. For instance, suppose we chose $\alpha = 650$ and $\beta = 2$. Then, on a day (like January 26, 2018) when the average temperature was 46 degrees Fahrenheit, our prediction of the number of crimes is

$$\text{Predicted Crime} = 650 + 2 \cdot 46 = 742.$$

Of course, the line's prediction won't be exactly right—we sacrifice some accuracy in order to get a parsimonious summary of the data. For instance, in reality, the number of crimes on January 26, 2018, was actually 759. The difference between the true value of the dependent variable and our line's prediction for any given observation is called that observation's *error*:

$$\text{error}_i = \text{Crime}_i - \text{Predicted Crime}_i$$

So, for instance, given our choice of α and β, the error for January 26, 2018, is $759 - 742 = 17$.

Put differently, for any given line we choose (i.e., values of α and β), we can describe any observation i as follows:

$$\text{Crime}_i = \underbrace{\alpha + \beta \cdot \text{Temperature}_i}_{\text{Predicted Crime}_i} + \underbrace{\text{error}_i}_{\text{Crime}_i - \text{Predicted Crime}_i}$$

Figure 5.2 draws a line with $\alpha = 650$ and $\beta = 2$ on top of the data and shows how the errors are measured. (As we will see later, this turns out not to be the line of best fit.) The errors are the vertical lines from a data point to the line. We only drew the errors for a few data points in order to avoid the figure getting too messy. However, to evaluate the fit of a line, we would actually start by calculating the error for every single data point.

The error for any given data point can be positive (if the data point lies above the line) or negative (if the data point lies below the line). But we want a measure of how far the data point is from the line. We don't care whether it is above or below. So, to get such a measure, we next square the error for each data point. The squared error is positive regardless of whether the data point lies above or below the line. It is just a measure of how far the data point is from the line.

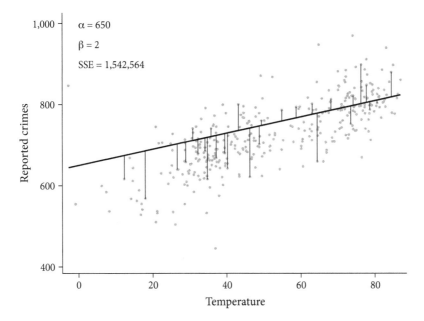

Figure 5.2. Fitting a line through crime and temperature (in degrees Fahrenheit), showing some of the errors.

We add up all those squared errors to get the *sum of squared errors* (SSE). The figure reports the SSE for this particular line in the upper left-hand corner.

We can follow this procedure to get the sum of squared errors for the line associated with any α and β. Different lines have different SSEs. The bigger the sum of squared errors, the further the data is from the line, on average.

The line we are looking for is the one with the smallest sum of squared errors. That is, we find (your computer knows how) the values of the parameters α and β that minimize the sum of squared errors. This process is call *ordinary least squares* (OLS) regression. We label the values of the parameters that minimize the sum of the squared errors as α^{OLS} and β^{OLS}. These values of the parameters are called the *ordinary least squares (OLS) regression coefficients*. The line associated with these parameters is the *OLS regression line*. It is our line of best fit.

There's a lot of lingo to describe finding the α and β that minimize the sum of squared errors. Sometimes we say that we're "regressing crime on temperature." When we're in a long-winded mood, we'll say that we're "running an ordinary least squares regression where crime is the dependent variable and temperature is the independent variable."

Figure 5.3 shows the crime and temperature data with four different lines drawn through it, corresponding to different combinations of α and β. For each line, the figure reports the α, β and the sum of squared errors. A few of the errors are shown visually with vertical black lines. The bottom-right panel shows the OLS regression line—the line that minimizes the sum of squared errors. Visually, we can see that this line is a better approximation of the data than the other three options. In practice, we don't have to use trial and error to find this line. Instead, we'll ask our computer to do the work for us, and it, using linear algebra, will find the values of α and β that minimize the sum of squared errors before you can blink.

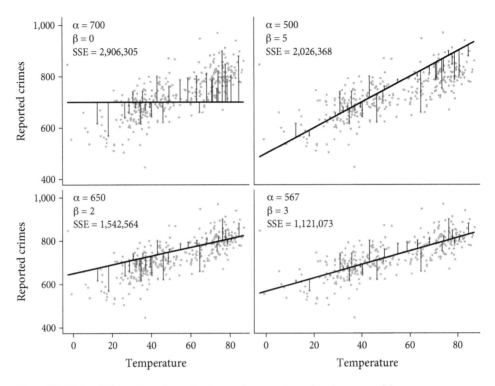

Figure 5.3. Fitting different lines through crime and temperature, showing some of the errors.

How do we interpret the OLS regression line? As we see in the figure, rounding to the nearest integer, the intercept (α^{OLS}) is 567 and the slope (β^{OLS}) is 3. In other words, the OLS regression line is telling us that, in 2018, on days when the average temperature at Midway Airport was 0 degrees, there were about 567 crimes on average, and for every additional degree Fahrenheit, the average number of crimes increased by about 3. So, for example, the predicted amount of crime on a day when the temperature was 46 degress (like January 26, 2018) is

$$\text{Predicted Crime} = 567 + 3 \cdot 46 = 705.$$

We didn't have to choose our regression line by minimizing the sum of squared errors. Depending on our goals, we could have instead minimized the sum of the absolute value of the errors. Or we could have minimized the sum of errors raised to the fourth power. The possibilities are endless.

We like the sum of squared errors for a couple reasons. First, minimizing the sum of squared errors turns out to provide the best linear approximation to another useful function: the *conditional mean function*. The conditional mean function is a function that tells you the mean (average) of some variable conditional on the value of some other variables. Here the particular conditional mean function we are interested in is the one that gives the mean number of crimes conditional on temperature.

Suppose that for, say, each degree Fahrenheit, you calculated the average number of crimes on days with that temperature and plotted them. That gives you a graph of a conditional mean function—for each degree of temperature, it tells you the average number of crimes. In figure 5.4, the light-gray dots are our raw crime and temperature data and the large black dots are the mean number of crimes conditional on being in a

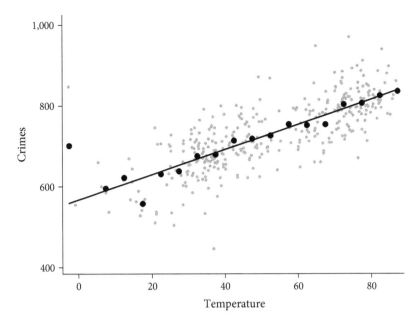

Figure 5.4. The regression line through the data is also the best linear approximation to the conditional means.

5 degree Fahrenheit bin (0–5 degrees, 6–10 degrees, and so on). Conditional means are another reasonable way to predict crime on the basis of temperature. However, the conditional mean function isn't as parsimonious as a line—to summarize the conditional mean function, you need a list of the average level of crime for each temperature bin, whereas a line is summarized by two parameters. But, as you can see, the regression line, in addition to being the line of best fit through the raw data, is also a very good approximation of these conditional means—indeed, it is the best linear approximation of them. So, if you are interested in conditional means, the line that minimizes the sum of squared errors is a good way to summarize them.

Of course, you might not be interested in means. Perhaps, instead, you want to describe or predict the conditional median. In that case, it turns out that you'd want to draw the line that minimizes the sum of the absolute values of the errors. As we said, there are a variety of reasonable choices.

The second reason that people focus on minimizing the sum of squared errors is historical. As indicated above, there is an easy way for your computer to calculate the values of α and β that minimizes the sum of squared errors using linear algebra; as a result, OLS coefficients can be calculated quite quickly. But back when people did this by hand, or even when computers were much slower, this was an important consideration. As computational speeds have improved, however, this consideration has become less relevant.

Linear Regression, Non-Linear Data

What do we do when we want to use linear regression but our data is not well described by a line? To start to think about this, let's return to the data we looked at in our discussion of voter turnout in chapter 2. Remember, there we wanted to describe the relationship between age and voter turnout—perhaps to know whether younger

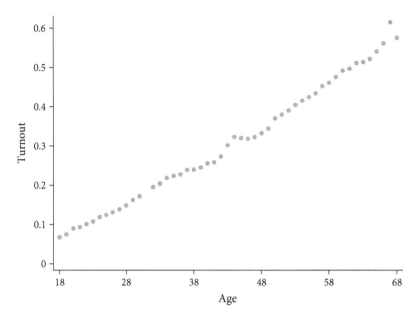

Figure 5.5. Voter turnout rate by age in the 2014 U.S. midterm election.

people are politically underrepresented or perhaps to decide whom to target with a get-out-the-vote drive.

Figure 5.5 shows the voter turnout rate for each year of age between 18 and 68 in the 2014 midterm elections. Notice, in this data, the observation is not an individual; it is an age cohort. As with temperature and crime, the relationship between age and turnout is potentially quite complex. What if we want to summarize the average relationship between age and turnout in a simple way? Or what if we didn't have the data for 31-year-olds (omitted from the figure) and we wanted to come up with our best guess for their turnout level? Or what if we wanted to predict turnout based on age in the 2018 election? Linear regression could be useful for all of these purposes.

Looking at the graph, the relationship between age and turnout appears approximately linear, at least for this range of the data. In other words, we could probably draw a line on this graph that comes pretty close to each of the data points. And if we did draw such a line, this would be fairly useful for both description and forecasting.

Let's try out OLS regression with our voter turnout data. We could again describe any line with the following regression equation:

$$\text{Predicted Turnout} = \alpha + \beta \cdot \text{Age}$$

Our statistical software program tells us that, for this data, $\alpha^{OLS} = -.1381$ and $\beta^{OLS} = .0103$. With these two numbers, we can draw the line that best fits the data, and we can generate predicted turnout for any given age. Figure 5.6 shows how the OLS regression line looks.

It is important to pause and think clearly about the substantive meaning of the regression line.

The number α^{OLS} is the intercept. It tells us that the predicted turnout rate of people age zero is $-.1381$, or about -14 percent. That's a pretty weird prediction. Turnout rates

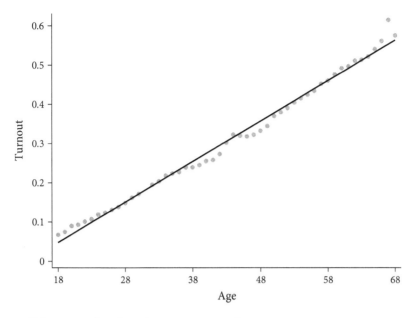

Figure 5.6. OLS regression line through voter turnout rate by age.

can't be negative. And infants can't vote. We know that the turnout rate for zero-year-olds is zero.

Does this mean that the regression is meaningless or wrong? No. It reflects the fact that the regression isn't super useful for describing or forecasting the voting behavior of babies. That isn't surprising. Our regression line was chosen to do a good job of approximating our data. We shouldn't expect it to do a terribly good job approximating the behavior of people with ages well outside the range of our data. And we don't have any data on people younger than 18.

The number β^{OLS} is the slope. It tells us that, on average, within the range of our data, each additional year of age corresponds to an increase in turnout of just over 1 percentage point. In other words, on average, between the ages of 19 and 68, people are about 1 percentage point more likely to vote than people who are just one year younger than themselves. That's interesting. And it accumulates across years, implying that 68-year-olds are approximately 50 percentage points more likely to vote than are 18-year-olds, which is exactly what we see in the data.

The regression line is doing its job pretty well. It gives us a fairly simple and quick summary of the relationship between age and turnout for people between the ages of 18 and 68 in the 2014 election. In this particular election, 18-year-olds voted at an approximate rate of 4.8 percent $((-.1381 + .0103 \cdot 18) \cdot 100 \approx 4.8)$, and then turnout increases by just over 1 percentage point for every additional year in age. Although this summary doesn't get turnout exactly right for each age group, it gets pretty darn close. And, in our view, what is lost in accuracy (compared to, say, just listing turnout rates by age) is more than made up for in parsimony and ease of communication.

We can also use α^{OLS} and β^{OLS} to predict turnout levels for voters whose ages are not in our data. For reasons we've already discussed, we don't want to extrapolate too far. We can't extrapolate back to infants, or even 17-year-olds, since they aren't eligible to vote. We probably also don't want to extrapolate to people too much older than 68.

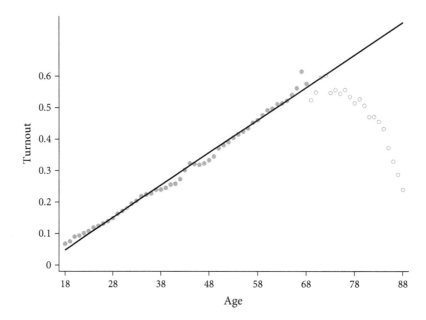

Figure 5.7. Using the regression line to predict voter turnout rate (poorly) for out-of-sample ages.

Our predictions are likely to be pretty good for 69- and 70-year-olds, for whom we predict turnout rates of approximately 57.3 percent $((-.1381 + .0103 \cdot 69) \cdot 100)$ and 58.3 percent $((-.1381 + .0103 \cdot 70) \cdot 100)$, respectively. But the further we get away from the range of our actual data, the more we should worry about the reliability of our predictions.

The spot where we might be most confident in our predictions is for 31-year-olds. For whatever reason, our graph shows no data on that age group. (Here that's because we purposefully omitted it for illustrative purposes. But if you start working with data you'll find that this sort of thing happens all the time. Maybe the county clerk spilled coffee on the voter returns for 31-year-olds.) But we have lots of data on people with ages on both sides of 31. So we can probably generate pretty good predictions for turnout by 31-year-olds. Let's see.

Our regression equation predicts a turnout rate for 31-year-olds of just over 18 percent $(-.1381 + .0103 \cdot 31) \cdot 100 = 18.12$. Since we actually do have the data, we can see how well our prediction pans out by adding the 31-year-olds back in to the graph.

Figure 5.7 plots the same regression line, fit to data on 18- to 68-year-olds, excluding 31-year-olds. But it introduces some previously excluded data points, plotting them as hollow circles. The new data include 31-year-olds, as well as folks ages 69–88.

With 31-year-olds, we hit the mark almost perfectly: we predicted a turnout rate of 18.12 percent, and the true rate was 18.11 percent. With 69- to 72-year-olds, we did okay, though not as well. But our predictions start performing really poorly for the oldest individuals.

That's because the relationship between age and turnout seems to be quite different for the elderly. For younger people, turnout is increasing in age. But once people get past the age of 70 or so, turnout appears to drop with age. As a result, trying to predict the difference in voter turnout between an 80-year-old and an 88-year-old using data on

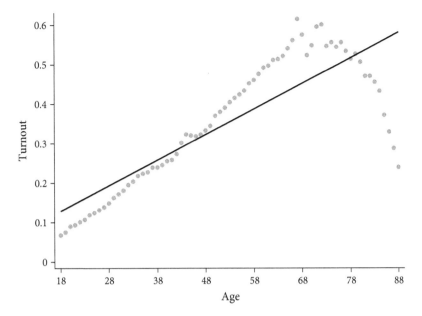

Figure 5.8. A regression of voter turnout rate on age for all ages.

voter turnout of 18- to 68-year-olds doesn't work very well. Just like with our prediction of a −14 percent turnout rate for infants, this illustrates what can go wrong when we try to extrapolate our predictions outside the range of the data that we used to generate the regression line on which those predictions are based.

Suppose we in fact wanted to analyze the relationship between age and turnout for everyone between the ages of 18 and 88. By just looking at the data, we can see that the relationship is not linear. How should we account for this non-linearity?

One approach would be to fit a new linear regression, now using all the data. Even if the data itself doesn't sit on a line, we can still find the line that minimizes the sum of squared errors. As you can see in figure 5.8, there is now a lot more error, since we are fitting a line to data that have a clearly non-linear relationship.

A second approach is to keep fitting regression lines, but use a different line for different parts of the data. For instance, we could find the line that minimizes the sum of squared errors for the data on people between 16 and 68, a second line that minimizes the sum of squared errors for the data on people ages 69–78, and a third line for that data on people ages 79–88. This would not be as parsimonious or easily communicated as running a single regression—instead of two parameters (α and β), we would have six parameters (a separate α and β for each regression line). But, as you can see in figure 5.9, the payoff we get for that lack of parsimony is a tighter fit to the data (i.e., less error).

We hinted at a third way to deal with non-linearity back in chapter 2. There's no reason that our regression equation has to have only one explanatory variable. If we know that there's a non-linear relationship between turnout and age, maybe we want to consider transforming the age variable into age-squared, age-cubed, and so on.

When we took this approach in chapter 2, we kept the regression simple. We just regressed the outcome variable on the explanatory variable squared. But we can do something more general than that. Instead of regressing voter turnout on just age or

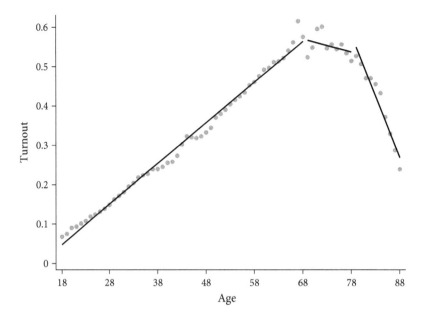

Figure 5.9. Separate regression lines through voter turnout rate and age for ages 16–68, 69–78, and 79–88.

just age-squared, we can regress it on both. This allows us to fit a function that is more flexible than a line to our data. Of course, for each new variable we include, that's a new coefficient that we have to vary when we minimize the sum of squared errors. But our computer can handle that.

In principle, we don't even have to restrict ourselves to different transformations of the age variable. We could also include other factors—average income or average voter registration status—which might further improve our predictions. We'll come back to that possibility in chapter 10. For now, let's stick to transformations of our age variable.

With just one explanatory variable, it is easy to visualize what we are doing when we run a regression. We are just drawing a line through the data in a two-dimensional space—in particular, the line that minimizes the sum of squared errors.

With two explanatory variables, things are a little more abstract, but still manageable. Now we can think about finding a line going through our data in a three-dimensional space. Just picture adding a third axis coming out of the page toward you in our graphs. That axis will have the scale of the second explanatory variable (perhaps age-squared). Now the data forms a cloud in that three-dimensional space. Regression is still just drawing a line that minimizes the sum of squared errors, but now the line passes through that cloud of three-dimensional data points. Describing this line requires three parameters instead of two: the intercept (α), the slope with respect to changes in the first explanatory variable (we can call this β_1), and the slope with respect to changes in the second explanatory variable (we can call this β_2).

Once we go beyond two explanatory variables, it's hard to visualize the regression line, since most of us can't think in four or more dimensions. But you can analogize. You understand what it means to find the line that minimizes the sum of squared errors with one or two explanatory variables. There is no reason we can't do the same with ten. Certainly your computer will have no trouble calculating the sum of squared errors and finding the OLS regression coefficients.

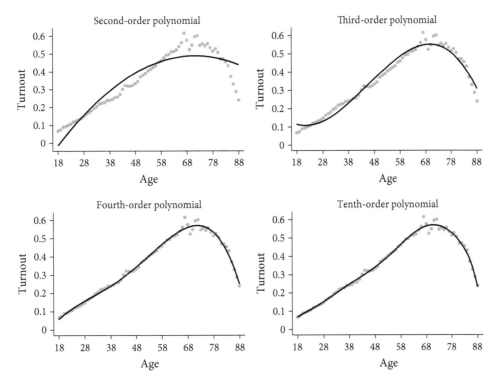

Figure 5.10. Fitting regressions through voter turnout rate with different polynomials of age.

Let's see how this works in practice. We replicated the regression of voter turnout on age but also included age-squared as an explanatory variable. That is, we considered the following equation:

$$\text{Predicted Turnout} = \alpha + \beta_1 \cdot \text{Age} + \beta_2 \cdot \text{Age}^2$$

Once our computer calculates the associated regression coefficients, we can plug in any value of age and the associated value of age-squared to get a predicted level of turnout. So, for instance, if we wanted to know the predicted turnout of 31-year-olds, we'd plug in 31 for age and $31^2 = 961$ for age-squared.

And we don't have to stop at age and age-squared. Figure 5.10 shows the predicted turnout from different regressions, one with age and age-squared as explanatory variables (this is called a second-order polynomial); another with age, age-squared, and age-cubed as explanatory variables (third-order polynomial); another with a fourth-order polynomial; and another with a tenth-order polynomial!

The overall relationship between age and turnout is pretty complicated. As we've seen, it's approximately linear from 18 to 68, but then it takes a hard turn sometime after that. As a result, if we just include age, we don't do a great job fitting the data. Similarly, we see here that a regression with age and age-squared also doesn't do that well because the relationship in the data is poorly approximated by a quadratic curve. Our predictions get better and better as we include more and more explanatory variables, since we have more and more parameters that we can play around with to fit the data. By the time we get to a fourth-order polynomial, the fit looks quite good.

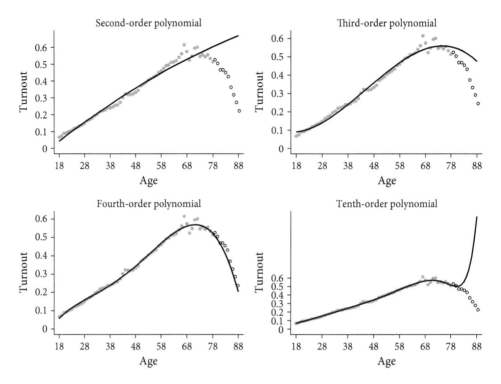

Figure 5.11. Using regressions through voter turnout rate and different polynomials of age to predict voter turnout for out-of-sample ages.

Of course, the tenth-order polynomial does the best job approximating the data—the more explanatory variables included in the regression, the better the fit. But that doesn't necessarily mean that you want to include as many explanatory variables as possible. There are trade-offs.

For one, remember that part of our goal is to describe the data in a simple and parsimonious manner that is easy to understand and communicate. Describing the data with eleven parameters (α plus β_1 through β_{10}) isn't much better in this regard than simply listing the turnout rate for each age group.

Furthermore, we often want to make *out-of-sample predictions*, forecasting voter turnout for age groups not actually observed in our data (like 90-year-olds). Adding more and more terms often results in worse out-of-sample predictions. The reason is that, as the function we use becomes more and more flexible, it can read every little bump and hiccup in the data as meaningful, even when they aren't.

To illustrate this point, we repeated the analyses above, but ran the regressions only using data on people ages 18–78. Then we can see how well we do making out-of-sample predictions of the turnout rates for people with ages above 78. (These predictions are out-of-sample because we purposefully removed voters over the age of 78 from our data.) Figure 5.11 shows the results. The data used for fitting the regression are plotted in black. The data we are attempting to predict are shown as hollow circles. And the gray curve represents the predicted values from the regression. As you can see, the fourth-order polynomial does well at predicting turnout for the oldest voters. But the tenth-order polynomial is a disaster!

The Problem of Overfitting

The example we just saw, where the tenth-order polynomial performed worse than the fourth-order polynomial at out-of-sample prediction, is an instance of a more general phenomenon called *overfitting*. If we test enough explanatory variables, we're bound to find some that correlate with the outcome in our data just by chance. The tenth-order polynomial regression was using meaningless correlations between high-order transformations of the age variable and voter turnout among one set of voters to try to predict turnout among another set of voters. Unsurprisingly, those meaningless correlations did not continue to hold. To better understand overfitting, let's talk about a somewhat more realistic forecasting problem.

Forecasting Presidential Elections

Americans are really interested in predicting the outcomes of upcoming presidential elections. When we tell people that we are political scientists, by far the most common question we get is "Who's going to win the next election?" We tend to disappoint with our answers, since election prediction is not what most political scientists spend their time on.

However, compared to most complex political phenomena, presidential elections are actually rather predictable. Even months before the election, we often have a pretty good idea of who is going to win based on how the economy is doing. And in the final weeks before Election Day, the average of polls usually gets within 1 or 2 percentage points of the final vote share. The journalist Nate Silver established himself as a giant of political data analytics by essentially averaging polls.

Of course, the fact that we can usually predict the vote share within 1 or 2 percentage points doesn't mean we always know who's going to win. Most presidential elections are highly competitive, and the Electoral College allows some candidates to win the election even while losing the popular vote. In close races, like in 2000 or 2016, given the available information on the morning of the election, there was probably no way an honest quantitative analyst could have been more than 90 percent sure that any particular candidate was going to win.

Although we said most political scientists don't spend much time trying to predict election outcomes, some do. The academic journal *PS: Political Science & Politics* typically publishes a symposium before each presidential election with various attempts to predict the outcome using quantitative data and analyses. Often, the goal of these analyses is to see how well researchers can predict the upcoming election results without using polling data. For example, we might see how well we could predict vote share if we just knew the fundamentals, like economic growth and incumbency status.

To make such a prediction, a researcher might run a regression using historical data in which each observation is an election, the outcome variable is the two-party vote share of the incumbent party in that election, and the various explanatory variables are features of that particular election like economic growth in the election year, whether the incumbent is seeking reelection, the number of war casualties over the past four years, and so on. Having obtained the regression coefficients based on data from previous elections, the researcher can then plug in the values for explanatory variables from the current election and obtain a forecast for the upcoming two-party vote share. Because many other analysts are doing the exact same thing, the goal is often to find some new variable to include in your own regression in order to improve its predictive power.

Mimicking this approach, we ran a regression predicting the incumbent's vote share in presidential elections between 1948 and 2012. To be thorough, we included ten different independent variables, all of which have been identified by political scientists as factors that might help us predict election results. Specifically, we included an indicator for whether the incumbent is a Democrat or Republican; an indicator for whether the incumbent is seeking reelection; GDP growth in years 1, 2, 3, and 4 of the most recent presidential term; an indicator for whether the country was involved in a major war at the time; a count of the number of consecutive terms in which the same party has been in power (many people expect that voters are more likely to replace a party that has been in power for a long time); the unemployment rate; and the change in the unemployment rate over the last four years.

We have good reasons to expect that these ten variables should help us predict presidential election results, and at first glance, it looks like they do. The r^2 statistic from the regression is .83, meaning that 83 percent of the variation in incumbent vote share appears to be accounted for by these variables. Furthermore, when we calculate predicted values from this regression, they only miss the actual vote share by an average of 1.7 percentage points.

The apparent success of our regression, however, is misleading. It turns out, if we had simply generated ten random variables (which we have done in computer simulations) and run the same regression using those meaningless numbers as our explanatory variables, we would have averaged an r^2 statistic of around .67 and an average error of 2.4 percentage points. This is almost as good as our predictions using real data, even though our ten randomly generated variables should contain no information about the likely outcome of the election at all.

This is quite surprising. Why is it true? When you generate a bunch of entirely random variables, some of them are going to end up correlated with your outcome just by chance. In a regression, those meaningless variables will appear to predict the outcome. But, of course, they don't really. If you try to use the forecasts generated by the relationship between those meaningless variables and past outcomes to predict future outcomes, you will fail miserably. Their predictive power is just an illusion created by chance.

One way to try to assess and mitigate overfitting is by holding some data out of your regression analysis and conducting out-of-sample tests—as we did with voters over the age of 78 in the previous section. In the context of predicting election outcomes, when generating a prediction for the vote share in 2012, we could leave the 2012 data out of the sample, run a regression using all the other elections, generate a predicted value for 2012 using those regression coefficients and the true values of the explanatory variables for 2012, and see how our predictions fare. In principle, we could do this for each year in our data set—remove one observation, run our regression, generate a predicted value for that observation, check our prediction against the truth, and repeat for each observation.

When we subject our regression with ten explanatory variables to out-of-sample testing, it fares much worse than it first appeared. The average prediction error jumps up from 1.7 to 5.6 percentage points. We doubt that any campaign would hire a statistical consultant who could only promise to predict the election results within 5 or 6 percentage points, on average. Even more embarrassing, a naive prediction based on a simple average of the other elections in the sample gets within 4.6 percentage points, on average. In other words, the overfitted regression that we thought was giving us such accurate predictions is actually worse than a regression that uses no explanatory variables at all.

Table 5.1. Output of regression of average voter turnout on age.

	DV = Voter Turnout
Age	.0103
	(.0001)
Constant	−.1381
	(.0066)
r^2	.991
Root-MSE	.151
Observations	50

Of course, when analysts are careful to avoid overfitting, they can generate useful predictions. A simple regression that uses only GDP growth in year 4 as an explanatory variable produces an out-of-sample prediction error of 3.8 percentage points, beating the model with no explanatory variables. And if we included poll results as Nate Silver does, we would do even better. Nonetheless, it's easy to trick yourself into thinking you're generating good predictions when you're not. Careful analysts only include variables in their regression that they believe are genuinely correlated with the outcome, they avoid having too many variables in their regression relative to the number of observations, and they validate their predictive strategy using out-of-sample testing.

How Regression Is Presented

Sometimes the outputs of a regression are presented graphically, as we have done thus far. But the most common form in which regression results are presented is in a table. For instance, table 5.1 shows how the output of a regression of voter turnout on age might be presented.

You don't quite know what everything in this table means yet (we will come to standard errors, the number in parentheses, in chapter 6), but most everything should be familiar. The number in the Constant row is the intercept, α^{OLS}. The number in the Age row is the slope of the regression line, β^{OLS}. We've also already discussed the idea of r-squared in chapter 2: it is the amount of the variance in voter turnout that can be predicted from age. And Root-MSE is the square root of the mean squared error, which gives you some sense of how far off, on average, our regression predictions are from the real data points.

A Brief Intellectual History of Regression

As far as historians of statistics can tell, regression was invented (or was it discovered?) around the end of the nineteenth century. The first published instance of a linear regression is in the appendix to a brief book entitled *New Methods for the Determination of the Orbits of Comets* by the French mathematician Adrien-Marie Legendre. This was work with important implications for geodesy—the study of the measurement of the earth, which was a high-stakes problem, given the economic and military importance of navigation in the eighteenth century.

Legendre's status as the discoverer of regression was contested by a contemporary, the great German mathematician Carl Friedrich Gauss. In his 1809 *Theory of the Motion of the Heavenly Bodies Moving about the Sun in Conic Sections*, Gauss staked his claim, writing, "Our principle, which we have made use of since 1795, has lately been published by Legendre." Legendre was not amused, and the two continued to snipe at one another over the matter throughout the early nineteenth century.

Neither Gauss nor Legendre referred to the method of drawing a line of best fit by minimizing the sum of squared errors as a *regression*. That term was coined by the late eighteenth-century scholar, Francis Galton. Galton, a cousin of Charles Darwin's who was also married to Darwin's niece, was a polymath (he dabbled and excelled in a lot of different areas). He also came up with the idea for the modern fingerprinting system and was the first person to quantitatively document the wisdom-of-the-crowds phenomenon.[1] More disturbingly, Galton was a eugenicist—a proponent of selective human breeding. To be clear, we do not support or approve of eugenics, but regression turns out to be useful for non-eugenicists as well.

Galton's interest in eugenics led him to want to study evolution and heredity quantitatively. He started by measuring the easy things like height. In one analysis, he collected data on the heights of parents and their children. After plotting the data, he assessed the average relationship between these two variables using what we now call a regression line.

Galton's analysis was actually a little complicated. He compared the height of children to the average height of their parents after first adjusting the heights so that women's and men's heights were measured on the same scale. We don't want to go through all that. So, to get the idea, imagine an analysis like Galton's that studies just the heights of fathers and sons. The unit of analysis is a father-son pair, and the regression equation looks like this:

$$\text{Predicted Son's Height} = \alpha + \beta \cdot \text{Father's Height}$$

When Galton measured α and β using OLS, what do you think he found? We might have expected $\alpha^{OLS} = 0$ and $\beta^{OLS} = 1$. That would mean, on average, sons tend to be the same height as their fathers—that is, we'd expect the son of a five-foot-tall father to also be five feet tall, the son of a six-foot-tall father to also be six feet tall, and so on. Instead, Galton was surprised to find $\alpha^{OLS} > 0$ and $\beta^{OLS} < 1$. Stop for a moment and think about why that might be.

Figure 5.12 demonstrates Galton's result graphically. The dashed black line shows the 45-degree line—that is, the line with $\alpha = 0$ and $\beta = 1$. The thick gray line shows the best fitting regression line, with $\alpha^{OLS} = 38.2$ and $\beta^{OLS} = 0.448$.

Let's start by interpreting these regression coefficients. The regression line lies above the 45-degree line for relatively short fathers and below for relatively tall fathers. This means that tall fathers tend to have sons that are taller than average but nonetheless shorter than they are. Similarly, short fathers tend to have sons that are shorter than average but nonetheless taller than themselves. Galton called this phenomenon "regression to mediocrity." Today, we typically call this phenomenon *regression to the mean* or *reversion to the mean*, and we'll devote the entirety of chapter 8 to understanding

---

[1] The idea is that if you ask enough people, even if they are non-experts, perhaps their errors will cancel out and you'll get a good answer. Galton showed that although most individuals are bad at guessing the weight of an ox, if you ask hundreds of people and average their answers, you'll get very close to the correct weight. Unfortunately, this doesn't always work.

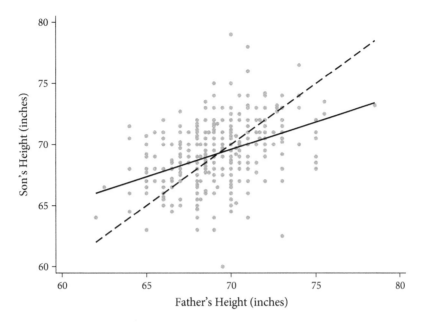

Figure 5.12. A regression line through son's height and father's height.

it. Since then, we've used the word *regression* to refer both to Galton's statistical technique and to the phenomenon that he discovered using it. So it's no coincidence that *OLS regression* and *regression to the mean* use the same word. They have a common intellectual history.

Wrapping Up

Regression is the most important tool we have for studying correlations. The slope of the line of best fit tells us the sign and magnitude of the relationship between two variables—as one goes up, how much does the other tend to go up or down? We can learn a lot from regressions, but we have to be vigilant about keeping our thinking clear. When using a technique that your computer can implement for you, it is easy to become complacent. You can guard against some of the pitfalls by plotting your data, considering the possibility of non-linear relationships, and being careful about overfitting.

A regression tells us the relationship between variables in our data. If we are just trying to describe the data, that is informative all on its own. But often we are trying to do more. For instance, we might be trying to infer the relationship between variables in some larger population from the relationship between those variables in our data, which may only be a small sample of the population. How do we know whether a relationship we found in our data is likely to hold in some larger population? Those concerns are the topic of chapter 6.

Key Terms

- **Dependent variable:** The variable associated with the outcome we are trying to describe, predict, or explain.

- **Independent or Explanatory variable:** A variable we are using to try to describe, predict, or explain the dependent variable.
- **Regression equation:** An equation linearly relating a dependent variable to some independent variables.
- **Regression parameters:** The parameters (intercept and slopes) that relate a dependent variable to some independent variables in a regression equation.
- **Error:** The difference between the value of the outcome variable for an individual data point and the predicted value for that same data point. This is sometimes also referred to as the residual.
- **Sum of squared errors (SSE):** For a given line, calculate the error for each data point by finding its vertical distance from the line. The sum of squared errors for that line is found by squaring each of the individual errors and adding them together.
- **Ordinary least squares (OLS) regression:** The method for finding the line of best fit through data that minimizes the sum of squared errors.
- **Regression line:** The line of best fit through the data that one gets from OLS regression.
- **Intercept:** In the context of a regression, the intercept tells us the predicted value of the outcome when the values of all the explanatory variables are set to 0. This is also referred to as the *constant term*. Sometimes the intercept has a substantive interpretation, but sometimes it doesn't because it doesn't make sense to think about situations where all the explanatory variables are zero (for example, predicted voter turnout for people with an age of zero). In any case, we always include the intercept when we run a regression (except in very unusual circumstances where we know from theory that the intercept should be zero).
- **Conditional mean function:** A function that tells you the mean (average) of some variable conditional on the value of some other variables.
- **Out-of-sample prediction:** Using regression (or another statistical technique) to predict the outcome for observations that were not included in the original data you used to generate your predictions.
- **Overfitting:** Attempting to predict a dependent variable with too many independent variables, so that variables appear to predict the dependent variable in the data but have no actual relationship with it in the world.

Exercises

Download SchoolingEarnings.csv and the associated README.txt, which describes the variables in this data set, at press.princeton.edu/thinking-clearly. This data set gives the average annual earnings for 41- to 50-year-old men in the United States in 1980 at each level of schooling. One observation gives the average earnings (in thousands of dollars) for men with eight years of schooling, another gives the average for those with nine years of schooling, and so on.

5.1   Run a regression with earnings as the dependent variable and schooling as the sole independent variable. Interpret the coefficients.

5.2   Suppose you wanted a parsimonious way to predict earnings using only years of schooling. What would you do?

5.3   Let's dig more deeply into whether the relationship between earnings and schooling is approximately linear.

(a) Start by making a scatter plot. Then plot the predicted values from your regression along with the raw data points, as we did in chapter 2. Does the regression line look like it's fitting the data well?

(b) Now run a fourth-order polynomial regression (i.e., include schooling, schooling^2, schooling^3, and schooling^4. Do those predictions meaningfully differ from the predictions coming from the linear regression?

(c) Now run different regressions for some different ranges of schooling. Do those lines look meaningfully different from the predictions you get from a single regression including all the data?

(d) Does all this make you think the simple linear approach was reasonable or unreasonable?

5.4   Similar to what we did with age and voter turnout, conduct some out-of-sample tests to evaluate your prediction strategy. Using only data for those with twelve years of schooling or less, see how well your different strategies from question 3 perform when predicting earnings for those with more than twelve years of schooling.

Readings and References

For more information on the early history of regression, see

Stephen M. Stigler. 1986. *The History of Statistics: The Measurement of Uncertainty before 1900.* Belknap, Harvard.

CHAPTER 6

Samples, Uncertainty, and Statistical Inference

What You'll Learn

- All quantitative estimates are the sum of three terms: the true quantity of interest, bias, and noise.
- Statistical hypothesis testing allows analysts to assess whether an estimate was likely to have arisen from noise.
- Statistical significance and substantive significance are not the same and should not be conflated.

Introduction

Chapters 4 and 5 articulated tools that allow us to describe a relationship between variables within a data set. We need variation in both variables and then we can describe the correlation between those variables using regression. But often we want to go further. We want to use the relationships between variables that we find in the data we have (our *sample*) to make inferences about relationships that hold between those variables in the larger world (the *population* of interest). For instance, once we've found that crime is higher on warm days in 2018, we'd like to know whether we are justified in concluding that this relationship is likely to hold in other years and isn't simply an artifact of the 2018 data. That is, we want to know whether an observed relationship in a sample of days reflects a genuine phenomenon in the population of days or whether it happens to be true in the sample of data that we looked at by chance (or dumb luck). In this chapter, we discuss some tools that help us to adjudicate between these possibilities.

Estimation

To start thinking about this question, we need a common language to talk about the differences between the things we observe in our sample and the phenomena in the population that we'd like to learn about. To do so, we are going to use the following simple equation, which will come up so often throughout the rest of the book that, from now on, we are going to start calling it *our favorite equation*:

$$\text{Estimate} = \text{Estimand} + \text{Bias} + \text{Noise}$$

We are going to explain each of these terms carefully as we go. But let's start with some basic definitions.

The *estimate* is the number we get as a result of our analysis. The *estimand* is the true quantity of interest in the population that we are trying to learn about. Our hope is that our estimate closely approximates our estimand. An estimate can differ from the estimand for two reasons: bias and noise. *Bias* refers to errors that occur for systematic reasons, and *noise* refers to idiosyncratic errors that occur because of chance.

Let's set the stage with a simple example that will allow us to define and understand these terms more clearly.

Suppose we conduct a poll to learn which of two candidates (a Republican and a Democrat) is going to win an upcoming election. We can think of this as a prediction problem: we are collecting data to forecast the future winner. But we can also think of this as pure description: we want to know the proportion of voters who support one candidate over the other.

In either case, a key challenge is that there are too many voters for us to ask all of them their opinions. Necessity forces us to poll a *sample*, constituting only a small proportion of the total *population* of voters. Thus, we need to figure out what we can conclude about political views in this larger population from evidence generated by a poll of only a relatively small sample.

In our example, we are interested in learning the proportion of voters in the population who support the Republican. Let's call that proportion, which is a number between 0 and 1, q. Since there are only two candidates, the proportion who support the Democrat is just $1 - q$. So q is our estimand. Until we actually hold the election, we don't get to observe q; we have to try to estimate it.

Suppose we poll a random sample of 100 voters and ask them whether they will support the Republican or the Democrat. We could estimate the number of voters in the population who support the Republican (which we can't observe) by calculating the proportion of people in our sample who support the Republican (which we can observe). Let's call our estimate from our sample $\hat{q}$, which we pronounce "q-hat." Following standard practice, we will notate estimands with a letter (it need not be q) and we will notate estimates of that estimand using that same letter with a hat over it. In this case, our hope is that our estimate, $\hat{q}$, is close to the estimand, q.

In this example, the *estimand* is the true proportion of Republicans in the population (q)—it is the unobserved quantity that we are trying to learn about with our data analysis. The process of sampling 100 voters and calculating the proportion who support the Republican is called the *estimator*—it is the procedure we apply to generate a numerical result. The proportion of Republicans in our sample ($\hat{q}$) is our *estimate*—it is the numerical result arising from the application of our estimator, which we hope approximates the estimand.

By understanding the distinction between estimates and estimands, we can take a first step toward making sense of our favorite equation:

$$\text{Estimate} = \text{Estimand} + \text{Bias} + \text{Noise}$$

The quantity we are interested in is the estimand. The quantity we observe in the data is the estimate. In an ideal world, the estimate would equal the estimand, so that our estimator would reveal to us the true quantity of interest. But our favorite equation says this isn't the case. Estimates differ from estimands because of bias and noise. To understand why, we need to learn more about those two troublesome quantities.

Why Do Estimates Differ from Estimands?

Bias and noise are both important to understand. But they differ, and their difference is often lost on people, leading to unclear thinking. So we'll take them in turn. But before discussing bias and noise in detail, an analogy might help.

Anthony likes to play the Scottish game of curling. In curling, two teams take turns sliding heavy granite stones down a long sheet of ice. As a stone slides, other team members sweep in front of the stone like crazy while running along the ice. We recommend watching a video; it's pretty fun. Anyway, the team with the stone closest to the center of a target on the far end of the sheet of ice (called the button) scores points.

Anthony's quite good at curling. He can more or less get his stones to go where he wants. But, despite his skill, sometimes his stones miss the button (you're not always trying to "draw to the button" in curling, but for the purposes of this discussion, we'll assume that this is your goal). Why is this? Well, there are all sorts of factors outside the control of the thrower that affect how a stone slides. Maybe there was some debris on the sheet, causing a well-aimed stone to divert off course. Or maybe Ethan slipped on the ice while trying to sweep and that accidentally "burned the stone." Anyway, for all of these reasons, Anthony's well-aimed stones might miss the button.

Ethan, by contrast, is terrible at curling. So when he goes curling with Anthony, his stones frequently miss the target, typically to the left (let's not even talk about distance). He'd like to claim it is because of idiosyncratic factors, like with Anthony's misses. But if that were true, he wouldn't be more likely to miss left than right. No, the truth is, Ethan's technique is poor, so his stones are systematically improperly aimed.

There is, we think, a useful analogy between curling and data analysis. Think of the button as the estimand: it is the truth you are aiming at. Think of your estimator as the act of sliding a stone down the ice. And think of the outcome of one stone throw as an estimate arising from one iteration of the estimator.

Your stone (estimate) might miss the button (estimand) for two reasons. First, like Anthony, you may have aimed well, but random factors may have moved the stone this way or that. These random factors are like noise. Since these factors are random, on average, they don't make Anthony miss more to the left or to the right. Indeed, on average, his stone's location is on the button. But that doesn't mean every individual stone finishes on the button; his misses just average each other out. This is what noise does—estimates can equal the estimand on average, but because of noise, any given estimate may not equal the estimand.

Second, like Ethan, you may systematically aim too far to the left. There is still noise, so you might sometimes miss to the right. But, on average, your stone finishes to the left of the button. These systematic errors are like bias. Unlike Anthony, Ethan's average stone misses the button. This is what bias does—when there is bias, even the average estimate doesn't equal the estimand, let alone any given estimate.

Okay, now that we have an analogy to help us see the difference between bias and noise, let's talk about them in a bit more detail.

Bias

One reason an estimator might give you an estimate that differs from the estimand is because it is *biased*. Imagine applying your estimator over and over again an infinite number of times, each time to a new, independent sample of data. Doing so would generate an infinite number of estimates. Because of noise, some of those estimates will be bigger than the estimand (i.e., you'll get a larger share of Republicans in some of your samples than there are in the population) and some of those estimates will be smaller than the estimand (i.e., you'll get a smaller share of Republicans in some of your samples than there are in the population). But you would like the average of that infinite number of estimates to be equal to the estimand. That is, you don't want to predictably (or systematically) over-estimate or under-estimate the number of Republicans. You want to be aimed at the truth. We say that an estimator is *unbiased* if the average value of the estimates it generates would equal the estimand if we repeatedly applied the estimator to new, independent samples an infinite number of times.

We also sometimes talk about the average value of a variable over an infinite number of draws in terms of *expectations*. So, we might say that an unbiased estimator equals the estimand, *in expectation*. Or we might say that the *expected value* of an unbiased estimator is the estimand.

There are lots of reasons a political poll might be biased. Suppose voters systematically lie to pollsters. Perhaps voters believe that pollsters are themselves likely to be Democrats and the voters want to please the pollsters, so some Republican voters report supporting the Democrat. Then our estimator will be biased in favor of Democrats—on average, reporting more voter support for Democrats than there really is. Or suppose Democrats are more likely to turn out to vote than Republicans, but equally likely to answer polls. Then poll respondents will differ from voters, and the estimates from polls will be biased in favor of Republicans—on average, reporting more voter support for Republicans than there actually is. Finally, what if pollsters contact people by phone and phone owners are systematically different in their political leanings than the population as a whole? This will also lead to bias. For lots of reasons, if we ran the poll an infinite number of times and averaged the estimates, that average might not equal the true proportion of Republicans in the population of voters, which is our estimand. Thus, the poll could be biased for any of these reasons.

In subsequent chapters, we will be very concerned with thinking about sources of bias. For the remainder of this chapter, however, we are going to ignore these potential sources of bias to focus on the second potential problem with estimators, noise.

Noise

When you take a sample of the population, you inevitably introduce some noise into your estimate. When you ask 100 randomly selected people out of 100 million their opinions on political candidates, sometimes by chance you happen to talk to a disproportionate share of Republicans and sometimes you happen to talk to a disproportionate share of Democrats. As a result, even without bias, any individual estimate need not equal the estimand. Suppose your estimand is unbiased. If you applied it an infinite number of times, you would not over-estimate Republican or Democrat support, on average. But each individual estimate would likely differ somewhat from the estimand because of noise—that is, natural variability that results from sampling. This natural variability is sometimes referred to as *sampling variation*, a common source of noise.

We have ways of quantifying the amount of noise associated with an estimator. Think about repeatedly applying an estimator with new, independent samples of data an infinite number of times. The closer the various estimates would be to each other, the more *precise* is the estimator. Thus, a more precise estimator is one with less noise.

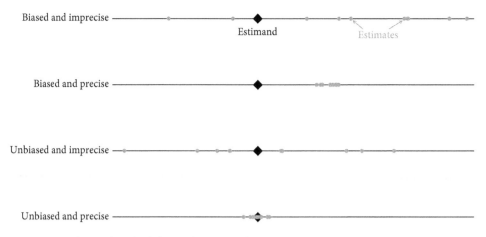

Figure 6.1. Understanding the difference between *unbiased* and *precise*.

What Makes for a Good Estimator?

In the end, we are trying to learn the true value of the estimand. Since our estimate can differ from the estimand because of bias or noise, what we really want is an estimator that is both unbiased and precise.

If our estimator is unbiased but imprecise, our estimates will typically differ from the estimand because there is so much noise. For instance, in our polling example, if we talk to just one voter at random, their opinion is an unbiased estimate of the average opinion in the electorate (if you did this an infinite number of times, q of those times you'd get a Republican, and $1 - q$ of those times you'd get a Democrat). But the sampling variation associated with estimating voter opinion by asking just one person's opinion is huge—we will always estimate either 100 percent Republicans or 100 percent Democrats.

If our estimator is biased but precise, our estimates will typically differ from the estimand because they are very precisely estimating the wrong quantity. For instance, if we sample ten thousand voters, but only do so in Republican neighborhoods, we will get answers clustered very tightly around each other, but they will systematically over-estimate the number of Republicans.

Figure 6.1 illustrates that estimators can be unbiased, precise, neither, or both. The black diamonds represent the estimand—the true value in the world we are interested in. The gray dots show various estimates that arise from repeated applications of a given estimator, each time with an independent sample of data. If the gray dots are symmetrically distributed around the diamond (like Anthony's curling stones around the button), the estimator is unbiased. That is, the estimates it provides are right on average. If the gray dots are clustered tightly together, the estimator is precise. That is, there is very little noise, so the estimator yields similar estimates with each iteration. All else equal, we would obviously like to have our estimator be less biased *and* more precise. However, sometimes there are trade-offs between these goals, and we have to decide how much bias we're willing to accept for a certain gain in precision.

For a concrete example of the possible trade-offs between bias and precision, let's return to the topic of polling. Suppose you have $2,000 and you'd like to conduct a reliable poll to understand how popular a political candidate, policy proposal, product, or potential advertising campaign would be. You could post the survey online, pay people twenty cents per response, and obtain ten thousand responses. Or you could pay a professional polling firm to obtain a random, representative sample at a cost of $20 per response, meaning you'll be able to afford only one hundred responses.

The online convenience sample is much larger, so your estimates of public opinion will be more precise, but they'll also likely be biased. The kinds of people who voluntarily take surveys for modest compensation are not likely to be representative of the general population. The professionally conducted survey will likely give you less biased estimates, but the sample size will be smaller, so your estimates will be less precise.

This kind of trade-off between bias and precision is quite common for data analysts, and we'll see more examples in part 3. The right way to make this trade-off will depend on your goals, the costs of different kinds of errors, and the particular question you are hoping to answer.

If an estimator is unbiased, we'd also like it to be as precise as possible. And as we've discussed, we might even allow for a little bias in exchange for a big gain in precision. But if an estimator is really biased, it's no longer obvious that precision is a good thing. For one thing, a precise biased estimator will never be anywhere close to the truth. Whereas with less precision, you might sometimes make good predictions despite the bias, albeit by accident. (Ethan would probably be better off if there was an earthquake just as he released his curling stone because at least sometimes his stone would stay in play.) Furthermore, precision might give you a false sense of confidence. Beware a precise estimate with an unknown bias.

Quantifying Precision

Remember the motivating question for this chapter: When we estimate something from a sample of data, how confident should we be in drawing inferences about the larger population? As we've seen, if our estimator is biased, we should certainly be worried. But even if our estimator isn't biased, we still have to be worried that our estimates do not reflect the true relationship in the larger population (the estimand) because of noise. In order to know how worried we should be about this possibility, we need to quantify the precision of an estimator. We do so through a statistic called the standard error, which we can then use to construct confidence intervals.

Standard Errors

In chapter 2, we talked about the standard deviation as one way to measure how spread out a variable's distribution is (or, equivalently, how variable the variable is). Well, imagine that we repeated our estimator an infinite number of times, each time with a newly drawn sample of data. In that thought experiment, we could think of the estimate itself as a variable. Each time we draw the data and run our estimator, we get a different value of the estimate because of the noise. So, we can imagine the distribution of estimates we would get after repeating our estimator an infinite number of times. That imagined distribution is called the *sampling distribution*. The standard deviation of that sampling distribution is called the *standard error*. The standard error, if we knew what it was, would give us a sense of how far any given estimate will be from the average estimate, since it measures how variable our estimates will be. If the estimator is unbiased, the average estimate equals the estimand. So, for an unbiased estimator, the standard error tells us approximately how far a typical estimate is from the estimand, which is the true value we are trying to learn about.

If the standard error is large, then the estimates would be very spread out and the estimator is relatively imprecise (i.e., there is a lot of sampling variation). If the standard error is small, then the estimates would be very close together and the estimator is relatively precise (i.e., there is little sampling variation). Look back at figure 6.1. The third row shows an example of some estimates from repeated runs of an estimator with a relatively large standard error—as a consequence, the estimates we see are quite spread out. (Of course, we aren't seeing the full sampling distribution since we don't have infinite estimates.) The fourth row shows an example of some estimates from repeated runs of an estimator with a relatively small standard error—as a consequence, the estimates we see are tightly clustered.

We can provide some insight into what makes an estimator precise or imprecise (i.e., when the standard error will be small or large). In our polling example, the standard error is approximately equal to $\sqrt{\frac{q(1-q)}{N}}$, where N refers to the sample size (the number of people polled). While we aren't going to show you how to derive this formula (a topic for a different book), we can learn some things about what makes an estimator more or less precise by thinking about the formula.

Let's start with understanding the numerator, $q(1-q)$. Notice this term is maximized at $q = \frac{1}{2}$ and decreases as q gets larger or smaller. So, suppose the true proportion of Republicans in the population, q, is either very large (close to 1) or very small (close to 0). This makes $q(1-q)$ very small and, therefore, makes the standard error small. Why? When q is very large or very small, there is little possibility of sampling error. If 99 percent of voters are Republicans, when you collect your sample of, say, one thousand voters, it will be very unlikely that you find many Democrats. By contrast, if q is close to one-half, the standard error is large. This reflects the fact that there is lots of room for sampling error. You could easily find a 55-45 or 45-55 split in your sample of data drawn from a 50-50 population. The closer q is to one-half, the more natural variation there is in our outcome of interest, making the standard error larger.

Now consider the denominator. It tells us that as the size of our sample increases, our standard error goes down. This makes sense. The problem of imprecision comes from the fact that our sample might not accurately reflect the whole population. When the sample is large, it will more closely approximate the population. We can more precisely estimate the opinions of a million people by talking to ten thousand people than by talking to ten people.

The formula for the standard error actually tells us something a little more subtle than just that small sample sizes lead to imprecision. It tells us that the standard error shrinks in proportion to $\sqrt{N}$. Suppose the true proportion of Republicans in the population is $q = .5$. Then, if we took a poll of 1000 voters, we'd have a standard error of $\sqrt{\frac{.5 \cdot .5}{1,000}} \approx .016$. Suppose we conducted a much larger poll of 10,000 people. Then our standard error is $\sqrt{\frac{.5 \cdot .5}{10,000}} = .005$. So increasing the sample size by a factor of 10 only improves the precision of the poll by approximately threefold. If we further increased the sample size to 100,000, we'd get another roughly threefold improvement in precision, ($\sqrt{\frac{.5 \cdot .5}{100,000}} = .0016$). In other words, there are diminishing returns to bigger and bigger sample sizes. The standard error of a survey with 10,000 respondents is already tiny, and adding more respondents doesn't meaningfully improve precision.

One tricky thing you might have noticed is that we need to know q in order to calculate the standard error. But we don't know q; that's why we're doing the poll to begin with. In practice, we approximate the standard error by substituting $\hat{q}$, our estimate of q, into the formula. Of course, this approximation would run into problems if you had a really small N or a value of q that was really close to 0 or 1. Suppose you talked to five people and found that none of them were Republicans. Thoughtlessly applying the procedures above, you would wrongly conclude that nobody is a Republican and that your standard error is 0. Of course that's wrong, and that's because with small samples and with extreme values of q, your approximation using $\hat{q}$ is misleading.

We should also point out that although there is a nice formula for approximating the standard error in our polling example, this won't always be the case. Fortunately, our computers can often produce reasonably reliable approximations of standard errors, even in more complicated circumstances.

Small Samples and Extreme Observations

It is worth pausing to note that the fact that small samples lead to imprecision explains a common phenomenon that you may have noticed out there in the world. If you look up data on the towns with the highest or lowest cancer rates or the highest or lowest average income, you will find a list of towns with a pretty small number of residents. Similarly, if you look up the schools with the highest or lowest average test scores, you will find a list of schools with a small number of students. Why is this?

Think of the average cancer rate or income in a town as an estimate of the national cancer rate or income, just like the average support for Republicans in a polling sample is an estimate of the average support for Republicans in the whole population. When the number of residents in a town is small, that is equivalent to having a small sample size. That leads to less precision (more noise) in your estimate. That means it is more likely your estimate will have an extreme value in either direction. Small towns tend to dominate the list of places with extreme cancer rates or average incomes, not because they are necessarily on average more or less cancer prone or more or less wealthy, but because their cancer rates and average incomes are more variable than places with more people to average over.

To see this in the extreme, imagine a town with just one resident. That town either has a 100 percent cancer rate or a 0 percent cancer rate. But a town with one hundred thousand residents is going to have a cancer rate somewhere in the middle, much closer to the national average.

Figure 6.2, inspired by a similar graph in Howard Wainer's *Picturing the Uncertain World*, illustrates the point. The figure plots data from California middle schools in 2012. We observe students' average academic performance (the Academic Performance Index, which is largely determined by standardized test scores) and the size of the student body for each school. The hollow data points represent the very worst performing schools (bottom 5 percent on academic performance), and the solid-black data points represent the very best performing schools (top 5 percent on academic performance). As you can see from the regression line, there is actually a positive correlation in this data between school size and academic performance—on average, larger schools perform better than smaller schools. But, more importantly for us, small schools are overrepresented in both groups.

Understanding that small sample sizes lead to imprecision is important for many reasons. One is that, as Wainer points out, failing to think clearly about the issue can lead to bad decision making. The Bill and Melinda Gates Foundation spent billions of dollars on an ultimately ineffective small schools initiative. The evidence that led

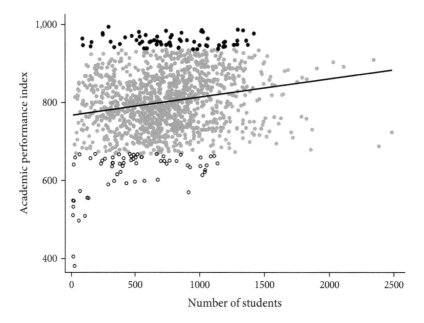

Figure 6.2. A scatter plot and regression line showing a slight positive correlation between average academic performance and school size for California middle schools in 2012.

them to make this misguided investment was the observation that schools with a small number of pupils were over-represented on lists of schools with the best test scores. Had they thought a little more clearly, they would have also checked the lists of schools with the worst test scores and found small schools over-represented on those lists too.

Confidence Intervals

Another way we often quantify precision is through a confidence interval.

An important mathematical fact, called the Law of Large Numbers, tells us that as our sample size gets really big, the noise will essentially disappear. But how big is big enough?

Another important mathematical fact, called the Central Limit Theorem, tells us that if our poll is indeed unbiased, then if we were to repeatedly run our poll, approximately 95 percent of our estimates ($\hat{q}$, Republicans in our sample) will end up being within approximately 2 standard errors of our estimand (q, Republicans in the population). Therefore, pollsters will often report what they call the *margin of error*, which is simply twice the standard error.

Researchers and pollsters also sometimes report what they call the *95% confidence interval*. This is the interval that ranges from the estimate ($\hat{q}$) minus two times the standard error up to the estimate plus two times the standard error.

The 95% confidence interval is a source of some confusion. Often, people will casually say that we're 95 percent confident that the true value lies within the 95% confidence interval. But that's not quite right. The correct statement is a lot clunkier. Technically, we can say that if there is no bias and if we repeated our estimator an infinite number of times, the true estimand would be inside the 95% confidence interval 95 percent of the time.

To get a picture in our head of how confidence intervals work, let's go back to our curling analogy. Suppose Anthony pushes an infinite number of stones down an infinite number of ice sheets. Think of the spot on the ice where the exact center of his stone comes to rest as the estimate. That estimate is extremely unlikely to be sitting exactly on the button—your estimate is almost never exactly equal to the true value of the estimand. But the stone is wider than that one spot. So we might ask how often the button will be touching some part of the stone. That will depend on how wide the stone is. (Of course, there is a regulation width in curling, but allow us a little poetic license. We aren't Scottish. And this isn't the Olympics.) We could find the exact width of a stone such that the button would be touching some part of the stone on 95 percent of Anthony's throws. This is like the 95% confidence interval. It isn't that, on any one throw, we're 95 percent confident that the button is covered by some part of the stone. It is that, on 95 percent of throws, the button is covered by some part of the stone.

This analogy can also help us think about confidence intervals other than the 95% confidence interval. Sometimes we want to be more confident than 95 percent. So we might be interested in the 99% confidence interval. Ask yourself whether the 99% confidence interval is wider or narrower than the 95% confidence interval. If Anthony wants 99 percent of his throws to end with some part of the stone touching the button, he is going to need to use a wider stone. So the 99% confidence interval is wider than the 95% confidence interval. We have to admit a larger range of possible Republicans if we want to be sure our estimate is within that range 99 percent of the time rather than just 95 percent of the time.

Statistical Inference and Hypothesis Testing

Now we can finally turn to this chapter's motivating question: How do we make inferences about populations using estimates from samples? Let's stick with our polling example. As we emphasized, when we conduct a poll, even if we think it is unbiased, we also want it to be precise because we want to know that it is giving us an estimate that's close to the truth. How can we assess this? How well does a sample of, say, one thousand voters estimate the views of the 140 million Americans that will determine who wins an upcoming presidential election? Let's see.

Hypothesis Testing

Often, we want to assess some particular hypothesis. For instance, we might want to know whether it is reasonable to believe that the estimand is greater than, less than, or different from some particular reference point. For that, we need to think about *hypothesis testing*.

In the example of an electoral poll, we might like to know which candidate is going to win the election. Suppose we conducted an unbiased poll of one thousand voters and this yielded an estimate of the Republican candidate's vote share of $\hat{q} = .532$ or 53.2 percent. How confident should we be that the Republican is actually going to win the election—that is, how confident should we be that more than 50 percent of voters will vote for the Republican or, put differently, that $q > .5$? Hypothesis testing provides a way for us to say something about that.

One way of thinking about this question is as follows. We have some evidence from our poll that the Republican candidate is more popular than the Democrat. But we want to know how good that evidence is. That is, we want to know how likely it is that we could have observed such evidence *even if the Republican is not more popular than the Democrat*. So we test how likely it is that we would have observed the evidence we observe if the two candidates were actually equally popular. This *no relationship* benchmark is typically referred to as the *null hypothesis*.

To understand the hypothesis test, start by assuming the null hypothesis is true—that is, the two candidates are exactly equally popular, so $q = .5$. Now ask how likely would it be for us to obtain a poll result at least as favorable for the Republican as the one we actually found, $\hat{q} = .532$.

We already have the information we need to answer this question. With a true vote share of $q = .5$ and a poll of one thousand voters, the standard error of our estimator is approximately 1.6 percentage points ($\sqrt{\frac{.5 \cdot .5}{1,000}} \approx .016$). Our estimate of .532 is 2 standard errors above the null hypothesis ($.5 + 2 \cdot .016 = .532$). (We didn't choose these numbers by accident.)

As we said earlier, the Central Limit Theorem tells us that 95 percent of estimates from an unbiased poll of the sort we ran will fall within 2 standard errors of the truth, meaning that only 5 percent of estimates will fall more than 2 standard errors from the truth. Moreover, in half of those unfortunate cases, the estimate will be 2 standard errors *below* the truth (showing the Democrat to be notably ahead). So if the null is true, the probability that we'd get a poll result as favorable for the Republican as the one we got is about 2.5 percent, or 1 in 40.

We obviously picked numbers that would make this calculation straightforward, but your computer can do this calculation for any poll result. Statisticians are in the business of developing methods for conducting these calculations. In statistics lingo, the analysis we just did is called a *one-sided z-test*. You don't need to know about z-tests to understand the rest of this book, but if you want to learn about them, you can consult virtually any statistics book. (Wikipedia is pretty reliable for such material as well.) More generally, the important thing is that hypothesis testing is a strategy for assessing the probability of getting a result as extreme as yours under the assumption that the null hypothesis is true.

Statistical Significance

We just saw that if the null is true, the probability we would have gotten a result as favorable to the Republican as what we found is only .025. This probability is called a *p-value*. If our *p*-value is really low, then we might conclude that the null is unlikely to be true. Thus, we have some statistically compelling evidence that the Republican is indeed favored by voters—if the true vote share were evenly split, it's quite unlikely that the poll result would be this favorable to the Republican (and even more unlikely if the true vote share favored the Democrat).

A common strategy is to pre-specify a particular threshold (most commonly, .05), and if the *p*-value is below that threshold, then we say we reject the null hypothesis and conclude that we have *statistically significant* evidence for the hypothesis we were testing against the null hypothesis.

Of course, hypothesis testing does not provide certain conclusions. With a significance threshold of .05, there's a 5 percent chance of obtaining a statistically significant result even if the null hypothesis is true. But hypothesis testing provides one way of thinking quantitatively about whether a pattern or result you have detected in your data set is likely to reflect a genuine phenomenon rather than simply being the product of noise.

One common error is to assume that the *p*-value tells you the probability that the null hypothesis is true. It doesn't. It tells you the probability of getting an estimate as extreme as the one you got if the null is true. Those two numbers are typically different. Indeed, to calculate the former quantity, you'd have to have a lot more information (e.g., how likely you thought it was that the null was true before you saw the evidence). We'll discuss these issues in part 4.

Statistical Inference about Relationships

So far, we've developed our ideas about bias, noise, and hypothesis testing in a simple setting where we are just trying to learn about the share of voters who support the Republican candidate. But all these concepts and tools of statistical inference can be applied to much more interesting problems, including estimating relationships like correlations.

Suppose we ran a regression to estimate the relationship between some outcome variable and some explanatory variable. The previous chapter discussed how we can utilize linear regression to find coefficients that describe the relationship between two variables in a data set. But now let's think about this in terms of estimation and statistical inference.

Suppose our data set consists of information on the income and education of a random sample of one thousand workers, but we are actually interested in the average relationship between income and education in the population of all workers. So we are trying to make inferences about a correlation in the population (our estimand) based on a correlation in the data (our estimate). How do we do this?

Start with the following equation, which describes the relationship between income and education in the population.

$$\text{Income}_i = \alpha^{OLS} + \beta^{OLS} \cdot \text{Education}_i + \text{error}_i$$

This equation is just like the one that we studied in chapter 5. Income_i is person i's income, Education_i is person i's years of education, and error_i is the difference between person i's income and the income predicted by the OLS regression line for a person with person i's education. The parameters α^{OLS} and β^{OLS} take whatever values minimize the sum of squared errors across the population. For example, β^{OLS} is the average extent to which income increases with each additional year of education in the population. These parameters α^{OLS} and β^{OLS} are features of the world. We don't know them. But, since we would like to know, on average, how income changes with education, β^{OLS} is our estimand.

We don't know β^{OLS} because we don't observe the income and education of every single person in the population. But we can estimate it by applying linear regression to our data on one thousand workers. Following our convention of labeling estimates with hats, let's call the estimate from that regression $\hat{\beta}^{OLS}$. It is the regression coefficient, and it reflects the correlation between education and income in our sample. (Often, people drop the OLS superscript and just talk about their estimate as $\hat{\beta}$, which is fine as long as it is clear what you are up to.)

Unfortunately, β^{OLS} and $\hat{\beta}^{OLS}$ are not the same thing. The former is an estimand and the latter is an estimate, which, as we know from our favorite equation, may differ from the estimand because of both bias and noise. Let's assume that our sample of workers was randomly selected from the population, so there is no bias. (We'll talk more about random sampling and unbiasedness in chapter 11). But there is still noise. So if we want to know how close $\hat{\beta}^{OLS}$ is likely to be to the true β^{OLS}, we're going to need to think about the standard error.

Just as $\hat{q}$, our estimate of the proportion of Republicans in the population, had a standard error, so too does our estimate of the relationship between income and education, $\hat{\beta}^{OLS}$. The standard error gives us a sense of how far, on average, our estimate would be from the truth if we repeated our estimator an infinite number of times with independent samples of data. Just as with the poll result, there are formulas for calculating this standard error. For now, you don't need to worry about the formula because a computer will calculate the standard error for you. Thinking more technically about standard errors is a topic for a different book.

Once you've estimated the standard error associated with a regression coefficient, you can do the same kinds of things that you did with the standard error of the poll result. For instance, you can construct a 95% confidence interval. You can also conduct hypothesis tests and compute p-values. All of this can help you assess how precise your estimate of the true relationship is.

One common question people are interested in is whether there is compelling evidence that there is any true relationship at all. That is, suppose you find a positive $\hat{\beta}^{OLS}$; income and education are positively correlated in your sample. Should you be confident, on the basis of that evidence, that they are positively correlated in the larger population?

You can start to answer that question by testing the null hypothesis that the true relationship between income and education is in fact zero. To do so, you ask how likely it is that you would have gotten an estimate as big as $\hat{\beta}^{OLS}$ if there was in fact no correlation between income and education in the population (i.e., $\beta^{OLS} = 0$). If you obtain a small p-value and reject the null hypothesis, then you have statistically significant evidence that there is a relationship between income and education in the population.

One reason statistical inference of this sort is so useful is that we're bound, from time to time, to find relationships in our data that do not reflect genuine relationships in the larger population. This is the nature of noisy data. So we need to check whether we have good reason to believe our findings aren't just the result of noise.

What If We Have Data for the Whole Population?

Sometimes we have data for an entire population of interest. For instance, suppose we want to know the correlation between participation in varsity athletics and GPA for University of Chicago students. It's conceivable that we could convince the university to give us the relevant data for every single student, in which case we wouldn't need to estimate the correlation in the population by calculating it in a sample. We could perfectly measure the true estimand, the correlation between athletics and GPA for the whole population of University of Chicago students.

Here's a tricky question. Does it still make sense to think about standard errors, confidence intervals, and statistical significance when we have data for the entire population? One argument is that these tools are irrelevant because there was no sampling. So there is no noise. The estimate is the estimand. As such, there's no need to think about statistical inference.

But we still think there are good reasons to pay attention to the concept of noise and the associated measures of uncertainty even if we have data for an entire population. Let's talk about why.

Suppose we found a small positive correlation between playing a varsity sport and GPA. It still seems reasonable to ask whether that difference arose for a reason or whether it arose just by coincidence.

What would it mean for a correlation to arise by coincidence? Suppose that there's no good reason to think there should be an on-average difference between the GPAs of athletes and non-athletes: the admissions standards are the same for both kinds of students, athletic participation has no effect on GPA, academic performance has no effect on athletic participation, and so on. Nonetheless, there are all kinds of idiosyncratic differences between students that lead their GPAs to be different from one another. And with any finite number of students, there's bound to be at least a slight difference between the GPAs of athletes and non-athletes, even if there's no good reason for the difference.

To assess whether this observed correlation arose by coincidence or for a reason, we can't collect more data. We already have all the data there is to have on University of Chicago students. However, it turns out that the tools of statistical inference and hypothesis testing still provide a useful way to think about whether an observed pattern was a coincidence or not.

One way to think about the problem is that, although we have data on all the actual students at the university, these actual students are just a small sample of a much larger hypothetical population of students that could have been at the university. We can start with the null hypothesis that the true correlation in that larger, hypothetical population is zero, and we can ask how likely it is that we would have observed a correlation at least as large as the one we observed among the actual students by chance. Of course, doing this requires a metaphysical leap from actual populations to hypothetical populations. But engaging in a little bit of metaphysics is a price probably worth paying to preserve our ability to think about whether some observed relationship reflects a genuine, predictable pattern or was just a fluke.

Substantive versus Statistical Significance

Statistical hypothesis testing is often helpful and informative because we want to know whether an observed phenomenon is likely to have arisen purely by chance (e.g., due to sampling variation). However, *statistical* significance (a low p-value indicating that a result was unlikely to have arisen by chance) is not the same thing as *substantive* significance, and we must be careful not to conflate these two concepts. Often, we don't want to know just whether some phenomenon *exists* or not, which is the question of statistical significance; we want to know how big or small the phenomenon is because that will tell us whether it is *important* or not, which is the question of substantive significance. For example, executives at Coca-Cola probably already know that their marketing has some effect on sales. But that doesn't tell them how much to spend on marketing. For that, they want to know how big the effects of marketing on sales are. Let us give you examples that illustrate the two ways quantitative analysts can be led astray by emphasizing statistical significance over substantive significance.

Social Media and Voting

In 2012, six researchers published a study in *Nature* showing that people were more likely to vote in the 2010 U.S. midterm elections if their Facebook pages displayed a banner indicating which of their friends voted. The study was notable for several reasons.

Facebook allowed the researchers to randomize the experience of sixty-one million voting-age Facebook users in the United States on Election Day. And indeed, the experimental intervention appears to have increased turnout—the estimated effect of seeing that a close friend voted is highly statistically significant ($p = .02$). The researchers concluded that "strong ties are instrumental for spreading both online and real-world behaviour in human social networks." And the study received significant press coverage for demonstrating how important social pressure is for voting.

What most observers failed to notice was that the estimated effect of the Facebook banners on voter turnout was less than 0.4 percentage points. This is a substantively small effect, arguably of little relevance for campaigning or understanding elections. The fact that 0.4 percent of eligible voters can be persuaded to vote through a Facebook banner reporting their friends' voting choices does not tell us that strong ties are instrumental for spreading behavior. Of course, with a sample size of sixty-one million, almost any non-zero estimate will be statistically significant. That's not a bad thing. Big sample sizes mean that our estimates are quite precise, so we will more reliably detect genuine relationships. However, we can't just assume that any statistically significant result is also substantively significant.

We've seen that statistically significant results can be substantively insignificant. Now let's see that the opposite is also true.

The Second Reform Act

In a 2011 article in the *Quarterly Journal of Political Science*, Samuel Berlinski and Torun Dewan estimate the effects of the Second Reform Act of 1867 on elections in the United Kingdom. Despite the fact that the Second Reform Act roughly doubled the size of the eligible electorate and brought working-class voters to the polls for the first time, the authors report that there was little effect on election outcomes: "There is no evidence relating Liberal [one of the major British parties] electoral support to changes in the franchise rules."

But is this the right way to interpret the evidence? When the authors say there is no evidence, what they mean is that their estimates of the effect of the Reform Act are not statistically significant. So they can't say that those results were unlikely to have arisen by chance. But, while not statistically significant, the evidence from the study actually suggests that the Second Reform Act had important consequences. The numerical estimates indicate that the Reform Act's doubling of the electorate increased the Liberal Party's vote share by 8 percentage points, a substantively large effect implying that the new, working-class voters enfranchised by the reform were much more likely to support the Liberal Party than were wealthier, previously enfranchised voters. However, although the estimate is substantively large, it is also imprecise and therefore not statistically significant. Focusing on this statistical insignificance, Berlinski and Dewan conclude that the Second Reform Act had little effect. But the evidence actually indicates that our best guess is it had a big effect. It's just that that guess is uncertain.

Although statistical significance is useful and informative, it is often misused and misunderstood. A theme throughout this book is that clear thinking and data are complements, not substitutes. Just because we're doing statistics doesn't mean we can stop thinking substantively about the questions we really want to answer. We should utilize statistical inference when possible. But we should also always remind ourselves to make substantive inferences from the evidence.

Wrapping Up

Estimates can differ from estimands for two reason: bias and noise. Bias will be a major focus of chapter 9. In this chapter, we focused on noise—differences between the estimate and the estimand that arise because of idiosyncratic features of our sample. Because noise is idiosyncratic, it would average out to zero if we were to follow our estimation procedure over and over again an infinite number of times, each time on an independent sample of data. But in any one sample, noise can be quite important.

The presence of noise means that we are always at least somewhat uncertain whether a relationship in a sample of data (the estimate) in fact reflects a real relationship in the larger population of interest (the estimand). We have discussed techniques for quantifying this uncertainty and for testing the hypothesis that an estimated relationship is real against the null hypothesis that the estimated relationship was the result of noise alone.

The presence of noise creates challenges beyond uncertainty. For instance, in chapter 7 we will consider the problem that, if the same study is run over and over again, some iterations will yield statistically significant results because of noise, even if the relationship under investigation isn't real. If only those statistically significant findings get reported, then the scientific enterprise may lead to systematically incorrect conclusions. In chapter 8 we will examine how the presence of noise creates the puzzling phenomenon of reversion to the mean—extreme observations tend to be followed by less extreme observations—which, if we don't think clearly, can lead to all sorts of misinterpretations of evidence.

Key Terms

- **Population:** The units in the world we are trying to learn about.
- **Sample:** A subset of the population for which we have data.
- **Estimand:** The unobserved quantity we are trying to learn about with our data analysis.
- **Estimator:** The procedure we apply to data to generate a numerical result.
- **Estimate:** The numerical result arising from the application of our estimator to a specific set of data.
- **Bias:** Differences between our estimand and our estimate that arise for *systematic* reasons—that is, for reasons that will persist on average over many different samples of data.
- **Noise:** Differences between our estimand and our estimate that arise due to *idiosyncratic* facts about our sample.
- **Unbiasedness:** An estimate/estimator is unbiased if by repeating our estimation procedure over and over again an infinite number of times, the average value of our estimates would equal the estimand.
- **Expectation or Expected value:** The average value of an infinite number of draws of a variable is the variable's expected value or its value in expectation.
- **Precision:** An estimate/estimator is precise if by repeating our estimation procedure over and over again, the various estimates would be close to each other. The more similar the hypothetical estimates from repeating the estimator, the more precise the estimate.

- **Sampling distribution:** The distribution of estimates that we would get if we repeated our estimator an infinite number of times, each time with a new sample of data.
- **Standard error:** The standard deviation of the sampling distribution. If the estimator is unbiased, the standard error gives us a sense of how far, on average, our estimate would be from the estimand if we repeated our procedure over and over with independent samples of data.
- **Margin of error:** Pollsters often multiply the standard error by 2 and report this as the margin of error.
- **95% confidence interval:** If we applied the estimator an infinite number of times, each time on a new sample of data, the estimand would be contained in the 95% confidence interval (newly calculated each time) 95 percent of the time. Importantly, it is not true that we are 95 percent confident that the true estimand lies in the 95% confidence interval.
- **Hypothesis testing:** Statistical techniques for assessing how confident we should be that some feature of the data reflects a real feature of the world rather than arising from noise.
- **Null hypothesis:** The hypothesis that some feature of the data is entirely the result of noise.
- **Statistical significance:** We say that we have statistically significant evidence for some hypothesis when we can reject the null hypothesis at some pre-specified level of confidence (typically, 95% confidence).
- **p-value:** The probability of finding a relationship as strong as or stronger than the relationship found in the data if the null hypothesis is true. We use p-values to assess statistical significance. For instance, if the p-value is less than .05, then we have statistically significant evidence (at the 95% confidence level) that the relationship is real. Importantly, the p-value is not equal to the probability that the null hypothesis is true.

Exercises

6.1   Consider the following strategies for conducting a political poll to predict the vote shares in an upcoming election. Discuss the likely extent of bias and precision for each one.

(a) Fox News asks their viewers to call in and tell them who they are supporting in the election. They get more than one hundred thousand responses.

(b) Nailbiter Polling (a new firm on the scene) conducts polls, and then, regardless of the answers, they always report that the race is a dead heat: 50 percent in favor of candidate A, and 50 percent in favor of candidate B.

(c) Surprising News Polls (another new player) conducts large, representative polls, computes the average support for each candidate, and then flips a coin. If the coin is heads, they add 10 percent to candidate A's support, and if the coin is tails, they subtract 10 percent from candidate A's support.

(d) Middle America Polling obtains a physical copy of the voter file (the list of registered voters), they flip to the middle page, and they contact and interview the ten individuals in the middle of that middle page.

6.2 Anthony's father, Pete, recently purchased a roulette wheel to run an underground casino in his garage. In case you're not familiar with roulette, the wheel is spun and a ball is dropped seemingly randomly into one of thirty-eight pockets on the wheel, each of which corresponds to a number and a color. On this wheel, there are eighteen red pockets, eighteen black pockets, and two green pockets. A gambler might bet on red, in which case they will double their money if the ball falls into a red pocket but lose their money otherwise. If the wheel is indeed fair, meaning that the ball is equally likely to fall in any pocket, Pete expects to make money on these bets because the gambler wins 18 out of 38 times, while Pete wins the other 20 out of 38 times. Of course, if the wheel is not fair, Pete could have just made a terrible investment. To test the wheel, Pete conducted three practice spins (with no gambling), and much to his dismay, the ball fell into a red pocket all three times. Given the information available to us thus far, what can we say from a statistical standpoint about whether the table is likely to be biased toward the red pockets?

(a) What's the null hypothesis?
(b) What's the p-value?
(c) Provide a substantive interpretation for the p-value and, importantly, explain what the p-value is *not*.
(d) Ignoring the legality of garage roulette, what additional advice would you give to Pete to help him figure out if his table is fair?

6.3 Let's return to the analysis of schooling and earnings from last chapter's exercises. When you regress earnings on schooling, in addition to giving you estimated coefficients, your computer also probably gave you some other numbers that you didn't understand until you read this chapter. For the coefficient associated with years of schooling, you should have obtained an estimate of 1.16, indicating that each additional year of schooling corresponds with increased earnings of about $1,160. What are the estimated standard error, p-value, and 95% confidence interval associated with that coefficient? Provide a substantive interpretation for each one.

Readings and References

If you are interested in the history of how scientists and statisticians came to settle on the widely accepted 5 percent threshold for statistical significance, which is surprisingly interesting, see

Michael Cowles and Caroline Davis. 1982. "On the Origins of the .05 Level of Statistical Significance." *American Psychologist* 37(5):553–58.

If you are generally interested in the history of probability and statistics (which you should be), have a look at

Ian Hacking. 2006. *The Emergence of Probability: A Philosophical Study of Early Ideas about Probability and Statistical Inference, 2nd Edition.* Cambridge University Press.

Ian Hacking. 1990. *The Taming of Chance.* Cambridge University Press.

For a fascinating history of statistical hypothesis testing and the problems that arise when scientists conflate statistical and substantive significance, we recommend

Stephen T. Ziliak and Deirdre N. McCloskey. 2008. *The Cult of Statistical Significance: How the Standard Errors Cost Us Jobs, Justice, and Lives.* University of Michigan Press.

Our discussion of small sample sizes, small schools, and the Gates Foundation drew on material from

Howard Wainer. 2009. *Picturing the Uncertain World: How to Understand, Communicate, and Control Uncertainty through Graphical Display.* Princeton University Press.

The data on academic performance and enrollment in California schools is from https://www.cde.ca.gov/re/pr/reclayout12b.asp.

The paper on Facebook and voter turnout that we mention is

Robert M. Bond, Christopher J. Fariss, Jason J. Jones, Adam D. I. Kramer, Cameron Marlow, Jaime E. Settle, and James H. Fowler. 2012. "A 61-Million-Person Experiment in Social Influence and Political Mobilization." *Nature* 489(7415):295–98.

The paper on the British Second Reform Act is

Samuel Berlinski and Torun Dewan. 2011. "The Political Consequences of Franchise Extension: Evidence from the Second Reform Act." *Quarterly Journal of Political Science* 6(34):329–76.

CHAPTER 7

Over-Comparing, Under-Reporting

What You'll Learn

- If analysts make lots of comparisons but report only the statistically significant ones, there will be lots of false positive results and over-estimates.
- These false positives can be the result of nefarious researcher behavior (*p*-hacking). But they can also arise in a community of entirely honest researchers (*p*-screening).
- There's no easy solution, but analysts and consumers have some tools at their disposal to reduce the risk of being misled.

Introduction

Although statistical hypothesis testing is a useful tool, it's far from foolproof. To understand why scientific studies and quantitative data analyses so often produce misleading or unreliable results, we're going to start in an unlikely place—the story of a seemingly impressive sea creature.

Can an Octopus Be a Soccer Expert?

In 2008 and 2010, Paul the Octopus made headlines for his apparent prowess in predicting the outcome of soccer matches. Before matches between two national teams, Paul's keepers would present him with two boxes of food, each marked with the flag of one of the competitor countries. The keepers interpreted the box Paul ate from first as his forecast for who would win the match. Paul was surprisingly accurate, and journalists and gamblers eagerly awaited his predictions.

Paul was the subject of much fascination and some scorn. According to Nick Collins of *The Telegraph*, an Argentinian chef was so angry after Paul correctly forecast Germany's defeat of Argentina that "he threatened to cook Paul in retribution." Gamblers were betting on the accuracy of Paul's predictions before he had even made them. Collins reported that "William Hill, the bookmaker, says it has taken so many bets on whether Paul will call the final between Spain and Holland correctly that it had to cut odds from evens to 10/11."

A skeptic might point out that, although octopuses are impressively intelligent, there's no way that Paul could actually have had special insight into the outcome of

Table 7.1. Ways to flip a coin 3 times.

	Three Heads	Two Heads	One Head	Zero Heads
Ways It Can Happen	HHH	HHT HTH THH	HTT THT TTH	TTT

soccer matches. Even experts have a hard time calling games in a sport in which, as far as we Americans can tell, basically no one ever scores. And Paul presumably knew nothing about the teams playing or even about soccer in general. Was Paul's success dumb luck?

As discussed in chapter 6, we have tools for assessing whether an observed pattern is likely to be the result of dumb luck or, more scientifically, noise. We can conduct a hypothesis test and calculate a *p*-value.

How does Paul fare in such a hypothesis test? Paul made 14 predictions over the course of his career, and he was correct in 12 of those 14 games. That's pretty good. Suppose the null hypothesis that this was dumb luck is true—that is, Paul was picking in a completely random fashion, with each box equally likely to be selected. To figure out whether it is plausible that Paul's record emerged from dumb luck alone, we want to know how likely it is that Paul would have guessed correctly at least 12 times if he was in fact just guessing at random.

This problem is simple enough that you can compute the *p*-value by hand. The basic idea is this. Assume Paul is guessing at random. Calculate how likely it is that he'd get exactly 12 correct, how likely it is that he'd get exactly 13 correct, and how likely it is that he'd get exactly 14 correct. The sum of those three probabilities is the probability Paul would have done at least as well as he did by dumb luck.

Before we go on with the Paul story, let's pause and learn how to calculate these probabilities. Doing so will help make sure we are all thinking clearly about what dumb luck really means.

It will help to start with a simplification of the problem. Our null hypothesis is that Paul the Octopus is guessing at random—that is, Paul predicting the winner of a game is analogous to a person flipping a coin and having it land on heads. So let's think about flipping a coin. Suppose you flip a coin 3 times (we'll get to Paul's 14 in a bit). Table 7.1 shows all the things that could happen.

Equivalently, if Paul forecast three games, then zero, one, two, or three of his predictions could be correct.

What is the probability that you get, say, exactly two heads? Well, there are eight total things that could happen, and if we're flipping a fair coin, they're all equally likely. Of those eight, three involve getting two heads. So the probability you get exactly two heads when you flip three coins is $\frac{3}{8}$. Analogously, if Paul was forecasting three games at random, the probability he would get exactly two correct is $\frac{3}{8}$.

But that isn't quite the quantity we want to know. We want to know the probability you get *at least* two heads or that Paul correctly forecasts at least two games.

Well, in addition to getting two heads, you could also get three heads. There is one way for this to happen, so the probability you get three heads is $\frac{1}{8}$. Hence, the probability you get at least two heads is $\frac{3}{8} + \frac{1}{8} = \frac{1}{2}$. Analogously, if Paul had called three games, and he was just guessing randomly, the probability he'd get at least two right is one-half.

But Paul didn't just forecast three games. He forecast 14. Making a table for fourteen coin flips would be pretty boring. So let's think about how to analyze this problem a little more generally.

Suppose you flipped a coin n times. How likely is it that you get exactly k heads? Let's start by calculating the probability that each of the first k coin flips lands on heads and the remainder land on tails. The probability that the first k flips land heads is $\frac{1}{2}^k$. The probability that the remainder lands tails is $\frac{1}{2}^{n-k}$. So the probability that the first k flips land heads and the remaining $n - k$ flips land tails is $\frac{1}{2}^k \times \frac{1}{2}^{n-k}$.

Of course, that's only one way to get exactly k heads. The k heads don't have to be the first k flips. They can be any group of k out of the n flips. There are $\frac{n!}{k!(n-k)!}$ different ways to get exactly k heads when flipping a coin n times. So the overall probability of getting exactly k heads out of n coin flips is

$$\frac{1}{2}^k \times \frac{1}{2}^{n-k} \times \frac{n!}{k!(n-k)!}.$$

The exclamation points above mean *factorial*. We refer to the expression $n!$ as *n factorial* and it's defined as the product of n and every positive whole number less than n. So, for example, $3! = 3 \times 2 \times 1 = 6$.

Let's see if this confirms our finding from before in our three-coin-flip example. If we flip a coin three times, what is the probability we get exactly two heads? Since $n = 3$ and $k = 2$, we calculate the probability as follows:

$$\frac{1}{2}^2 \times \frac{1}{2}^{3-2} \times \frac{3!}{2!(3-2)!} = \frac{1}{4} \times \frac{1}{2} \times \frac{3 \times 2 \times 1}{2 \times 1 \times 1} = \frac{3}{8}$$

And now we can calculate the probability that Paul the Octopus would correctly predict 12 or more games out of 14, if he was picking at random. The probability he gets exactly 12 right is

$$\frac{1}{2}^{12} \times \frac{1}{2}^{14-12} \times \frac{14!}{12!(14-12)!} \approx .00555.$$

The probability he gets exactly 13 right is

$$\frac{1}{2}^{13} \times \frac{1}{2}^{14-13} \times \frac{14!}{13!(14-13)!} \approx .00085.$$

The probability he gets all 14 right is

$$\frac{1}{2}^{14} \times \frac{1}{2}^{14-14} \times \frac{14!}{14!(14-14)!} \approx .00006.$$

So the probability Paul calls twelve or more games correctly is approximately $.00555 + .00085 + .00006 \approx .0065$, around 1 in 155. In other words, if Paul had no special insight into soccer, it's highly unlikely that he would have been as accurate as he was. That's, of course, precisely why everyone was obsessed with Paul. And it seems like perhaps they were right to be. Using the standard statistical hypothesis testing approach that we introduced in chapter 6, we can reject the null hypothesis that Paul is just guessing at random and conclude that we have statistically significant evidence that Paul is indeed an expert soccer forecaster.

The analysis above is pretty similar to what two mathematicians, Chris Budd and David Spiegelharter, did when they were interviewed about Paul back in 2010. But if we look at Paul's games a little more closely, we can see that this analysis may be overly generous to Paul's psychic powers.

Paul lived in Germany, and he was primarily asked to predict the outcome of games in which Germany was competing. In fact, 13 of the 14 games involved Germany. Furthermore, Paul had a strong tendency to pick Germany. Maybe he liked that flag because he'd been seeing it for years. Maybe the German box happened to be his favorite box for reasons unbeknownst to us. Maybe Paul's handlers subconsciously trained Paul to pick Germany. Who knows? It also turns out that Germany is good at soccer—they win most of the time. So maybe Paul's success isn't so shocking. Let's redo the analysis above with this information in mind.

Paul predicted the outcome in 13 games involving Germany and he picked Germany to win 11 of those games. Germany in fact won 9 of them. Our null hypothesis is again that Paul's predictions were dumb luck, in the sense of having no special insight into soccer. But this time, instead of imagining that he was equally likely to choose either box, imagine he was predisposed to pick the German box. Let's assume his predisposition meant that his probability of picking Germany was $\frac{11}{13}$ in any game Germany played, since that's the frequency with which Paul in fact selected Germany. If Germany won 9 of 13 games and Paul selected Germany with a probability of $\frac{11}{13}$ each time, how likely is it that he would have been correct 11 or more times just by pure chance? This p-value could be computed by hand, but it is complicated to do so. So instead we ran a simple simulation on our computer to approximate it. With these tweaked assumptions, the chances that Paul gets 11 or more games right out of 13 is about .03 or 1 in 33—still unlikely, but much more likely than 1 in 155.

Now, what do we think? It still looks pretty unlikely that Paul's success is attributable purely to dumb luck. Even if he was predisposed to predict the strong German team, there was only a 3 percent chance that Paul would be as successful as he was. Therefore, a traditional hypothesis test with a .05 threshold would still lead us to reject the null. We continue to have statistically significant evidence that Paul is good at predicting soccer matches.

You won't be surprised to learn that we're still skeptical. But why? Paul is not the only octopus out there. What if there were actually ten octopuses scattered around Germany, each trying to predict the outcomes of soccer matches? The world, of course, would only ever hear about the most successful one. If this is right, then we still haven't tested the right hypothesis to figure out how likely it is that Paul's accuracy was due to dumb luck. If there really were ten octopuses trying to predict soccer matches, and if Paul just happened to be the one who did well and therefore became famous, instead of asking how likely it is that Paul would be so accurate by luck, we have to ask how likely it is that any one of the ten octopuses would be that accurate by luck. Because if it had turned out that Paulina the Octopus was right 12 out of 14 times instead of Paul, then we'd be talking about Paulina and we'd never have heard of Paul.

Figuring out how likely it is that some octopus out of the ten would have been as accurate as Paul is relatively straightforward. But to do the calculation, we need to understand one more fact about p-values. Recall that the p-value is the probability of observing an outcome at least as extreme as the one you observe if the null hypothesis is true. So, if the null hypothesis is true, how often will you observe an outcome as extreme as an outcome with a p-value of .05? Exactly 5 percent of the time. And if the null hypothesis is true, how often will you observe an outcome as extreme as an outcome with a p-value of .2? Exactly 20 percent of the time. And so on for each and every p-value. This is just a restatement of the definition of the p-value.

But from this fact, we learn something important. When the null hypothesis is true, we should observe a p-value less than or equal to .05 in 5 percent of cases, p-values less than or equal to .2 in 20 percent of cases, p-values less than or equal to .5 in 50 percent of cases, and so on. Hence, it must be that, when the null hypothesis is true, you are equally likely to find each p-value. (The technical jargon for this is that p-values are *uniformly distributed under the null*.)

So, what's the probability that at least one of our German octopuses would generate a record of prediction with a p-value at least as good as Paul's record of .03 by dumb luck alone? We just saw that the probability that any one octopus generates a p-value of .03 or lower by dumb luck alone is .03. Therefore, the probability that any one octopus generates a p-value higher than .03 is .97. If there are two octopuses and they're making their guesses independently, the probability that neither of them generates a p-value better than .03 is therefore $.97^2$. So the probability that at least one of them generates a p-value of .03 or better is $1 - .97^2$ (i.e., one minus the probability that both generate a p-value worse than .03). If ten octopuses are taking random guesses, the probability that at least one generates a p-value as good as Paul's is $1 - .97^{10} \approx .26$. In other words, if ten German octopuses went through the same ridiculous prediction exercise as Paul, there's about a 1 in 4 chance that at least one of them would have accumulated a record of predictive accuracy at least as glorious as Paul's, even if none of the octopuses were in fact soccer experts. This should make us much more skeptical of Paul's abilities.

We don't know how many German octopuses were in the soccer forecasting business. But we do know that lots of other animals got in on the action. No joke, Leon the Porcupine, Petty the Hippopotamus, Anton the Tamarin, and Mani the Parakeet all forecast the winners of soccer matches around the same time as Paul. And those are just the ones that made the news. Presumably, there were dozens more that we never heard about. And this discussion only includes soccer. What about all the other sports? And what about all the non-athletic things there are to predict? If Judy the Badger were good at predicting the winners of college football games, Steve the Cat were good at predicting the winners of congressional elections, and Fran the Otter were good at predicting stock market shifts, they would be celebrities too. But their predictions turned out to be no better than chance, so we never heard about them.

Budd and Spiegelharter, the mathematicians, were quick to point this out. Spiegelharter notes that "if someone flips a coin and gets the same result 9 or 10 times, it is not remarkable in itself, but it will seem remarkable to the person flipping the coin." In other words, if enough people flip coins, one of them is bound to flip a bunch of heads in a row. And despite the fact that somebody was bound to have a lucky streak of heads by chance, that person might wrongly conclude that they have an unfair coin or that they are a particularly skilled coin flipper. Unfortunately, as we'll see, this problem applies to much more serious situations than coin flipping and soccer forecasting, with far-reaching implications.

Publication Bias

Statistical hypothesis testing and *p*-values are clearly useful. When we find patterns in data, we want to know if they reflect genuine phenomena or if they could have easily been produced by random chance.

But there is a problem, which the story of Paul the Octopus highlights. Neither the public nor the broader scientific community gets to see all the hypothesis tests that were (or could have been) conducted. Often, the only results reported and published are the statistically significant ones. It's just not that interesting to write about Mary the Octopus, who is about as good as a coin flip at predicting soccer matches. But if there are twenty different animals out there making soccer predictions, we'd expect one of them to have a *p*-value less than .05 by pure luck, even if none of them actually have any special insight into soccer. Only that 1 in 20 case will be written up or reported in the news. So if we base our beliefs purely on what gets reported, we will have systematically misguided beliefs.

Making a lot of comparisons, *over-comparing*, while selectively reporting only the interesting or statistically significant ones, *under-reporting*, is a dangerous combination. But it is widespread. And because of it, when we hear about a new, exciting scientific result, it is much harder to know how likely it is to reflect a genuine phenomenon than the simple logic of hypothesis testing suggests.

This problem of over-comparing and under-reporting doesn't just affect how confident you should be that one particular finding is genuine. It also affects our ability to accumulate knowledge over time in a field. We know that any one estimate, even if unbiased, may be far from the true estimand because of noise. The hope is that as a field accumulates estimates, the noise averages out, so that the average of a large number of unbiased estimates gets very close to the true estimand. Over-comparing and under-reporting means that this may not work for the collection of published estimates, a troubling phenomenon called *publication bias*. To see why, let's go back to our favorite equation:

$$\text{Estimate} = \text{Estimand} + \text{Bias} + \text{Noise}$$

Suppose there are a large number of studies, all on the same question. Each study is really well designed, producing an unbiased estimate of the phenomenon under consideration. So the only reason the estimates differ from one another or from the true quantity of interest in the world (the estimand) is because of noise.

But let's also suppose, in the spirit of under-reporting (i.e., not reporting every result), that we only hear about the results of studies in which the evidence is strong enough to reject the null hypothesis that the true estimand is zero (i.e., that our estimate was the result of noise). For a result to be statistically distinguishable from zero, the estimated relationship must be sufficiently large, relative to the standard error. So if we only hear about statistically significant results, we are only hearing about the estimates that were sufficiently large in magnitude.

This means that, for any given true estimand, the estimates that end up being reported will be those for which the noise happened to be large enough in magnitude to push the magnitude of the estimate far enough away from zero to make it statistically significant. So, as a result of over-comparing and under-reporting, not only will our

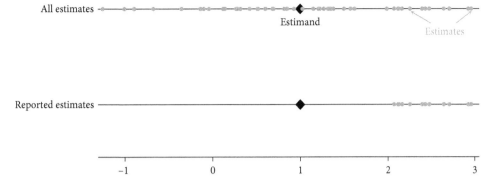

Figure 7.1. Only reporting statistically significant estimates creates publication bias.

p-values be wrong, but the collection of estimates that we learn about from published studies will systematically over-estimate the magnitude of the true estimand.

Distressingly, even though we started by assuming no bias in our estimates, we've learned that the process of over-comparing and under-reporting introduces bias, not into any one estimate but into the overall distribution of estimates reported in a scientific literature. So, when we average all the estimates, we do not get close to the true estimand, even if the number of estimates is very large. That is, we have what is called *publication bias*.

Figure 7.1 illustrates how this works. In the top figure, we see fifty unbiased but imprecise estimates. The true estimand is 1, and since our estimates are unbiased, the average of all estimates is also 1.

We calculate the standard error and find that the 95% confidence interval is from -2 to 2. That is, the probability an estimate would have arisen even if there was no relationship (i.e., the true estimand was 0) is less than 5 percent only if that estimate is greater than 2 in magnitude. So only the estimates larger than 2 are deemed statistically significant (we don't have any estimates less than -2). The statistically significant estimates are in the lower figure.

Suppose that only these statistically significant estimates are ever reported. Now, of course, the reported estimates are systematically greater than the estimand. So if we based our beliefs about the true value of the estimand on these published estimates, we'd be systematically over-estimating the truth. This is publication bias.

Over-comparing and under-reporting that results in publication bias can arise in a variety of ways. Let's consider a couple.

p-Hacking

One way we might end up with over-comparing and under-reporting is through bad or dishonest behavior by individual analysts. The scientific community calls the behavior of playing around with the data or tests until a p-value below a particular threshold emerges *p-hacking*. For instance, suppose a scientist does an experiment and doesn't quite get statistically significant evidence for the expected or desired result. That scientist might reason that something probably wasn't quite right in the initial attempt, and so try a slight tweak on the experiment. Indeed, the scientist can keep trying similar experiments until one comes up statistically significant. Because of noise, if they try the experiment enough times, eventually they will get a result, even if there is no real phenomenon being studied. That's the problem of over-comparing. And, of course, if an unscrupulous scientist only reports the results from the one experiment that yielded a statistically significant result, we have the problem of under-reporting and, thus, publication bias.

Or maybe the analyst has some flexibility in how a particular statistical test is implemented. Suppose you are asked to do an analysis at work about the relationship between productivity and having a standing desk. Should you pool the entire workforce together or run separate regressions for different age groups? Should you include higher-order polynomials of age? Should you separate women and men in the analysis? How about people with different job responsibilities, medical histories, and so on? As you can see, there are lots of reasonable ways to think about doing the analysis. If you keep trying out different ones, you'll eventually find a statistically significant result, even if there is in fact no real relationship between productivity and standing. Searching over specifications is, thus, another way of over-comparing.

Yet another way of over-comparing is by trying out lots of different outcomes. Suppose you want to evaluate the efficacy of some new pill for heart disease. You might run an excellent clinical trial that generates no bias at all. But perhaps you collected data on lots of outcomes for the experimental subjects: mortality, heart attacks, strokes, cholesterol, days of hospitalization, ability to exercise, subjective sense of well-being, and so on. You can then test whether the pill has a statistically significant effect on each of these outcomes. If you have enough different outcomes, you're likely to find a statistically significant result on one of them just due to noise—that is, the people given the pill and the people given the placebo will happen to differ on some outcome, even if the pill doesn't actually do anything. And, if you lack the proper ethics, you might just report the results for that one outcome in the hope of convincing doctors to prescribe your new pill.

As we've seen, p-hacking can take many different forms, and you have to work hard to avoid it as a quantitative analyst and to detect it as a consumer of quantitative evidence.[1]

p-Screening

Of course, p-hacking is a big concern. But it need not be the case that any individual is acting in a dishonest or negligent way for the problem of over-comparing and under-reporting to occur. It can happen even if absolutely everyone behaves in a completely honest and responsible manner!

Imagine that twenty scientists around the country all have the same scientific hunch. Let's suppose it's about the efficacy of a potential new cancer drug. In truth, the hunch is false—the drug doesn't work. But there is no way for the scientists to know this at the outset. So, as scientists do, they design studies to test the drug. Indeed, all twenty of their labs, independently and unaware of the others, run the same high-quality experiment, but on different samples. They each recruit a large sample of patients with the relevant type of cancer. At random, they assign half of them to receive the new drug. The other half receives a placebo sugar pill. At the end of the study period, they assess whether the

[1] Fun fact: The term p-hacking was coined by Joseph Simmons, Leif Nelson, and Uri Simonsohn in a clever study in which they showed, among other things, that by using standard methods in social science, they could provide statistically significant evidence that listening to the song "When I'm Sixty-Four" by the Beatles makes subjects younger!

group that received the drug was more likely to go into remission than the group that received the placebo.

Nineteen out of the twenty labs find no statistically significant evidence—the remission rates among those who received the drug and those who received the placebo are indistinguishable—and conclude that the drug doesn't work. Such null results aren't considered very exciting. "Another drug doesn't cure cancer" isn't a great headline. So scientific journals are reluctant to accept papers reporting null results for publication. As a consequence, these labs may not bother to write up their results, instead just moving on to more promising lines of research. This is sometimes called the *file drawer problem* because statistically insignificant results get locked away in a file drawer. Even if the labs do write up their findings, they might have trouble finding a journal interested in publishing them. In either case we get under-reporting, and the scientific community and the public fail to learn about these nineteen null results.

One (un)lucky lab out of the twenty finds statistically significant evidence suggesting the drug works. We know the drug doesn't work (though the scientists don't), so we know this is sheer chance. It just so happens that, for reasons having nothing to do with the drug, the people assigned to receive the drug in this experiment also had higher remission rates than the people assigned to receive the placebo. These things happen. The estimate can differ from the estimand, even absent bias, because of noise.

Since the other studies were either never written up or never accepted for publication if they were written up, as far as the scientist in charge of this one lab is aware, all existing evidence points toward this new drug working. So this one lab, appropriately, writes a scientific paper on their findings. Because the result is surprising and noteworthy, it is likely to be well published and reported on by the scientific press. And, indeed, if you look at this one study, it looks great. The lab ran a good, unbiased experiment. They made only the one appropriate comparison about the one appropriate outcome. There was no *p*-hacking. And the data support their hypothesis. So everyone believes this result even though it is in fact completely wrong and, if we had access to all the data (i.e., from the nineteen "failed" experiments), we'd see that the preponderance of the evidence points in exactly the opposite direction. That is, we end up with publication bias.

There isn't a term in common usage that describes both scientists not bothering to write up results that find small or no effects because they'll be hard to publish (which is the file drawer problem) and journals being reluctant to publish such findings even if they are written up. But we think these two phenomena are usefully thought of together, since they both give rise to publication bias despite no individual acting inappropriately. So, by analogy to *p*-hacking, we call this problem *p-screening*. The issue here isn't that some individual researcher is *p*-hacking their way to a statistically significant result. The issue is that the scientific community, through its publication practices, screens out studies with *p*-values that are above some threshold. Under *p*-hacking we don't see null results because dishonest researchers hide them. Under *p*-screening we don't see null results because honest researchers can't publish such results. Either way the outcome is the same. The results we do see suffer from publication bias due to lots of comparisons being made but only the statistically significant ones being reported.

Yikes! Because of *p*-screening, the scientific record (and our knowledge in a lot of other areas) can be unreliable even when everyone behaves just as they should. This should make you worry that it is going on all the time. In fact, stop and ask yourself, For how many things I believe might this story characterize the state of knowledge? Once you start thinking clearly about the problem, you'll see its potential everywhere.

Are Most Scientific "Facts" False?

As we've seen, over-comparing and under-reporting gives rise to publication bias. And these practices are pretty deeply entrenched in a lot of scientific practice and culture. This realization has led to something of an existential crisis in many scientific fields, with practitioners wondering whether many widely accepted scientific facts are actually false, the artifacts of over-comparing and under-reporting.

This is a real concern. It is surely the case that many things that we believe are true are in fact false because of publication bias. But certainly not everything. And analysts have started to think more clearly about how we might diagnose when a scientific consensus or literature is or is not likely to suffer from severe publication bias. To see how, we are going to talk through a couple examples of the problem and various attempts to address it. We'll even discuss some tips on how to detect p-hacking.

ESP

In 2010, Cornell psychologist Daryl Bem made news by publishing a study in the *Journal of Personality and Social Psychology*, a prestigious academic psychology journal, claiming that human beings have extrasensory perception (ESP). Often, academic researchers and quantitative analysts are the ones debunking claims about the paranormal, but in this case, a respected, tenured Ivy League professor was the source of the outlandish claim.

In Bem's experiment, students were asked to predict which virtual curtain on their computer screen (left or right) had an object of interest hiding behind it. Bem reported statistically significant evidence that his subjects were better than chance at predicting the future and identifying the correct curtain.

This is a very exciting finding if you are a journal editor who cares about notoriety or a science journalist who cares about readership. The result is cool. The scientist in question works at a reputable university. The article is published in a major scholarly journal. There is no reason to think the data are faked. The study provides scientific evidence of, to say the least, a surprising phenomenon. What journalist with blood running through their veins could resist the story?

This study and all the media attention it received notwithstanding, we're fairly confident that people don't have ESP. So what is going on?

There are, of course, the normal concerns with statistical hypothesis testing. If an analyst uses a significance threshold of .05, there's a 5 percent chance of finding support for a result (i.e., rejecting the null), even if the result is false (i.e., the null is true). And as we'll see in part 4, if you already have good reasons to believe that people do not have ESP, then you shouldn't shift those beliefs much in response to this one study.

But we have other concerns based on the themes of this chapter. This is a case where many researchers might be conducting experiments, but only the one with statistically significant evidence of an unlikely phenomenon gets published. Presumably, nobody is going to publish a paper that reports that people are no better than chance at guessing the correct curtain. That's what we all already believe. So we should worry a lot about publication bias due to p-screening.

We should probably also consider the possibility that the results were p-hacked. Bem reported the results of nine different experiments carried out over the course of ten years. These experiments are relatively inexpensive to conduct. Since Bem was, by all accounts, committed to the study of ESP, it doesn't seem far-fetched to imagine that he might have conducted more ESP experiments over this ten-year period. And, if so, the nine experiments that were reported on might well have been the ones with the strongest confirmatory evidence of ESP.

There are also some signs of over-comparing and under-reporting within the study itself. For example, Bem doesn't find evidence of ESP in general; he only finds it when the object behind the curtain is erotic in nature. For other kinds of objects, he finds no evidence of the paranormal. Of course! Wouldn't it make sense for humans to have evolved ESP that allows us to detect erotic activity around the corner but not other kinds of activity? Furthermore, in some tests, he only finds effects for women, not men; in others, he finds results only for those who are easily bored. Given all of the different tests conducted by Bem, it would be surprising if he *hadn't* stumbled upon a few statistically significant results, just by chance.

Reassuringly, the community of psychologists remained skeptical and responded quite quickly to Bem's paper. Several follow-up studies tried and failed to replicate the findings. Disappointingly, however, the *Journal of Personality and Social Psychology* initially refused to publish the replication studies debunking Bem's claim. The editor justified this decision on the grounds that the journal has a long-standing policy of refusing to publish *mere replication*. Fortunately, the journal eventually had a change of heart and published a meta-analysis of replication attempts, which strongly suggested that the original result was unreliable. This illustrates one important corrective to the problem of over-comparing and under-reporting: a vigilant commitment to investigating whether findings replicate within a scientific community. We will discuss replication in more detail later in this chapter.

Get Out the Vote

Political campaigns engage in lots of activities—phone calls, direct mail, door-to-door canvassing—to try to get out the vote. Since the 1990s, scholars have teamed up with campaigns to conduct experiments to learn about the efficacy of these efforts. In such studies, some people are randomly assigned to treatment (e.g., a direct mailing with information about the date of the election or the location of their polling place) and other people are randomly assigned to control (e.g., not getting any extra information). We can learn about the average effect of get-out-the-vote efforts on voter turnout by comparing the turnout rates in the two groups.

In the published record, the average estimated effect of a get-out-the-vote intervention is about a 3.5 percentage point increase in voter turnout. Moreover, almost no published paper reports an effect of less than 1 percentage point. So, if a campaign consulted the published record, it would conclude that get-out-the-vote efforts are quite effective.

But there have been many more get-out-the-vote experiments than there are scientific papers published on the topic—which means that some of those experiments did not result in publication. Why not?

If our fears about over-comparing and under-reporting are right, we might expect that the answer is *p*-screening—experiments that yielded no statistically significant evidence of an effect did not result in a published paper. If this is true, then there is publication bias. So we should expect that the true average effect of get-out-the-vote interventions is smaller than what is suggested by the published findings.

Three political scientists, Don Green, Mary McGrath, and Peter Aronow, decided to investigate this possibility quantitatively. They managed to get their hands on the data from over two hundred experiments done by a variety of scholars over many years. Some of those experiments had resulted in published papers. Others had not. They did an analysis to find the average effect of get-out-the-vote interventions across all two hundred of these interventions. The result: half a percentage point! Dramatically less than the 3.5 percentage point average effect shown in the published record. The unpublished record is, indeed, much less supportive of the efficacy of get-out-the-vote efforts than is the published record.

The efficacy of get-out-the-vote efforts is one of the most rigorously studied topics in the social sciences. And so, candidates or campaigns wanting to figure out the best way to allocate scarce resources might naturally turn to published studies to inform their decision. However, we now know that doing this would lead them to over-estimate how effective get-out-the-vote efforts are by a factor of 7, demonstrating again that *p*-screening can have serious consequences.

p-Hacking Forensics

It's always hard to know for sure if *p*-hacking took place in an individual study. And it is a good practice to be charitable, assuming that most people are attempting to behave in an above-board and honest manner most of the time. That said, clear thinking can help us get a sense of how widespread the *p*-hacking problem is. The best evidence comes from observing the *p*-values in actual published scientific literature. Doing so doesn't tell us whether any individual study is *p*-hacked. But it can help us sniff out whether an overall literature looks like it has a bunch of *p*-hacking going on.

Here's how it works. You start by thinking about what the distribution of *p*-values in a literature would look like in four different possible states of the world:

1. If there is no real relationship in the world and there is no *p*-hacking;
2. If there is a real relationship in the world and there is no *p*-hacking;
3. If there is no real relationship in the world and there is *p*-hacking; or
4. If there is a real relationship in the world and there is *p*-hacking.

You are then going to compare the actual distribution of reported *p*-values in a scientific literature to the distributions you would get in each of these four states of the world to try to figure out which state you are most likely to be in. For what follows we are going to assume there is still *p*-screening going on (so there are no *p*-values greater than .05). We just want to figure out if the literature is also *p*-hacked. But everything we are going to say is true even without *p*-screening.

The logic of the cases can be understood with reference to figure 7.2, which is adapted from a 2014 study by Simonsohn, Nelson, and Simmons, who first proposed examining the distribution of *p*-values in order to assess *p*-hacking.

Start with case 1: there is no real relationship in the world and there is no *p*-hacking. If there is no real relationship out there in the world, that means the null hypothesis is true. And, as we've already discussed, if the null hypothesis is true, then all *p*-values are equally likely to emerge in any given study. So, if there is no *p*-hacking, the observed distribution of *p*-values in published studies should look approximately uniform—that is, between 0 and .05, different *p*-values should appear with approximately equal frequency. This is illustrated by the light-gray line in figure 7.2.

There are two reasons we might see a deviation from this uniformity. The first is that there is a real relationship in the world. The second is that there is *p*-hacking.

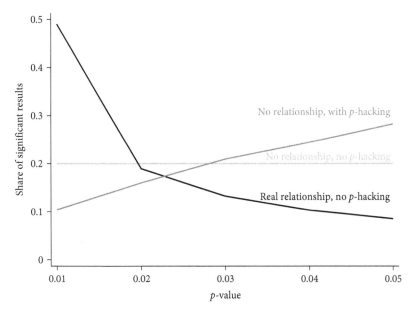

Figure 7.2. *p*-hacking distorts the distribution of *p*-values in a literature.

This brings us to case 2: there is a real relationship in the world (i.e., the null hypothesis is false) and there is no *p*-hacking. If we are actually studying a real relationship in the world, we are more likely to detect a statistically significant relationship than if there is no real relationship in the world. So, in case 2, where there is a real relationship and no *p*-hacking, we expect a distribution of *p*-values in the published record that is skewed such that there are more low *p*-values. That is, reflecting the fact that we are detecting a real relationship, there should be more low *p*-values in case 2 than in case 1. So, if we see a distribution with more low *p*-values, that is suggestive evidence that the literature is detecting a real relationship in the world. This is illustrated by the dark curve in figure 7.2.

The other reason we might see a deviation from case 1 is because of *p*-hacking. This takes us to case 3: there is no real relationship in the world and there is *p*-hacking. As we've already discussed, when there is no real relationship in the world, every *p*-value is equally likely. But, what happens in the presence of *p*-hacking? Well, suppose a researcher finds a *p*-value below .05. They can just report that statistically significant result. But suppose they find a *p*-value close to, but above, .05. They might be tempted to *p*-hack, playing around with specifications, subgroups, and so on until they find a *p*-value below .05 that they can report as statistically significant. The consequence of this *p*-hacking will be a whole bunch of reported *p*-values close to, but just below, .05. So, unlike in case 2, where we saw more low *p*-values than high *p*-values among statistically significant results, in case 3, we should expect more high *p*-values than low *p*-values among statistically significant results. This is illustrated by the medium-gray curve in figure 7.2.

Case 4 combines cases 2 and 3. If there is a true relationship, that skews things toward low *p*-values. If we also *p*-hack, that skews things back toward high *p*-values. So it is hard to know what to expect in this case. But, nonetheless, just with the distinctions between cases 1, 2, and 3, we can make some progress diagnosing *p*-hacking in a literature.

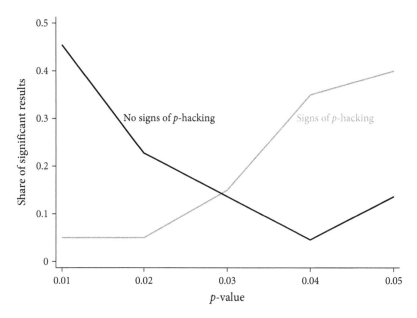

Figure 7.3. Using the distribution of *p*-values to diagnose *p*-hacking.

Sadly, many academic literatures exhibit a distribution of *p*-values consistent with case 3. Simonsohn, Nelson, and Simmons examined papers in a prominent psychology journal to see if there were any red flags that might indicate *p*-hacking. They identified certain words that might be a sign of over-comparing. For instance, one of their words of concern is *excluded*, as in "I excluded this variable (or group, or outcome) from my analysis because it didn't give the result I wanted." Another is *transformed* as in "I transformed age into age^2, age^3, age^4, and so on until the results supported my hypothesis." The darker curve in figure 7.3 shows the distribution of *p*-values for studies that don't use words that are signs of *p*-hacking. Reassuringly, for these studies, we see more low *p*-values, indicating that they are identifying genuine relationships in the world (case 2). The lighter curve in figure 7.3 shows the distribution of *p*-values for studies that do use words that are signs of *p*-hacking. Disturbingly, for these studies, there is reason to suspect *p*-hacking; we see more high than low *p*-values (case 3). So, while these forensics don't tell us exactly which papers are *p*-hacked, they allow us to look at the distribution of *p*-values in a literature and ask how worried we should be that any scientific consensus based on those studies is biased by *p*-hacking.

Potential Solutions

Publication bias is an insidious problem for science. And so scientists have started thinking about how they might change scientific practice to reduce the problem of over-comparing and under-reporting.

Reduce the Significance Threshold

Maybe we can solve the problem of publication bias by using a more stringent significance threshold for *p*-values. Maybe the conventional .05 threshold makes it too easy to hunt around until you find a statistically significant result. In 2017, seventy-two researchers across various fields published a letter in *Nature Human Behaviour* urging the scientific community to adopt a dramatically lower significance threshold of $p < .005$.

On the one hand, a lower significance threshold would certainly make it harder to conjure up a statistically significant result by over-comparing. On the other hand, lowering the significance threshold would likely increase incentives for p-hacking by making statistically significant results rarer and, thus, more valuable. It might even increase complacency about these issues, leading us all to think a little less critically. And, while a threshold of .005 means fewer false positives (i.e., rejecting the null hypothesis when it is true), that comes at the cost of more false negatives (i.e., failing to reject the null hypothesis when it is false). It's not obvious where we should draw the line to balance that trade-off. The answer probably depends on the particular question.

Adjust p-Values for Multiple Testing

The p-value is supposed to tell us the probability of obtaining a result at least as strong as your result if the null hypothesis is true. As we've seen, if researchers engage in over-comparing and under-reporting, the p-value doesn't reflect this probability. It is too low.

If we know how many tests were run, we can try to correct the p-value. As we discussed in the case of Paul the Octopus, if researchers conduct ten independent tests but only report their lowest p-value of .03, the true p-value is more like $1 - (1 - .03)^{10} \approx$ .263. Correcting p-values in this way to account for the number of tests run is a good way for researchers to be transparent and for consumers of quantitative information to better assess the state of the evidence. Unfortunately, this is also not a panacea. The kind of simple calculation done above only works if the tests are truly independent. If the tests are closely related to each other—for example, if we're testing the same hypothesis with the same data but using slightly different variables in a regression or focusing on slightly different subgroups of observations—if may be much less clear how to adjust the p-values correctly.

Don't Obsess Over Statistical Significance

The threshold .05 is just an arbitrary number. Substantively important effects may be statistically insignificant, and statistically significant results may be substantively unimportant. Statistical hypothesis testing is a useful tool for quantifying uncertainty, but it can be abused. We should use p-values when appropriate. But they're not the end-all-be-all for assessing the believability of a quantitative finding. You can't just calculate; you have to keep thinking clearly. In part 4, we'll talk about how to incorporate quantitative evidence with other knowledge in order to think clearly about what our beliefs should be after seeing some new evidence.

Pre-Registration

At least in some settings—such as when the researchers are creating the data themselves with a new survey or experiment—researchers can pre-commit to exactly the tests they are going to do before they ever see the data. To do so, they pre-register their study, writing down and publishing exactly what they plan to test for and how they plan to do so, before actually doing the study. As long as they pre-register a reasonable number of tests, this prevents them from over-comparing. It also makes it harder to under-report.

People will be suspicious if a scientific paper only includes the results from 3 out of 10 promised tests. Moreover, some scientific journals are now willing to accept scientific studies for publication based only on the pre-registered plan—committing to report the results regardless of what the researcher finds, which also helps with under-reporting.

Pre-registration is a useful tool for mitigating the problems of over-comparing and under-reporting. Let's see an example of it in action, so we can get a sense of its merits and its limits.

Requiring pre-registration in drug trials

The problem of over-comparing and under-reporting is an important one in clinical trials for new drugs—a company that has invested a lot in a new drug might be tempted to search over specifications, subgroups, or outcomes until they find some result that suggests the drug is efficacious for some outcome on some group of people. The National Heart, Lung, and Blood Institute (NHLBI) has funded many clinical trials of new drugs and dietary supplements since 1970, and in 2000, they came up with a clever way to use pre-registration to combat this problem. They required the developers of a drug or supplement to announce beforehand the goals of the product. Under these new rules, a clinical drug trial is only declared a success if the researchers show a statistically significant effect on the pre-registered outcome of interest.

A 2015 study by Robert Kaplan and Veronica Irvin shows that after the NHLBI started requiring pre-registration, the rate of successful trials dropped from 57 percent to 8 percent. This suggests that many of the "successful" trials prior to pre-registration were the result of over-comparing rather than of any genuine effect of the drug or supplement. This was a big success for pre-registration.

Importantly, even if pre-registration is working to curtail over-comparing and under-reporting, we still have to worry about all the other problems of statistical inference. Think about the 8 percent success rate after pre-registration. Kaplan and Irvin use a significance threshold of .05, which means that even if none of the drugs or supplements were effective, we'd expect 5 percent to generate statistically significant evidence of efficacy just by chance. So the 8 percent success rate is not much higher than what we'd expect even if none of the drugs work. That means that even after we observe a successful, pre-registered trial, we still should not be that confident that the drug is effective. In fact, it looks like there's still a 5 in 8 chance that a positive, pre-registered result is a false positive.

Replication

One way to assess whether an estimated effect is genuine is to replicate it on new, independently generated data. Replication isn't foolproof. But, as we saw with the ESP studies, it can help provide some evidence of whether an estimated effect is genuine or just the result of over-comparing and under-reporting.

Suppose we do just one comparison and use a significance threshold of .05. The likelihood of finding statistically significant evidence of a relationship, even if none exists, is .05. But if we run the study twice, using independent data each time, the probability of finding statistically significant evidence in *both* studies if no real relationship exists is $.05 \times .05 = .0025$. If we do it a third time, the probability we find evidence for the non-existent relationship in all three studies is $.05^3 = .000125$, pretty unlikely. By replicating, we reduce the chance that we reach a spurious positive conclusion. This is especially true if the replication is done by independent teams who don't have a vested interest in validating the initial finding.

Of course, replication is not a panacea, and we have to keep thinking clearly. Failure to reject the null hypothesis is not proof that the null is true. So, if we only believe results if they replicate multiple times, we might sometimes wrongly reject real effects, especially if we conduct replications on sparse or noisy data, where effects are hard to detect. Ideally, we'd get lots of data and replicate on large samples.

Sometimes such replication is feasible and sometimes it's not. If researchers conducting a drug trial for a cholesterol drug happen to collect weight data and find an unexpected effect of the drug on weight loss, researchers can recruit a new pool of subjects and see if the new treatment group shows similar weight loss relative to the new control group. But if we discover a phenomenon regarding twentieth-century gubernatorial elections, the behavior of the moons of Venus, or leadership strategies in the run-up to World War I, there's just one sample of them. There's no way to go collect more data. In that case, we may want to think less literally and more conceptually about replication. We do this not by directly replicating the existing findings but by asking something like, "If this phenomenon is genuine, what are some other hypotheses that should also be true?" Let's see an example.

Football and elections

Anthony has a paper with Pablo Montagnes that illustrates this approach. The paper re-examines a prominent study by Andrew Healy, Neil Malhotra, and Cecilia Mo, published in the *Proceedings of the National Academy of Sciences*, that claims that the outcome of college football games affects who wins elections. Specifically, the incumbent party reportedly performs better in congressional and gubernatorial elections in the home counties of teams that won prior to the election. This kind of finding makes some people worry about democracy. (Not us, but that is a topic for another day.)

Anyway, the Healy et al. study is in many ways good. Football wins and losses seem pretty random, so there isn't lots of reason to be concerned about bias. But this is exactly the kind of setting where you might worry about a false positive resulting from over-comparing and under-reporting. For instance, there is almost certainly a *p*-screening problem—would a prestigious scientific journal have published a paper showing that college football games do *not* appear to have any influence on elections? Moreover, there are lots of sports that might have been used to predict incumbent success: other research teams, studying the effects of basketball or curling losses on elections, may have found no relationship and, thus, not published papers. So we shouldn't leap to conclusions just because one published paper presents evidence supporting the claim that losses in one particular sport are associated with election outcomes.

Anthony and Pablo couldn't conduct a purely independent replication because there's no way to re-run decades of college football games and elections. Instead, they thought about independent theoretical predictions—additional hypotheses that seem like they should also hold if football losses really do affect elections. For instance, if football losses affect elections, you might expect the relationship to be particularly strong in places that care a lot about college football. If voters blame incumbent politicians for bad football outcomes, you might expect the impact of a football loss on the incumbent's party to be bigger when the incumbent is actually seeking reelection relative to when some new candidate from the same party is running. And so on. Testing such hypotheses, which speak to the underlying mechanism, is a way to probe whether some estimated effect is likely to reflect a real relationship in the world or is the result of noise (i.e., a false positive).

Here are some examples of what Anthony and Pablo found. It turns out that the estimated effect of football games is smaller in counties where more people follow college football than in counties where fewer people follow college football, no greater when an incumbent actually runs for reelection as opposed to just the incumbent's party running a candidate, and just as strong outside the home county of the team as inside the home county of the team. Furthermore, they found no evidence of a relationship between football losses and electoral outcomes for NFL games, despite the fact that NFL teams have the same kind of regional support as college football teams and NFL games are roughly ten times more popular than college football games.

Anthony and Pablo tested multiple, independent theoretical predictions that seemed like they should have held if the relationship between football and elections was real, but none of them received support in the data. From this, they concluded that it seems unlikely that college football games really do influence elections. This isn't a classic replication. But it shows how looking at the evidence for additional hypotheses that are related to the mechanism underlying the original hypothesis can help shed light on the strength of the evidence for surprising results.

Related to the idea of independent replication is the use of hold-out samples, which we discussed in chapter 5 when we talked about overfitting. Suppose you have a large sample of data and want to explore it for relationships. It might be a smart idea to hold out a randomly selected subset of that data from the exploration. For example, you could randomly select half the observations and use them as an exploratory data set. Then, after you've found a few interesting relationships, you could test whether those relationships also appear in the hold-out sample of data that you have not yet analyzed. If over-comparing produced a false positive in your initial analysis, we would expect that the same relationship is unlikely to appear in the hold-out sample. But if you've identified a real phenomenon, then we should expect it to persist in the hold-out data.

Test Important and Plausible Hypotheses

If you read a study that would have never been published had the researchers found the opposite of what they found (e.g., failed to reject the null), you should be particularly worried about over-comparing and under-reporting. But if a study answers a question for which we care about the answer intrinsically, regardless of what that answer turns out to be, a lot of the problems of over-comparing and under-reporting disappear. In particular, if the findings can be published regardless of the result, we can worry less about p-screening and we might think the researcher has less incentive to engage in p-hacking.

Happily, many important scientific questions fall into this latter category. If a study is testing a serious theoretical hypothesis, exploring a medical treatment that there are good reasons to think might work, or evaluating a real policy intervention, the answer is interesting, whatever it turns out to be.

By contrast, a lot of fun-sounding questions with surprising answers fall into the former category. And, unfortunately, such studies appear irresistable to much of the science press. Think of the ESP study. No one would be interested in a paper that found no evidence for ESP. So there were concerns both about incentives to p-hack and about the file drawer problem. An example will illustrate the point.

The power pose

A famous study by Amy Cuddy, Dana Carney, and Andy Yap purportedly shows the remarkable efficacy of adopting a simple power pose. Our attitudes, the argument goes, often cause our behaviors, rather than the other way around. And small changes to the way you hold yourself can change your attitude. In particular, by standing in a posture that you associate with being powerful, you will inspire feelings of assertiveness and will then behave accordingly.

Though the underlying science is strongly disputed, its promoters continue to argue that striking the right pose causes people to experience feelings of power and leads to physiological changes, including increased testosterone and cortisol levels. There were no pre-existing good reasons to think this might be true. And it is hard to imagine a major journal publishing a study showing that adopting a power pose had no effect on anything. So readers should have been skeptical from the outset. Nonetheless, because the findings were fun, surprising, and optimistic, the study got enormous attention. It was published in a prestigious scientific journal and written up in major media outlets, and Cuddy was invited to give what turned out to be a wildly popular TED Talk.

Not surprisingly, the result turns out to be wrong. Multiple attempts at replication fail to find similar effects. And one of the coauthors, Dana Carney, eventually went so far as to disavow the work, documenting the many ways in which the finding was the result of *p*-hacking.

Beyond Science

We have focused on the ways in which over-comparing and under-reporting create deep challenges for the scientific community. But, as the story of Paul the Octopus illustrates, the problem is broader than that. Indeed, we suspect you run into it on a regular basis, often without noticing.

Suppose someone is trying to sell you something—perhaps a car, financial advice, or a subscription to a dating app. The salesperson might tell you, "This car was rated number one in customer satisfaction five years after purchase!" Sounds great. But you might want to ask yourself how many measures of satisfaction they looked at before finding the one on which this car was rated number one. Did they look at reliability, repair record, safety, longevity, gas mileage, and resale value in addition to customer satisfaction? Did they also look one year from purchase, two years from purchase, three years from purchase, and so on? If so, they made a lot of comparisons and told you about the one that puts the car in the best possible light. This is not an unbiased estimate of the car's quality; it reflects the salesperson's equivalent of *p*-hacking.

Similarly, your financial advisor might tell you, "This mutual fund outperformed the S&P 500 for seven of the last eight years." That sounds good. But how did it do relative to the Dow Jones or a broad market index? How did it do over the last nine years, ten years, fifteen years? Did the advisor choose to compare to the S&P over the last eight years because that was the natural comparison or because it was the comparison that made the mutual fund look best?

In general, then, you need to think clearly about the problems of over-comparing and under-reporting not just when formally thinking about hypothesis testing and statistical significance. Whenever you are offered a piece of evidence, you should be asking yourself whether this particular comparison is the natural one or the first one you would have thought to look at. If not, you might pause to contemplate how many plausible comparisons there are and, thus, how difficult it would have been to come up with some comparison that made whatever point the speaker was trying to make.

In the spirit of appreciating the fact that this problem is, indeed, everywhere, let us leave you with one final story that illustrates yet another way in which over-comparing and under-reporting frequently rears its head—identifying superstars.

Superstars

We like to admire and study people who are really successful. We've already seen one reason why this can produce misleading inferences: correlation requires variation. Another reason that we shouldn't be so quick to admire and study superstars is that there may not be anything particularly special about them beyond good luck.

Bill Miller majored in economics in college, served as a military intelligence officer, dabbled in a doctoral program in philosophy, and worked as treasurer for a steel and cement company before taking a position at Legg Mason Capital Management as director of research in 1981, at the age of thirty-one. Miller was clearly a smart guy with a promising career ahead of him. The next year, he began running the Legg Mason Value Trust mutual fund. For the first decade or so, the fund's performance was mediocre, slightly underperforming the market average. But Miller eventually hit his stride, scoring some big returns in the late 1990s and early 2000s. By 2006, fellow investors and reporters noticed that Legg Mason Value Trust had outperformed the market for fifteen years running, an unprecedented streak that launched Bill Miller into the upper echelons of finance stardom.

Inevitably, everyone wanted to know Miller's secret. What made him such a successful investor? Perhaps surprisingly, Miller didn't achieve his success by developing intimate knowledge of niche industries or technical trading algorithms. His fund primarily invested in a small number of already well-known companies like Google, Amazon, eBay, J.P. Morgan, and Aetna. When describing his investment philosophy in a 2006 letter to investors, Miller reported that he simply looks for the "best value." He further speculated on what separates his fund from so many competitors: "We differ from many value investors in being willing to analyze stocks that look expensive to see if they really are. Most, in fact, are, but some are not."

Miller makes it sound easy. He just invests in companies that are undervalued. But before we conclude that Bill Miller is a genius investor, let's consider the possibility that Miller was simply lucky, like Paul the Octopus.

There is an idea in finance called the efficient-market hypothesis. It more or less says that no fund or investment strategy should be able to systematically beat the market average over the long run. Loosely, the logic goes like this. If some genius investor came up with an investment strategy that predictably beat the market, other investors would mimic that strategy. This would change the prices of the assets traded under that strategy. Investors would keep doing this until that strategy no longer beat the market. For instance, if a company's stock price fully reflects all available information about the value of that company, which we'd expect in a large market with lots of people trading on the best available information, there should be no way to systematically predict whether the stock price will go up or down without insider knowledge.

If the efficient-market hypothesis is right, then Miller and the other fund managers and stock pickers are just doing the equivalent of flipping coins. And we know that if enough people flip coins, a few of them will flip a long string of heads by sheer luck. So, to assess whether Miller is indeed a genius, we need to ask how likely it is that he just happens to be the one guy who hit a long string of heads by luck.

To get started, let's imagine that beating the market is really just like flipping heads with a fair coin. This is our null hypothesis. Then we want to ask, If our null hypothesis is true, how likely is it that someone would flip 15 heads in a row?

The chances that a given investor in a given 15-year period beats the market every single year by chance is really low. The probability that some investor beats the market by luck in one year is $\frac{1}{2}$. The probability that an investor beats the market by luck two years in a row is $\frac{1}{2} \times \frac{1}{2}$. Extending this logic, the probability that a given investor beats the market 15 years in a row by sheer luck is $\frac{1}{2}^{15}$, or about 1 in 30,000. So maybe Miller is a genius; if he was just flipping coins, there's only a 1 in 30,000 chance that he would be so successful. But maybe not. Let's make sure we are thinking clearly about a few things.

There are lots of investors out there, and if any one of them beat the market 15 years in a row, they would have been just as famous as Miller, and we'd be discussing them instead of him. Therefore, the relevant question is not how likely it is that one particular fund manager, Bill Miller, would beat the market 15 years in a row by chance. The relevant question is how likely it is that some fund manger would beat the market 15 years in a row by chance.

Notice, this is just like publication bias or the problem of Paul the Octopus. With publication bias, we only hear about the few studies out of many with statistically significant results. With Paul, we only heard about the one animal out of many who correctly forecast a lot of soccer games. And, similarly, we only hear about the few investors who have really long winning streaks. In all three cases, if we only think about the studies, animals, or investors we get to hear about, we over-estimate how likely it is that their success reflects a real phenomenon in the world.

In any given year, there are at least 24,000 professional funds trading, and presumably each will continue trading if it beats the market. So let's assume (as our null hypothesis) that there are 24,000 fund managers, none with any special insight. That means that whether each of them beats the market in any given year is a 50-50 proposition. So figuring out how likely it is that one of them beats the market 15 years in a row is just like figuring out how likely someone is to flip 15 heads in a row if 24,000 people each flips 15 fair coins.

Doing the same kind of calculation we did for Paul the Octopus, the answer is about .52 or 1 in 2.[2] It is very unlikely that any particular investor will beat the market 15 years in a row by sheer luck. But when you consider the thousands of investors out there, it's actually more likely than not that one of them will beat the market 15 years in a row, even if none of them has any special insight and they're all just flipping coins.

These calculations look even worse for Miller if we consider that a 15-year streak would have seemed just as impressive had it started in another year. Once we consider all the funds and all the possible 15-year periods, it seems extremely likely that some fund manager would have such a streak at some point just by chance. These calculations, combined with our knowledge of the efficient-market hypothesis, should make us skeptical of anyone who claims to know the secrets to beating the market. The sheer

---

[2]The probability that one investor gets 15 years in a row right is $.5^{15}$. So the probability that one investor doesn't gets 15 years in a row right is $1 - .5^{15}$. So the probability that none of 24,000 gets 15 years in a row right is $(1 - .5^{15})^{24,000}$. So the probability that at least one investor does get 15 years in a row right is $1 - ((1 - .5^{15})^{24,000})$, which is approximately .52.

number of traders and funds means that there are bound to be some exceptionally good track records. And those are the ones we hear about. So, before handing over your life savings to an investment manager, you should ask whether you would invest the same money betting on Paul the Octopus's soccer picks. If not, let us recommend that you consider low-cost index funds.

What do you think happened to Bill Miller after his flurry of press coverage in the mid-2000s? The streak ended in 2006. His fund lost 55 percent of its value during the 2008 financial crisis, the fund continued to trail the market for several more years, and he eventually stepped down from his post in 2012. Looking across the full thirty-year period in which Miller managed Legg Mason Value Trust, it actually *underperformed* the market. Alas, his historic winning streak still earns him regular appearances on cable news programs, where he pontificates on market conditions and hot stock picks. In 2017, his new fund, Miller Opportunity Trust, was once again making news for impressive returns in 2017. The secret? A big bet on Apple, the most highly valued company in the world.

Wrapping Up

Over-comparing and under-reporting can happen because of nefarious researcher behavior (*p*-hacking) or in a community of entirely honest researchers (*p*-screening). In either case, it results in publication bias—the phenomenon whereby published results are systematically misleading because there is a bias toward publishing statistically significant findings. There is no simple solution to the problem of over-comparing and under-reporting. But once we learn to think clearly about it, we can get a better sense for when it is likely to be occurring and come up with some practices that at least mitigate the problem.

In chapter 8, we turn to another challenge created by the presence of noise: reversion to the mean. Once we learn to think clearly about reversion to the mean, we will see that it, in combination with over-comparing and under-reporting, helps to explain what appears to be a truly puzzling phenomenon—the tendency of scientific estimates to shrink over time.

Key Terms

- **Publication bias:** The phenomenon whereby published results are systematically over-estimates because there is a bias toward publishing statistically significant results.
- *p*-**hacking:** Searching over lots of different ways to run an experiment, make a comparison, or specify a statistical model until you find one that yields a statistically significant result and then only reporting that one.
- *p*-**screening:** A social process whereby a community of researchers, through its publication standards, screens out studies with *p*-values above some threshold, giving rise to publication bias.

Exercises

7.1   Briefly return to the question from chapter 6 about Pete's roulette wheel. Would you revise any of your advice or conclusions in light of the lessons from this chapter?

7.2   In late April 2020, the National Institutes of Health announced the results of a study on the use of the drug remdesivir to treat COVID-19. Some COVID-19 patients were randomly given remdesivir; others were given a placebo. The study found statistically significant evidence that treatment with remdesivir reduced recovery time, as measured by the number of days it took for a patient to be discharged from the hospital after being put on the drug. The study was double blind (neither the patients nor doctors knew whether a subject had been put on the real drug or the placebo). The study size was reasonably large (hundreds of patients). And treatment assignment was random.

(a) On the basis of the lessons of this chapter, identify two more pieces of information that would help you assess how confident you should be in the efficacy of remdesivir.

(b) It turns out the study was pre-registered. The pre-registration plan identified twenty-eight outcomes that the scientists were going to measure. How does this change your beliefs about whether the findings identify a real effect in the world? Why?

(c) The pre-registration plan also identified one outcome as the primary outcome of interest. That primary outcome of interest was the one reported: how long it took for a patient to be discharged from the hospital. Does this affect your answer to the previous question? Why or why not?

(d) But wait, there is one final twist. The pre-registration plan was actually revised during the course of the study. It turns out that the length of hospitalization was not listed as the main outcome of interest until a revision on April 16, 2020. Prior to that, the primary outcome of interest was listed as a patient's score on an eight-point scale measuring disease severity. This is reflected in the April 2, 2020, version of the plan. The researchers, in a statement, explained that they had not seen the data coming out of the study prior to changing their primary outcome of interest. Reflect on how all of this affects your views on the study's findings.

7.3   Download "VoterSurveyData2016.csv" and the associated "README.txt," which describes the variables in this data set, at press.princeton.edu/thinking-clearly. Suppose we want to know whether prior exposure to Donald Trump before he was a politician affected political behavior in the 2016 U.S. presidential election. To proxy for exposure to Trump, a survey asked people whether they watched *The Apprentice*, a television show starring Trump, and whether they watched *Home Alone 2*, a movie featuring a cameo by Trump.

(a) Using the data available, try to find at least three interesting, statistically significant relationships suggesting that prior exposure to Trump corresponded to political behaviors in the 2016 presidential election.

   If you're struggling to find statistically significant relationships, think about all the different things you can test for. You could use having seen *The Apprentice*, *Home Alone 2*, or both as your measure of prior Trump exposure. You can use support for Trump, support for Hillary Clinton, or voter turnout in 2016 as your outcome of interest. You can subset the data to look specifically at voter subgroups of interest (e.g., women, Blacks, Southerners, rich, young, and so on).

(b) Once you've found three statistically significant relationships, interpret them substantively and think about what they mean. Did you learn something interesting about American electoral behavior?

(c) The data you just analyzed is real survey data from the 2016 Cooperative Congressional Election Study. We randomly selected one thousand respondents and shared a subset of their responses with you. However, we lied above when we said that respondents were asked whether they watched *The Apprentice* or *Home Alone 2*. We made those variables up. (Sorry, we won't lie to you again.) Furthermore, the values for those variables were generated completely at random. Explain why you were nonetheless able to find a relationship between those variables and political behavior. Would you expect that relationship to continue to hold if we provided data on another thousand respondents and again randomly generated the exposure data?

7.4   Find a recently published academic study for which you are worried about the problems of over-comparing and under-reporting. Explain your concerns. Without collecting additional data, is there anything the authors could do to address or mitigate your concerns? Is there additional information you'd like the authors to disclose? Are there additional analyses you'd like them to conduct?

Readings and References

For more on *p*-hacking, see

Joseph P. Simmons, Leif D. Nelson, and Uri Simonsohn. 2011. "False-Positive Psychology: Undisclosed Flexibility in Data Collection and Analysis Allows Presenting Anything as Significant." *Psychological Science* 22(11):1359–66.

Uri Simonsohn, Joseph P. Simmons, and Leif D. Nelson. 2014. "P-Curve: A Key to the File-Drawer." *Journal of Experimental Psychology* 143(2):534–47.

To see the ESP study and to read about some of the failed replications, see

Daryl J. Bem. 2011. "Feeling the Future: Experimental Evidence for Anomalous Retroactive Influence on Cognition and Affect." *Journal of Personality and Social Psychology* 100(3):407–25.

Jeff Galak, Robyn A. LeBoeuf, Leif D. Nelson, and Joseph P. Simmons. 2012. "Correcting the Past: Failures to Replicate Psi." *Journal of Personality and Social Psychology* 130(6):933–48.

For more on *p*-screening in the context of get-out-the-vote studies, see

Donald P. Green, Mary C. McGrath, and Peter M. Aronow. 2013. "Field Experiments and the Study of Voter Turnout." *Journal of Elections, Public Opinion and Parties* 23(1):27–48.

The essay by seventy-two researchers on lowering our threshold for statistical significance is

Benjamin, Daniel J., et al. 2017. "Redefine Statistical Significance." *Nature Human Behavior* 2:6–10.

The study on the frequency of null results in NHLBI studies before and after pre-registration is

Robert M. Kaplan and Veronica L. Irvin. 2015. "Likelihood of Null Effects of Large NHLBI Clinical Trials Has Increased over Time." *PLoS One* 10(8).

To read more about whether college football outcomes influence elections, see

Andrew J. Healy, Neil Malhotra, and Cecilia Hyunjung Mo. 2010. "Irrelevant Events Affect Voters' Evaluations of Government Performance." *Proceedings of the National Academy of Sciences* 107(29):12804–09.

Anthony Fowler and B. Pablo Montagnes. 2015. "College Football, Elections, and False-Positive Results in Observational Research." *Proceedings of the National Academy of Sciences* 112(45):13800–04.

There is a good discussion of the whole power pose episode on Andrew Gelman's blog, which frequently covers issues related to publication bias: https://statmodeling .stat.columbia.edu/2017/10/18/beyond-power-pose-using-replication-failures-better -understanding-data-collection-analysis-better-science/. The original study on power poses and the first replication attempt are

Dana R. Carney, Amy J. C. Cuddy, and Andy J. Yap. 2010. "Power Posing: Brief Nonverbal Displays Affect Neuroendocrine Levels and Risk Tolerance." *Psychological Science* 21(10):1363–68.

Eva Ranehill, Anna Dreber, Magnus Johannesson, Susanne Leiberg, Sunhae Sul, and Roberto A. Weber. 2015. "Assessing the Robustness of Power Posing: No Effect on Hormones and Risk Tolerance in a Large Sample of Men and Women." *Psychological Science* 26(5):653–56.

Carney's disavowal can be found at http://faculty.haas.berkeley.edu/dana_carney /pdf_my%20position%20on%20power%20poses.pdf.

If you would like to see the full history of revisions of the pre-analysis plan for the remdesivir study mentioned in exercise 2, you can find it at https://clinicaltrials.gov /ct2/history/NCT04280705.

CHAPTER 8

Reversion to the Mean

What You'll Learn

- Lots of things tend to revert toward the mean, meaning that extreme observations are often followed by less extreme observations.
- This phenomenon will arise for virtually any outcome that is a function of both signal (i.e., something real in the world) and noise.
- If you don't think clearly about reversion to the mean, it is easy to misinterpret evidence.
- We shouldn't expect reversion to the mean for things that reflect our beliefs about the future, like election projections or stock prices.

Introduction

As emphasized by our favorite equation, the world is noisy, and most quantitative measurements reflect both the thing we meant to measure and noise. This has lots of implications for the ways that we study and understand the world.

One of the most common yet least understood consequences of living in a noisy world is *reversion to the mean*. Loosely speaking, unusually large or small measurements tend to be followed (and preceded) by measurements that are closer to the mean.

Although reversion to the mean is not a standard topic in books on quantitative reasoning and data analysis, its pervasiveness means that you will often be misled by quantitative information if you don't understand this phenomenon. So we think it is important to devote some time to it.

Does the Truth Wear Off?

In chapter 7 we saw that, because of over-comparing and under-reporting, we should often be skeptical of new, surprising scientific findings. And so, when such findings are initially reported, often the first question that gets asked is "Does the result replicate?" That is, if we were to run a new, independent study designed similarly to the original study, would we find a similar effect? The instinct to ask this question is solid: we are worried that some reported results reflect the vagaries of chance, rather than real phenomena in the world. So, before hanging our hats on new findings, we want to see that they hold up in multiple studies. And, in fact, researchers often fail to replicate hyped results in follow-up studies. Indeed, in some fields of study this is so common that people have started talking about a *replication crisis* undermining confidence in entire bodies of scientific enquiry.

Jonathan Schooler, a prominent psychologist at UC Santa Barbara, famously noticed such a pattern of replication failures in some of his own most influential studies. Interestingly, the effects Schooler estimated typically didn't disappear entirely when replicated, but they did get systematically smaller. He asked around and found that many colleagues had experienced the same thing; replicated results were often smaller than the original findings.

One potential explanation for this pattern is that once you've done a study and subjects are aware of the results, they change their behavior. This phenomenon, whereby subjects alter their behavior because they know they're being studied, is sometimes called the *Hawthorne effect*.[1] Another term—*demand effects*—refers to situations where the subjects behave differently because they know what the experimenters are looking for and are trying to please them.

Schooler and his colleagues quickly ruled out the Hawthorne effect and other similar explanations because they found the same pattern in studies of birds, who presumably have no idea what's being studied and don't care one way or the other about pleasing human researchers. So what else could explain the peculiar pattern of disappearing effects?

Schooler (perhaps jokingly) started referring to this phenomenon as *cosmic habituation*. He wondered whether there is some unknown force in the universe that causes effects to shrink every time they're studied. One analogy he gives is to the habituation of human sensory perception. When something first touches your arm, you are acutely aware of it. However, over time, you habituate, and your sensation of being touched diminishes. Maybe the universe is like that. The first time we observe some phenomenon, there is an acute effect. But, over time, the universe habituates to our studies and we observe the effect less and less. In other words, scientists actually alter reality every time they study it. Spooky.

Schooler's theory of cosmic habituation has received significant media attention, including an episode of the popular radio show and podcast *Radio Lab* and an article in the *New Yorker* entitled "The Truth Wears Off." But before we follow Schooler down the path of hypothesizing new cosmic forces, let's see if thinking a little more clearly can help us resolve the puzzle of shrinking effect sizes a bit less mystically.

Francis Galton and Regression to Mediocrity

As we described back in chapter 5, Francis Galton made a similarly eerie discovery in the 1860s. He collected data on the size of parents and their children. He did this for human height. He also did it for plants, collecting data on the size and weight of the seeds of parent and child sweet-peas.

Galton drew scatter plots of these kinds of data, putting the parents' size on the horizontal axis and the children's on the vertical axis. Then he plotted a regression line

---

[1] Fun fact: The term *Hawthorne effect* comes from a study of the relationship between working conditions and productivity at the Hawthorne Works factory outside Chicago. But it turns out that the data were analyzed badly. The economists Steven Levitt and John List reanalyzed the original data and showed that what looked to the original researchers like a Hawthorne effect was more likely attributable to other factors, such as differences across days of the week, rather than the subjects changing their behavior in response to being studied.

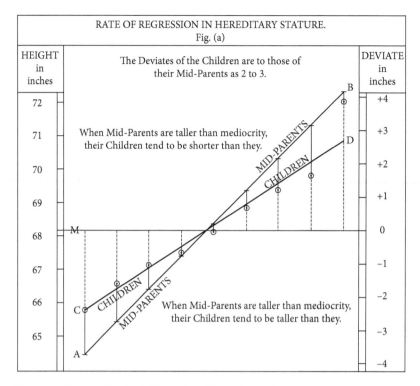

Figure 8.1. A reproduction of Galton's illustration of reversion to the mean.

through the data. You can see one of Galton's plots, for the heights of parents (adjusting for biological sex) and their children, in figure 8.1.

Originally, Galton expected the regression line would be a 45-degree line—that is, its intercept would be 0 and its slope 1. That seems a reasonable guess. It would be true if, on average, children are the same size as their parents (again, adjusting for biological sex).

As it turns out, however, this guess is not correct for humans or for sweet-peas. Let's look at Galton's figure. In that figure, the 45-degree line is labeled "Mid-Parents." The phrase refers to Galton's measure of the average height of a child's parents, after first adjusting to put female and male heights on the same scale. The (unlabeled) horizontal axis corresponds to parents' height. Then, the line tracing out parents' height must be the 45-degree line. The line labeled "Children" is the regression line running through the data that takes as its x-value the parents' height and as its y-value the children's height.

As you can see in the figure, Galton's regression shows a positive y-intercept—at the lowest value on the horizontal axis (parents' height), the regression line lies above the 45-degree line. And Galton's regression line has a slope that is positive but distinctly less than 1—the regression line is increasing more slowly than the 45-degree line.

What does this regression imply about the relationship between parents' height and children's height? The fact that the slope is positive means that, on average, the taller the parents, the taller their children. As you can see in the figure, the fact that the y-intercept is positive means that particularly short parents tend to have children who are taller than they are. On the left-hand side of the horizontal axis (where parents are short), the regression line lies above the 45-degree line. But because its slope is less than 1, the regression line increases less quickly than the 45-degree line. And, indeed, the two lines cross in the middle. As such, on the right-hand side of the horizontal axis (where parents are tall), the regression line lies below the 45-degree line. Particularly tall parents tend to have children who are shorter than they are.

As we mentioned in chapter 5, Galton referred to this phenomenon as "regression to mediocrity." And it is because of this word choice that we now use the word *regression* to refer to the practice of fitting lines to data. It is also why some people refer to the phenomenon whereby things tend to revert toward the mean (which is the subject of this chapter) as *regression to the mean*. However, to avoid confusing the two concepts, we will refer to the latter by its other common name, *reversion to the mean* also sometimes referred to as *mean reversion*.

Galton's findings sound a lot like cosmic habituation. Perhaps there is some unseen force in the universe that pushes size within families toward the average. Maybe when the universe sees tall parents or big sweet-pea seeds, it restores order by making their offspring smaller. Or perhaps when Galton measured the heights of the parents and the diameter of sweet-pea seeds, he somehow made their offspring shrink! Galton was probably perplexed by his unexpected findings. But he wasn't so quick to jump to supernatural conclusions.

Eventually, Galton realized what was going on. Size is determined by many factors. For the purposes of seeing Galton's idea as clearly and simply as possible, let's think about sweet-pea seeds. And let's imagine that a sweet-pea seed's size is influenced by just two things: (1) the genes it inherits from its parent and (2) the amount of direct sunlight it gets while growing. Inheriting genes for largeness from its mother make a seed larger, all else equal. And getting more sunlight make a seed larger, all else equal.

Under this simple model, let's think about how a seed can end up especially large or especially small. Suppose you find a really large sweet-pea seed. It could be large because it got genes for really large size from its mother. It could also be large because it happened to grow in a year with uncommonly good sun. Or it could be some combination of the two. Odds are, if a seed is *really* large, it had both factors working in its favor: a parent with genes for large size and excellent sun.

So what should we expect if these really big seeds are planted and produce offspring of their own? They'll pass along their genes for larger-than-average size. But, most likely, the child seed won't experience the same outstanding sunlight as its parent did. On average, it will grow in average sun. So the child will be larger than average because of the genes it inherited. But the child will probably be smaller than its parent because its parent got particularly lucky with respect to sun exposure. The same holds for the children of very small seeds. They get their parents' genes for small size. But they are likely to experience better sunlight than their parents did and, thus, be larger than their parents.

So, if this simple model were correct, we would observe exactly Galton's pattern. Larger plants tend to have larger children (the regression line has a positive slope). But size reverts toward the mean—really small parents tend to have children who are smaller than average but larger than they are, and really large parents tend to have children who are larger than average but smaller than they are (the slope of the regression line is less than 1).

Obviously, seed size is more complicated than this. Many things influence it other than genes and sun. But the example makes the point. We should expect reversion to the mean if size is partly determined by genes that are systematically transmitted from parent to child and partly determined by idiosyncratic or random factors that are uncorrelated across generations (like sun exposure). The same goes for human height, as we see in Galton's plot.

More generally, there will be reversion to the mean for any outcome that's partly a function of systematic factors (which we sometimes call *signal*) and partly a function of random or idiosyncratic factors (which we sometimes call *noise*). Imagine an outcome observed over and over, where with each observation, the outcome reflects a combination of a systematic signal (e.g., the genes) and random noise (e.g., sunlight). Extreme outcomes typically arise because of extreme values of both the signal and the noise. In other iterations, while the signal stays fixed, the noise takes a new, random value. And, in expectation, the value of the noise will be average. So extreme values in one iteration are expected to revert toward the mean in other iterations.

Many phenomena in the world have this signal and noise structure. So we should expect reversion to the mean to pop up a lot. Therefore, thinking clearly about evidence requires anticipating and accounting for reversion to the mean. In what follows, we first delve a little more deeply into the nature of reversion to the mean to make sure we are clear about exactly what is going on. We then consider a variety of different real-world settings to understand when we should and should not expect reversion to the mean to appear.

Reversion to the Mean Is Not a Gravitational Force

One common misconception about reversion to the mean is that it reflects something like a gravitational pull—that is, that the world is full of outliers and that ineluctably, over time, things are being pulled toward the mean. This isn't right.

To see if you are thinking clearly about reversion to the mean, try answering each of the following questions:

1. John Junior is exceptionally tall. If you had to guess, would you guess that John Junior's son, John III, is
   (a) shorter than John Junior?
   (b) the same height as John Junior?
   (c) taller than John Junior?

2. John Junior is exceptionally tall. If you had to guess, would you guess that John Junior's father, John Senior, is
   (a) shorter than John Junior?
   (b) the same height as John Junior?
   (c) taller than John Junior?

Before we turn to the answers, let's start by noting that you should have given the same answer to both questions. Understanding why is essential.

For many people, once they learn about reversion to the mean, question 1 is pretty intuitive. John III is probably shorter than John Junior. John Junior is particularly tall. So he probably has genes for tall height (signal). And he also probably had idiosyncratic things happen that led him to grow particularly tall (noise). His son, John III, will likely inherit his genes for tallness. But, if you had to guess, you'd guess the idiosyncratic other factors will likely be more average. This is the logic of reversion to the mean as explained by Galton.

But, in our experience, question 2 is often a bit more vexing. You may be inclined to reason as follows. John Junior is really tall. And there is reversion to the mean in the world. So John Junior's height is probably closer to the mean than was his father's.

Factoring in reversion to the mean, for John Junior to be so tall, his father must have been a virtual giant! Hence, one might reason, while the answer to question 1 is (a), the answer to question 2 must be (c).

It's okay if you thought something along those lines. The argument has a certain appeal. But it is wrong, and it's important that you see why. The answer to both questions 1 and 2 is (a). And the logic for John Junior's father is identical to the logic for John Junior's son: the logic of reversion to the mean. Here's how it goes, one more time.

Suppose you observe some outcome made up of signal and noise and that outcome is surprisingly large. (The argument, of course, works for surprisingly small too.) Then suppose you are going to observe another outcome, where the signal is the same as your first observation, but there will be a new, independent draw of the noise. Since the first observation is so large, it probably reflects a large value of the signal and a large value of the noise. The new observation again has a large signal value, but the value of the noise is likely to be smaller. So that new observation will likely be smaller.

Importantly, in making this argument, we said nothing about which outcome was determined first in time. We just talked about the order in which you observed them. Reversion to the mean is not a gravitational force pulling things toward the average over time. For the logic of reversion to the mean, it makes no difference which came first temporally. So, if John Junior is very tall, and his son has the same signal (genes) but independent noise, then his son is probably shorter than him. And, if John Junior is very tall, and his father has the same signal (genes) but independent noise, then his father is also probably shorter than him.

The easiest place to see this in the real world is in data from athletic competitions, where we observe the same competitor doing the same task over and over again. And, what we see in those settings is that reversion to the mean characterizes the data, moving forward and backward in time.

Figure 8.2 is a scatter plot of scores from the first two rounds of the 2019 U.S. Women's Open golf tournament. Players' scores from round 1 are on the horizontal axis and from round 2, on the vertical axis. What do you see here?

On average, there is a positive correlation between scores in the two rounds; the regression line is sloping upward. The players who did better (in golf, lower scores are better) in round 1 also tended to do better in round 2. That makes sense: some players are better than others (that's the signal). But the slope of the regression line is far less than 1; the regression line is shallower than the 45-degree line. If a player's round 1 score was worse than average, their round 2 score tended to be better than their round 1 score. And if a player's round 1 score was better than average, their round 2 score tended to be worse than their round 1 score. It's exactly the same as the pattern with the heights of parents and children or the size of mother sweet-peas and their offspring discovered by Galton. And we can assure you that we didn't cherry pick this example. It's a virtual guarantee that you'll see this same pattern for any golf tournament.

A golf commentator might look at this data and tell a story to explain the scores. Maybe the players who had a really good first round succumbed to the pressure. They choked. And that explains why they did worse in round 2. And maybe the players who had a bad first round realized they had to put in more practice, change strategy, or really focus. And they accordingly improved their scores.

That's possible. But it could also just be reversion to the mean. Golf scores are a function of both skill (signal) and luck (noise). The players with the best score in a given round are probably better than the average player in the field. But they probably also had some luck on their side. A few putts went in that could have just as easily lipped

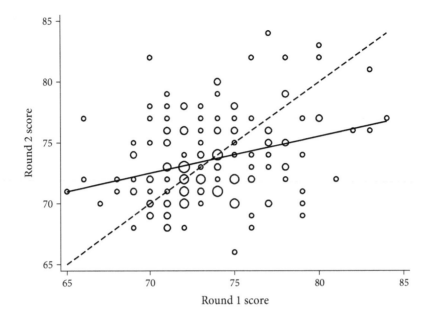

Figure 8.2. Scores across rounds in the 2019 U.S. Women's Open golf tournament. In cases where multiple players had identical scores, the size of the circle is increased to reflect the number of players. The 45-degree line is dashed, and the actual OLS regression line is solid.

out. Their few bad shots got fortunate bounces, keeping them out of trouble. And so on. In their other rounds, they're still better-than-average players, so we expect their scores to be better than average. But they probably won't have the same good luck, so their score will probably be worse than in that exceptional round.

Notice, nothing in the previous paragraph's logic depended on which round came first. That's because reversion to the mean isn't some gravitational force pulling things toward the mean over time. This realization allows us to probe which story—the commentator's or reversion to the mean—is more likely to be true.

Think about a player who has a particularly good score in round 2. Should we expect their round 1 score to be better or worse than their round 2 score? The old temptation was to think that because of reversion to the mean, in order for them to have a good score in round 2, they must have had a really good score in round 1, allowing them to still have a good round 2 score despite reversion to the mean. But we now know better.

The logic of reversion to the mean has nothing to do with time. The score in each round of golf is a combination of signal and noise. If a player had a particularly good round at some point, we should expect a different round by that player (with the same signal but different noise) to be worse, regardless of which round came first. And if a player had a particularly bad round at some point, we should expect a different round by that player to be better, regardless of which round came first.

Figure 8.3 shows the same graph you saw before, but with the axes flipped so that round 2 is on the horizontal axis and round 1 is on the vertical axis. The overall pattern is almost exactly the same. People who had particularly good scores in round 2 were better than average in round 1 but still worse in round 1 than in round 2. Just like with John Junior and John Senior, reversion to the mean works backward in time just as well as it works forward in time.

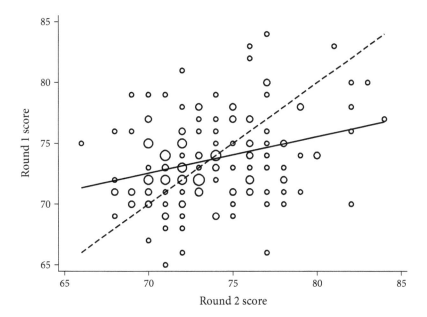

Figure 8.3. Scores across rounds in the 2019 U.S. Women's Open golf tournament, with flipped axes.

Seeing both versions of the graph demonstrates why the commentator's explanation is unlikely to be right. It is hard to believe that a good score in round 2 causes players to feel extra pressure, which somehow goes backward in time, making their round 1 score worse. And yet, we see the same pattern whether we look forward or backward in time. The explanation is reversion to the mean.

Seeking Help

Reversion to the mean can be particularly problematic for clear thinking in settings where we seek help when things have gone unexpectedly wrong (e.g., you suddenly become ill or you do poorly on an exam). Why is this?

If things have gone unexpectedly wrong, that suggests we have some underlying expectation of how things should be going—perhaps formed on the basis of long past experience—and that we have deviated from that expectation in a bad direction. We might think of the expectation of how things should be going as reflecting the signal. And deviations from that expectation might reflect noise.

Let's think about that in a couple of concrete settings.

Suppose you are a relatively healthy person. You might think of good health as reflecting the true underlying signal for you. Even most fundamentally healthy people feel unwell from time to time—because of the flu, a back ache, or what have you— for idiosyncratic reasons that perhaps do not reflect any fundamental change to their underlying state of healthiness. And most healthy people also have days when they feel particularly vigorous and well. Thus, we might think of a day when you feel fine as reflecting your true signal, with very little noise. Days when you feel sick can be thought of as days with particularly negative values for the noise. And days when you feel like you could go out and conquer the world can be thought of as days with particularly positive values for the noise.

Or maybe an example about school will speak more directly to our readers. You have some underlying level of academic skill that reflects how strong a student you are in any given area. That is your true signal. But some days you do way better than normal on a test—perhaps reflecting a particularly lucky draw of questions or a particularly good night's sleep. And some days you do way worse than normal on a test—perhaps reflecting an unlucky draw of questions or a late night. These idiosyncratic features constitute noise.

Now, what does this have to do with reversion to the mean? Ask yourself, On which days is a person likely to seek help from, say, a chiropractor? Probably on days when they wake up with a back ache that feels worse than normal—that is, on days when the noise is particularly negative. And ask yourself, Which students seek out help from a test prep company? Probably students whose performance on an important standardized test was worse than they had anticipated given their sense of their underlying ability. If this is right, then reversion to the mean tells us that, even if chiropractic adjustments or test prep strategies don't actually help at all, we should expect people who seek out this kind of assistance to see improvements. And, if they aren't thinking clearly about reversion to the mean, they are likely to give too much credit to the chiropractor or the test prep company. Reversion to the mean can be a good business model.

This kind of problem is pervasive. We've already seen an example in chapter 1, where we discussed broken-windows policing. Recall that, in New York City, when the police rolled out a new strategy, they targeted the highest crime precincts and found that, after the change of strategy, crime went down in those precincts. But this is just what we'd expect from reversion to the mean, even if broken-windows policing doesn't work at all. The highest-crime precincts will tend to get better and the lowest-crime precincts will tend to get worse, regardless of any policy change. Because of this reversion to the mean, policing strategies that target the highest-crime precincts will look to the naive observer as if they are really effective, even if they aren't.

And, actually, reversion to the mean was lurking underneath another of our examples in chapter 1. Remember when Ethan's son's doctors recommended that he try out a gluten-free diet because he was underweight? Their idea was that, if his weight percentile increased once he went on the gluten-free diet, that would be evidence of gluten intolerance. But reversion to the mean says that we should have expected Abe's weight percentile to increase even with no intervention. Month to month, a baby's weight is a function of both signal (e.g., health, genetics) and noise (e.g., random features of the environment, idiosyncrasies in the growth trajectory). If a kid has off-the-charts low weight in one month, he probably had extremely low values on the noise terms that month. Over time, we should expect more average values on the noise, so his weight percentile should increase. It would be a mistake to interpret this, on its own, as evidence that some change in behavior (e.g., going gluten-free) explains the weight increase.

Once you think about it clearly, you'll see that all kinds of interventions and treatments will look like they work even if they do nothing. People typically seek out help when things are at their worst. We'd expect things to improve, even without an intervention, because of reversion to the mean. Let's look at one particularly striking example that scientists have actually investigated to see whether this is going on.

Does Knee Surgery Work?

There are many expensive medical treatments for which the best available evidence is not so different from the evidence for broken-windows policing or SAT prep. For instance, there are no randomized trials validating the efficacy of a variety of kinds of surgery. Consider a patient who goes to the surgeon with joint pain of some sort. The doctor recommends surgery. At the end of a recovery period, the patient says they feel better. Now, the doctor may have all sorts of knowledge about body mechanics and physiology that provides some good reasons for believing the surgery did help. But we should at least entertain the possibility that reversion to the mean is also at work—that is, that many patients would have experienced at least some significant improvement without surgery.

Indeed, once a randomized trial is run, researchers sometimes find that a common surgery does not in fact provide the hypothesized benefits. For example, in a 2002 study of arthroscopic surgery for osteoarthritis of the knee, researchers found that the commonly prescribed surgeries had no detectable effect on knee pain. Yes, patients reported less knee pain two weeks after surgery, but other subjects who simply received skin incisions and were told that they received the surgery reported the same reduction in knee pain. That's right: doctors actually gave sham surgeries to some of their patients, and those deceived patients were no worse off than those who received the real surgery. Why did all the patients seem to feel better? Presumably, you only go under the knife for knee pain when it's especially severe, so most of those patients might have felt better in a few weeks even without the surgery.

Reversion to the Mean, the Placebo Effect, and Cosmic Habituation

We've just seen that, if we fail to think clearly about reversion to the mean, we are likely to misinterpret the extent to which certain kinds of interventions, including medical interventions, are actually responsible for improved outcomes. But, it turns out, reversion to the mean can even create problems when we try to do careful scientific studies. Let's see why this is the case in a couple different settings. First, we will consider the much discussed *placebo effect*. Then we will revisit the problem of cosmic habituation with which we opened this chapter.

The Placebo Effect

Few phenomena in medicine are cited more often than the so-called *placebo effect*. Many people suspect that the belief that we've undergone treatment somehow activates the body's own healing powers, independent of the direct effects of the treatment itself. For this reason, medical researchers are careful to compare the effectiveness of new drugs or treatments to placebos. They want to account for the possibility that believing you're receiving a treatment will heal you all on its own. So they use things like sugar pills or fake surgeries, so that experimental subjects don't know whether they are getting a real treatment or not.

Why do medical researchers, and others, think that there's a placebo effect? One source of evidence comes from medical trials themselves. In such experiments there is a treatment group that gets the drug and a control group that gets a placebo pill. And often, in such studies, both groups' health improves. The improvement of the control group is taken as evidence for the placebo effect.

But now you can see that this kind of evidence for the placebo effect is unconvincing. The people in the control group (and the treatment group) entered the medical study because they were unwell. We might expect them to tend to get better even in the absence of any treatment. This need not be because their minds are healing their bodies. It could just be reversion to the mean.

If you actually wanted to test for a placebo effect, you'd want to divide the pool of experimental subjects into a group that got a placebo pill and a group that got no treatment at all. (Of course, you could also have a group that got the real medicine. Let's not forget why we are here in the first place.) Few studies explicitly test for the effect of a placebo treatment relative to no treatment. The ones that do typically find no evidence of a placebo effect. Moreover, those studies that do find evidence for a placebo effect typically concern purely subjective outcomes. So people may perceive themselves to be feeling better after taking a placebo, even if they aren't objectively healthier.

For example, in 2011, a team of researchers from Harvard Medical School published a paper in the *New England Journal of Medicine* comparing the effects of real medical treatments, placebo treatments, and no treatment for asthmatic patients. Interestingly, both the real treatment (an albuterol inhaler) and the placebo treatments (a placebo inhaler or acupuncture) led patients to report that they felt better. But when the scientists actually measured the subjects' lung capacity, only the real treatment had an effect; the placebo treatments were no better than doing nothing. So to the extent that there's evidence for a placebo effect, it's evidence of mind over mind, not mind over matter.

In short, once we think clearly about reversion to the mean, we see that there's little compelling evidence of a placebo effect in medicine. Yet somehow, almost everyone believes in the placebo effect because they're bad at recognizing and correctly interpreting reversion to the mean. Even some of the greatest medical researchers have fallen victim to this confusion. Vitamin C is widely believed to provide significant health benefits, despite little evidence. (To be clear, a small amount of vitamin C is necessary to avoid scurvy, but for almost everyone in the developed world who naturally consumes some vitamin C, there is little evidence that additional vitamin C is beneficial.) An important source of this widely held superstition is Linus Pauling, a world-famous chemist and two-time Nobel Prize winner, who strongly advocated for vitamin C. Some argue that Pauling knew that vitamin C had little effect, but he believed in the placebo effect, and he thought that telling people that a vitamin C supplement, or a glass of orange juice, would heal them was a cheap and easy way to get the placebo effect working, inducing the human body to somehow cure itself.

Cosmic Habituation Explained

If you are paying particularly close attention, you might have noticed a connection between the talk of signal and noise in this chapter and our favorite equation. Recall, our favorite equation says that an estimate from data is made up of three things—the true estimand, bias, and noise:

$$\text{Estimate} = \text{Estimand} + \text{Bias} + \text{Noise}$$

Imagine a study that is really well designed to learn about an estimand so that there is no bias. The estimate generated by that study will be made up of the true estimand and noise from things like sampling variation. The true estimand stays constant across different studies of the same phenomenon. But the resulting estimates nonetheless vary from study to study because of the noise. So, if we imagine multiple studies of the same phenomenon, we can think of the true estimand as the signal. And we can think of the noise as, well, the noise.

Given this, we should expect repeated scientific studies of the same phenomenon to exhibit reversion to the mean. If the first study found a particularly large relationship, it is probably the case that the true relationship in the world is big, and it is also probably the case that the sampling variation happened to create noise in the positive direction in that study. In the next study, we should expect to find a smaller estimate because, while the true relationship (i.e., the estimand) is still probably large, the noise from the sampling variation will probably not be as large this time around.

With this realization, we are now, finally, ready to return to the idea of cosmic habituation and see why it probably isn't best explained by a mystical force whereby the universe accustoms itself to the activity of scientists here on earth.

If it isn't mystical forces, why do estimated effects tend to get smaller when replicated? Part of the answer is reversion to the mean. But that's not the whole answer. To really understand what is going on with cosmic habituation, you need to combine our new understanding of reversion to the mean with our discussion of publication bias from chapter 7. Let's see why.

Imagine several scientists, independently studying some phenomenon—say, whether giving people time to think leads them to make better decisions, which is one of Jonathan Schooler's areas of interest. Each scientist does a study. One finds that people who are given time to think make dramatically worse decisions. Another finds that people who are given time to think make slightly worse decisions. A third finds no relationship. And a fourth finds that people who are given time to think make slightly better decisions. Given the sample size of the various studies, only the large finding is statistically significant.

What generates these different estimates? Presumably, there is some true effect of giving people time to think on the quality of their decisions. This is the estimand in our favorite equation. We can also think of it as the *signal* that is common across each of these studies. But then there are lots of idiosyncratic features, the *noise*, that affect the observed relationship (the estimate) in any given study. For instance, even though these are experiments, in any one of them, by happenstance, it could occur that the people given time to think turn out to be intrinsically much worse decision makers than the people not given time to think. This large negative noise term would lead that study to find a particularly large negative effect. In another study the people given time to think might happen to be intrinsically slightly better decision makers than the people not given time to think. This positive noise term would lead that study to find a more favorable relationship between thinking time and decision making. So, we can see, the results of these studies are made up of both signal and noise. Thus, we should expect replications to experience reversion to the mean.

Now let's think about which of the findings are most likely to be replicated. From our earlier discussion of *p*-screening and publication bias, if we had to guess, we'd guess that only one of these studies is notable enough to the original researcher or the scientific community to warrant an independent replication—the one with the large, statistically significant negative relationship between time to think and the quality of decision making. This study has two things going for it over the other studies. First, it has a statistically significant finding, so it is more likely to be published. Second, that finding is pretty surprising—who would have thought that thinking things through leads to worse decisions?

Imagine that this is what happens. One large surprising finding gets published. It was found in a well-designed study, so people think it is probably true. But, because it is an important result, scientists will also want to see if it replicates. What should we expect them to find? Well, we just saw that a finding is more likely to get published and warrant replication (both because of its surprise value and because it is more likely to pass the statistical significance threshold) when the estimated effect size is particularly large in magnitude. But we also know that particularly large estimates are probably the result of both large values of the signal *and* large values of the noise. So, because of reversion to the mean, when we go to replicate this study, we should expect to find a smaller (in magnitude) estimated effect size (as, indeed, the other three, unpublished studies had found). That is, because of a combination of publication bias and reversion to the mean, we should expect to see cosmic habituation!

Cosmic Habituation and Genetics

Figure 8.4 is our favorite illustration of the phenomenon of cosmic habituation resulting from publication bias and reversion to the mean. The figure describes the changing evidence on the link between particular genes and particular diseases. The different curves represent different hypothesized gene-disease linkages. Each data point shows the sign and size of the estimated relationship, taking into account all the available data at any given point in time. In this particular graph, a value of 1 on the vertical axis means that the evidence shows no relationship at all between the gene and the disease. A value below 1 means that the evidence shows a negative relationship between the gene and the disease. And a value above 1 means that the evidence shows a positive relationship between the gene and the disease. The farther from 1, the larger (in magnitude) the estimated relationship.

The data points on the far left of the plot are the estimated relationships between genes and diseases from the very first study published on the topic. Moving to the right, the next data point shows the estimated relationship taking into account the data from both the first and second published studies. This continues as we move to the right, until we get to the most recent published study.

What you can see in figure 8.4 looks like cosmic habituation. The first published study finds a large relationship between a gene and a disease. This is the kind of study that gets published in a prestigious journal and covered in the press. But as scientists engage in replication, reversion to the mean kicks in. The magnitude of the estimated effects is typically smaller in subsequent studies. As we add more and more information, we get closer to the truth, which is quite far from the over-estimate reported in the initial study. As we see, by the end, the evidence suggests at most a very weak relationship between the gene and disease in question. The follow-up newspaper story is rarely written.

Beliefs Don't Revert to the Mean

Once you understand reversion to the mean, you should start to worry about it a lot. Commentators, analysts, and casual observers constantly misunderstand it, introducing complex theories to explain patterns that reflect a simple statistical phenomenon. The preceding discussion makes it sound like we should expect reversion to the mean almost everywhere, and to a close approximation, that's right. We should see reversion to the mean for any variable that is influenced by signal and noise. So instead of listing all the instances of reversion to the mean, let's think about situations where we shouldn't expect it.

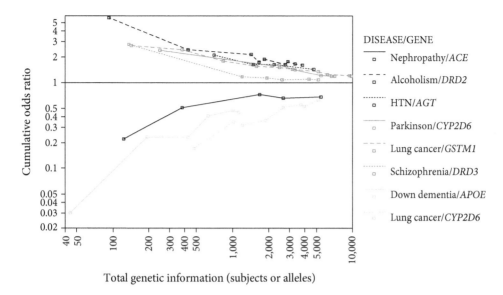

Figure 8.4. The estimated effect size shrinks as more data is accumulated in genetic studies.

First, if the signal is much greater than the noise, then we wouldn't expect to see much reversion to the mean. Suppose we repeated our earlier golf analysis, but instead of plotting scores from two different rounds within one tournament, we plotted average scores from two different seasons on the LPGA Tour. An average score from an entire season contains a lot more information about a player's ability. Much of the good and bad luck that constitutes the noise across rounds averages out, so there will be less reversion to the mean in that picture (but still some).

But there are some situations where we should expect no reversion to the mean at all. Let's think about the stock market. Should we expect to find reversion to the mean in stock prices? Maybe we could beat the market and become billionaires by exploiting reversion to the mean.

Reversion to the mean would seem to predict that, on average, companies with low stock prices should rebound in the future, and companies with high prices should drop. It also seems to predict that increases should be followed by decreases and vice versa. Could we exploit this information by buying the stocks that just dropped and selling the stocks that just increased?

The answer to this question is almost surely no. Suppose it were the case that there was reversion to the mean in stock prices. Clever investors would realize this, follow the strategy described above, and make a lot of money. But with enough investors following this strategy, the reversion to the mean would go away, because the prices of the low stocks would increase and the prices of the high stocks would decrease in response to the market's buying and selling decisions. The efficient-market hypothesis, discussed briefly in chapter 7, says that with enough traders looking for these kinds of opportunities, we shouldn't be able to predict changes in stock prices, and therefore, we shouldn't expect reversion to the mean.

Reversion to the mean is quite prevalent in the business world. We see it for corporate revenues and profits, despite the desire by startups and venture capitalists to project future revenues by making linear or sometimes exponential projections from past revenues. So why don't we see reversion to the mean for stock prices? The main reason is that stock prices reflect beliefs about the future, while revenues don't. The price of the stock is driven by investors' beliefs about the long-term value of the firm. And if there were reversion to the mean, it would suggest that investors are making systematic mistakes in forming those beliefs. If there were a stock that we could expect to increase in price, investors would all buy it, driving the price up, erasing our expectation of a change.

The stock market is just one example of a general phenomenon. There should be no reversion to the mean when it comes to beliefs. It wouldn't make sense to say something like "Today, I believe that Republicans have a 60 percent chance of winning the House in the next election, but come Election Day, I expect my belief to be lower." That doesn't make sense because your belief is just your belief about the future—nothing else. If you expect that your belief will be 55, rather than 60, percent on Election Day, then your belief should be 55 percent today.

Wrapping Up

In part 2 we have learned how to quantify correlations and how to assess whether correlations found in data are likely to reflect real phenomena or just noise. We then turned to other challenges created by the presence of noise—over-comparing and under-reporting and reversion to the mean.

Importantly, our favorite equation told us that noise is not the only reason an estimate might not equal the estimand. We also have to worry about bias. For reasons that we started to learn about in chapter 3, bias is a particularly important concern when we are trying to learn about causal relationships—when we say correlation doesn't imply causation, what we mean is that the correlation between two features of the world may be a biased estimate of the causal relationship between them. In part 3, we will focus on causal relationships, first examining the sources of bias in more detail and then learning about strategies for estimating causal relationships in an unbiased way.

Key Words

- **Hawthorne effect:** The phenomenon whereby subjects change their behavior because they know they are being studied.
- **Demand effect:** A specific instance of a Hawthorne effect in which research subjects change their behavior to try to please the researcher.
- **Signal:** The systematic component of an outcome that is persistent across observations.
- **Noise:** Random components of an outcome that change from observation to observation.
- **Reversion to the mean:** The phenomenon whereby, if one observation of an outcome made up of signal and noise is particularly large (respectively, small) other observations will typically be smaller (respectively, larger).

Exercises

8.1   Early on in every baseball season, someone appears to be on pace to break the home-run record, but they almost never do. Let's think about why.

Suppose you hit a phenomenal number of home runs in the first twenty games of the season, and you're on pace to break the record.

(a) In the next twenty games, are you more likely to hit an above-average or below-average number of home runs? Why?

(b) In the next twenty games, are you likely to hit fewer home runs, the same number of home runs, or more home runs than you hit in the first twenty games? Why?

(c) A commentator notices that players on pace after the first twenty games almost never break the record. The commentator argues that this shows that players lose their nerve when they start thinking about setting the record. What data might you want to collect, and how might you want to analyze it in order to see if this interpretation is right?

8.2   Anthony once took a course from a famous econometrician who made the following argument: Paul's son John has a genius-level IQ. Therefore, because of mean reversion, Paul himself must have had a super-genius-level IQ.

(a) What's wrong with the econometrician's reasoning? If you had to guess, is Paul's IQ lower or higher than average? Is it lower or higher than John's?

(b) How would your answer change if we told you that the Paul in this example is Paul Samuelson, a Nobel Prize winner considered by many to be the foremost academic economist of the twentieth century?

8.3   At the time of this writing, the stock price of Zoom (a company specializing in online video conferencing, with which many of us became all too familiar in the year 2020) has just fallen by about 18 percent in response to Joe Biden winning the 2020 U.S. presidential election and the release of promising results on COVID-19 vaccines. Because of mean reversion, your friend argues that now would be a great time to buy Zoom stock.

(a) Explain to your friend, in layperson's terms, what's wrong with their reasoning.

(b) Without knowing any additional details except that Zoom stock recently fell, would you expect your friend to make money, lose money, or break even on this investment?

8.4   Psychologists argue that the extent to which someone can accurately assess their own ability in some domain depends on their ability in that domain. Perhaps people who lack ability in a particular area don't even know enough to know how deficient they really are. Named after the researchers who first developed this hypothesis, this phenomenon is often called the Dunning-Kruger effect.

The typical evidence offered in favor of the Dunning-Kruger hypothesis is shown in the figure below. Subjects were first asked to predict their own IQ, and they later took an IQ test. The figure shows a scatterplot of these two scores for each subject. The regression line is shown in gray, and the dashed, 45-degree line is in black. People with low IQs (as measured by the test) tended to over-estimate their score, and people with high IQs (as measured by the test) were, on average, correct.

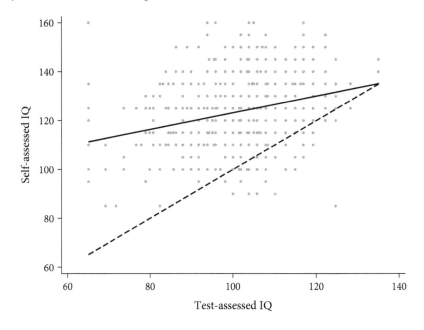

(a) Can you come up with another explanation for this empirical phenomenon that wouldn't necessarily imply that high-IQ people are better at assessing their own IQs? You'll want to think about mean reversion, but that alone won't do the trick since the high-test-score people didn't under-estimate their IQ. Perhaps you'll also want to think about bias. Remember our favorite equation.

(b) To check your intuitions, simulate some data on your computer that generates a similar result even though the assessments of high-ability people are just as noisy as those of low-ability people. (Hint: It will help to remember that the test-assessed IQ is not a perfect measure of true intelligence.)

(c) Download "IQdata.csv" and the associated "README.txt," which describes the variables in this data set, at press.princeton.edu/thinking -clearly. These are the data used to produce the figure. (We obtained the data from a 2020 study by Gignac and Zajenkowski.) Let's think about how we can assess whether high-IQ people really are better at assessing their own IQs.

   i. First, compute the absolute value of the error for each subject (that is, how far off were their self-assessed IQs from their test-assessed IQs?).

   ii. Now, regress this absolute error on the test-assessed IQ and interpret the results.

(d) As you can see in the figure, people tend to over-estimate their own IQs.

   i. Estimate the average extent of this bias in this data.

    ii. Subtract this estimate of the average bias from everyone's self-assessed IQ to get a bias-corrected self-assessment.

    iii. Using this bias-corrected self-assessment, recompute the absolute value of the errors—that is, calculate how far off, on average, a person's bias-corrected self-assessment is from their test-assessed IQ.

    iv. Finally, regress this new measure of error on the test-assessed IQ and interpret the results.

(e) Provide your final assessment of the Dunning-Kruger hypothesis on the basis of this data. Are high-intelligence people better at assessing their own intelligence?

8.5   Find a recent example where an analyst failed to consider mean reversion when they should have. Specifically, look for evidence that is presented in favor of a particular theory or phenomenon that could also easily be explained by mean reversion. Your example might come from a newspaper article, an academic study, a policy memo, or a statement by a politician, business leader, or sports commentator. Summarize the claim being made by the analyst and the evidence that purportedly supports the claim. Explain why the data is equally consistent with mean reversion. As a bonus, think about ways that you could potentially adjudicate between the analyst's claim and mean reversion.

Readings and References

The *New Yorker* article on cosmic habituation is:

> Jonah Lehrer. 2010. "The Truth Wears Off: Is There Something Wrong with the Scientific Method?" *The New Yorker*. December 13.

The study we mentioned reanalyzing the evidence for the Hawthorne effect is

> Steven D. Levitt and John A. List. 2011. "Was There Really a Hawthorne Effect at the Hawthorne Plant?: An Analysis of the Original Illumination Experiments." *American Economic Journal: Applied Economics* 3(1): 224–238.

The source for Figure 8.1 is Galton's original paper on the subject

> Francis Galton. 1886. "Regression towards Mediocrity in Hereditary Stature." *Journal of the Anthropological Institute of Great Britain and Ireland* 15:246–263.

The study comparing real knee surgeries to sham surgeries is

> J. Bruce Moseley, Kimberly O'Malley, Nancy J. Petersen, Terri J. Menke, Baruch A. Brody, David H. Kuykendall, John C. Hollingsworth, Carol M. Ashton, and Nelda P. Wray. 2002. "A Controlled Trial of Arthroscopic Surgery for Osteoarthritis of the Knee." *New England Journal of Medicine* 347(2):81–88.

The article showing that, among asthma patients, the placebo effect appears to exist for subjective measures but not for objective measures is

> Michael E. Wechsler, John M. Kelley, Ingrid O. E. Boyd, Stefanie Dutile, Gautham Marigowda, Irving Kirsch, Elliot Israel, and Ted J. Kaptchuk. 2011. "Active Albuterol

or Placebo, Sham Acupuncture, or No Intervention in Asthma." *New England Journal of Medicine* 365(2):119–126.

Figure 8.4 is taken from

John P. A. Ioannidis, Evangelia E. Ntzani, Thomas A. Trikalinos, and Despina G. Contopoulos-Ioannidis. 2001. "Replication Validity of Genetic Association Tests." *Nature Genetics* 29:306–309.

The exercise on the Dunning-Kruger effect is inspired by

Gilles E. Gignac and Marcin Zajenkowski. 2020. "The Dunning-Kruger Effect Is (Mostly) a Statistical Artefact: Valid Approaches to Testing the Hypothesis with Individual Differences Data." *Intelligence* 80:101449.

PART III

Is the Relationship Causal?

CHAPTER 9

Why Correlation Doesn't Imply Causation

What You'll Learn

- Correlation does not necessarily imply causation.
- There are two key reasons why an observed correlation might be a biased estimate of a causal relationship: confounders and reverse causation.
- If we think clearly, we can sometimes sign this bias.
- There is an important distinction between confounders and mechanisms.

Introduction

As we discussed in chapters 2 and 3, information about correlations and information about causal relationships are useful for different purposes. Knowledge of correlations, on its own, can help us describe the world and forecast the presence of certain features of the world on the basis of the presence of other features of the world. Knowledge of causal relationships is particularly valuable for decision making because it can tell us how the actions we take will affect the world. Remember our definition of causation from chapter 3. A *causal effect* is a change in some feature of the world that would result from a change to some other feature of the world.

So when we say that some action has a causal effect on some outcome, we're asserting that the outcome would be different in a counterfactual world in which the action was different. Knowing the effects of our actions allows us to anticipate and weigh their costs and benefits.

From a pragmatic perspective, this distinction is why the maxim "Correlation doesn't imply causation" is so important. If we mistakenly take knowledge of a correlation as implying knowledge of a causal relationship, we might end up making big mistakes, taking actions because of a misguided belief about how those actions will affect outcomes we care about. In this chapter, we are going to learn to think clearly about the difference between correlation and causation, discuss the sources of bias that can make correlations unreliable estimates of causal effects, and start considering what that means for how we learn about causal effects.

To give you a sense of how important this topic is, let's talk through an example where high-stakes decisions are being made about how to deploy resources and where we can disentangle correlation from causation with some confidence. The example concerns the topic of charter schools in the United States.

Charter Schools

In his heart-rending movie *Waiting for Superman*, David Guggenheim tells the story of several young children from poor families. In each case, a child is enrolled in a substandard public school. And, in each case, the parents are working hard to get their child into a charter school (or, in some cases, a magnet school).

Charter schools are operated at public expense but independently of the public school system. Some charter schools are run by not-for-profit organizations and others by for-profit corporations. The idea behind the charter school movement is to encourage innovation and choice. Charter schools are free from some of the constraints (e.g., union contracts, legacy curricula) that public schools face. Hence, the argument goes, they can innovate in curriculum, teacher incentives, and the like in ways that regular public schools cannot. And, because they have to compete for students, they will be motivated to come up with new and potentially better approaches to education. Whether charter schools in fact succeed in improving educational outcomes is a matter of heated debate.

In many areas, there are more kids applying to attend charter schools than can be accommodated. By law, when a charter school is oversubscribed it must admit students by random lottery. Families apply to the school, and after that, luck determines which kids get the coveted spots. As the movie powerfully illustrates, the odds are stacked against the children. Some of the charter schools have hundreds of applicants for a couple dozen spots.

During the course of the movie we are told a slew of facts about the performance of the charter schools to which the students are seeking admission. Compared to public schools with socioeconomically similar populations of students, these charter schools have better test scores, higher graduation rates, less crime, and so on. Indeed, the charter schools featured in the movie perform much better than public schools with respect to virtually every measurable outcome.

As the movie ends, we discover that few of the students we've been following were admitted to the school of their choice. Instead, they will be enrolled in "failure factories" where, we are left to believe, in all likelihood, their potential will be wasted.

But is this the right inference? Does getting into a charter school really improve a child's educational outcomes? There is more at stake here than our feelings about the kids in the movie. Over the past several decades, charter schools have emerged as one of the dominant approaches to school reform in the United States. Expansion of charter schools as an alternative to traditional public schools has received bipartisan support—it was, for instance, pushed aggressively by both the Bush and Obama administrations. The share of public school students attending charter schools has risen from less than 1 percent in 1999 to more than 6 percent in 2021. But critics raise concerns about the possibility that this expansion has led to a decline in resources available to traditional public schools, perhaps harming the students enrolled in those schools. So we'd really like to know whether charter schools have a positive effect on academic outcomes for students.

Here's what we know. There is definitely a correlation between charter school attendance and academic performance. Within a city, on average, low-income students who go to charter schools have better educational outcomes than low-income students who go to traditional public schools.

As an example, consider the Preuss School, a charter school created by the University of California at San Diego. The Preuss School serves low-income middle and high

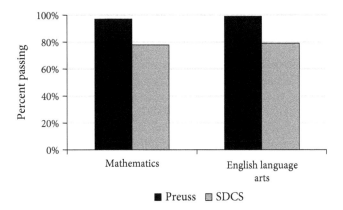

Figure 9.1. Standardized test scores at Preuss School and San Diego City Schools (SDCS).

school students from all over San Diego County. By all accounts, it is a remarkable school, sending almost 100 percent of its students, who typically come from families with no history of college attendance, on to higher education. The school has garnered praise from many sources, including *Newsweek* magazine, which named Preuss the "top transformative high school" in the country multiple times.

And, indeed, it is certainly the case that students at the Preuss School perform much better than their peers at the San Diego public schools. For instance, look at the data in figure 9.1, showing the difference in the percentage of students who pass standardized tests in math and English at Preuss versus the San Diego City Schools (SDCS).

Just like in the stories from *Waiting for Superman*, from these data, it sure looks like the Preuss School is having a huge impact on the academic performance of its students.

But before we jump to conclusions, let's think about this a little more clearly. These data show a positive correlation between going to Preuss and academic performance. But does the fact that students going to Preuss (or other charter schools) perform better academically than students at public schools imply that going to a charter school is *causing* them to perform better? That is, in the counterfactual world in which some other kids go to Preuss and these kids go to the public schools, would those other kids perform better academically and the current Preuss students perform worse? Does the correlation imply causation? That's what we need to know if we are going to figure out whether investing resources in charter schools is a good decision.

Of course, it could well be that charter schools are genuinely causing students to perform better, meaning that in the counterfactual world where the charter school students had attended regular public schools, they would have performed worse and their replacements from the public school would have performed better. But another possible explanation, as *Waiting for Superman* so eloquently illustrates, is that the students and families who choose charter schools are themselves different from the average public school student in important ways. That is, perhaps the explanation for the correlation isn't a better school, but better students. If that is the case, then, in the counterfactual world in which these better students had not gone to a charter school, can we be so sure that they wouldn't still have outperformed their peers?

Ask yourself, Under what circumstances are economically disadvantaged parents likely to sign up their child for the lottery to get into a charter school? Two circumstances occur to us. First, if the parents believe their child is particularly talented, they might be particularly motivated to get their child into a school with a good reputation. Second, if the parents themselves are particularly invested in their child's education, they might be more likely to do the work necessary to get that child into the lottery.

Natural talent and parental involvement are themselves pretty important determinants of student achievement. Suppose that the pool of students in the charter school lotteries (and, hence, at those schools) are, on average, more talented and come from families more interested in education than the population at large. Then, even if the charter schools themselves have no effect on the performance of their students, those students would nonetheless outperform the general population simply by virtue of their greater ability and more supportive family. Put differently, if all children went to the exact same school, the children who are currently at the charter schools would still be above average because they are more talented and have more dedicated parents.

Remember the question we care about: Can sending a child to a charter school be expected to improve the performance of that child relative to what they would have achieved at their local public school? The discussion above shows that we can't know the answer to this crucial question by comparing the performance of students currently in charter schools versus traditional public schools. We'd be comparing a group of particularly talented, ambitious kids from highly dedicated families to the general population. How would we know whether differences between these groups arose because of the effects of charter schools, because of underlying differences between groups, or both? In simpler terms, we'd be comparing apples to oranges.

To determine whether the charter schools are actually a cause of their students' excellent outcomes, we need to make a comparison that comes closer to capturing the counterfactual nature of causality. To do this, we need a way to compare apples to apples. The ideal question we'd like to answer is something like this: If everything else about two children were identical, would the child who went to the charter school do better than the child who went elsewhere? We obviously can't answer this question. But we can get closer by trying to answer something like this: If everything else about two groups of children was identical on average, would the kids who went to charter schools do better on average than kids who went to public schools?

To take a shot at this latter question, we have to move beyond just comparing charter school kids to all other public school kids. We do so by narrowing our focus to just the children who tried to get into charter schools. All of those children were promising enough or had families dedicated enough to apply to a charter school. But, as a result of the admissions lottery, some lucky students got into the charter school and others did not. Since the lottery was random, the pool of lottery winners and the pool of lottery losers should have the same characteristics, on average (that is, if we ran the lottery over and over again, the kids winning the lottery would be no more or less motivated or talented than those who lost). So we can learn a lot more about the actual effect of attending a charter school by comparing the academic performance of those who entered and won the admissions lottery to those who entered but lost the lottery. If the positive correlation between charter school attendance and academic performance is still there in this narrower comparison, we will feel much more secure in giving it a causal interpretation because now we're comparing apples to apples.

This comparison has been done for many charter schools. Let's start by looking at what happens when you make that comparison for the Preuss School. We don't have data on this comparison for the same standardized test as in figure 9.1, but we do for another important standardized test, shown in figure 9.2.

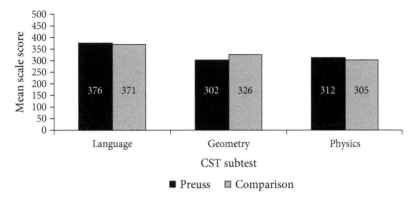

Figure 9.2. Comparing standardized test scores of kids who did and did not win the Preuss School admission lottery.

This comparison demonstrates the importance of comparing apples to apples. Yes, the students at the Preuss School tend to outperform the students in the San Diego City Schools as a whole. But when lottery-winning students are compared to lottery-losing students, the correlation disappears—there is no performance difference.

Similar findings emerge from studies of many other charter schools. To be sure, different studies find different things. Researchers in Boston find that kids admitted to charter schools run by the Knowledge is Power Program do better than kids who applied to but lost the lottery. But our sense is that the following, from another study of school choice programs in San Diego, is more typical of the literature:

> In the vast majority of cases, we found no evidence that winners and losers of a given lottery fared differently in these achievement tests one to three years after the admissions lottery was conducted. We interpret this to mean that winning a lottery neither helps nor hurts achievement growth.

Think about what this means. When we make an apples-to-apples comparison, the high-performing charter schools appear to have little to no effect on student performance. Most of the apparent effects of these schools come from the fact that the students who enter the charter school lotteries are already academically different from the average student. Those students would have done better than average anyway. Separating correlation from causation in this way may change your views about how we should spend education resources.

Thinking Clearly about Potential Outcomes

When can a correlation between two variables be plausibly interpreted as compelling evidence of a causal relationship? We just saw an example of how we might mistakenly think a correlation indicates causation and how it can really matter for decision making. But let's try to be a bit more systematic about why correlations aren't always evidence for causation, so we can think more clearly about when we do and don't have a credible estimate of a causal relationship.

Remember, we define causal relationships counterfactually. In chapter 3, we introduced the notion of potential outcomes, which helps us think more clearly about such counterfactuals.

Let's suppose we're trying to estimate the effect of going to a charter school on academic performance, as measured by standardized test scores. So the *outcome* of interest is standardized test scores, and the *treatment* of interest is attending the charter school.

Represent the outcome, standardized test scores, with Y. And represent the treatment, going to the charter school, with a binary variable T. If $T = 1$ for some individual, that means they attended the charter school. If $T = 0$ for some individual, that means they attended a public school. We sometimes say that a unit with $T = 1$ is *treated* and a unit with $T = 0$ is *untreated*, although it's often arbitrary which groups are labeled *treated* versus *untreated* (e.g., we could similarly talk about the effect of attending traditional public schools versus charter schools).

In a metaphysical sense, for each individual there is some standardized test score that they would have gotten had they gone to the charter school and some standardized test score that they would have gotten had they not gone to the charter school. However, we only ever get to observe one of these. Nonetheless, having notation for each of these potential outcomes helps us think clearly about counterfactuals:

$$Y_{1i} = \text{outcome for unit } i \text{ if } T = 1$$

$$Y_{0i} = \text{outcome for unit } i \text{ if } T = 0$$

Using this notation, the effect of going to the charter school on person i's test scores is

$$\text{Effect of Charter School on } i\text{'s Test Scores} = Y_{1i} - Y_{0i}.$$

We say that causality is about counterfactual comparisons because we can only observe, at most, one of the two quantities—Y_{1i} or Y_{0i}—for any individual at a particular point in time. This means that we can't directly measure the effect of going to the charter school on an individual.

Maybe we can instead hope to estimate the average effect of going to a charter school across a bunch of individuals in some population of interest. For whatever population we are interested in, let's define notation for the average test score *if everyone went to the charter school* and the average test score *if everyone went to the public school* as follows:

$$\overline{Y}_1 = \text{average outcome if all units had } T = 1$$

$$\overline{Y}_0 = \text{average outcome if all units had } T = 0$$

With this notation, we can now think about the *average treatment effect* (ATE):

$$\text{ATE} = \overline{Y}_1 - \overline{Y}_0$$

Of course, we can't directly observe this average effect any more than we can observe the effect of charter schools on an individual. We never see all units both treated *and* untreated. Indeed, at any given time, each unit is only one or the other. But we can try to estimate the ATE.

A first thing we might do to try to estimate the average treatment effect is simply look at the correlation—comparing the average test scores of students who go to the charter school (treated) to the average test scores of students who go to the public schools (untreated).

Start by thinking of our population as divided into two groups, those who went to charter schools ($\mathcal{T}$) and those who went to public schools ($\mathcal{U}$). Denote the average test scores in each of these groups by

$$\overline{Y}_{1\mathcal{T}} = \text{average outcome among units with } T = 1$$

$$\overline{Y}_{0\mathcal{U}} = \text{average outcome among units with } T = 0.$$

We will refer to the difference in the average test scores between these two groups as the *population difference in means*. (Remember that *mean* is usually just another word for *average*, and in the context of this book, the two terms are used interchangeably.) It is just

$$\text{Population Difference in Means } = \overline{Y}_{1\mathcal{T}} - \overline{Y}_{0\mathcal{U}}.$$

Of course, we might not observe the whole population; we might observe just a sample. For instance, perhaps we only observe the students from one particular charter school. So the difference in average test scores that we observe in our sample is equal to the difference in average test scores among students who go to charter and public schools in the whole population plus some noise. So, we have

$$\text{Sample Difference in Means } = \underbrace{\overline{Y}_{1\mathcal{T}} - \overline{Y}_{0\mathcal{U}}}_{\text{Population Difference in Means}} + \text{Noise,}$$

which is just a measure of the correlation between standardized test scores and attending a charter school in our sample.

Of course, we want to know the average *effect* of going to the charter school, not just the correlation. To start thinking about the difference between these, it helps to introduce two more concepts—the *average treatment effect on the treated* (ATT) and the *average treatment effect on the untreated* (ATU). The ATT is the average effect of going to the charter school among those students who in fact went to the charter school. That is,

$$\text{ATT} = \overline{Y}_{1\mathcal{T}} - \overline{Y}_{0\mathcal{T}}.$$

And the ATU is the average effect of going to the charter school among those students who in fact went to the public schools. That is,

$$\text{ATU} = \overline{Y}_{1\mathcal{U}} - \overline{Y}_{0\mathcal{U}}.$$

Notice two things. First, the ATE is just a weighted average of the ATT and the ATU, where the weights depend on how many kids are in each group.[1] Second, just like the ATE, the ATT and ATU are both fundamentally unobservable. We don't observe the test scores that students who go to the charter school would have made had they gone to the public schools ($\overline{Y}_{0\mathcal{T}}$). And we don't observe the test scores

---

[1] A weighted average is just an average where we put different weights on different items. For example, suppose 75 percent of the population is treated and 25 percent of the population is untreated; then the ATE is the weighted average of the ATT and the ATU with 75 percent of the weight on the ATT. That is,

$$\text{ATE} = \frac{75 \cdot \text{ATT} + 25 \cdot \text{ATU}}{75 + 25} = .75 \cdot \text{ATT} + .25 \cdot \text{ATU}$$

students who go to the public schools would have made had they gone to the charter school ($\overline{Y}_{1\mathcal{U}}$).

Okay, now that we have all that notation, we should be able to think clearly about the difference between correlation and causation. To start doing so, let's compare the difference in means that we in fact observe (which is our measure of the correlation) to the ATT—the effect of going to charter schools among students who went to charter schools. This will help us build some intuition that we will then be able to apply to thinking about the comparison of the difference in means to the ATU and, ultimately, the ATE.

We are going to want to get back to working with our favorite equation:

$$\text{Estimate} = \text{Estimand} + \text{Bias} + \text{Noise}$$

That is, we want to find a way to write

$$\text{Sample Difference in Means } = ATT + \text{Bias} + \text{Noise}.$$

How do we do this?

Let's start by remembering, from above, that

$$\text{Sample Difference in Means } = \underbrace{\overline{Y}_{1\mathcal{T}} - \overline{Y}_{0\mathcal{U}}}_{\text{Population Difference in Means}} + \text{Noise}.$$

Now, we are going to cleverly rewrite the population difference in means by adding and subtracting $\overline{Y}_{0\mathcal{T}}$ from it. We know that seems weird. But, trust us, it's going to help. And, for now, it should at least be clear that we aren't doing any harm since, by adding and subtracting the same term, we are really just adding zero. Anyway, when we do that, we get

$$\text{Sample Difference in Means } = \overbrace{\overline{Y}_{1\mathcal{T}} - \overline{Y}_{0\mathcal{T}}}^{\text{ATT}} + \overbrace{\overline{Y}_{0\mathcal{T}} - \overline{Y}_{0\mathcal{U}}}^{\text{Bias}_{\text{ATT}}} + \text{Noise},$$

where we've subscripted *Bias* with ATT to indicate that this is the bias we get when using the difference in means to estimate the ATT.

Our algebraic trick was actually pretty cool, right? By adding and subtracting the same term, we were able to write things in terms of our favorite equation. The sample difference in means (estimate) is equal to the ATT (estimand) plus a bias term plus noise!

But what exactly does that bias term say? If we are trying to estimate the effect of going to a charter school, our comparison of test scores among students who did and did not go to the charter school is biased if we expect that those two groups of students would have made different average scores on their standardized tests even in the counterfactual world where they all went to the public schools (i.e., $\overline{Y}_{0\mathcal{T}} - \overline{Y}_{0\mathcal{U}} \neq 0$). When this is the case, we say the two groups have *baseline differences*.

So far, we've seen how the difference in mean test scores between charter public school students might be a biased estimate of the true effect of charter school attendance on those students who attend charter schools (the ATT). We could do a similar analysis for the effect of charter school attendance on those students who attend public schools (the ATU):

$$\text{Sample Difference in Means} = \overbrace{\overline{Y}_{1\mathcal{U}} - \overline{Y}_{0\mathcal{U}}}^{\text{ATU}} + \overbrace{\overline{Y}_{1\mathcal{T}} - \overline{Y}_{1\mathcal{U}}}^{\text{Bias}_{\text{ATU}}} + \text{Noise}$$

Here we find a similar bias, but now the baseline differences we are worried about have to do with differential outcomes between the treated and untreated groups if both groups were to receive treatment (i.e., $\overline{Y}_{1\mathcal{T}} - \overline{Y}_{1\mathcal{U}} \neq 0$). Since the overall average treatment effect (ATE) is itself just a weighted average of the ATT and the ATU, the bias associated with using the difference in means to estimate the ATE comes from both of these kinds of baseline differences.

Think back to the difference in academic performance between students at the Preuss School (treated) and the students at the San Diego City Schools (untreated). We were concerned that the relationship might not be causal because, say, the students at Preuss were more academically talented, on average, than the students at the San Diego City Schools. If the Preuss students are in fact more academically talented, then there are baseline differences between the two groups of students—a difference in academic performance would exist between the treated and untreated students even if all students in both groups attended the same school (i.e., $\overline{Y}_{0\mathcal{T}} - \overline{Y}_{0\mathcal{U}} > 0$ and $\overline{Y}_{1\mathcal{T}} - \overline{Y}_{1\mathcal{U}} > 0$). Because this comparison is so clearly not apples-to-apples, we can't be certain that the difference in average performance between the two groups is evidence of an effect of the Preuss School. Even if the ATE was zero, we would still expect to find a positive difference in means. This is exactly what it means to say correlation doesn't imply causation.

The lottery was convincing evidence precisely because it randomized people into treated and untreated. Randomization guarantees that, on average, the two groups are the same with respect to potential outcomes. That is, if we ran the randomization over and over again, on average the two groups would have the same baseline outcomes. (Of course, for any one run of the randomization, there could still be non-causal differences in academic performance between the two groups, just because of sampling variation or other kinds of noise.) Hence, a difference in average outcomes between lottery winners and lottery losers is an unbiased estimate of the causal effect of the school.

When talking about causality, we often use language that evokes experiments, as we have here by discussing treatment. We do so because experiments provide a clear way to think about inferring causality from a correlation. If there is experimental randomization into treatment, then there are no systematic baseline differences between the treated and untreated groups.

Importantly, though, in many circumstances where we are interested in causality, we don't actually get to run an experiment. Instead, some people get the treatment and others do not, for reasons that we are not in charge of. In those circumstances, we have to be very careful about interpreting a correlation between outcome and treatment status as an estimate of the causal relationship. As we saw, the positive correlation between test scores (outcome) and going to the Preuss School (treatment) in the overall population was not in fact indicative of a causal relationship. The reason is because, out there in the world, social processes gave rise to baseline differences between the treated and untreated groups.

Sources of Bias

To take the proper care in interpreting correlations, we need to be able to think clearly about when there will be systematic baseline differences, because it is these baseline differences that give rise to bias. There are two main sources of such differences: *confounders* and *reverse causality*. Understanding these is a big step toward being able to think about when you can and cannot learn something credible about causality from a correlation.

Confounders

A *confounder* is a feature of the world that satisfies two conditions:

1. It has an effect on treatment status.
2. It has an effect on the outcome over and above the effect it has through its effect on treatment status.

Confounders create baseline differences and, thus, bias. Suppose some feature of the world makes people more likely to receive treatment. And suppose it also makes people more likely to have a particular outcome. Then, because of the confounder, there will be a correlation between that outcome and treatment, for reasons separate from any actual effect of the treatment. Hence, if there are such confounders (and we haven't done anything to account for them, which we will discuss in coming chapters), then it is a mistake to interpret a correlation between an outcome and a treatment as an unbiased estimate of the causal effect of the treatment.

To be a little more concrete, remember our concern that the correlation between going to the Preuss School and academic achievement was not convincing evidence of a causal relationship. That concern was about baseline differences that resulted from more academically talented kids being more likely to seek out (or have families that seek out) the Preuss School. Another way of expressing that same concern is that the underlying academic talent of a kid is a confounder. Academic talent has an effect on treatment status—kids who are more academically talented are more likely to be in the treatment group (i.e., go to Preuss). And academic talent has an effect on outcomes over and above the effect it has through its effect on treatment status—more academically gifted kids are going to do better on tests for reasons over and above the fact that they seek out better schools. Looking at the lottery winners and losers helped to tease out causality because it broke the link between talent (the confounder) and going to Preuss (the treatment).

Consider one further example. Many studies show a strong negative correlation between a country's economic productivity and whether it experiences civil war. There are reasons to think that there could be a causal relationship underlying that correlation—for instance, perhaps when the economy is doing better, people have better lives and, thus, are less likely to be willing to mobilize to fight. But before interpreting the correlation as causal, one needs to think about whether there are potential confounders. One confounder you might worry about has to do with politics. A democratic political system, by incentivizing the government to adopt better public policy, is likely to positively affect a country's economy. Moreover, by giving people a non-violent means to express various grievances, democracy may also directly reduce the risk of civil war. Hence, democracy is a potential confounder. And, so, we are not justified in interpreting the

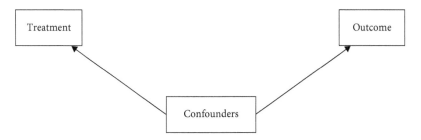

Figure 9.3. Confounders have an effect on treatment status and an independent effect on outcome.

correlation between economic prosperity and civil war risk as an unbiased estimate of the causal relationship.

So the first step in assessing whether a correlation is evidence of a causal relationship is to ask yourself whether there are any confounders. The schematic picture in figure 9.3 might help you remember to do so. The question the figure asks is, For any given treatment and outcome, are there any factors that you suspect belong in the confounders box? To fit in the box, two things must be true. First, the arrow from confounder to treatment has to make sense—that is, you must believe the confounder might exert an effect on the treatment. And second, the arrow from the confounder to outcome has to make sense—that is, you must believe the confounder might exert an effect on the outcome that doesn't run through the treatment. If you can fill in factors that satisfy both these conditions, then you have a reasonable concern about confounders and should be wary of giving a causal interpretation to the correlation between treatment status and outcome.

Reverse Causality

The second source of bias we need to worry about is reverse causality. There is *reverse causality* if the outcome affects treatment status. Reverse causality creates baseline differences because, if an outcome affects whether or not a unit receives treatment, there will be systematic differences in outcomes between the treated and untreated groups that are not due to the effect of the treatment.

Consider, again, our example of the negative correlation between the state of a country's economy and civil war. We've already seen that there could be confounders underlying this relationship. But there might also be reverse causality. For instance, during the course of fighting a civil war, infrastructure is destroyed, production is disrupted, and people are killed. All of these effects of civil war directly reduce economic prosperity. Hence, a negative correlation between a measure of economic prosperity and civil war might reflect the effect of war on the economy, rather than the effect of the economy on war. The potential for such reverse causality is yet another reason that a causal interpretation of this correlation is not justified.

The schematic picture in figure 9.4 is a way of helping to remind yourself to check for reverse causality before interpreting a correlation as causal. The question the figure asks is, For any given treatment and outcome, are there potential sources of reverse causality? That is, can we think of reasons that a causal arrow might run from the outcome to the treatment? If so, then you have a legitimate concern about reverse causality and should be wary of giving a causal interpretation to the correlation between treatment and outcome.

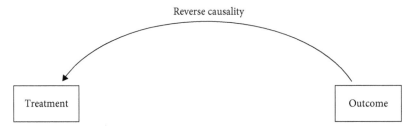

Figure 9.4. Reverse causality is when the outcome affects treatment status.

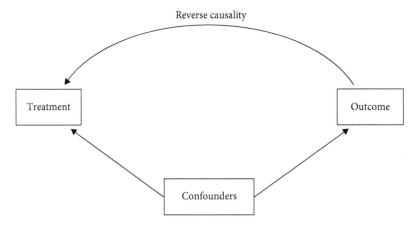

Figure 9.5. Confounders and reverse causality—two key sources of bias for estimating causal relationships.

In general, if someone shows you a correlation between an outcome of interest and a treatment of interest, without some additional information and investigation, you might have no way of knowing whether that correlation arose because the treatment affects the outcome, the outcome affects the treatment, confounders affect both the treatment and the outcome, or some combination of all of these possibilities.

Figure 9.5 provides an overall schematic for thinking about the two sources of bias we've discussed. Now that we've got the conceptual material summarized in figure 9.5 firmly in hand, let's get some practice thinking clearly about correlation versus causation, confounders, and reverse causality by talking through a couple examples in some detail.

The 10,000-Hour Rule, Revisited

You probably don't know the name Dan McGlaughlin, but he got quite a bit of press back in 2010. In April of that year, McGlaughlin quit his job as a photographer to pursue the dream of playing professional golf. He planned to practice golf for at least thirty hours every week for more than six years, until he had put in 10,000 hours of deliberate practice. He believed that by the end of those 10,000 hours he would be an expert golfer, ready to qualify for the PGA Tour. It hasn't quite worked out as McGlaughlin planned. He didn't make the PGA Tour but did open what appears to be a pretty cool artisanal soda company.

McGlaughlin's quixotic plan should sound familiar. He took Malcolm Gladwell's 10,000-hour rule, which we discussed back in chapter 4, to its (il)logical extreme. Talent, the argument goes, is secondary; great success is all about putting in those 10,000 hours. So any of us can achieve virtually anything, even a career in professional sports, if we just commit ourselves to 10,000 hours of really serious practice.

As we've already discussed, Gladwell's evidence for the 10,000-hour rule—even just as a statement about a correlation—is dubious because of lack of variation. But McGlaughlin did not hang his hat entirely on this evidence. He was also inspired by research done by the psychologist K. Anders Ericsson of Florida State University.

Ericsson argues that the key to super-high performance at anything is deliberate practice. Once a certain level of expertise has been achieved at some task, he claims, people's performance tends to plateau even if they keep gaining experience or general practice. The only way to continue improving at that point is through deliberate practice—working on exercises specifically targeted to particular aspects of performance. The more deliberate the practice is, the better the performance will be. What distinguishes true masters of an activity from good, but not great, experts, is the amount of time devoted to deliberate practice.

The 10,000-hour idea derives from a seminal study of expert musicians by Ericsson and collaborators. Unlike Gladwell, Ericsson does have variation. He studied violin students at an elite music school in Berlin. All of the students in the study were expert violinists. But they could nonetheless be distinguished in terms of quality. Ericsson asked the faculty to identify three groups—the very best violinists who were likely to go on to careers as soloists or in major orchestras, good violinists who were less likely to have successful performance careers, and the weakest group of violinists, who would likely become teachers. (We are trying not to take offense.)

The violinists were interviewed about their history of practice—age at which they started, hours per week, the type of activities they engaged in during practice, level of concentration, and so on. They were also asked to keep diaries recording their practice habits. Armed with this information, the researchers were able to compare the practice behaviors of the different groups of violinists. The finding: The best violinists had practiced at least 10,000 hours by the time they were eighteen, while the less accomplished violinists in the second group had only practiced about 7,500 hours, and the future teachers in the third group had practiced only about 5,000 hours. Moreover, the best violinists were distinguished by spending a greater share of their practice time deliberately. For example, they spent more time on difficult tasks designed to improve performance rather than simply playing enjoyable pieces that they had already mastered. Similar studies report analogous findings for chess players, athletes, and others. So the data show a positive correlation between deliberate practice and high performance.

Given this evidence, it looks like both the 10,000-hour rule and the focus on deliberate practice might not be so far-fetched. The highest-performing experts, in an array of fields, don't seem to be distinguished by measurable physical characteristics. The key appears to be that the best performers are those who practice the longest number of hours and in the most focused way. So maybe practicing deliberately for 10,000 hours really can make you world-class. Maybe Dan McGlaughlin had a pretty good shot at becoming the next Tiger Woods.

But before you stop reading to go become a professional golfer, let's think a bit more. Ericsson didn't make Gladwell's mistake. He had variation and so established a correlation between deliberate practice and achievement. But that doesn't mean the correlation reflects a causal effect. To reach that conclusion, we need to think about confounders and reverse causality.

Here's one possible concern. Suppose innate natural talent really is important. Imagine two kids, both of whom love to play the violin. One kid is more innately talented than the other. They both practice hard, putting in many hours. The hard work pays off and both progress rapidly. But over time the talent differential starts to manifest itself. The more talented kid masters difficult pieces of music more quickly and with greater precision. She receives more accolades and performance opportunities than the less talented kid.

Time progresses and the two kids become teenagers. New opportunities and distractions—dating, sports—arise. Each teen has to decide how much time and energy to continue to devote to violin practice. The more talented of the two teens finds that every time she devotes a day to violin, she masters new skills and repertoire. This progress and achievement is inspiring. It creates a positive feedback loop whereby practice leads to success, which inspires further practice and greater focus. So she continues to devote herself to deliberate violin practice, achieving those magic 10,000 hours by the time she is eighteen.

The less talented of the two teens also progresses each time he devotes a day to the violin, but he does so more slowly and with less proficiency. A piece that takes the more talented teen a week to master might take him a month. Even then, he plays it with less technical accuracy and musicality. His achievements are slower to come and met with fewer accolades. This lack of progress is frustrating. Met with less positive feedback, he finds practicing less rewarding. As a result, he still loves and continues to work hard at violin, but as new opportunities come up, he is more likely to take a few hours or a day off of violin practice to pursue them. And even while practicing, perhaps he is less focused because he has other things to think about. By the time he is eighteen, he's put in only three-quarters as much practice time as his more talented friend, and less of it is deliberate.

Two young people like those we've just described could easily have ended up music school classmates in Ericsson's study. The more talented of the two would have been identified by the faculty as one of the best violinists, while the less talented would have been identified as good but not great. Comparing them, Ericsson would have found, as he did, that the stronger of the two violinists put in 10,000 hours of deliberate practice, while the weaker put in only about 7,500 hours of less deliberate practice.

From this comparison, Ericsson concludes that practice caused the difference in their success. But as we've seen, this causal interpretation of the correlation is not warranted. As highlighted in figure 9.6, innate talent could well be a confounder—affecting the amount of deliberate practice (treatment) and having a direct effect on performance (outcome) over and above its effect through practice. Differences in talent cause baseline differences in achievement.

Of course, in the story we told, it's not as if practice has no effect. Success is surely influenced by talent, practice, and the combination of the two (the most innately gifted person in the world could not become a great violinist without practice). But in our hypothetical example, the more talented student would likely still be a better violinist than her classmate even if she had only practiced for 7,500 hours, and the less talented student would still be worse than his classmate even if he had forced himself to practice for 10,000 hours.

The extent to which the correlation reflects a causal relationship versus the bias from a talent differential is important here. To see why, think back to Dan McGlaughlin.

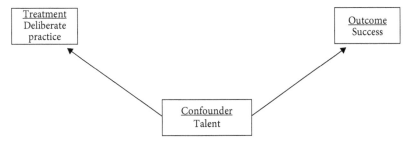

Figure 9.6. Is the correlation between deliberate practice and performance an unbiased estimate of the causal relationship?

Before quitting his job, McGlaughlin hadn't shown any of the signs of a world-class golfer. That fact might help explain why he hadn't previously put in thousands of hours of deliberate practice. If a significant portion of the correlation between practice and success is due to both of them being affected by innate talent rather than being the causal effect of practice, then McGlaughlin's efforts were unlikely to yield the desired outcome. Profoundly talented people practice a lot and have great success. That doesn't mean that a person who lacks profound talent but forces himself to practice a lot will find that same success. And so, perhaps, he should have anticipated that his journey would end as it did, in an artisanal soda company rather than a PGA Tour card. (For what it is worth, Ethan thinks running an artisanal soda company sounds *way* more fun than playing professional golf. Anthony disagrees.)

Diet Soda

Speaking of fizzy beverages, at the time of this writing, there is a near consensus among nutrition experts that diet soda is bad for you. Studies by experts in respected scientific journals have linked diet soda consumption to a range of health problems including obesity, diabetes, and heart attacks.

Curiously, despite all of the purportedly hard evidence on the dangers of diet soda, scientists don't yet have a compelling explanation (aside from the adverse dental consequences of diet soda—acid is bad for your teeth). They have been racking their brains to explain why beverages with virtually no calories are somehow making people overweight.

Several theories have been put forward. One explanation is that diet soda has *chemicals*, which might be bad for us. Of course, everything we consume has chemicals, so this isn't much of an explanation, and it just kicks the can of soda one more step down the road. Another explanation is that diet soda confuses your body and makes it somehow want more calories. After consuming diet soda, the story might go, your brain expects you to receive some calories from this sweet beverage, and when it doesn't, it urges you to raid your pantry for cookies and chips. In this way, your brain is like a child who is told they're about to get some candy only to have it revoked at the last minute. A third explanation is that diet soda (and presumably anything sweet) desensitizes your taste buds, meaning that you need to eat more and more sugary foods to get your fix.

We aren't nutritionists, but none of these explanations sounds overwhelmingly compelling to our untrained ears. Indeed, we could have imagined similarly convincing stories for why the effect should go in the opposite direction. Diet soda might allow someone with a sweet tooth to enjoy a refreshing treat without consuming extra calories. And diet soda might even trick your brain into thinking you've ingested calories and therefore speed up metabolism, which could be good for health and weight management. As we say, we're not experts, but it seems at least as plausible that diet soda is good for health, especially as a substitute for sugary beverages. So why have experts so strongly agreed that diet soda is bad for your health?

We have scoured the studies, and the extent of the evidence seems to be the following. There is a negative correlation between drinking diet soda and health outcomes. People who drink diet soda are more likely to be obese, have diabetes, and suffer from a range of other health problems than are people who do not drink any kind of sweet beverages.

Before agreeing with the nutritionists that this correlation reflects a genuine causal effect of diet soda on health, we should think about whether there are confounders or reverse causality.

What if, for example, snacking makes people more likely to both drink soda (because the soda goes well with the snacks) and, for reasons unrelated to soda, more likely to be obese? Then snacking would be a confounder. Or perhaps it's reverse causality—what if obesity or diabetes makes people more likely to drink diet soda? Presumably, if you like soda and become diabetic, you'll switch to diet soda. Similarly, we ourselves could imagine switching from diet soda to sugary beverages if only we were healthier. Clearly, confounders and reverse causality are serious concerns, and we should not treat the correlation between diet soda and health outcomes as a credible estimate of the causal effect.

How Different Are Confounders and Reverse Causality?

While we are thinking about confounders and reverse causality, it is worth pausing to reflect on how they relate to one another. Often a problem that appears to be about reverse causality can also be thought of in terms of confounders, where the relevant confounder is simply the anticipated outcome.

To see what we mean, think back again to our example of the negative correlation between the economy and civil war risk. We've seen that there are both confounders and reverse causality that invalidate a causal interpretation of this correlation. Consider one more problem. Suppose that, for a variety of reasons (e.g., lack of democracy, ethnic divisions, nearby civil wars), people believe some country is at high risk for a civil war. This risk of civil war might deter investment in the country, lead to capital flight, cause a brain drain, and so on. In this way, anticipation of a future civil war can cause the country to have a weaker economy. You could think of this as a case of reverse causality: civil war risk causes economic weakness. But it may be more clarifying to think of it as a case of confounding, where the confounders are whatever factors lead people to believe the country is at high risk of civil war. Those factors cause economic weakness by deterring investment and causing brain drain. And, presumably, they lead people to believe the country is at high risk of civil war precisely because they exert an independent effect on civil war occurring.

Let's consider another example—campaign spending.

Campaign Spending

Political candidates spend huge amounts of time raising money for their campaigns. Members of Congress, for example, often spend several hours per day in a call center phoning wealthy constituents and asking them to help fund their next reelection effort. (It turns out that being in Congress isn't a particularly glamorous job.)

Of course, politicians do this because they believe that campaign dollars are essential for their electoral prospects. And campaign consultants constantly advise candidates about how much they should be spending on television ads, digital ads, direct mail, and personal voter outreach. Electoral campaigns are clearly a big business predicated on the notion that candidates can improve their chances of success by raising and spending more money.

Given the scale of campaign spending, political scientists have devoted a lot of time and effort to estimating the returns on these efforts. Can spending on advertising really influence election results? And are those effects big enough to justify the millions of dollars donated to finance campaigns and the thousands upon thousands of hours spent raising those dollars?

One of the earliest and most influential studies of campaign spending was conducted by Gary Jacobson in 1978. Jacobson concludes that campaign spending seems to significantly help challengers' electoral prospects but has little benefit for incumbents. Indeed, campaign spending by incumbents might even be counterproductive, hurting their electoral fortunes!

What is Jacobson's evidence for this claim that campaign spending helps challengers but not incumbents? Challenger spending is strongly positively correlated with challengers' vote shares. But incumbent spending is negatively correlated with incumbents' vote shares.

One explanation for these correlations, Jacobson speculates, is that incumbents typically raise and spend more money than challengers. Maybe some initial amount of spending at the levels that we typically see for challengers helps a candidate to obtain name recognition and persuade voters. But perhaps too much spending from an already well-known incumbent annoys and turns off potential supporters. On this account, incumbents are making systematic mistakes, both in spending their time raising money and in spending that money once they've raised it.

Of course, the comparisons underlying these correlations may not be apples-to-apples. We need to think about confounders and reverse causality.

One big concern along these lines has to do with electoral strength. Which kinds of challengers tend to be able to raise and spend lots of money? Presumably, popular challengers with a real shot at victory. It is those electorally strong challengers that donors are likely to be willing to invest in. But, of course, strong challengers are those who were expecting to do well in the election even before they raised the money—perhaps they are charismatic, well-known, or particularly talented. So it would be a mistake to interpret the positive correlation between challenger spending and electoral performance as purely causal. It, at least in part, reflects baseline differences in electoral strength between challengers who can and can't raise a lot of money.

The thing we want you to notice in this example is that you can think of the problem of electoral strength as one of reverse causality or as one of confounding. Thought of as reverse causality, you might describe it as follows: "When a challenger is going to do well, she can raise and spend more on her campaign." Thought of as a confounder, you might describe it as follows: "When a challenger has characteristics that make her competitive, this affects both her ability to raise and spend money and how well she does in the election." Both sentences describe the same concern, just framed slightly differently.

A similar argument holds for incumbents. In general, although they spend and raise a lot of money, most incumbents in U.S. elections are electorally pretty safe. The ones who really need to exert a lot of effort raising and spending money are those who are electorally vulnerable. So we might expect exactly the opposite relationship for incumbents as for challengers. Incumbents spend a lot of money not when they are strong but when they are weak. And, again, you can view this problem in terms of reverse causality—"Electorally weak incumbents spend more money"—or in terms of confounders—"Characteristics that weaken incumbents, making the race competitive, separately cause them to spend more money and lead to worse than average electoral outcomes."

Subsequent studies using randomized experiments and other clever approaches to try to tease out the causal relationship generally suggest that campaign spending does have positive effects for both challengers *and* incumbents, although the substantive size of those estimated effects is typically small. A campaign might have to spend hundreds of dollars to swing a single vote, which means that meaningfully influencing the outcome of a large election through campaign donations is typically unaffordable. For example, consider a gubernatorial or senatorial race in a large U.S. state. Even in a race thought to be very close, the outcome will likely be decided by hundreds of thousands of votes. This means that if donors wanted to influence the outcome of the election, they would have to spend tens of millions of dollars and hope that their spending does not trigger an offsetting response from supporters of the opponent. Because of this, even the very largest donors have likely swung very few elections.

As you can see, there isn't a ton at stake as to whether we think about such cases as reverse causality or as confounders. What really matters is that we interrogate correlations for possible baseline differences, whether from confounders or reverse causality, and if there are baseline differences, that we show proper caution before interpreting a correlation as implying causation.

Signing the Bias

When there are confounders or reverse causality, the correlation between treatment and outcome is not an unbiased estimate of the true causal relationship of interest (whether the ATE, ATT, ATU, or other causal quantities that we'll discuss in later chapters). But sometimes we can make some progress on learning about causality by asking whether the correlation over- or under-estimates the causal effect.

Let's think back to our favorite equation, this time written in terms of causal inference:

Observed Correlation (Estimate) = True Causal Effect (Estimand) + Bias + Noise

Suppose the observed correlation between administering some medical treatment and survival rates following a stroke is positive. But also suppose there are confounders that you have not accounted for, so there is bias in your estimate of the true causal effect. If you have reason to believe that the bias is positive, then the observed correlation is an *over-estimate* of the true causal effect of the treatment. This means that you can't be confident, on the basis of the observed positive correlation, that the treatment does anything at all. Even if the true causal effect is zero, you would observe a positive correlation on average due entirely to confounders creating positive bias.

But now suppose you have reason to believe that the bias is negative instead of positive. In this case, the observed correlation is an *under-estimate* of the true causal effect of the treatment. So, if you are confident that the observed correlation is positive, you should be even more confident that the true causal effect is positive. And this can be useful to know. For instance, suppose administering the treatment would be a good idea (given its various costs) even if the true effect was equal to the observed correlation. Then the fact that the observed correlation is an under-estimate of the true effect suggests that you should administer the treatment.

Note, of course, you could still end up being wrong because of noise. Even if you are under-*estimating* the true causal effect, on average, that doesn't mean that any one estimate is in fact lower than the true effect. It just means that your estimates will be lower than the true effect on average.

Because this kind of thinking about the sign of the bias in an estimate can sometimes be valuable, it is useful to spend a little time thinking conceptually about when confounders imply that an observed correlation over-estimates the true effect and when they imply that an observed correlation under-estimates the true effect.

Start with our discussion of the relationship between votes and the campaign spending of challengers, where we worried that electoral strength was a confounder. Does this confounder tend to make the correlation between votes and campaign spending an over- or under-estimate of the causal effect? It seems likely that electoral strength has a positive effect on both fundraising and votes for challengers. So some of the extra votes received by high-spending challengers are actually the result of their electoral strength rather than an effect of the spending. As such, we should expect the correlation between spending and votes to be an over-estimate of the true effect.

To see another example, let's return to our discussion of the positive correlation between attending a charter school and standardized test scores. There, we said, one possible confounder is that students who go to the trouble of applying to a charter school may on average be more academically gifted than the general student population. And the fact that those students are more academically gifted or motivated may have a direct effect on their test scores.

If this story is right, does this confounder tend to make the correlation between charter school attendance and standardized test scores an over- or under-estimate of the true effect? Let's think about it. Being academically gifted has a positive effect on the likelihood a student goes to a charter school. And it also has a positive effect on test scores. That means part of the observed positive relationship between going to a charter school and test scores is the result of differential academic talent. Hence, this confounder is pushing the observed correlation to be an *over-estimate* of the true effect. That is, the bias in our favorite equation is positive.

It is straightforward that the same would be true if we had a confounder that negatively affected both attending a charter school and test scores. Indeed, this is simply the same case but with relabeling. If we think of the confounder as "lack of academic talent" instead of "academic talent," then that confounder has a negative effect on the treatment and outcome but still, obviously, leads the observed correlation to be an over-estimate of the true effect. Thus, as illustrated in figure 9.7, if you have a confounder that has the same sign effect on both treatment and outcome (whether negative or positive), then failing to account for this confounder will create positive bias. In such circumstances, the observed correlation will tend to be larger than the true effect.

Now let's think about a confounder that has differently signed effects on treatment and outcome. For instance, suppose students from poor neighborhoods are more motivated to apply to charter schools (perhaps because their local public schools are underfunded), but are also expected to do worse academically because of challenges in their living environment. This, again, is a confounder—it exerts an effect on both

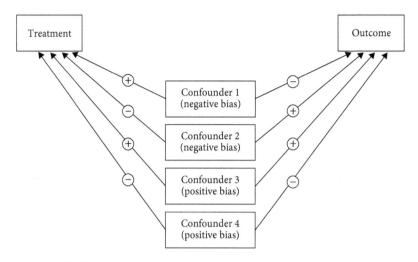

Figure 9.7. Signing the bias from a confounder.

the treatment (whether or not a student attends a charter school) and the outcome (performance on standardized tests). But unlike the case of academic talent (which positively affects the treatment and the potential outcomes), this confounder will create negative bias. Hence, the observed correlation between charter school attendance and standardized test scores is an under-estimate, rather than an over-estimate, of the true effect.

Why is this the case? In our new story, living in a poor neighborhood has a positive effect on the likelihood a student goes to a charter school. And it has a negative effect on test scores. That means the observed correlation between going to a charter school and test scores reflects the fact that the kids at charter schools over-represent poor neighborhoods, relative to the full population. This fact tends to lower test scores for charter school students for reasons having nothing to do with the effect of the charter school. If charter schools and public schools had the same proportion of kids from wealthier and poorer neighborhoods, the positive correlation between charter school attendance and test scores would be even more positive. Hence, this confounder is pushing the observed correlation to be an *under-estimate* of the true effect.

It is again straightforward that the same would be true if we had a confounder that negatively affected the likelihood of attending a charter school and positively affected the outcome. Thus, as illustrated in figure 9.7, if you have a confounder that has one sign effect on treatment and the opposite sign effect on outcome, this confounder creates negative bias. In such circumstances, the observed correlation will tend to be smaller than the true effect.

Signing the bias is even easier in the case of reverse causality. The outcome is, by definition, positively related to itself. So, if the outcome also has a positive effect on the treatment, the bias is positive. This means the observed correlation is an over-estimate of the true causal effect. And if the outcome has a negative effect on the treatment, the bias is negative, so the observed correlation is an under-estimate.

In addition to simply signing the bias, if we had a lot more information, we might be able to say something about the magnitude of the bias. Under some assumptions, the bias induced by a confounder is simply the effect of the confounder on the outcome multiplied by a measure of the correlation between the confounder and the treatment (measured by the coefficient you would get from regressing the confounder on the treatment).

As we'll see in chapter 10, if we have data on this confounder, we can try to remove this bias by controlling. But if we don't have that data, one could still make some guesses about the extent to which the confounder affects the outcome and is correlated with the treatment in order to gauge the extent of the bias.

The discussion above illustrates that we can learn something about causal effects even from biased estimates. It's not as if we have to throw away all our analyses just because there might be confounders, and if we have good guesses about the direction and magnitude of the biases, then we might still be able to learn a lot. But often, it's difficult to know how much an observed correlation is the result of bias, which is why simple correlations are not our preferred approach for learning about causal relationships. Less naive and more informative approaches to causal inference are the focus of the subsequent chapters.

A related approach to learning about causal effects from potentially biased correlations is to work in reverse. Instead of inferring how big an effect is by making guesses about the magnitude of the bias, we can start with the assumption that the true effect is zero and then ask how big the bias would have to be to explain an observed correlation. If the extent of that bias is implausibly large, then we can conclude that the effect probably is not zero. This kind of analysis is often referred to as *sensitivity analysis*. We won't discuss the details in this book, but as a general rule of thumb, it's good to think about sources of bias, their likely signs, their likely magnitudes, and what that implies for the effect you are trying to estimate.

With an understanding of different sources of bias and their likely signs, you can more deeply understand why correlation is not necessarily evidence of a causal relationship. The true effect could be zero, but the observed correlation could have emerged because of confounding or reverse causation. Similarly, as we discussed in chapter 3, causation need not imply correlation. Even if some treatment has a large, positive effect, confounding or reverse causality could create a large, negative bias. This could lead to an observed correlation that is small, zero, or even negative (as in the case of campaign spending and votes for incumbents), despite the positive treatment effect. So, not only does correlation not necessarily imply causation. Causation does not necessarily imply correlation.

With all of this in mind, let's think through a more extended example.

Contraception and HIV

One of the greatest public health scourges of our time is the spread of HIV and AIDS in Africa. Researchers have worked hard to determine why these diseases are spreading so quickly and to try to stem the tide. One hypothesis that has received attention from scholars and public health officials alike is that the use of hormonal contraception by women may increase the risk of HIV transmission by inducing changes in the immune system or body tissue.

In a 2012 study in *The Lancet Infectious Diseases*, researchers presented evidence supporting this hypothesis. The researchers analyzed data on more than 3,500 couples in which one partner was infected with HIV and the other was not. They had data on a variety of self-reported behaviors—for example, condom use, other sexual partners—and on whether the woman received hormonal contraception from the clinic that was conducting the study. The data also reported whether the non-infected partner

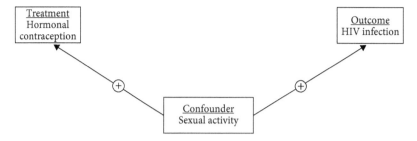

Figure 9.8. Underlying level of sexual activity tends to make the correlation between hormonal contraception use and HIV transmission an over-estimate of the true causal relationship.

contracted HIV over the course of a year or two. Finally, for those partners who did contract HIV, genetic screening provided information on whether it was transmitted partner to partner or from some third source.

There were two big findings. First, HIV-negative women who used hormonal contraception were twice as likely to acquire HIV from their infected male partners as were HIV-negative women who did not use hormonal contraception. Second, HIV-infected women who used hormonal contraception were twice as likely to transmit HIV to their HIV-negative male partners as were HIV-infected women who did not use hormonal contraception. These results held true controlling for self-reported condom use. (We'll talk more about what *controlling* means in the next chapter.) From these findings, the authors, the *New York Times*, National Public Radio, and many other sources reported that hormonal contraception likely increases the risk of HIV transmission.

This study was a major improvement over existing studies on this critically important issue. But it was a long way from comparing apples to apples. What might be going wrong?

The biggest worry is the possibility of confounders—women who take hormonal contraception are different from women who don't in lots of unmeasured ways, some of which may also be relevant for HIV transmission risk. If this is the case, then the observed correlation between hormonal contraception use and HIV transmission may be a biased estimate of the true causal relationship.

One concern is that women who intend to be more sexually active might also be more likely to use hormonal contraception. The researchers who authored the *Lancet* study were not able to randomly assign some women to take hormonal contraception and other women not to. Women received hormonal contraception if they wanted it. Sexual activity is a risk factor for HIV transmission. So, independent of anything else, more sexually active women are at greater risk of HIV transmission. If the women who are taking hormonal contraception are systematically engaging in more sexual activity, they will have higher transmission rates, even if the contraceptives themselves are playing no direct biological role.

In which direction would this confounder bias the estimates? As highlighted in figure 9.8, the thought is that sexual activity increases the use of hormonal contraception and also increases HIV transmission for reasons unrelated to contraception. So the bias is positive. As such, this confounder tends to make the observed correlation an over-estimate of the true causal relationship between hormonal contraception and HIV transmission.

The *Lancet* authors are aware of these types of concerns and make some attempts to address them. In particular women were asked about past sexual behavior and condom

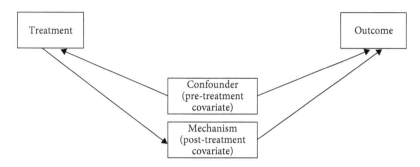

Figure 9.9. The distinction between confounders and mechanisms.

use. But self-reported behavior is notoriously unreliable, especially for sensitive topics like sexual activity and condom use.

Mechanisms versus Confounders

It is easy to get a little confused about what is and what is not a confounder. One particularly common error is to mistake the mechanisms by which a treatment affects an outcome for confounders. A *mechanism* (sometimes also called a *mediator*) is some feature of the world that the treatment affects, which then, in turn, affects the outcome. So a mechanism, rather than being a confounder, is part of the way that the treatment has its effect on the outcome.

For instance, one way that a charter school might cause students to get better test scores than they would if they went to their local public school is by providing more advanced placement (AP) classes that better prepare students for tests. When looking at a correlation that says charter school students perform better than public school students on standardized tests, it is tempting to say, "Yeah, but that is confounded by the fact that those charter school students had access to more advanced placement classes." But this isn't right.

Remember, a confounder is not simply a feature of the world that is correlated with treatment and outcome (which, in this story, AP classes are). It is a feature of the world that *affects* both treatment and outcome. But, in our story, access to AP classes doesn't affect whether a student goes to a charter school (treatment). Rather, it is affected by the student going to a charter school and then, in turn, affects the student's performance on standardized tests. Thus, access to AP classes is not a confounder; it is one of the mechanisms by which charter schools improve test scores. We sometimes describe confounders as *pre-treatment covariates*—that is, variables that were correlated with treatment and outcome before the treatment occurred—and describe mechanisms as *post-treatment covariates*—that is, variables that become correlated with treatment and outcome after treatment occurs. Figure 9.9 illustrates the distinction (note the direction of the arrows).

As we say, it is easy to get confused about these issues. So, let's talk through a couple examples.

Suppose that a medical study of middle-aged men finds that those who take statins are less likely to die of heart attacks. You note that those men who take statins are on average wealthier and have lower cholesterol. Which of these is a confounder and which might be a mechanism? Think about it for a moment before we tell you the answer.

Let's start with wealth. Remember, when assessing whether some feature of the world is a potential confounder, you need to ask whether it could affect both treatment and outcome. So we ask two questions:

1. Could a man's wealth affect whether he takes statins? Surely the answer is yes. Wealthier men are, presumably, better able to afford medication and also probably more likely to see a doctor who would prescribe that medication to them.
2. Could a man's wealth affect his risk of dying from heart disease? Again, the answer is yes. Wealthier men might be better able to afford heart-healthy lifestyles (e.g., joining a gym) and are more likely to get swift access to health care in the event of a heart attack.

Thus, we should worry that wealth is a confounder here.

What about lower cholesterol? Medical evidence suggests that higher cholesterol might affect the likelihood of having a heart attack (although it's hard to tease out the causal effect). But does cholesterol affect whether or not a person takes statins? Here, we might need a little more information—in particular, when exactly the cholesterol levels were measured.

If cholesterol was measured before the person started taking statins, then it is a good candidate for a confounder. After all, people typically choose to take statins when they have high cholesterol. (Using your skills from the previous section on "signing the bias," does this confounder make you think the study under- or over-estimates the efficacy of statins?)

But if cholesterol levels were measured after the person started taking statins, then it is a mechanism. We suspect that one of the ways that statins might reduce the risk of heart disease is by lowering cholesterol. If this is true, and if we randomly assigned some people to take statins and others not to, we would expect the ones who took the statins to have lower cholesterol (and lower risk of heart disease). This difference in cholesterol levels isn't a problem for inferring the efficacy of statins; rather, it is a mechanism by which that efficacy is achieved.

Here's another example. Suppose we are interested in whether a good economy helps reduce the risk of civil war. We find that there is indeed a negative correlation between per capita income and the frequency with which a country experiences civil war. But we also note that democracy is positively correlated with per capita income and negatively correlated with civil war risk. Should we think of democracy as a confounder or a mechanism in this case?

This is a tricky one. You can certainly see how democracy might be a confounder. Having a democratic form of government might improve the quality of governance. And good governance might cause a country's economy to grow. Moreover, being a democracy might give people non-violent ways to resolve political disputes, thereby directly reducing the risk of civil war. In this story, democracy is a confounder, since it has a direct causal effect on both treatment (per capita income) and outcome (civil war).

But you can also see how democracy might be a mechanism. Perhaps as countries become richer, citizens become more informed, better educated, more able to take actions for their own benefit, and so on. In this way, having a higher per capita income might directly increase the probability that a country becomes a democracy. And then, for the reasons already stated, democracy might decrease the risk of civil war. In this story, rather than being a confounder, democracy is part of the mechanism by which higher per capita income reduces civil war risk.

As this example highlights, the distinction between a confounder and a mechanism is important, but not always cut-and-dry. For now, it is important to see the distinction at a conceptual level, even if in many real-world scenarios you are not always sure whether some factor is the one or the other. We will return to this theme in the next chapter, when we talk about the benefits and limitations of *controlling*.

Thinking Clearly about Bias and Noise

We'd like to pause to make sure you don't forget the lessons from part 2—about assessing whether a relationship exists—just because we've now turned our attention to thinking about causal questions. In this spirit, let's think about the questions you should ask yourself when someone shows you a correlation and interprets it as an estimate of some causal relationship.

First, are we actually observing a correlation? Recall from chapter 4 that people often think they have measured a correlation when they haven't because they didn't collect data with variation in one of the key variables. So, for instance, you need to make sure that they didn't just look at instances when the outcome of interest occurred or the purported treatment was always present. If they made this kind of mistake, you can't even know from the data presented whether the variables are correlated, let alone related causally.

Second, does the estimated correlation reflect a genuine relationship in the world? For example, suppose someone shows you that peanut butter consumption is correlated with appendicitis in a sample of 100 people—within that sample, people who ate more peanut butter were more likely to get appendicitis. You might ask yourself a series of questions. Is the correlation statistically distinguishable from the null hypothesis of no correlation? Why do they only have data on 100 people? Did they collect the data with the goal of measuring this particular correlation? Would they have told you about this finding if they had found no correlation? If you're worried about *p*-hacking or *p*-screening, then you might be skeptical that there's actually a correlation between peanut butter and appendicitis in the broader population, and you'd want to collect an independent sample of data to see if the correlation persists in that new sample. If it doesn't, you should worry that the true estimand (the correlation in the population) is zero and that they found a positive correlation in their 100-person sample because of noise.

Third, is this correlation convincing evidence of a causal relationship? You'd want to ask whether they're comparing apples to apples—are there confounders or reverse causation that biases the estimated correlation away from the true causal relationship? For example, if someone shows you that ice cream consumption is correlated with sunburns across days of the year, you'd probably believe that they've identified a genuine correlation. If they collected a new sample, they'd probably continue to find a strong correlation between ice cream and sunburns. But that doesn't mean the correlation constitutes evidence that ice cream causes sunburns. It might. Maybe eating ice cream inspires people to go outside. But a far more likely explanation is that sunshine increases both ice cream consumption (for reasons unrelated to sunburns) and sunburns (for reasons unrelated to ice cream).

To help us put all of this together, let's return to the special case of our favorite equation when we are doing causal inference:

$$\text{Observed Correlation (Estimate)} = \text{True Causal Effect (Estimand)} + \text{Bias} + \text{Noise}$$

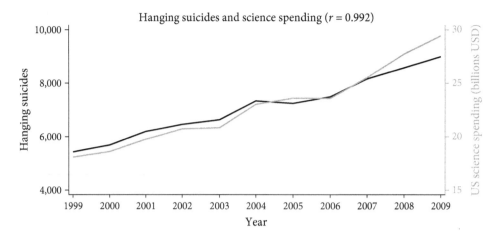

Figure 9.10. The strong correlation over time between suicides by hanging and government spending on science.

There are two kinds of ways an estimated correlation can deviate from the causal effect of interest. First, there could be noise. *Noise* here refers to idiosyncratic factors that affect our estimate. This could come from sampling variation in cases where you care about a population but you only have data on a sample of the whole. Or noise could come from other idiosyncratic variation in your variables of interest that are independent of any kind of causal connection (e.g., you might measure the variables with error). We might think that, since the noise is zero on average, we can just ignore it. But the fact that the noise is zero on average doesn't mean it is zero in any particular sample. And furthermore, in the presence of p-hacking and p-screening, even the average noise won't be zero. This was the focus of chapter 7. Second, in addition to noise, there could be bias—that is, confounders or reverse causation that makes the estimate different from the estimand on average, which is the focus of this chapter.

When confronted with a correlation that is presented as evidence of causation, it helps to consider all three factors—a true causal effect, bias, and noise—and try to think through the role each plays in explaining the correlation. Of course, it is often the case that an estimate reflects some combination of all three.

In some cases, it's tricky to separate bias and noise or even to think about them in a conceptually clear way. Let's see some examples of this. Tyler Vigen's book *Spurious Correlations* identifies pairs of trends over time that happen to correspond with one another, even though there's no good reason to think that those two trends are causally or logically connected in any way. The term *spurious correlation* is certainly apt, although we tend to avoid it because it doesn't clarify whether the person using the term thinks the correlation arose because of bias or noise.

Figure 9.10 illustrates one of Vigen's examples. It shows the correlation over time between suicides by hanging and government spending on science in the United States. Although it's not presented in a conventional way, this figure shows a positive correlation. If you think of each year as a unit of observation, it's clear that years with more hanging suicides than usual also have higher-than-average spending on science. In fact, the correlation coefficient (r) is .992, essentially the strongest correlation one can find without making up the data.

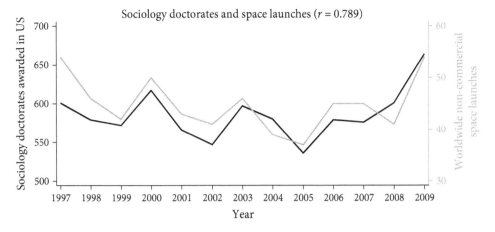

Figure 9.11. The quirky correlation over time between sociology doctorates and space launches.

What's going on here? Is this correlation attributable to a true causal effect of science spending on suicides, to bias, or to noise? It's theoretically possible, but very unlikely, that science spending has a large, positive effect on suicide by hanging (or vice versa). Noise certainly seems like a plausible explanation. If you look at enough variables, you're bound to find two of them that happen to correspond by chance, and we know that this is exactly what Vigen did. He checked for correlations over time for many variables and selectively reported the correlations that were significant.

But maybe it's also bias. What's an example of a confounder here? Could there be a variable that affects both hanging suicides and also science spending? One potential confounder is population. Over this period (1999–2009), the U.S. population grew steadily from about 279 million to 307 million. And population growth could plausibly increase both suicides and science spending.

To explore whether bias or noise is the more important explanation for the observed correlation, it might help to think about whether you expect this correlation to also hold for years before 1999 and after 2009. If you suspect that this correlation would likely hold more generally outside this sample of data, then it can't just be noise. Alternatively, if you think that this correlation is just a fluke, unlikely to hold outside the short period for which Vigen collected data, then it's just noise, due to neither a causal relationship nor bias.

Let's take a look at another couple examples. Figure 9.11 shows the correlation over time between sociology doctorates awarded in the United States and worldwide non-commercial space launches. Again, there's a strong correlation. Furthermore, it's not so easy to simply attribute the result to population growth (or something else changing over time) because the correlation is not driven by the two variables generally increasing over time. On average, space launches and sociology doctorates aren't increasing or decreasing, but the years with more space launches also tend to be years with more sociology doctorates.

We're pretty comfortable chalking this one up to noise. There's idiosyncratic variation from year to year in space launches and sociology doctorates, and they happened to line up during this period. But we suspect that if we looked at the next thirteen years of data, the correlation would be close to zero.

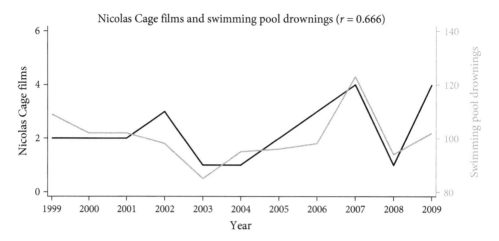

Figure 9.12. The metaphysically challenging correlation between Nicolas Cage movies and swimming pool drownings.

Finally, figure 9.12 shows the correlation over time between the number of movies in which Nicolas Cage starred and swimming pool drownings. This one feels like another straightforward case of noise. There's surely no causal connection, and there's also probably no compelling confounder. And, as with sociology and space launches, we're willing to bet that this correlation won't continue to hold in future years.

However, the Cage-drowning correlation poses a different conceptual conundrum. Suppose that this analysis included all of the years during which Nicolas Cage was acting and all of the years during which people had swimming pools (this is obviously not the case, but just imagine with us). If Nicolas Cage no longer made movies and people no longer had swimming pools, we couldn't assess the correlation between these two variables in some future period. So how could we think about whether this correlation was the result of noise? Furthermore, what would it even mean to say that this correlation was the result of noise if we had all the data there was to have on Nicolas Cage movies and swimming pool drownings? If you have observed the entire population (here, of Nicholas Cage movies), there is no sampling variation.

One way to resolve this puzzle is to make the metaphysical leap we discussed back in chapter 6 when we talked about statistical inference when we have data for the whole population. Sure, there's an observed correlation between Nicolas Cage movies and swimming pool drownings in this world, but that's just a small sample of a broader population of alternative, hypothetical worlds that might have been. Those worlds are just like our own, but all of the idiosyncratic, unrelated factors happen to play out differently. Do we have any reason to expect that Nicolas Cage movies would be correlated with swimming pool drownings in those worlds? If the answer is *no*, we might say that the correlation we observed is just noise, even though we have all the data there is to have about Nicolas Cage and swimming pool drownings.

Wrapping Up

We've seen that a correlation is often a biased estimate of a causal relationship because of confounders or reverse causality. This is what we mean when we say that correlation does not imply causation.

If we know what confounders to look out for, and if we can measure them, can we correct the bias and obtain a better estimate of the causal relationship? How to do so is the topic of chapter 10.

Key Terms

- **Causal effect:** The change in some feature of the world that would result from a change to some other feature of the world.
- **Average Treatment Effect (ATE):** The difference in average outcome comparing two counterfactual scenarios—one where everyone in the population is treated and one where everyone in the population is untreated.
- **Average Treatment Effect on the Treated (ATT):** The difference in average outcome comparing the scenario where everyone in the subgroup of people who in fact received treatment is treated and the counterfactual scenario where everyone in that subgroup is untreated.
- **Average Treatment Effect on the Untreated (ATU):** The difference in average outcome comparing the counterfactual scenario where everyone in the subgroup of people who did not receive treatment is treated and the scenario where everyone in that subgroup is untreated.
- **Difference in means:** The difference in average outcome comparing the subgroup of people who in fact received treatment to the subgroup of people who in fact did not receive treatment.
- **Baseline differences:** Differences in the average potential outcome between two groups (e.g., the treated and untreated groups), even when those two groups have the same treatment status.
- **Confounder:** A feature of the world that (1) has an effect on treatment status and (2) has an effect on the potential outcome over and above the effect it has through its effect on treatment status.
- **Reverse causality:** When the outcome affects treatment status.
- **Over-estimate:** When the bias is positive, so that the estimate is larger than the true effect in expectation.
- **Under-estimate:** When the bias is negative, so that the estimate is smaller than the true effect in expectation.
- **Mechanism (or mediator):** A feature of the world that the treatment affects, which then, in turn, affects the outcome.
- **Pre-treatment covariate:** A variable that is correlated with treatment and outcome before the treatment occurs.
- **Post-treatment covariate:** A variable that becomes correlated with treatment and outcome after treatment occurs.

Exercises

9.1   At the end of our discussion of violent and non-violent resistance in chapter 1 we asked you the following:

> Why might the fact that there are more government crack-downs following violent protests than non-violent protests *not* mean that switching from violence to non-violence will reduce the risk of crack-downs?

We promised that you would be able to give a compelling answer by the end of this chapter. So, please identify at least one reason why the fact that violent protests are more often met with a government crack-down than non-violent protests is not compelling evidence that the use of violent protest tactics causes government crack-downs.

9.2   Let's think about over-estimates and under-estimates in two of our examples.

(a) In our discussion of violin practice, we noted that a musician with greater talent might both practice more and play the instrument better for reasons having nothing to do with how much she practices. Does this suggest that the correlation between practice and playing quality is an over-estimate or an under-estimate of the true effect of practice on playing?

(b) In our discussion of campaign spending, we argued that incumbents are likely to spend heavily on their campaigns when they are electorally weak. Does this suggest that the observed lack of (or even negative) correlation between campaign spending and electoral performance of incumbents is an over-estimate or an under-estimate of the true effect of spending on votes?

9.3   Ethan was once at a meeting where he was briefed on the ways in which data analytics can improve universities' operations. The example the presenter was most excited about was from a data analytics team in a major research university's development (which is jargon for *fundraising*) department. The data analytics team had discovered the following correlation by analyzing years of data: alumni who donate to the university six years in a row are way more likely to be lifelong givers than are alumni who only donate five years in a row.

The presenter was excited because, in their view, this finding from the analytics team suggested a clear strategy to improve fundraising and alumni engagement. In particular, on the basis of this analysis, they had decided to make a major push to encourage alumni who had already given for five years in a row to give a sixth—the idea being that the evidence of a correlation between giving for six years and giving in the future suggested that giving in that sixth year had a big causal effect on future giving, so resources spent encouraging five-year givers to become six-year givers were being put to the best possible use.

Provide two arguments, using the clear thinking skills you acquired in this chapter, to explain why this might not be a good plan.

9.4   Shortly after Harvard psychologist Daniel Gilbert's book, *Stumbling on Happiness*, was released, he was on TV, where he informed Stephen Colbert that "marriage is one of the best investments you can make in happiness." That advice implicitly rests on a causal claim: marriage causes happiness.

Much recent research documents a positive correlation between marriage and happiness. But is the relationship causal?

(a) Provide an argument for why the correlation between marriage and happiness might be the result of reverse causation (happiness causing marriage, rather than the other way around).

(b) Identify two confounders that you think might make a causal interpretation of the correlation between marriage and happiness problematic. For each, explain why you believe the confounder might affect both treatment (being married) and outcome (happiness).

(c) Sign the bias for each of the confounders you identified. Having done so, explain whether each tends to make the observed correlation between marriage and happiness an over- or under-estimate of the true causal effect.

(d) A study by Anke Zimmermann and Richard Easterlin follows people from up to four years prior to their first marriage through several years after getting married. The basic finding is illustrated in the left-hand panel of the figure on this page, which shows the life satisfaction of people who got married during the study period relative to those who never got married during the study period. As we go from left to right, we see how the life satisfaction of a person changes over time as they first cohabitate with a partner, then get married, and continue that marriage for more than a year.

    i. Compare the life satisfaction of people who have been married for a while to that of people who are not married but are living with their partner. Do you find this evidence supportive of or contrary to Gilbert's advice?

    ii. Identify a confounder that this comparison suggests may have existed in the original correlation.

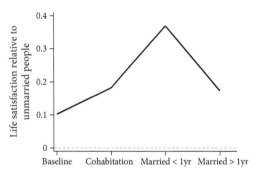 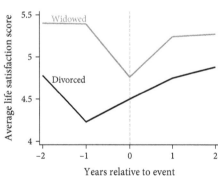

Life satisfaction and marriage.

(e) A study by Jonathan Gardner and Andrew Oswald also follows individuals over time but asks a different question. It considers what happens to people's happiness when marriages end. The study looks at two ways a marriage might end: divorce or death of a spouse. The results are summarized in the right-hand panel of the figure.

The horizontal axis shows years relative to an important event (divorce or widowhood) at time 0. The vertical axis shows life satisfaction. Life satisfaction is shown in black for those who became divorced and in gray for those who became widowed.

  i. Notice the initial difference in life satisfaction between those who became widowed and those who got divorced, even before the event occurred. Does this difference make you more or less confident in Gilbert's causal interpretation? Why?
  ii. Now consider the widows and widowers (gray line). How does their happiness change before, during, and after the year in which their spouses passed away? Does this make you more or less confident in Gilbert's causal interpretation? What does this comparison make you think might be going on in Gilbert's original correlation?

9.5   Download "HouseElectionsSpending2018.csv" and the associated "README.txt," which describes the variables in this data set, at press.princeton.edu/thinking-clearly.

  (a) Run a linear regression that finds the relationship between incumbent vote share and incumbent spending. (Note: This may require you to recode some of the variables in the data set or generate your own variables that better suit your goal.)

     i. Is the correlation positive or negative?
     ii. According to this data, do incumbents who spend more do better or worse?
     iii. Interpret the magnitude and direction of the correlation between incumbent spending and incumbent vote share.

  (b) Do the same as above for challengers.
  (c) Let's think about whether the regressions you've run constitute compelling evidence of the effect of campaign spending of vote shares.

     i. Identify three confounders you are worried about.
     ii. Do you have any variables in this data set that measure those confounders? If so, identify a variable that might plausibly measure a confounder that is in the data set.
     iii. Using linear regression, assess whether incumbent spending and challenger spending (the treatments) are in fact correlated with one of the potential confounders measured in the data set.

9.6   Find an example of a researcher, journalist, policy maker, or analyst who you believe has made an error by wrongly interpreting a correlation as credible evidence of a causal relationship. Your example should not be closely related to any example discussed in class or in the readings. Explain the evidence presented, and explain why you think this correlation is not persuasive evidence of the purported causal relationship. Discuss the likely direction of the bias. As a bonus exercise, continue to think about your example as you read through the next four chapters. Can you think of a better way to more credibly estimate the causal relationship of interest?

Readings and References

The study of the Preuss School is

Larry McClure, Betsy Strick, Rachel Jacob-Almeida, and Christopher Reichher. 2005. The Preuss School at UCSD. Research report of The Center for Research on Educational Equity, Assessment and Teaching Excellence. create.ucsd.edu/_files/ publications/PreussReportDecember2005.pdf.

The study on the Knowledge is Power Program is

Joshua D. Angrist, Susan M. Dynarski, Thomas J. Kane, Parag A. Pathak, and Christopher R. Walters. 2012. "Who Benefits from KIPP?" *Journal of Policy Analysis and Management* 31(4):837–60.

The quote about many null findings in the literature studying the effects of charter schools is from

Julian R. Betts, Lorien A. Rice, Andrew C. Zau, Y. Emily Tang, Cory R. Koedel. 2006. *Does School Choice Work?: Effects on Student Integration and Achievement.* Public Policy Institute of California.

The study of practice and skill among violinists is

K. Anders Ericsson, Ralf T. Krampe, and Clemens Tesch-Römer. 1993. "The Role of Deliberate Practice in the Acquisition of Expert Performance." *Psychological Science* 100(3):363–406.

The study of hormonal contraception and HIV is

Renee Heffron, Deborah Donnell, Helen Rees, and Connie Celum. 2012. "Use of Hormonal Contraceptives and Risk of HIV-1 Transmission: A Prospective Cohort Study." *The Lancet Infectious Diseases* 12(1):19–26.

The study examining the correlation between electoral success and campaign spending for incumbents and challengers is

Gary C. Jacobson. 1978. "The Effects of Campaign Spending in Congressional Elections." *American Political Science Review* 72(2):469–91.

We discussed several examples drawn from:

Tyler Vigen. 2015. *Spurious Correlations: Correlation Does Not Equal Causation.* Hachette Books.

We discussed three studies of happiness in exercise 4. You can find a general discussion of happiness research in

Daniel Gilbert. 2007. *Stumbling on Happiness.* Vintage.

The study of happiness before and after marriage is

Anke C. Zimmermann and Richard A. Easterlin. 2006. "Happily Ever After? Cohabitation, Marriage, Divorce, and Happiness in Germany." *Population and Development Review* 32(3):511–28.

The study of happiness before and after the ending of a marriage is

Jonathan Gardner and Andrew J. Oswald. 2006. "Do Divorcing Couples Become Happier by Breaking Up?" *Statistics in Society* 169(2):319–36.

CHAPTER 10

Controlling for Confounders

What You'll Learn

- If we can observe a confounder, we can control for it and mitigate the bias arising from it.
- The most common way to control for a confounder is by including it in a regression, although there are other approaches.
- Through graphs and simple examples, you will develop an intuitive understanding of how this works.
- Controlling is not magic. It doesn't remove bias arising from unobserved confounders or reverse causation.
- We should typically control for confounders but not mechanisms.

Introduction

In chapter 9, we saw that confounders are a big problem when we're trying to learn about causal relationships from correlations. Here, we are going to talk about the first line of defense against confounders, controlling.

You likely have heard people talk about controlling before, but what does it really mean? *Controlling* involves using statistical techniques to find the correlation between two variables, holding the value of other variables constant. The easiest way to begin to understand the idea is through some examples.

Party Whipping in Congress

A not terribly surprising fact about the United States Congress is that Republicans are more likely to vote in a conservative manner than Democrats. One way of measuring this, quantitatively, is through the scores given to each congressional representative by the right-leaning interest group the American Conservative Union (ACU). Each year, the ACU chooses twenty-five important bills and gives each congressperson a score between 0 and 100 based on how they voted on those bills. Since the ACU leans right, a higher score indicates a more conservative voting record.

We can back up the claim that being a Republican is correlated with a conservative voting record by checking whether Republicans have higher ACU scores than Democrats on average. Table 10.1, based on data from the House of Representatives

Table 10.1. Comparing the voting records of Republicans and Democrats in the U.S. Congress.

	Average ACU Score
Republicans	83
Democrats	19
Difference	64

in 1997, shows that they do. Democratic congressional representatives have an average ACU score of 19, while Republicans have an average ACU score of 83. On average, Republicans vote 64 ACU points more conservatively than do Democrats.

This data indicates that Republican and Democratic congressional representatives vote quite differently. What might explain such polarization?

One idea advanced by many political scientists is that party pressure causes the divergence in legislative voting behavior. Parties have lots of tools at their disposal to pressure rank-and-file members to vote the party line. Perhaps most important among these tools is help with fundraising for reelection campaigns.

But before we interpret the correlation between party membership and voting record as evidence for the effect of party discipline, we should consider possible confounders. A confounder, in this case, is some other feature of the world that affects both congressional representatives' party membership and their voting records.

As illustrated in figure 10.1, ideology is one obvious candidate for a confounder. The Republican party has a conservative reputation. The Democratic party has a liberal reputation. Hence, a conservative may be more likely to run as a Republican and a liberal may be more likely to run as a Democrat. Moreover, a politician's personal ideological leanings may well influence how they vote on legislation once in Congress. If people sort into the parties according to ideology in this way, there is reason to think that Republican representatives would vote more conservatively and Democratic representatives would vote more liberally, even if the parties exercised no discipline. So personal ideology is plausibly a confounder. In light of this, it would be a mistake to interpret the correlation between party membership and voting record as an unbiased estimate of the causal impact of party discipline on the voting behavior of representatives.

In order to address this potential confounder, we would like to control for it. In its simplest form, controlling for ideology simply means looking at the correlation between party membership and voting record, holding personal ideology constant. To do so, we first need a measure of personal ideology. Fortunately, we have a plausible candidate.

In 1996, a non-partisan organization called Project Vote Smart administered a survey, the National Political Awareness Test (NPAT), to congressional candidates. The survey asked candidates their views on a wide array of issues. From their answers, Project Vote Smart then generated a liberal to conservative ranking. Seventy-six percent of candidates responded to the survey, so we have a measure of the political ideology of a large number of congressional representatives.[1]

To control for personal ideology in our analysis of the relationship between party membership and voting record, we simply compare the voting records of Democrats

---

[1] Response rates declined considerably in subsequent elections, which explains why we're showing data from the late 1990s, even though it precedes the birth of many of our readers.

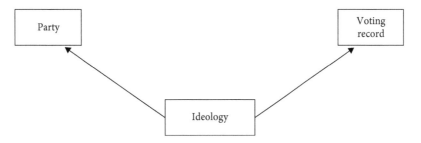

Figure 10.1. Ideology affects what party a politician joins and how that politician votes when in office. Hence, it is a confounder.

Table 10.2. NPAT scores controlling for party.

| | | Liberal ⟵ NPAT Percentile ⟶ Conservative | | | | |
		1–20	*21–40*	*41–60*	*61–80*	*81–100*
Republicans	*Avg ACU Score*	n/a	44	68	86	94
	# of People	0	4	45	69	69
Democrats	*Avg ACU Score*	10	18	41	96	84
	# of People	70	66	24	1	1
Difference in Average ACU Score		n/a	26	27	−10	10

and Republicans with similar NPAT scores. If the NPAT is doing a good job of measuring personal ideology, these comparisons will tell us about the difference in voting records of Republicans and Democrats, holding personal ideology constant (or, controlling for personal ideology).

Table 10.2 sorts congressional representatives into five bins, based on their NPAT scores. The left-most bin has representatives with the most liberal ideology according to their NPAT answers. The bins become progressively more conservative as we move to the right.

Looking at the data broken down in this way, a few things immediately jump out. First, and most importantly, in no column is the difference between Republican and Democratic voting records anywhere close to the 64-point difference we found before controlling for personal ideology. This suggests that personal ideology was an important confounder in that correlation—a large portion of the difference in voting record between Democrats and Republicans was due to the members of those two parties having different underlying personal preferences about policy rather than to party pressure. The reason, of course, is as we said earlier. More conservative people tend to become Republicans and more liberal people tend to become Democrats. This fact is reflected in the observation that the number of people in each cell is increasing in conservatism for Republicans and decreasing in conservatism for Democrats (i.e., almost all the Republicans are in the NPAT 41st–100th percentile and almost all the Democrats are in the NPAT 1st–60th percentile).

Second, within a party, as you move across the ideological bins, average ACU scores are, for the most part, going up. There is one exception—Democrats in the 61st–80th percentile vote more conservatively than Democrats in the 81st–100th percentile—but this comparison is not especially informative because it involves the comparison of only two people, since there are so few ideologically conservative Democrats.

Third, the difference between average Republican and average Democratic voting records varies across the columns. That is, the correlation between party and voting depends on ideology. This is fine. But often we want a single, overall measure of the correlation between partisanship and voting record controlling for personal ideology, rather than an ideology-by-ideology measure. To get that single number, we will need to take some sort of a weighted average of the differences from the various columns. But how do we decide what weights to give to each column?

As we start to think about the correct weights, note that there is clearly one column that is more informative than the others about the different voting behavior of Democrats and Republicans with similar personal ideologies—the column for the NPAT 41st–60th percentile. In each of the other columns, there are either very few Republicans or very few Democrats. But in the 41st–60th percentile column there are a large number of representatives from both parties. This isn't surprising—the place to look for ideological overlap across the parties is in the ideological center. So we probably want our weighted average to put a lot of weight on that column.

More generally, it is useful to think back to chapter 5, where we learned about how ordinary least squares (OLS) *regression* fits a line to data to minimize the sum of squared errors. (When we refer to regression in this chapter, we will always be referring to OLS regression.) OLS is one principled way to choose weights for the five columns. So consider the following regression:

$$\text{ACU Rating} = \alpha + \beta_1 \cdot \text{Republican} + \beta_2 \cdot \text{NPAT}_{21-40} + \beta_3 \cdot \text{NPAT}_{41-60}$$
$$+ \beta_4 \cdot \text{NPAT}_{61-80} + \beta_5 \cdot \text{NPAT}_{81-100} + \varepsilon$$

In this regression, the unit of analysis is an individual representative. The variable *ACU Rating* is an individual representative's ACU score. The variable *Republican* is what we call a *dummy variable*: it takes the value 1 if the representative is a member of the Republican party and the value 0 if the representative is a member of the Democratic party. The various *NPAT* variables are also dummy variables, taking a value of 1 if the representative is in the relevant percentile range and a value of 0 otherwise.[2] The greek letter ε (*epsilon*) represents the error.

The coefficient β_1 in this regression gives us the weighted average we have been talking about—that is, β_1 is the correlation between ACU score and being a Republican, controlling for personal ideology (as measured by NPAT percentile). We will also get estimates for the coefficients on the four included NPAT categories and the intercept (α). These also have interpretations. However, we are running the regression because we are interested in the correlation between ACU score and Republicanism controlling for ideology, so we focus on β_1.

---

[2] Since everyone is in one of the five NPAT categories, one of them must be omitted. Here, we have omitted the 1st–20th percentile. This is analogous to the fact that we can't include both a Democrat and a Republican variable in the regression when every member is either one or the other. We couldn't separately identify the effect of being a Democrat and the effect of being a Republican, so we just include a Republican variable and interpret the coefficient as the effect of being a Republican versus being a Democrat.

Running this regression on our data yields an estimate of β_1, which we label $\hat{\beta}_1$, equal to 24. (It is an estimate because our data is a sample drawn from the population of all congressional representatives, so the observed correlation also reflects noise.) Not surprisingly, this is very close to the difference between average Republican ACU score and average Democratic ACU score in the column corresponding to the 41st–60th percentile, which, as we said, is where almost all the information is. The regression, of course, puts a little weight on the other columns, dragging the estimate down from 27 to 24. But that column is basically telling us the answer.

Having controlled for ideology, we still probably don't have a terribly credible estimate of the causal effect of party discipline on the voting records of congressional representatives. This is because there could be many other confounders beyond personal ideology. That is, within an NPAT bin, there may be lots of other factors that lead some people to become Democrats and others to become Republicans that also have an independent effect on their voting behavior in Congress. For instance, even holding fixed personal ideology, Democrats may tend to represent districts with more liberal voters and Republicans may tend to represent districts with more conservative voters. If politicians choose how to vote on bills with an eye toward how their voters will react, then these differences in constituencies are yet another confounder. We are sure you can think of others.

As the list of confounders grows, making a table that breaks down the data into all the different possible cells becomes more difficult and unwieldy. But, as long as you can measure the potential confounders, you can control for them in a regression. Doing so will always get you an estimate of β_1 reflecting the weighted average of the various cells in that (imagined) big table that minimizes the sum of squared errors. Given this, regression will be our most important tool for controlling for confounders. Therefore, it is useful to have a better understanding of exactly how controlling with regression works.

A Note on Heterogeneous Treatment Effects

As we discussed in chapter 3, for almost all interesting examples of causal relationships, the effects of interest are heterogeneous—that is, they're not the same for every unit of observation. This was true in our flu shot example, where the flu shot prevented some people from getting the flu who otherwise would have, but didn't prevent other people from getting the flu, either because they weren't going to get it in the first place or because they were and the flu shot didn't work for them. It's probably also true for the above example about party effects on voting. To the extent that parties affect roll-call voting by members of Congress, this effect is probably not the same for every member of Congress. Perhaps some members of Congress are strong ideologues who will vote the same way regardless of any party pressure, so that there is no treatment effect. Perhaps others depend on their party's support for reelection and would do whatever their party leaders asked, so that there is a strong treatment effect. And perhaps others are somewhere in between.

It's important to think clearly about such heterogeneity when controlling because, as our discussion around table 10.2 showed, once we start controlling for confounders, we're no longer estimating the average effect of the treatment across all units. In our example, to estimate the relationship between party and voting, controlling for ideology, we put more weight on members of Congress with moderate ideologies. This is because there isn't much variation in party among members of Congress with extreme ideologies—basically, all strong conservatives are Republicans and all strong liberals are Democrats. If the effect of party membership is different for ideological moderates than it is for ideological extremists, we have to acknowledge that we're focusing on the former effect.

This acknowledgement raises a thorny problem. If controlling for a potential confounder meaningfully changes our causal estimate, this could be a sign that the estimate without controlling was biased and that controlling reduced that bias. This is to the good. But it could also be a sign that there are heterogeneous treatment effects, and we've changed the subset of units for which we're estimating the average effect. To the extent that the estimand we really care about is the average treatment effect across all units, this could be to the bad.

These challenges will arise for other methods beyond controlling that we'll discuss later in the book. We will refer back to this discussion when relevant. Sometimes we'll say that instead of estimating the average treatment effect (ATE) as our estimand, we can only estimate a local average treatment effect (LATE) as our estimand, where *local* refers to the subset of units for which we can generate a credible estimate. When treatment effects are heterogeneous across units, the LATE need not be the same as the ATE. So if the ATE is the estimand we really care about, we need to think clearly about the extent to which estimates of the LATE may or may not be informative about the ATE. But, as the economist Guido Imbens says of situations where we can only credibly estimate a local average treatment effect, "Better LATE than nothing."

The Anatomy of a Regression

The key ingredients in any regression for causal inference are

- the *dependent variable* (also called the *outcome variable*),
- the *treatment variable*, and
- a set of *control variables*.

The dependent variable is the outcome you are trying to understand. The treatment variable is the feature of the world whose effect on the dependent variable you are trying to estimate. And the control variables are potential confounders that you are including in the regression to reduce bias.

In the simple case where there is only one control variable, we write the regression equation as

$$Y = \alpha + \beta \cdot T + \gamma \cdot X + \varepsilon \tag{10.1}$$

where Y is the dependent variable, T is the treatment variable, and X is the control variable. The regression parameters (i.e., the quantities we'd like to estimate) are the intercept α, the effect of the treatment β, and the "effect" of the control variable γ. There is also an error term, ε, reflecting the fact that units differ from their predicted outcome for idiosyncratic reasons.

There's nothing in the regression equation that distinguishes the treatment variable from the control variable. This distinction is conceptual and is driven by the question you are trying to answer. If you want to know the effect of party on voting, controlling for ideology, the party variable is your treatment and NPAT is your control. But if you had wanted to know the effect of ideology on voting, controlling for party, this would be reversed.

This is also why the word *effect* is in scare quotes above when referring to the effect of the control variable. Often, we don't actually care about the regression parameter associated with a control variable (here, γ). What's important is that β is an effect of interest, and we are going to try to estimate it in an unbiased way.

One way to read Equation 10.1 is to take it literally. We can pretend that we know the data-generating process. Each individual i's outcome (Y_i) equals a common intercept (α) plus $\beta \cdot T_i$ plus $\gamma \cdot X_i$ plus idiosyncratic factors (ϵ_i). Another way to read the equation is to acknowledge that we don't know the data-generating process, but nonetheless, we'd like to estimate β—the average linear relationship between Y and T, controlling for X.

As we noted in chapter 5 (though we didn't quite put it this way), whatever the data-generating process, OLS regression always gives us the *best linear approximation to the conditional expectation function* (BLACEF). So we don't have to pretend to know the data-generating process in order to run a regression. If there are no baseline differences across values of T after controlling for X, then the BLACEF corresponds to the average effect of T on Y. In this case, knowing β is very valuable.

Just as in our discussion from chapter 5, when we run this regression, we get estimates $\hat{\alpha}$, $\hat{\beta}$, and $\hat{\gamma}$ by computing the values of α, β, and γ that minimize the sum of the squared errors. Let's see what that means.

For any arbitrary values of the regression parameters—say α', β', and γ'—the associated prediction of Y_i for an individual i is

$$\alpha' + \beta' \cdot T_i + \gamma' \cdot X_i.$$

Let's label the idiosyncratic errors associated with this regression ε'. For each observation i, they are the actual outcome minus the predicted outcome:

$$\varepsilon_i' = Y_i - \left(\alpha' + \beta' \cdot T_i + \gamma' \cdot X_i\right)$$

The OLS estimates—$\hat{\alpha}$, $\hat{\beta}$, and $\hat{\gamma}$—are the particular values of the regression parameters that minimize the sum of the square of these errors. Our computer can compute them really quickly.

Suppose we know that once we control for X, there are no other omitted confounders. So the regression of Y on T and X gives an unbiased estimate of the effect of T on Y. One question we might ask is how biased our results would have been if we failed to control for X.

It turns out, we can answer that question. Call Equation 10.1 above the *long regression* because it includes X. Now suppose we ran the following *short regression* instead:

$$Y = \alpha^S + \beta^S \cdot T + \varepsilon^S \tag{10.2}$$

The superscript S here indicates that we are talking about the short regression. Importantly, there's no guarantee that β^S from the short regression will be the same as β from the long regression. In fact, they won't be the same if X is a confounder.

We can quantify the bias associated with failing to include X in the regression. Consider a regression that treats the control variable (X) as a dependent variable and regresses it on the treatment (T):

$$X = \tau + \pi \cdot T + \xi$$

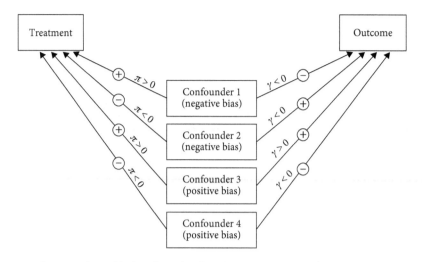

Figure 10.2. The omitted variables bias formula tells us how to sign the bias from an omitted confounder.

You'll notice that we've used different Greek letters for the regression parameters here. We now call the intercept τ (the Greek letter *tau*), the coefficient on the treatment π (the Greek letter *pi*), and the error ξ (the Greek letter *xi*). We did this for a couple reasons.

First, and most importantly, we didn't want to use the same letters here that had different meanings above. The parameter π, here, describes the correlation between T and X—it's the slope relating changes in T to changes in X. We didn't want you to confuse that with the two β's we've seen in this section (β and β^S, each of which describes some version of the relationship beween the treatment and the outcome Y). Second, we also don't want you to think that there's something special about certain Greek letters. It's not the case that α must always represent the intercept, β the coefficient on the treatment, and so on. After all, these are just symbols. We would like you to be able to look at the equation and figure out what the constant is, what the coefficient on the treatment is, what the error is, and so on, even if someone uses completely different symbols than the ones we use.

The bias from excluding X from the regression of the outcome on the treatment is $\beta^S - \beta$. It turns out, this bias is equal to $\pi \cdot \gamma$. That is,

$$\text{Bias} = \beta^S - \beta = \pi \cdot \gamma.$$

We sometimes call this the *omitted variable bias* formula.

What this formula tells us is that the short regression gives a biased estimate of the effect of the treatment on the outcome if the control variable is correlated with the treatment variable (so that $\pi \neq 0$) and the control variable influences the outcome variable (so that $\gamma \neq 0$).

If we can't observe X, we can't control for it by including it in the regression. But the omitted variable bias formula gives us a way to think about the direction and extent of the bias. Indeed, the omitted variable bias formula formalizes our ideas from chapter 9 about how to sign the bias, as summarized in figure 10.2, which repeats figure 9.7 but points out that the regression parameters π and γ directly measure the relationships relevant for determining the sign of the bias.

Table 10.3. The omitted variable bias formula helps us think about whether failing to control for a confounder results in an over- or under-estimate of the causal effect.

	Omitted Variable Positively Correlated with Treatment $\pi > 0$	Omitted Variable Negatively Correlated with Treatment $\pi < 0$
Omitted Variable Positively Correlated with Outcome $\gamma > 0$	Positive bias $\pi \cdot \gamma > 0$	Negative bias $\pi \cdot \gamma < 0$
Omitted Variable Negatively Correlated with Outcome $\gamma < 0$	Negative bias $\pi \cdot \gamma < 0$	Positive bias $\pi \cdot \gamma > 0$

If there's an unobserved confounder that we suspect is positively related to both T (so $\pi > 0$) and Y (so $\gamma > 0$), then the omitted variable bias formula tells us that $\beta^S - \beta > 0$, so we are over-estimating the effect of T. The same is true if the confounder is negatively related to both T and Y (so that π and γ are both negative)—again, the bias is positive and we are getting an over-estimate. If the confounder is positively related to T but negatively related to Y (so $\pi > 0$ and $\gamma < 0$) or vice versa (so $\pi < 0$ and $\gamma > 0$), the bias is negative and we under-estimate the effect of T. This is summarized in table 10.3.

How Does Regression Control?

We've seen that controlling for a variable (X) can change the coefficient describing the relationship between some other variable of interest (T) and an outcome variable (Y). In particular, controlling for X will change the estimated relationship between T and Y if X is correlated with T and has an independent relationship with Y. Here's one way to think, graphically, about what the regression is doing when we control for a variable.

Suppose we want to know the effect of height on income, in which case both our outcome and treatment variables of interest are continuous (they can, in principle, take an infinite and uncountable number of possible values). Figure 10.3 shows some data on income and height from the National Longitudinal Survey conducted by the U.S. Bureau of Labor Statistics. A representative sample of U.S. residents born between 1980 and 1984 were asked about their heights and their incomes in 2014, when they were between the ages of 34 and 38.

To allow for easier visualization, we grouped respondents by height and gender, so every dot in figure 10.3 corresponds to a group of fifteen or more individuals of the same gender and height (measured in inches). The figure plots the average income of each group, measured in thousands of dollars above $20,000, and the average height, measured in feet above 5 feet. (You'll see in a moment why we scaled our variables in such an unusual way.) The hollow dots correspond to groups of men and the solid dots correspond to groups of women.

Visually, we see a strong, positive correlation between height and income. What would we get if we ran a regression of income on height with this data, ignoring gender?

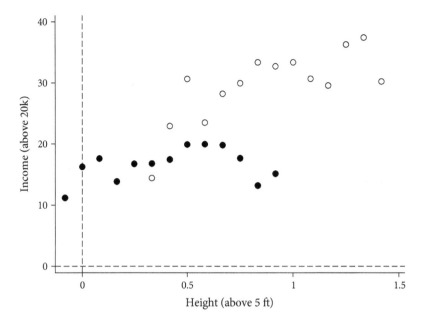

Figure 10.3. Income and height among 34- to 38-year-old Americans in 2014.

As we've seen previously, this would simply involve finding the line that best fits the data. Figure 10.4 plots that line. Indeed, the best-fitting line has a strong positive slope, indicating that, on average, taller people earn higher incomes.

To be a little more precise, the regression finds the line that best fits the data by identifying the values of α and β that minimize the sum of squared errors in the following equation:

$$\text{Income} = \alpha + \beta \cdot \text{Height} + \varepsilon$$

These two values are illustrated by figure 10.5. The height of the line when Height $= 0$ (i.e., when a person is 5 feet tall) is $\hat{\alpha}$, and the slope of the line is $\hat{\beta}$. For this particular data set, we estimate a slope of about 14.8. On average, people who are one foot taller earn an extra \$14,800 of income per year!

Of course, before we draw a causal interpretation from this regression coefficient, we should think about confounders. Gender is one possibility. Men are, on average, taller than women. And we suspect that men, on average, earn higher incomes than women for reasons unrelated to height. (This could be the result of gender discrimination in labor markets or other societal factors. Although the reasons are, of course, very important, we don't need to know them in order to control for gender as a confounder.) Indeed, we can see in the picture that women do seem to have lower heights and lower incomes, on average. So gender is a confounder that we might want to control for in this regression.

One way we could start addressing this concern would be to run separate regressions for men and women:

$$\text{Income} = \alpha^M + \beta^M \cdot \text{Height} + \varepsilon^M$$

$$\text{Income} = \alpha^W + \beta^W \cdot \text{Height} + \varepsilon^W$$

If we did that, we would fit two regression lines, as shown in figure 10.6.

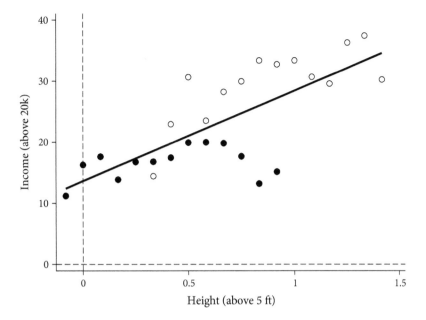

Figure 10.4. Regressing income on height.

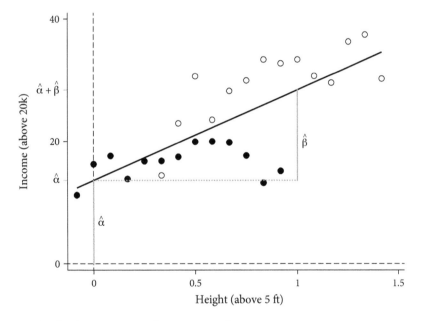

Figure 10.5. Graphical interpretation of regression coefficients.

The separate regression lines for men and women are shown in gray, while the previous regression line that pooled everyone together is still shown in black. Interestingly, the correlation between height and income is smaller within each gender than it is across the population as a whole. That is, both $\hat{\beta}^W$ and $\hat{\beta}^M$ are smaller than $\hat{\beta}$ from our earlier regression. Also notice that the slope is greater for men than it is for women, $\hat{\beta}^M > \hat{\beta}_W$.

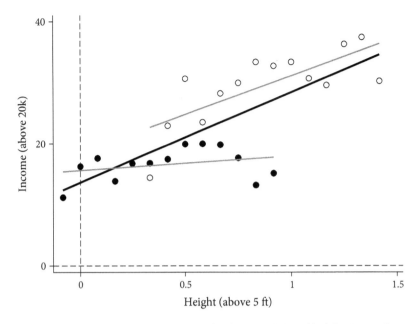

Figure 10.6. Representing both the regression line for the pooled data (black line) as well as separate regression lines for men and women (gray lines).

This procedure of splitting the data and running separate regressions tells us the correlation between income and height separately for men and women. Thinking back to our congressional politics example, this is analogous to the cells at the bottom of table 10.2, which told us the difference in average ACU score between Republicans and Democrats for each bin of NPAT scores.

While the separate correlations are good to know, just as in the congressional politics example, we might want to have one summary estimate of the correlation between income and height, controlling for gender. That number will be a weighted average of the slopes of the two gray lines in figure 10.11 (just as in the congressional politics example, where the single number was a weighted average of the individual differences at the bottom of table 10.2.). But we need to know how to assign the weights.

The most straightforward way to do this is to run a regression of income on both height and gender. The regression equation would look like this:

$$\text{Income} = \alpha + \beta \cdot \text{Height} + \gamma \cdot \text{Male} + \varepsilon$$

Graphically, how will this regression separately estimate α, β, and γ? Instead of finding one line that best fits the data, we can think of finding two lines that best fit the data—one for men and one for women. But unlike when we ran separate regressions, we now constrain those two lines to have the same slope ($\hat{\beta}$). Figure 10.7 shows how those two lines look if we do that and compares them to the lines we got when we ran separate regressions for men and women.

Notice that the slope of the two black lines is identical, by construction. And the slope is somewhere in between the slope for those we got running the two separate regressions (the gray lines). That is, it is a weighted average of the two. Figure 10.8

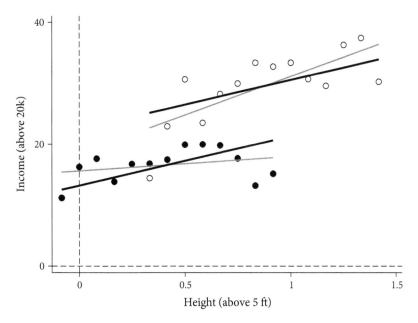

Figure 10.7. Representing the regression where we control for gender by including it in the regression of income on height (black lines) as well as separate regression lines for men and women (gray lines).

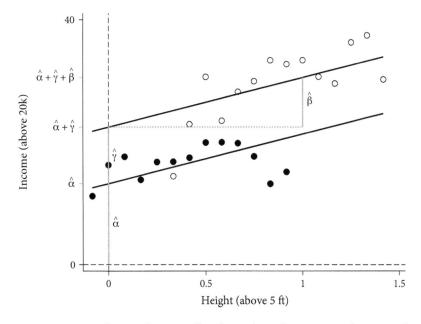

Figure 10.8. Regression coefficients when controlling for gender in the regression of income on height.

shows how, having estimated these two parallel lines that best fit the data, we've also estimated the regression parameters.

The intercept of the line for women (Male = 0) is $\hat{\alpha}$. The distance between the two lines is $\hat{\gamma}$. And the slope of the two lines is $\hat{\beta}$. Put differently, $\hat{\alpha}$ is the predicted income for women who are 5 feet tall; $\hat{\gamma}$ is the predicted difference in income between men and women of the same height; and $\hat{\beta}$ is the average relationship between height and income, controlling for gender.

Not surprisingly, controlling for gender has significant implications for the estimated relationship between height and income. Instead of 14.8, our new estimate for the slope is about 8.1. The change is due to the fact that gender is a confounder—it affects both height and income. Using our tools for signing the bias from chapter 9, we know that if the confounder is positively correlated with both treatment and outcome, as is the case here, it creates positive bias. Since 14.8 was an over-estimate of the true effect of height on income, when we control for gender, we get a smaller estimate.

It is worth noting that controlling for gender affects not only our estimate of the relationship between income and height but also the precision of that estimate, although the direction of that effect is theoretically ambiguous. On the one hand, adding a control that is correlated with the outcome reduces the residual variation in that outcome, which improves precision. On the other hand, adding a control that is correlated with the treatment reduces the residual variation in the treatment, which increases the uncertainty of our estimates. Whether controlling for a confounder improves or harms precision will depend on the relative impact of those two forces.

Given the discussion above, it might be tempting to add additional control variables to your regression, not for the purpose of reducing bias but with the goal of improving precision. Indeed, if you can find pre-treatment variables that are strongly correlated with the outcome but not the treatment; including them in a regression will tend to improve the precision of your estimates. However, if you keep trying control variables until you get a statistically significant estimate, that's p-hacking, and it's a bad idea.

Since we've talked about the analogy between what we've just done and our congressional politics example, let's revisit that example in a regression framework. Notice, in this case, the treatment (Republican or Democrat) is binary, but the potential confounder (ideology) is measured continuously by the NPAT score.

Again, start with a scatter plot, this time of the American Conservative Union rating on the vertical axis and the NPAT conservative score on the horizontal axis. In figure 10.9, the hollow dots correspond to Democrats and the solid dots correspond to Republicans.

Since the treatment is binary, we can start with a simple comparison of the average ACU rating for Republicans and for Democrats. Consider the following regression equation:

$$\text{ACU Rating} = \alpha + \beta \cdot \text{Republican} + \varepsilon$$

To minimize the sum of squared errors, the coefficient $\hat{\alpha}$ equals the average ACU rating for a Democrat (Republican = 0) and the coefficient $\hat{\beta}$ is the difference between the average ACU rating for a Republican and for a Democrat. Thus, as we've already seen, $\hat{\alpha} = 20$ and $\hat{\beta} = 84 - 20 = 64$. This is illustrated in figure 10.10, where the horizontal lines correspond to the average ACU ratings for Democrats and Republicans.

Our concern, of course, is that personal political ideology is a confounder in this regression, so that $\hat{\beta}$ does not estimate the true effect of party on congressional voting behavior. So we would like to control for personal ideology. We will do so using the NPAT Conservativeness score, measured on the horizontal axis.

In our income-height example, we were concerned about a confounder that was measured as a binary variable—gender. Our first step in building intuition about controlling was to consider running the original regression (income and height) separately for each

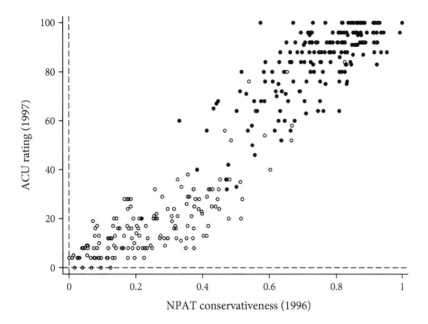

Figure 10.9. ACU score and NPAT conservative score.

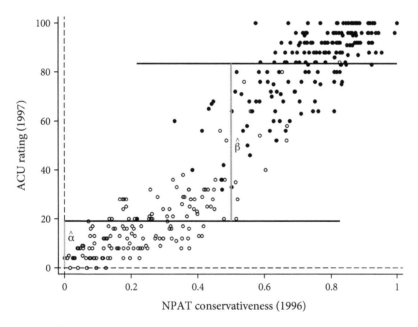

Figure 10.10. Coefficients in regression of ACU score on party.

value of the confounder. Then we saw that the final regression coefficient on height controlling for gender was a weighted average of the slopes of these two separately estimated regression lines.

Here, in our congressional politics example, because our confounder is continuous, we cannot do a separate regression for each value of the confounder. But we can

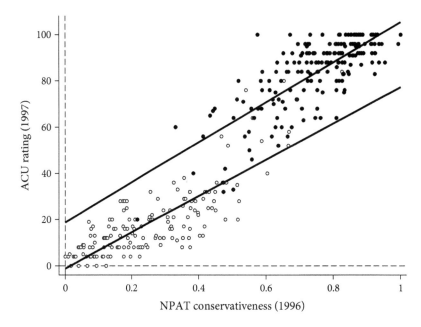

Figure 10.11. Controlling for NPAT score (ideology) in the relationship between ACU score and party by running two separate regressions, one for each party.

do something similar: run a regression of ACU Rating on NPAT Conservativeness separately for Democrats and for Republicans (the superscripts P on the regression coefficients refer to the idea that this is the regression for party P):

$$\text{ACU Rating} = \alpha^P + \gamma^P \cdot \text{NPAT Conservativeness} + \varepsilon^P$$

That gives us two regression lines, one for Republicans and one for Democrats, as in figure 10.11.

For each value of NPAT Conservativeness, the predicted ACU Rating of a Republican with that NPAT Conservativeness score is

$$\hat{\alpha}^R + \hat{\gamma}^R \cdot \text{NPAT Conservativeness}$$

And for each value of NPAT Conservativeness, the predicted ACU Rating of a Democrat with that NPAT Conservativeness score is:

$$\hat{\alpha}^D + \hat{\gamma}^D \cdot \text{NPAT Conservativeness}$$

This means that at any given value of NPAT Conservativeness, the gap between the two lines is the difference in predicted ACU Rating between Republicans and Democrats with that NPAT score. Hence, this regression allows us to get a continuous analogue of our earlier binary comparison. It tells us, for each value of NPAT Conservativeness, what the predicted difference in mean ACU Rating is between Republicans and Democrats.

But we aren't done. As before, the goal is to get a single measure of the relationship between ACU Rating and party membership, controlling for NPAT Conservativeness.

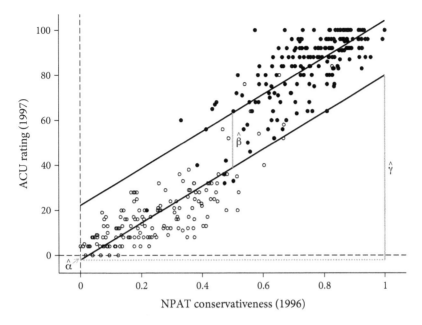

Figure 10.12. Controlling for NPAT score (ideology) in a regression of ACU score on party.

Currently, we have a separate measure of that relationship for each value of NPAT Conservativeness. The final step in controlling, then, is to use regression to create the weighted average of these differences that minimizes the sum of squared errors. We do so with the following regression:

$$\text{ACU Rating} = \alpha + \beta \cdot \text{Republican} + \gamma \cdot \text{NPAT Conservativeness} + \varepsilon$$

Figure 10.12 illustrates this regression. The parameter $\hat{\alpha}$ tells us the average ACU Rating of a Democrat with NPAT Conservativeness of 0. The parameter $\hat{\gamma}$ tells us the slope of the relationship between ACU Rating and NPAT Conservativeness. Importantly, unlike our previous two regressions, where $\hat{\gamma}^R$ and $\hat{\gamma}^D$ were different, this regression imposes that the slope of the relationship between ACU Rating and NPAT Conservativeness be the same for both parties. Hence, this slope $\hat{\gamma}$ is a weighted average of $\hat{\gamma}^R$ and $\hat{\gamma}^D$. Finally, the coefficient $\hat{\beta}$ is the gap between the two lines. This gap is constant across NPAT Conservativeness scores because we forced $\hat{\gamma}$ to be the same for both parties, making the lines parallel. Hence, $\hat{\beta}$ estimates the average difference in ACU Rating between Republicans and Democrats controlling for NPAT Conservativeness.

Controlling and Causation

While controlling allows you to mitigate or remove the biases arising from specific confounders that you are able to measure and include in your regression, we are typically still skeptical in most cases that controlling alone allows us to uncover unbiased estimates of causal relationships. Remember from chapter 9 that if we want to interpret a correlation as an unbiased estimate of a causal effect, we must believe that there are no baseline differences between the treated and untreated units. In other words, our comparison has to plausibly be apples-to-apples. If we regress Y on T and X (and other possible confounders), we're still making a similar assertion if we give the coefficient on T a causal interpretation. We are saying that, other than the set of variables we controlled for, we believe there are no confounders in the relationship between Y and T and no reverse causality. Put differently, for controlling to give an unbiased estimate of a causal effect, we must control for *all* the confounders.

In our experience, it is hard to find situations (other than randomized experiments, which we will discuss in chapter 11) where it feels plausible that there are really no omitted confounders. Typically, even if the analyst controls for lots of things, you can think of other potential confounders that are either unobservable or unmeasured in the data and, thus, can't be controlled for. For instance, ask yourself whether you can think of any potential confounders beyond gender in the relationship between income and height. The answer is, of course, yes, including economic, biological, cultural, health, and other characteristics. For instance, wealthy parents might provide their children with better nutrition, which might make them taller, and might also help their children in other ways that allow them to earn higher incomes. It is hard to imagine that you would be able to measure and control for all possible confounders.

Reverse causation is another reason we don't generally think controlling for confounders can uncover causal relationships on its own. In chapter 9, we talked about how both confounders and reverse causation can prevent us from making an apples-to-apples comparison. The idea of controlling is to try to account for confounders as best we can, but if there is reverse causation, meaning the outcome affects the treatment, there's no amount of controlling that can make that problem go away.

Let us give you an example.

Is Social Media Bad for You?

There is widespread concern that exposure to social media is bad for people. And, indeed, many studies show a negative correlation between social media usage and various measures of a person's subjective well-being and mental health.

Of course, that correlation may not reflect a causal effect of social media on well-being. For instance, there might be reverse causality—perhaps people who are sad, lonely, or distressed spend more time on social media than people who are happier or more socially connected. Or there might be confounders—perhaps socioeconomic status, education, or geography affect both social media usage and subjective well-being.

A first thing you might think to do to get at an estimate of the causal relationship is to control for some of these confounders. How well will that controlling strategy do at estimating the true causal effect?

There is a study that can provide some insight into that question. A group of scholars interested in the effects of social media ran an experiment. They first identified a large group of Facebook users willing to participate in their study. (The participants didn't know what the study was about.) From each of these people they elicited measures of subjective well-being, Facebook usage, and how much they'd have to be paid to turn off Facebook for a month. Then the experimenters randomly selected some of these people and in fact paid them to turn off Facebook for a month (which they were able to monitor). The others didn't turn off Facebook but continued to be part of the study as a control group. The researchers then measured subjective well-being again at the end to see whether turning off Facebook had changed the subjective sense of well-being for

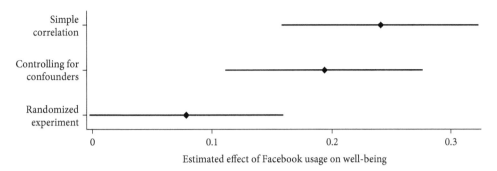

Figure 10.13. Estimates of relationship between Facebook usage and subjective well-being.

those in the treatment group, relative to those in the control group who did not turn off Facebook.

The nice thing about this study, for our purposes, is that the experiment, by randomly assigning Facebook usage, gives an unbiased estimate of the effect of Facebook usage. The researchers also asked about Facebook usage and subjective well-being at the start of the study, so by comparing levels of well-being across people with different levels of Facebook usage at the beginning of the study, they could also replicate the simple correlation reported in earlier studies. Moreover, the researchers, also observed a bunch of details about the individuals in their study and so could control for some potential confounders—for example, income, age, sex, education, race, political affiliation.

If they were able to control for all confounders, then the estimate of the relationship between Facebook usage and subjective well-being from controlling and from the experiment would be the same in expectation. So, by comparing the simple correlation, the correlation controlling for these potential confounders, and the experimental estimate, we can start to get a sense of how well controlling does, in this setting, at recovering the true causal effect.

Figure 10.13 shows the simple correlation, the correlation controlling for potential confounders, and the estimate from the experiment (each surrounded by a 95% confidence interval). All are measured in units of average Facebook use per day. As you can see, the simple correlation gives the biggest estimate of Facebook's negative relationship with subjective well-being. Controlling for potential confounders reduces that estimate a bit. But the experimental estimate is about one-third the size of the estimates from the simple correlation and about one-half the size of the estimate controlling for potential confounders. This suggests that the strategy of controlling, here, still leaves us with a substantial over-estimate of the true effect.

Reading a Regression Table

You've seen graphical representations of regression. But when you run a regression on your computer or see regression results discussed in a report, they are often presented in the form of a table. So it is worthwhile to be able to understand and interpret the different parts of a regression table. We first saw regression tables in chapter 5, but we now know enough to go into more detail.

Let's go back to our analysis of the relationship between congressional voting records and party. In that setting, we ran three regressions.

First, we regressed our measure of roll-call voting on party without controlling for anything:

$$\text{ACU Rating} = \alpha + \beta \cdot \text{Republican} + \varepsilon$$

Second, we controlled for ideology by including indicators for different ranges of the NPAT score:

$$\text{ACU Rating} = \alpha + \beta_1 \cdot \text{Republican} + \beta_2 \cdot \text{NPAT}_{21-40} + \beta_3 \cdot \text{NPAT}_{41-60}$$
$$+ \beta_4 \cdot \text{NPAT}_{61-80} + \beta_5 \cdot \text{NPAT}_{81-100} + \varepsilon$$

This is what we did to find the correct weighted average in our discussion surrounding table 10.2.

Third, we controlled for ideology by including the continuous NPAT variable:

$$\text{ACU Rating} = \alpha + \beta \cdot \text{Republican} + \gamma \cdot \text{NPAT Conservativeness} + \varepsilon$$

Each column of table 10.4 presents the results from one of these three regressions.

Let's talk about how to read this table. The first column simply contains labels. The second column shows the results from our first regression: ACU Rating on Republican, controlling for nothing. The third column shows the results from our second regression: ACU Rating on Republican, controlling for NPAT category. The fourth column shows the results from our third regression: ACU Rating on Republican, controlling for the continuous NPAT Conservativeness score.

Along the first row, we see the name of our dependent variable. For these regressions, this is always ACU Rating. For each of our regressions, the row labeled *Republican* shows three pieces of information. The top number is our estimate of the coefficient on Republican in our regression. The bottom number in parentheses is the standard error on that estimate. And the stars indicate whether the result is statistically significantly different from zero (and at what level). Looking across this row, we see that in the first regression, the coefficient on Republican is 64.32. But once we control for NPAT score, it drops dramatically. If we control with NPAT categories, it drops to 23.74. And if we control with the continuous NPAT Conservativeness score, it is 24.28. (Not surprisingly, it doesn't much matter exactly how we control for ideology.)

Going down the table, we then get the coefficient estimates, standard errors, and statistical significance for each of our control variables. This is why the next five rows are blank in the second column—we didn't control for anything in that regression. In the third column, the four rows associated with the NPAT categories are filled in, but the row associated with the NPAT Conservativeness score is blank. And in the fourth column, the NPAT category rows are blank, but NPAT Conservativeness is filled in. For all three regressions, the row called *Constant* is filled in. This is the estimate of the intercept ($\hat{\alpha}$) from that regression.

The table contains two more pieces of information. For each regression, the table tells us how many observations there were in the data. Here, the answer is 349, reflecting the number of congresspeople who filled out the NPAT survey in 1997.

And, for each regression, the table reports the r-squared statistic. Recall from chapter 2 that this is the proportion of variation in one variable that can be predicted by variation in other variables. So a value of .93 in our final regression says that, within the sample of data we have, you can predict 93 percent of the variation in a congressperson's ACU rating using party and NPAT score.

Table 10.4. Relationship between ACU rating and party.

Variables	ACU Rating	ACU Rating	ACU Rating
Republican	64.32**	23.74**	24.28**
	(1.71)	(2.25)	(1.98)
$NPAT_{21-40}$		8.01**	
		(1.76)	
$NPAT_{41-60}$		32.74**	
		(2.29)	
$NPAT_{61-80}$		52.27**	
		(2.83)	
$NPAT_{81-100}$		59.77**	
		(2.83)	
NPAT Conservatism			82.05**
			(3.44)
Constant	19.09**	10.29**	−2.10
	(1.25)	(1.24)	(1.18)
Observations	349	349	349
r-squared	.80	.92	.93

Standard errors in parentheses. $**p < .01$

While that sounds pretty good, we urge you not to over-interpret the r-squared statistic. In fact, when we run regressions, we often don't even report it. Typically, our goal is not to predict or model the variation in our dependent variable. It is to learn whether our key treatment variable matters for our outcome. For that, what we are really interested in is the coefficient estimate on that variable. Moreover, getting a high r-squared statistic, on its own, isn't very meaningful. One easy way to successfully predict a lot of the variation in your data is to just include lots of control variables in your regression. But this doesn't mean you've understood what is going on at all. Think back to our discussion of overfitting in chapter 5. Just because you fit the data really well (which is all that a high r-squared means) by including lots of variables doesn't mean you can do a good job predicting what the outcome will be when you look at observations not from your data set. And in some cases, you can have a reliable, unbiased estimate of your quantity of interest even though your r-squared is low.

Controlling for Confounders versus Mechanisms

Thinking clearly about controlling gets dicier when there is some variable that affects both the treatment and the outcome but is also affected by the treatment. What can we do in this situation? That variable is a confounder: it affects both the treatment and the outcome. So it seems that we should control for it. But as we discussed in chapter 9, that variable is also a mechanism: it is affected by the treatment and affects the outcome. So it seems that we should not control for it, since it is part of the pathway by which the treatment affects the outcome. What are we to do?

To make this conundrum more concrete, let's return to our example from chapter 9 where we were interested in the effect of per capita income on civil war. On the one hand, democracies might implement better policies that improve income and might also provide better opportunities for non-violent expression of political grievances, which might directly affect civil war risk. From this perspective, whether a country is a democracy or not is a confounder—that is, a pre-treatment covariate—and, thus, should be controlled for. On the other hand, perhaps as a country becomes richer, its citizens become more informed and start demanding greater democracy, which then reduces the likelihood they turn to civil war. From this perspective, democracy is one of the mechanisms by which GDP affects the likelihood of civil war—that is, a post-treatment covariate—and, thus, should not be controlled for.

There really isn't a solution in such situations. You are damned if you do and damned if you don't—which means that you aren't in a position to learn much about the causal relationship you are interested in. To do that, you'd need a more creative approach, which will be the subject of the next several chapters.

There Is No Magic

People would really like to believe that they can estimate causal relationships by just controlling for all the confounders. And they'd like you to believe it too. But, as we've just discussed, in many important settings you will only believe there are no omitted confounders if you aren't thinking clearly. And so, sometimes, people will use mathematical jargon, cool-sounding statistical methods, complicated computer programs, and other technical wizardry to try to get you to not think clearly. It is important to not be fooled. No matter what fancy techniques an analyst uses, if the fundamental strategy is to control for the confounders, and if there are plausible confounders that are either unobservable or unmeasured in the data, then they can't possibly have controlled for them. Computers aren't magical. They can control for observable confounders. But they cannot make unobservable confounders observable.

To see what we mean, consider the case of a perfectly fine and useful statistical technique called *matching*. Here's the idea. Suppose you have a continuous variable, X, that you'd like to control for. You could match each treated unit to whatever untreated unit has the most similar value of X. Then, you might compute a difference of means (or run a regression) on that matched data set in order to estimate the effect of T on Y. This is called *nearest neighbor matching*.

So, in our congressional politics example, you would start by matching each Democratic congressperson to the Republican congressperson with the most similar NPAT score. Then, in this matched sample, you would compute the difference in average ACU score between matched pairs of Republicans and Democrats, which is another way of estimating the relationship between ACU score and political party, controlling for NPAT score.

If you had multiple variables you wanted to control for, you'd have to define some summary measure of how similar any two observations are across those variables. There are lots of strategies for doing this. Some of them get pretty fancy in terms of computation, which can make it hard to keep thinking clearly. You must try to keep your wits about you.

Matching has some advantages over regression as a technique for controlling. One nice feature of matching is that it allows for more flexibility in the way in which the control variable might influence the outcome of interest. For instance, whereas regression assumes the relationship is linear, matching makes no such assumption. Matching also has disadvantages relative to regression. One downside of matching is that it's often less precise than regression because you're using less information. Another downside is that matching estimates can be biased because the best match for a treated observation will have, in expectation, a higher value of X if, for example, X is positively correlated with T. There are statistical solutions to that problem as well, which can again start looking pretty technical and fancy.

Matching, like regression, is a good statistical technique for controlling. We have no objection to it. We get concerned because analysts sometimes like to present some very technical matching algorithm and then say things like "Matching creates an experiment-like comparison of units that differ in the treatment but are otherwise the same." Such claims are an attempt to blind you with science. Matching is just a tool for controlling. It creates no more of an experiment-like comparison than does a regression that includes control variables. That is to say, it controls for the variables that were observed and matched on—nothing more. Your computer, no matter how fancy the statistical algorithm, can't make the unobservables observable. Because that would be magic. And there is no magic.

Wrapping Up

Controlling is a way to account for confounders and obtain better, less biased estimates of causal relationships. There are lots of different ways to control, but they're all fundamentally trying to do the same thing—generate more credible estimates by comparing treated and untreated units with similar values of other observable pre-treatment covariates.

While controlling is a valuable tool, it's not a silver bullet. In most interesting cases, there will still be unobservable confounders that we can't control for, reverse causation, or variables that are part confounder and part mechanism. So even when researchers have controlled for lots of potential confounders, we should still worry about biased estimates.

If controlling is typically an unconvincing strategy for estimating causal relationships, what can we do that would be more convincing? One way—perhaps the only way—to ensure unbiased estimates is to randomize the treatment yourself. Therefore, the next chapter focuses on the so-called gold standard for causal inference—the randomized experiment.

Key Terms

- **Controlling:** Using a statistical technique to find the correlation between two variables, holding the value of other variables constant.
- **Dummy variable:** A variable that indicates whether a given unit has some particular characteristic, taking a value of 1 if the unit has that characteristic and 0 if the unit does not.
- **Dependent or Outcome variable:** The variable in your data corresponding to the feature of the world that you are trying to understand or explain with your regression.
- **Treatment variable:** The variable in your data corresponding to the feature of the world whose effect on the dependent variable you are trying to estimate.
- **Control variable:** A variable in your data that you include in your statistical analysis in an attempt to reduce bias in your estimate of a causal effect.

- **Omitted variables bias:** The bias resulting from failing to control for some confounder when attempting to estimate a causal effect.
- **Local average treatment effect (LATE):** The average treatment effect for some specific subset of the population.

Exercises

10.1   Download "HouseElectionsSpending2018.csv" and the associated "README.txt," which describes the variables in this data set, at press.princeton.edu/thinking-clearly.

(a) Run a regression of incumbent vote share (your dependent variable) on both incumbent spending and challenger spending.

   i. Note that if challenger spending is positively correlated with higher challenger vote shares, it must be negatively correlated with incumbent vote share. In light of this, how should we interpret the estimated coefficients associated with your independent variables?

   ii. Are the results you obtained different from those you obtained when you ran separate regressions of incumbent vote share on incumbent spending and incumbent vote share on challenger spending in chapter 9? Why or why not?

(b) Let's add some controls to your regression in an attempt to obtain more reliable estimates of the effect of campaign spending. As you may know, 2018 was a good year for Democrats in House elections.

   i. Is the overall good performance of Democrats in 2018 a potential confounder in your regression?

   ii. Create a new variable indicating whether the incumbent is a Republican—call it *republicanincumbent*. It should take a value of 1 if the incumbent is a Republican and a value of 0 if the incumbent is a Democrat.

   iii. Re-run your regression, but include that variable as a control.

   iv. Interpret the estimated coefficient associated with your new republicanincumbent variable.

   v. Does including this control variable meaningfully change your estimated coefficients of interest (i.e., the coefficients on incumbent and challenger spending)? Why or why not, do you think?

(c) Now add in a control for the vote share that the incumbent's party received in that district in the 2016 presidential election.

   i. What kind of concern might including this control variable address?

   ii. Interpret the estimated coefficient associated with this control variable.

   iii. Does including this control variable meaningfully change your estimated coefficients of interest (i.e., the coefficients on incumbent and challenger spending)? Why or why not, do you think?

10.2   Produce a regression table that shows the results of each of the regressions from exercise 1, along with the number of observations and the *r*-squared.

10.3   In chapter 2, we discussed a study that finds a correlation between taking advanced math classes in high school and college completion, which the researchers presented as evidence of a causal relationship. Of course, we might worry that the kinds of students who take advanced math courses are different from those who do not, so the authors of the study run regressions that control for gender, socioeconomic status, race, cognitive ability test scores, and eighth-grade reading and math scores.

(a) Do these control variables assuage your concerns about potential confounders?
(b) Even after controlling for these background variables, name a potential omitted confounder that concerns you. What is the likely direction of the bias associated with this potential confounder?

Readings and References

For more details on controlling, as well as more details on experiments, instrumental variables, difference-in-differences, and regression discontinuity (topics we will cover in the next three chapters), we recommend

Joshua Angrist and Jorg-Steffen Pischke. 2014. *Mastering 'Metrics*. Princeton University Press.

For more information on political polarization, including details on increasing polarization in the U.S. Congress over the past seven or so decades, we recommend

Nolan McCarty. 2019. *Polarization: What Everyone Needs to Know*. Oxford University Press.

For more on the LATE versus the ATE, including a defense of credible estimates of a LATE, see

Guido W. Imbens. "Better LATE than Nothing: Some Comments on Deaton (2009) and Heckman and Urzua (2009)." *Journal of Economic Literature* 48(2):399–423.

The study on Facebook and subjective well-being is

Hunt Allcott, Luca Braghieri, Sarah Eichmeyer, and Matthew Gentzkow. 2020. "The Welfare Effects of Social Media." *American Economic Review* 110(3):629–76.

CHAPTER 11

Randomized Experiments

What You'll Learn

- Randomizing treatment can yield unbiased causal estimates.
- All the tools of statistical inference and hypothesis testing work in experimental settings for adjudicating between genuine effects and noise.
- Even with a randomized experiment, numerous complications can arise and must be planned around.
- When experimental subjects fail to comply with their experimental assignment, it is important to make comparisons based on randomized assignment.
- Even when researchers can't implement their ideal experiment, sometimes they can find instances in which their treatment of interest was randomized for non-research purposes. Such "natural experiments" are often fruitful, fortuitous opportunities to answer important causal questions.

Introduction

We love regression, so we had a pretty good time with chapter 10. But we can see how the message that you can basically never get unbiased estimates of causal relationships just by controlling for confounders might be something of a downer. We are going to try to make it up to you in the next three chapters. We'll do so by showing you that there are better ways to learn about causality. Those ways are called *research designs*. Using research designs to learn about causality often involves quite a bit of cleverness and creativity. This makes research design one of the most fun topics you must master in order to think clearly with data.

In this chapter, we consider the research design called a randomized experiment. Randomized experiments are great because, if you can randomize treatment, there are no confounders. So you can eliminate bias from your estimates. An analogy to randomized experiments also helps to explain why the approaches we consider in the next two chapters are called research designs. When you run a randomized experiment, you literally get to *design* the way in which treatment is assigned.

In chapters 12 and 13, we will turn to other research designs that are a little less "designy." In particular, those research designs are ways of trying to learn about causality from data that you observe in the wild—that is, where the world, rather than an experimenter, decided how treatment would be assigned. But before we go there, let's spend some time learning about randomized experiments and how they work.

Breastfeeding

At the time of this writing, it is a virtual article of faith in the developed world that babies should be breastfed. Consider, for example, this official statement from the World Health Organization: "Adults who were breastfed as babies often have lower blood pressure and lower cholesterol, as well as lower rates of overweight, obesity and type-2 diabetes. There is evidence that people who were breastfed perform better in intelligence tests." Similarly, in 2011, the Surgeon General of the United States issued a call to action to support breastfeeding, which she said is "one of the most highly effective preventive measures a mother can take to protect the health of her infant." The accompanying report claimed that breastfeeding prevents a host of childhood scourges, including ear infection, eczema, diarrhea, respiratory disease, asthma, obesity, type 2 diabetes, leukemia, and sudden infant death syndrome (SIDS). Indeed, an enormous scientific literature documents the positive correlation between breastfeeding and good health outcomes for children.

But before you jump to conclusions about the causal benefits of breastfeeding, consider this fact. In developing countries, breastfeeding seems to be correlated with worse, not better, health outcomes for children. In countries as diverse as Ghana, Kenya, Egypt, Brazil, Peru, Bolivia, and Thailand, breastfeeding has been found to be correlated with malnutrition and decreased height and weight.

What is going on? Is it possible that breastfeeding is good for kids in the industrialized world and bad for kids in the developing world? Maybe, but let's make sure we are thinking as clearly as possible. You have already learned that correlation does not necessarily imply causation. And in this case, the comparison of mothers who do and do not breastfeed is most likely not an apples-to-apples one.

First, think about the developing world, where breastfeeding is negatively correlated with children's physical well-being. One possibility is that breastfeeding causes these adverse outcomes. It's also possible that some confounding factor, like poverty, causes both breastfeeding and malnourishment. Breastfeeding costs a lot in terms of a mother's time, but it doesn't cost much money. Formula, by contrast, costs a lot of money but less time. So we might expect that economically distressed families are more likely to breastfeed their children. And children from those same economically distressed families may be more prone to health problems for reasons entirely unrelated to breastfeeding. Reverse causality is also a concern. Perhaps adverse health in an infant directly leads a mother to be more likely to breastfeed.

Indeed, confounding factors and reverse causality appear highly relevant in the developing world. A 1997 study published in the *International Journal of Epidemiology* tracked the health outcomes of 238 toddlers in a village in Peru. The study's data included information on child size, breastfeeding, complementary food intake, and diarrhea. The study found a negative correlation between breastfeeding and size—children who were breastfed were smaller on average, suggesting they were in poorer health. This relationship was strongest among those children who were getting the least complementary food and were the most sickly. It turns out that, because breastfeeding is widely believed to have health benefits, mothers whose children were sickly or lacked access to complementary food weaned their children later. Consequently, children who were already sick and malnourished were more likely to be breastfed. Thus, the study concludes, it is not breastfeeding that causes children not to grow in the developing world. Rather, children who are not growing because they are sick and malnourished are more likely to be breastfed.

Now think about the developed world, where parents are inundated with the message that breastfeeding is good for their children. Remember, breastfeeding is said to reduce the risk of heart disease, asthma, obesity, leukemia, SIDS, ear infections, and a host of other ailments. Unfortunately, the evidence underlying this conventional wisdom once again doesn't withstand much scrutiny. Surely you can think of lots of reasons why comparing breastfed children to children who are not breastfed might not be an apples-to-apples comparison. For instance, once official organizations issue statements on the efficacy of breastfeeding, we would expect wealthy, educated mothers to be particularly likely to hear this news and follow the advice. But their children were likely to have better health outcomes anyway.

Breastfeeding or not is such a high-stakes decision, and so many different factors influence this decision, that it might be impossible to find an apples-to-apples comparison out there in the world. However, perhaps we could generate our own apples-to-apples comparison through a randomized experiment. A team of researchers in Belarus tried to do exactly this.

The team's strategy was to run a randomized experiment. Clearly, for both ethical and practical reasons, they couldn't force mothers to breastfeed or not, just for the benefit of their study. But they could make it more likely that a randomly selected group of mothers would choose to breastfeed through randomly assigned encouragement. To achieve this, in some randomly selected hospitals the researchers implemented a program to encourage and facilitate breastfeeding. In other randomly selected hospitals, they did not implement this program. For all the hospitals, they recorded how children were fed and tracked a variety of the children's health (and other) outcomes over time. And, indeed, mothers in the hospitals that had the breastfeeding program were much more likely to breastfeed their newborns.

Despite the claims from the World Health Organization, the Surgeon General, the American Academy of Pediatrics, and the parenting industry more generally, they found surprisingly scant evidence for the large benefits breastfeeding is supposed to provide. Babies from the hospitals that received the program were slightly less likely to have eczema and gastrointestinal infections, but the researchers obtained null results (i.e., no statistically significant evidence of effects of breastfeeding) for many more outcomes. In a follow-up study, conducted when the children were between six and seven years old, the investigators explored whether the children whose mothers were encouraged to breastfeed performed better on any observable physical, psychological, or cognitive outcomes. They found no evidence that breastfeeding provided benefits in terms of the risk of eczema, allergies, asthma, obesity, emotional problems, conduct problems, hyperactivity, or peer problems. Indeed, if anything, the evidence went the other way, showing some limited evidence of a negative association between breastfeeding and these outcomes. The one piece of evidence they found in support of breastfeeding was that children from the hospitals that received the breastfeeding program performed slightly better on IQ tests. But in thinking about this one finding, don't forget the lessons about over-comparing we discussed in chapter 7. If you look at that many outcomes, you're pretty likely to find at least one statistically significant finding just because of noise.

Overall, our view is that the experimental evidence is not nearly strong enough to encourage every mother around the world to breastfeed. Although there are strong correlations between breastfeeding and health outcomes in various settings, and some reasonable arguments about the biological mechanisms through which breastfeeding might work, the best available evidence suggests that the average effect of breastfeeding is likely small. Without the power of randomized experimentation, it would be easy to over- or under-estimate the benefits of breastfeeding.

Randomization and Causal Inference

What makes randomized experiments such a powerful tool for learning about causal relationships? To start to see the answer, let's return to our discussion of potential outcomes and Body Vibes.

Suppose we want to know the effect of some treatment, say Body Vibes, on some outcome of interest, say skin health. In general, it is difficult to estimate the effect of Body Vibes because of all the issues discussed in previous chapters. We want to know how different a person's skin would be in the world in which they use Body Vibes versus the world in which they do not use Body Vibes. Unfortunately, for any given person, we only get to observe one of those potential outcomes. For example, if a person uses Body Vibes, we can observe their skin health in that situation, but we don't know what their skin would be like if they hadn't used Body Vibes.

If we just compared the average skin health of people who do and don't use Body Vibes, that's not comparing apples to apples. That is, there are a variety of confounders that imply that this difference in means is not an unbiased estimate of the average treatment effect. For instance, perhaps those who use Body Vibes just care more about their skin, and they also use more moisturizer and sunscreen. Or maybe the bias goes the other way. Perhaps the people who use Body Vibes have bad skin, they've tried everything else, and they're getting desperate. Either way, because of such confounders, we can't get an unbiased estimate of the effect of Body Vibes just by comparing the average skin health of people who do and do not use them.

One way, perhaps the best way, to get rid of this bias and be sure that we're making an apples-to-apples comparison is to randomize the treatment. Our comparison of those using and not using Body Vibes is biased because these groups likely have baseline differences. That is, on average, they would likely have different skin health even if none (or all) of them used Body Vibes. However, if we randomly assign people to use or not use Body Vibes, then those two groups would, in expectation, be the same in terms of their pre-existing skin health and all other prior characteristics. That is, there would be no confounders. Why is this the case?

If a treatment of interest is determined by the flip of a coin, a random-number generator on your computer, or another random process, then the only thing that distinguishes people in the treated group and the untreated group is pure chance. There is no reason why people in the treated group should be systematically taller, smarter, richer, more motivated, or have better skin than those in the untreated group before we deliver the treatment.

In terms of our potential outcomes notation, suppose we randomly assign some group (the treated group $\mathcal{T}$) to receive Body Vibes and another group (the untreated group $\mathcal{U}$) not to receive them. We observe the average skin health of the treated group with Body Vibes, $\overline{Y}_{1\mathcal{T}}$. And we observe the average skin health of the untreated group without Body Vibes, $\overline{Y}_{0\mathcal{U}}$. Thus, if we compare the average skin health in the two groups we get the difference in means:

$$\overline{Y}_{1\mathcal{T}} - \overline{Y}_{0\mathcal{U}}$$

But, because of randomization, there are no systematic differences between either of these groups and the population as a whole. Thus, the average skin health of the treated group wearing Body Vibes is an unbiased estimate of the average skin health of the whole population in the hypothetical world in which everyone wears Body Vibes:

$$\overline{Y}_{1\mathcal{T}} = \overline{Y}_1 + \text{Noise}_1$$

And similarly for the untreated group:

$$\overline{Y}_{0\mathcal{U}} = \overline{Y}_0 + \text{Noise}_0$$

Hence, the observed difference in means is an unbiased estimate of the average treatment effect,

$$\overbrace{\overline{Y}_{1\mathcal{T}} - \overline{Y}_{0\mathcal{U}}}^{\text{Observed Difference in Means}} = \overbrace{\overline{Y}_1 - \overline{Y}_0}^{\text{ATE}} + \text{Noise},$$

where this noise is just the difference of the two noise terms above.

As in the examples from previous chapters, noise can come from sampling variability. Perhaps there's a broader population about which we care, and we happened by chance to get an unusual sample of subjects in our experiment. It can also come from measurement error. And now, when we're doing an experiment, noise also comes from the random assignment of the treatment to subjects. Even for the same sample of subjects, different randomizations could have produced different estimates, and this also contributes to the noise.

Because of noise, for any small-scale experiment, there will be some differences in average potential outcomes between the treated and untreated groups, just by chance. But those differences won't be systematic—if we were to run many iterations of the experiment, we would not expect to find the same pattern of differences repeated over and over. This is what we mean by the phrase *in expectation* several paragraphs above.

Think back to our favorite equation:

$$\text{Estimate} = \text{Estimand} + \text{Bias} + \text{Noise}$$

Randomization guarantees that the bias is zero. So noise is the only reason that the estimate we get from comparing the mean outcome in the treated and untreated groups in a properly randomized experiment differs from the true causal effect (i.e., the estimand).

As we increase the number of subjects in any given experiment, we expect the two groups to become more and more similar. That is, as the sample size gets big, the noise becomes small.

Randomization gives you comparability of the treated and untreated group in expectation—generating unbiased estimates. A large sample size gives you a very small amount of noise—generating precise estimates. So randomization plus a large sample size gives you comparability in your actual, realized sample—generating estimates that are very likely to be close to the true estimand.

If you think clearly about it, you'll realize that randomization is essentially the only way to guarantee unbiased estimates of causal relationships. Suppose you tried to conduct an experiment, but instead of randomly assigning subjects to the treated and untreated groups, you tried to carefully divide the groups so that they were as similar as possible to each other. Since you can't possibly observe and quantify all of your subjects' relevant characteristics, you'd have to make some judgment calls. Maybe you'll do this really well, and maybe you won't. What if your own subconscious biases lead you to put slightly different people in the treated and untreated groups—perhaps because you're subconsciously hoping the experiment will show a big effect? You'll have no way of knowing whether you actually did a good job. Therefore, why take the risk? Why not actually flip a coin and assign the treatment randomly? If this point seems obvious now, it wasn't obvious to a lot of smart people in the past. It's only since the work of R. A. Fisher in the 1920s that scientific researchers have understood the value of randomization.

There is one way in which this thought about trying to make the treated and untreated groups as similar as possible on observable characteristics does make some sense. As we know from our favorite equation, there are two ways our estimates might differ from the true causal effect: bias and noise. Randomization eliminates bias. But there could still be lots of noise, especially if the sample size is small or the experimental subjects are quite different from one another on characteristics that matter for the outcome. That is, in any given iteration of an experiment, the treated and untreated groups could end up looking very different *in reality*, even though they are the same *in expectation*.

One thing you can do to reduce this problem is to start by grouping people on the basis of their observable similarities. Then you can randomly assign individuals to be treated or untreated within those groupings. This is called *blocking* or *stratification*. For example, you might be concerned that men and women, on average, have very different levels of skin health. It would introduce a lot of noise into your experiment if, by chance, you ended up with a treated group made up of mostly men and an untreated group made up of mostly women, or vice versa. This won't happen in expectation (i.e., if you did the experiment an infinite number of times, the average proportion of men and women will be the same in the treated and untreated groups). But it could happen in any given iteration of your randomization. To eliminate this source of noise, you could start by dividing your experimental population by biological sex. Then you randomly assign half the male group to be treated and half to be untreated, and likewise for the female group. You'd still have randomized treatment assignment, so you'd still get unbiased estimates. But you'd also have reduced the noise by making sure that your treated and untreated groups were similar in terms of biological sex, not just in expectation but in reality.

Extending this logic, an analyst could identify many different blocks or strata of subjects with similar pre-treatment characteristics and conduct their randomization within these strata or blocks. The most extreme version of this would be a matched-pair design, where an analyst identifies pairs of individuals that they believe are most similar to one another and for each pair randomly assigns one to be treated and the other to be untreated. This can be a great way to improve the precision of one's estimates. But you must make sure that the treatment is assigned randomly within each pair.

Estimation and Inference in Experiments

In chapter 6, we discussed statistical inferences about relationships. All of those lessons apply in the case of an experimental estimate as well. In the simplest scenario, we can analyze the results of an experiment by calculating a difference in means—that is, comparing the average outcome in the treated and untreated groups. In fact, as we saw in chapter 5, if we regress the outcome on a binary measure of treatment status, the regression coefficient associated with the treatment variable is just the difference in means. And since regression coefficients and differences in means are just quantitative relationships, we can apply all of the statistical tools of chapter 6 to experiments as well.

Standard Errors

Suppose we conduct a randomized experiment and estimate the average treatment effect by comparing the average outcome for subjects with the treatment to the average outcome for subjects without the treatment. This estimate is unbiased. But it might be imprecise (i.e., there may be lots of noise).

We'd, of course, like to know how close our estimates are to the true effect of interest (i.e., the estimand). We can estimate the standard error associated with our experimental estimate just like we estimated the standard error of poll results and regression coefficients in chapter 6. The standard error gives us a sense of how far, on average, our estimate would be from the truth as a result of noise if we repeated our experiment an infinite number of times, each time using the same procedure to generate an estimate of the treatment effect. Similar to our discussion of poll results, the true standard error depends on quantities that are unobservable, but there are various approximations that practitioners use for estimating the standard error.

You don't need to memorize formulas for standard errors; you can always look them up or just let your computer calculate them for you. Nonetheless, it's useful to think about how various features of experiments influence the amount of noise. Suppose we conduct an experiment with N subjects, of whom m receive the treatment and $N - m$ do not. All else equal, the greater N is, the less noise and, thus, the smaller the standard error. This should be intuitive. When the sample size is larger, the treated and untreated groups will be more similar to each other with respect to other characteristics, reducing noise, and making our estimates closer to the true causal effect.

What about m? Suppose we have five hundred people in our study. How many of them would we like to put in the treated group and in the untreated group? Obviously, we can't put all of them in either group because then we wouldn't be able to make a comparison (remember that correlation requires variation). Extending that logic, we can see that we don't want too few subjects in either group. If either the treated group or the untreated group is very small, then our estimates will be imprecise because the average outcome for whichever group is small will be quite sensitive to the idiosyncratic features of just a few subjects. Typically, then, you'll get the most precise estimates when the sizes of the treated and untreated groups are roughly equal.

With that being said, there are often cases where an optimal experimental design might have different numbers of subjects in each condition. Suppose you have 100,000 potential subjects. You only have enough resources to put 100 people in your treated group, but it's costless to put more subjects in your untreated group. You might as well randomly assign 100 people to the treated group and everybody else to the untreated group. Your estimates won't be nearly as precise as if you had 50,000 people in each group, but they'll be much more precise than an experiment with 100 people in each group.

The last factor that influences the noisiness of experimental estimates is how variable the outcome is in both the treated and untreated groups. If we study outcomes with little variance within each treatment condition, our estimates will be more precise than if we study outcomes with greater variance. This is because, if the outcome doesn't vary much based on non-treatment characteristics, then there is very little scope for noise—we'll get similar outcomes for each group across iterations of the experiment. This is why, for example, doctors and government regulators often have precise estimates of the effect of some heart medication on blood pressure (a relatively low variance outcome) but imprecise estimates of the effect of the same drug on heart attacks (a high variance outcome). Of course, sometimes, we have no control over this. The outcome of interest is what it is. And sometimes the most interesting or important outcomes (e.g., heart attacks) are high variance. But other times it might be possible to identify outcomes or methods for measuring those outcomes that reduce noise.

Hypothesis Testing

We can also apply the tools of hypothesis testing that we learned in chapter 6 to experimental results to assess statistical significance. For instance, dividing the estimate by the standard error generates a value called a t-statistic, which can be used to estimate a p-value. And because we often do hypothesis testing with experimental results, we need to keep thinking clearly about the risks of over-comparing, under-reporting, and reversion to the mean. Recall from chapter 7 that analysts can reduce these risks by stating up front the questions of interest the experiment is designed to address, pre-specifying the hypotheses they plan to test and regressions they plan to run (so they can't just go fishing for a statistically significant finding), and reporting the results regardless of what they find.

We should also interpret experiments with these issues in mind. If analysts are not transparent about the steps they took to avoid over-comparing and under-reporting, we should be skeptical of their findings. And, the more surprising the findings, the more skeptical we should be. Remember that the ESP result arose in an experimental study! Or, more seriously, think again about the breastfeeding experiment with which we began this chapter. That study had many virtues. But one potential problem is that, because the study designers collected information on so many outcomes, when we see no evidence of an effect of breastfeeding on eczema, allergies, asthma, obesity, emotional problems, conduct problems, hyperactivity, or peer problems, but we do see an effect on IQ, we are worried that the apparent effect on IQ arose just by chance.

Problems That Can Arise with Experiments

Things rarely work as beautifully in practice as they do in our idealized examples. In theory, you can design a randomized experiment and estimate the average treatment effect simply by comparing means. In practice, however, problems arise that make analysis and interpretation less straightforward. Let's discuss some of those problems and the ways in which careful analysts can deal with them. Thinking about these issues now will have benefits beyond the context of experiments because these problems can arise for virtually any strategy for estimating causal relationships.

Noncompliance and Instrumental Variables

One common problem in experiments is that subjects fail to comply with their assigned treatment. We call this *noncompliance*. For instance, it is pretty common in medical studies for some subjects to simply stop taking their medication. There was also noncompliance in the breastfeeding experiment. Recall, because it is unethical to force a mother to breastfeed or not, the researchers randomly assigned mothers into groups where they received more or less encouragement to breastfeed. Encouragement designs like this allow researchers to experimentally study lots of topics that would otherwise be off-limits for logistical or ethical reasons. But such studies inevitably involve the additional complications that arise from noncompliance, since surely some mothers who were encouraged nonetheless did not breastfeed and some mothers who were not encouraged did breastfeed.

Suppose we designed a randomized experiment to estimate the effect of Body Vibes on skin health. We randomly assign some individuals to the treatment condition—we give them Body Vibes and, for the sake of science, try to convince them to wear them. We also randomly assign some individuals to an untreated condition—they are given no Body Vibes and told to go about their normal lives. Then, despite our best efforts, some of the subjects in the treated group forget or simply refuse to wear their Body Vibes. And amazingly, a few of the more gullible members of the untreated group hear about Body Vibes elsewhere, spend their hard-earned money on the product, and wear them. Shoot! What do we do?

One idea would be to simply compare people who did and didn't wear Body Vibes, ignoring whether each subject was initially assigned to the treated or untreated group. But this won't work. It brings us right back to the problem we were trying to solve through our randomized experiment. The people who voluntarily wear or do not wear Body Vibes are likely different from one another, so a comparison of those two groups is not apples-to-apples.

Another idea would be to drop the subjects that did not comply with their treatment assignments. In other words, we could remove from our analysis the people who were assigned to the treated group but didn't wear Body Vibes and the people who were assigned to the untreated group but did wear them. After doing that, we might just proceed as normal, comparing the mean skin health among the remaining members of the treated and untreated groups.

Unfortunately, this is still not an adequate solution. To see why, think about the people who were in the treated group but refused to wear Body Vibes. They might be special in important ways—for example, they may have better skin health or be less gullible. Presumably, there were also people just like them in the untreated group. But, because we didn't ask those people to wear Body Vibes in the first place, we can't figure out who they are. So we can't similarly remove them from the untreated group. Thus, if we throw this group of people out of the treated group, the comparison of the treated and untreated groups will no longer be apples-to-apples. The kinds of people who wouldn't wear Body Vibes even if given to them would be present in the untreated group but not the treated group.

So what can we do in light of noncompliance? Well, one thing we can always do is estimate the effect of being assigned to the treated group (as distinct from the effect of the treatment itself). We sometimes call this the *intent-to-treat* (ITT) effect or the *reduced-form* effect. We do this by comparing the outcomes for the people assigned to the treated and untreated groups, regardless of whether they actually comply with their treatment assignment. This comparison won't give us an unbiased estimate of the effect of wearing Body Vibes. But it will give us an unbiased estimate of the effect of being given Body Vibes and encouraged to wear them.

There are situations where a policy maker or decision maker actually cares more about intent-to-treat effects than actual treatment effects. Suppose a charitable organization is trying to decide whether it should provide free Body Vibes to high school kids with bad skin. They know that not everyone provided with Body Vibes will wear them. Furthermore, all they can do from a policy perspective is provide the Body Vibes; they can't force anyone to use them. They conduct an experiment to estimate the benefits of free Body Vibes. What quantity should go on the benefits side of their cost-benefit analysis to inform them about whether this is a good policy? It's not the average effect of Body Vibes for an individual who uses them. It's the average effect of being provided Body Vibes, regardless of whether an individual uses them or not, since this is what the charitable organization can actually do. So the intent-to-treat effect is the relevant number. More seriously, in many settings, all a policy maker or organization can do is provide a service; they can't force people to take it up. In any such situation, the intent-to-treat effect may in fact be the most important quantity.

In other situations, however, we are interested in the actual effect of the treatment, not just the intent-to-treat effect. Suppose, for instance, that we're trying to decide whether we should wear Body Vibes ourselves. Or, more seriously, suppose someone is deciding whether to try an experimental medical treatment, a new study regimen, a new teaching technique, or a new productivity-enhancing management strategy. In those cases, we want to know more than just the intent-to-treat effect. We want to know the likely effect of taking up the treatment. So what more can we do with our experimental results, plagued as they are by issues of noncompliance?

To make some additional progress, let's think about the different ways a subject can respond to our experimental encouragement to wear or not wear Body Vibes. Our sample consists of up to four different kinds of people.

1. There are *compliers*, who will wear Body Vibes if they're assigned to treatment and will not wear them if they're not assigned to treatment.
2. There are *always-takers*, who will wear Body Vibes regardless of whether or not they are assigned to treatment.
3. There are *never-takers*, who will not wear Body Vibes regardless of whether or not they are assigned to treatment. (We are both never-takers when it comes to Body Vibes.)
4. And, in principle, there could be a perverse group of *defiers*, who won't wear Body Vibes if they're in the treated group but will wear Body Vibes if they're in the untreated group.

Obviously, when we do an experiment, we're hoping for lots of compliers. The whole idea of an experiment is that we want to randomly assign treatment, and the compliers are those subjects who are willing to let us do that.

Every subject in an experiment fits neatly into one (and only one) of these categories. However, we can't just look at our experimental subjects and figure out which people are compliers, always-takers, never-takers, or defiers. Why is that? Suppose we see that someone is in the untreated group and doesn't wear Body Vibes. We know that they are either a complier or a never-taker. But we have no way of knowing which, because we don't know whether they would have worn Body Vibes if they were in

Table 11.1. Who takes the treatment in a Body Vibes experiment?

	Treated Group	Untreated Group
Wore Body Vibes	Compliers & Always-Takers	Always-Takers & Defiers
Didn't Wear Body Vibes	Never-Takers & Defiers	Compliers & Never-Takers

Table 11.2. Who takes the treatment in a Body Vibes experiment, assuming there are only compliers and never-takers?

	Treated Group	Untreated Group
Wore Body Vibes	Compliers	N/A
Didn't Wear Body Vibes	Never-Takers	Compliers & Never-Takers

the treated group. Table 11.1 illustrates this issue more generally for our Body Vibes experiment.

Dividing people up into these groups helps us think clearly about when we are or are not making an apples-to-apples comparison. In particular, in order to ensure that we don't have confounding, we want the groups we compare (say, treated and untreated groups) to have the same share of compliers, always-takers, never-takers, and defiers.

To get a sense of how this helps us understand the problem, let's start by assuming that everyone is either a complier or a never-taker. In other words, none of those people who might buy and wear Body Vibes on their own happened to participate in our experiment. (We'll relax this in a bit.) Table 11.2 shows what our experiment looks like in a world with only compliers and never-takers.

Now let's revisit the various ways we might deal with experimental subjects who don't behave according to their treatment assignment. It's easy to see why we can't just compare people who did and didn't wear Body Vibes, ignoring their treatment assignment. The group that wears Body Vibes is made up of just the compliers in the treated group. The group that doesn't wear Body Vibes is a combination of the compliers in the untreated group, the never-takers in the untreated group, and the never-takers in the treated group. So the comparison of Body Vibes wearers to non–Body Vibes wearers is not apples-to-apples.

Similarly, it's easy to see why we can't just drop the people who visibly don't comply with our experiment. We would drop the never-takers from the treated group. But we wouldn't drop anyone from the untreated group. As a result we'd be comparing the compliers from the treated group to a combination of the compliers and the never-takers from the untreated group—again, not an apples-to-apples comparison.

It seems like we're still stuck in a place where all we can do is compare the treated and untreated groups, estimating the intent-to-treat effect. But, actually, we can do better. Let's see how.

A key step in doing better involves estimating the proportion of compliers in our sample. We don't know exactly who the compliers are. But, in our simplified example with only compliers and never-takers, we can estimate what proportion of the sample is compliers. We do so by calculating the proportion of the treated group that takes up the treatment. This is the proportion of compliers in the treated group. And, because

Table 11.3. Observed differences between the two experimental groups.

	People Assigned to Be Treated	People Assigned to Be Untreated
Average Skin Health	7.8	6.2

of random assignment, the treated and untreated groups have the same proportion of compliers in expectation. Therefore, the proportion of compliers in the treated group is an unbiased estimate of the proportion of compliers in the whole sample (i.e., the treated group and untreated group combined).

We now have unbiased estimates of both the intent-to-treat effect (by comparing the average outcomes in the group assigned to be treated and the group assigned to be untreated) and the proportion of compliers in the sample. How does that help us?

We want to know the effect of Body Vibes on some outcome like skin health. If we assume that the only way that treatment assignment could have influenced skin health is through the actual use of Body Vibes, then what is the intent-to-treat effect? Under our assumption, the never-takers were not affected by the treatment assignment, and the effect of the treatment assignment for the compliers is just the effect of Body Vibes. So the expected intent-to-treat effect is the average effect of Body Vibes for compliers times the proportion of compliers in the sample. That means if we divide the ITT effect by our estimate for the proportion of compliers, we'll have an unbiased estimate of the average effect of the treatment for compliers.

Let's do a little example to see how this works. Imagine that Body Vibes actually work. (Remember, a lot of this book is about counterfactual worlds.) In particular, suppose that you could measure skin health on a scale of 1–10, with 10 being perfect skin and 1 being very bad skin.

Now let's imagine we conducted an experiment on 100 people to study the effects of Body Vibes. We randomly assigned 50 people to receive the treatment and 50 people not to. The people assigned to receive the treatment got Body Vibes. The other people did not. A month later, we measured the skin health of each person on our 1–10 scale. Suppose the data looked like that in table 11.3.

Our estimate from the data of the intent-to-treat effect is 1.6—that is, on average, people given Body Vibes had a skin health score that was 1.6 points higher than people not given Body Vibes.

You dig a little deeper and discover that, while no one in the group assigned to be untreated went and bought Body Vibes, only 40 of the 50 people assigned to treatment wore them. From this you estimate that the proportion of compliers in your sample is 80 percent ($\frac{40}{50}$) and the proportion of never-takers in your sample is 20 percent. You can now estimate the true effect of Body Vibes on the compliers.

How does this work? To make sure we are thinking clearly, let's return to our potential outcomes notation. Let Y_{0c} be the average skin health of a complier without treatment (i.e., without Body Vibes); let Y_{1c} be the average skin health of a complier with treatment (i.e., with Body Vibes); and let Y_{0n} be the average skin health of a never-taker without treatment. Given that we have 80 percent compliers and 20 percent never-takers, we have the following two equations:

$$7.8 = 80\% \cdot Y_{1c} + 20\% \cdot Y_{0n}$$

$$6.2 = 80\% \cdot Y_{0c} + 20\% \cdot Y_{0n}$$

The first equation says that the average skin health for those assigned to the treated group (7.8) is a weighted average of the average skin health of compliers with treatment (with weight 80%) and of never-takers without treatment (with weight 20%). Similarly, the average skin health for those assigned to the untreated group (6.2) is a weighted average of the average skin health of compliers without treatment (with weight 80%) and of never-takers without treatment (with weight 20%).

We can subtract the left-hand sides of these two equations from one another and the right-hand sides of these two equations from one another to get

$$1.6 = 80\% \cdot (Y_{1c} - Y_{0c}).$$

The left-hand side is the intent-to-treat effect: the difference in average outcomes between the group assigned to be treated and the group assigned to be untreated. On the right-hand side, "80%" represents the proportion of compliers in the sample. And the term in parentheses is the average effect of the treatment for compliers (usually called the *complier average treatment effect* or CATE). So, we can recover the complier average treatment effect by dividing both sides by 80 percent:

$$\frac{1.6}{80\%} = \overbrace{Y_{1c} - Y_{0c}}^{\text{CATE}}$$
$$= 2.$$

It is important to note the distinction between the complier average treatment effect and the overall average treatment effect. It is possible that wearing Body Vibes has the same effect on skin health for everyone. In this scenario, we would say that there are *homogeneous treatment effects*. But this need not be the case—Body Vibes could differentially affect the skin health of different people, and the average effects might be quite different for the kind of person who would never use them (never-takers) and the kind of person who uses them if encouraged (compliers). In this case, we say there are *heterogeneous treatment effects*. As the algebra above shows, dividing the intent to treat effect by the share of compliers estimates the complier average treatment effect. If there are homogeneous treatment effects, the complier average treatment effect is the same as the overall average treatment effect. But if there are heterogeneous treatment effects, they are not the same and we have to keep in mind that we are only able to estimate the average treatment effect for this specific subgroup. The intuition for why is straightforward. It is only the compliers who are actually changing their behavior in response to treatment. So they are the only part of the population about whom we are actually gaining information.

It was relatively easy to see how all this works in a simplified world where everyone was either a complier or a never-taker. But we can do the same basic thing even if we move away from this simplified world and also allow for the possibility of always-takers. For now, let's continue to assume that there are no defiers, because they muddy the waters. (There are lots of situations, including this hypothetical Body Vibes experiment, where we think that there will be few to no defiers.)

Table 11.4 shows how different types of subjects appear in our experimental sample in this more complicated world.

How do we estimate the proportion of compliers when there are compliers, never-takers, and always-takers? First, the people in the group assigned to be treated who

Table 11.4. Who takes the treatment in a Body Vibes experiment, assuming there are no defiers?

	Treated Group	**Untreated Group**
Wore Body Vibes	Compliers & Always-Takers	Always-Takers
Didn't Wear Body Vibes	Never-Takers	Compliers & Never-Takers

actually wear Body Vibes are either compliers or always-takers. So the size of this group gives us an estimate of the proportion of always-takers plus compliers. Second, the people in the group assigned to be untreated who wear Body Vibes are definitely always-takers. So the size of this group gives us an estimate of the proportion of always-takers. By subtracting this second number from the first, we get an estimate of the proportion of compliers. With that in hand, we can again proceed as above—calculating the ITT effect and dividing it by the share of compliers to get the CATE.

Therefore, our general procedure for estimating the complier average treatment effect is as follows. First, estimate the ITT effect—that is, the effect of being assigned to the treated group on the outcome of interest. Second, estimate the effect of being assigned to the treated group on the actual take-up of the treatment. This is sometimes called the *first-stage effect*. Assuming there are no defiers, this gives us an unbiased estimate of the proportion of compliers. We then recover an estimate of the CATE by dividing the intent-to-treat effect by the proportion of compliers. This ratio is called the *Wald Estimator*, after the statistician Abraham Wald, who first developed it, though in a different context.

The Wald Estimator is a special case of what is called *instrumental variables* (IV) analysis. This kind of analysis is appropriate when the treatment of interest is not randomly assigned but there is some other variable (called an instrument) that (1) affects the treatment of interest, (2) does not affect the outcome of interest except through the treatment, and (3) is randomly assigned (or, there is some other way to credibly estimate its effect on the treatment and the outcome).

To be more precise, there are four key conditions that must hold for IV analysis to work:

1. **Exogeneity**: The instrument must be randomly assigned or be "as if" randomly assigned, allowing us to obtain unbiased estimates of both the first-stage and reduced-form (ITT) effects.
2. **Exclusion restriction**: All of the reduced-form effect must occur through the treatment. In other words, there is no other pathway for the instrument to influence the outcome except through its effect on the treatment. If this isn't the case, then the reduced-form effect includes both the effect of the treatment on the outcome for compliers and these other pathways. Then, even after we divide by the first-stage effect, the resulting estimate still includes these other pathways and, thus, does not reflect the CATE.
3. **Compliers**: There must be some compliers.
4. **No defiers**: If there are defiers, then our estimate will give us a weighted average of the average effect for compliers and the average effect for defiers, but with the defiers getting negative weight (since their behavior changed in the wrong direction). How big a problem the presence of defiers is depends on how many of them there are and how different the treatment effects are for compliers

and defiers. If there are very few defiers, then the bias that comes from their presence is negligible. But if there are many defiers, they are a big problem for the IV analysis.

In the case of our Body Vibes experiment, the experimental assignment to be treated or untreated was an excellent instrument. It clearly satisfied exogeneity because we randomized treatment. It also seems unlikely that being assigned to the treated group had any way of affecting skin health other than through Body Vibes, so it quite plausibly satisfied the exclusion restriction. So, as long as there were compliers (i.e., people who actually used the Body Vibes because they were assigned to) and no defiers, our analysis yielded an estimate of the complier average treatment effect.

There are more flexible ways to implement IV analysis than the Wald Estimator. In particular, it can be implemented using regression, which is important because that allows us to accommodate control variables, if necessary, as well as situations with multiple instruments or treatments and instruments that are not binary.

Some analysts think of IV as a method or research design unto itself. For example, an analyst might implement our design above and say that they estimated the effect of Body Vibes using instrumental variables. That's technically true but misleading. The important research design in our example is the randomized experiment. We're using instrumental variables to deal with noncompliance, acknowledging the additional assumptions (above and beyond randomization) that doing so requires. In particular, the exclusion restriction is defensible in our example because all the experiment did was hand out stupid stickers to some people and not to others. In other contexts, however, the exclusion restriction will be harder to justify and will require a lot of thought. We will return to this later, when we discuss natural experiments.

Chance Imbalance

Randomization guarantees that the treated and untreated groups are, in expectation, the same in terms of potential outcomes. But the term *in expectation* is important. Just because two groups are the same in expectation doesn't mean they are the same in actuality. As we've discussed, in any given experiment, the treated group could differ from the untreated group in lots of ways, just due to chance, and we might call this a *chance imbalance*. This is why there is a noise term, in addition to a bias term, in our favorite equation.

Experimenters often assess the *balance* between their treated and untreated groups by comparing them in terms of measurable pre-treatment characteristics. For example, in our Body Vibes experiment, we could compare the average age, gender, weight, diet, and skin health of the subjects in the treated and untreated groups before the treatments are delivered. We could even test for statistically significant differences. The hope, of course, is that we don't find any differences. If we do, we must worry that, even though our estimate is unbiased, it might nonetheless be quite different from the true effect because of noise.

What should a careful analyst do if, despite randomization, the treated and untreated groups turn out to differ in substantively or statistically significant ways? Let's consider three potential responses.

1. **Throw out the "broken" experiment.** You had good intentions when you ran the experiment, but you got unlucky and now you can't trust your results, so

you should just forget the experiment and move on. Maybe you should do another one and hope for better balance.

We think this is an inappropriate response. Remember the problem of over-comparing. If you test for balance on enough pre-treatment variables, you are virtually guaranteed to find statistically significant imbalance on some of them. Therefore, by this logic, the more pre-treatment variables you can measure, the more likely you are to have to throw out the experiment, which seems perverse. Moreover, even "broken" experiments contain information. Importantly, they are unbiased (remember, bias is about getting the answer right on average, across lots of iterations of the experiment). And, so, the information could be pooled with other evidence (perhaps from other iterations of the same experiment) and incorporated into a larger analysis that will ultimately contribute to knowledge.

Our response here assumes that the analyst is confident that the treatment was indeed randomly assigned. Our recommendations would change if this wasn't the case. Suppose you (or your computer) didn't do the randomization directly. Instead, suppose you were running a large-scale experiment and the randomization was implemented by a big team or by a partner organization. In a situation like this, if you detect enough imbalance, you might start to worry that your planned randomization wasn't faithfully implemented. In that case, throwing out the experiment (probably following some investigation into whether your suspicions are well founded) could be appropriate.

2. **Proceed as normal.** Unbiasedness is a property *in expectation*, so the experimental estimate is still unbiased. You could report the imbalance for the sake of transparency while still estimating the treatment effect as you originally planned. Of course, the treated and untreated groups are sometimes different by chance. That's exactly why we report standard errors or other measures of noise.

   This strategy may seem unsatisfying. As you'll recall from chapter 6 and our favorite equation, even an unbiased estimate can be very far from the truth. When we find an imbalance between the treated and untreated groups that we think is strongly related to the outcome of interest, we might worry that this chance imbalance reflects getting one of those draws of our procedure that result in an estimate that is far from the truth, despite the absence of bias. Nonetheless, there is still some merit to proceeding as planned and reporting your unbiased (if probably quite wrong) estimate. This is especially the case if we are talking about the kind of experiment that will be replicated lots of times, so that the lack of balance in any one iteration will be washed out in the long run through averaging across many iterations of the experiment.

   But we also might wonder whether there is some way that we can account for the imbalance and generate an estimate that is likely to be closer to the right answer right now—which leads us to our third possible response.

3. **Use the techniques discussed in chapter 10 to control for any unbalanced variables.** As we learned in chapter 10, controlling for pre-treatment variables could improve precision by accounting for the variance in the outcome that is due to those variables. This is the sense in which controlling may help you get closer to the truth. But it has disadvantages as well. Because of randomization, you can be sure that estimating the treatment effect without controlling (e.g., just comparing the average outcome in the treated and untreated groups) leads

to an unbiased (if potentially very far from correct) estimate of the true effect. By contrast, controlling for variables after the fact can produce a biased (if more precise) estimate. This means that if you were to run your experiment lots of times and always control for whatever variables turn out to be imbalanced, the average of your estimates might not converge on the true effect. So there are trade-offs to think about between reducing noise and increasing bias.

Another concern with this approach is that by controlling for pre-treatment variables, the researcher is exercising additional degrees of freedom that should raise concerns about over-comparing and under-reporting. As we learned in chapter 7, savvy consumers should be skeptical when they see an analyst play around with their specification, and if an experimental result depends upon a particular set of control variables that were not necessitated by the design, we probably shouldn't have much faith in that result.

There is no easy answer or quick fix to the problem posed by chance imbalance following randomization. Our view is that you should probably do some combination of options 2 and 3. Also, whenever feasible, you should try to replicate experiments multiple times. No matter what, be honest and transparent about the choices you make.

Of course, what we'd really like is to avoid these difficult decisions by avoiding chance imbalance in the first place. And there are ways to do this. If you can identify and measure important characteristics ahead of time, you can design your experiment to ensure balance. We've already briefly mentioned how—by using a *blocked* or *stratified* experimental design. Prior to treatment, divide your sample into groups based on those characteristics and then randomize within those groups. Recall that earlier in this chapter we suggested that you might be concerned that Body Vibes differentially affect men and women, so you want to make sure your treated and untreated groups are balanced by biological sex. You achieve this by first dividing your sample into a male group and a female group. Then you randomize treatment assignment within these groups. This guarantees that biological sex is balanced between the treated and untreated groups (reducing noise), while still assigning treatment randomly (preserving unbiasedness). We can save ourselves a lot of headaches by following a procedure like this for pre-treatment characteristics that would cause us concern if they turned out to be imbalanced after the fact.

Lack of Statistical Power

Sometimes, an otherwise excellent experiment yields inconclusive results because the standard error is so large that we don't learn much, and even a reasonably sized effect would not be statistically distinguishable from zero. In this case, we say that the experiment lacked the *statistical power* to detect the effect of interest. Ideally, an experimenter would think about this problem beforehand and take steps to improve the precision and statistical power of the experiment—for instance, by increasing the sample size.

That said, sometimes, because of costs or other constraints, it turns out that you've run an underpowered experiment. If you've already run the experiment and obtained imprecise estimates, what can you do? Here, the debate mirrors that around chance imbalance. You can try to improve precision by controlling for some variables, but, as we've already discussed, that has downsides. Sometimes, you may just have to accept that you don't have a convincing answer to your question and you haven't learned much, even after running an experiment.

Thinking back to chapter 7, you might be wondering whether burying the results of an underpowered experiment contributes to the file-drawer problem. The answer is, yes. And this is a good reason not to run underpowered experiments. But if the results of an experiment are so imprecise that we learn virtually nothing, there isn't much use publicizing them. So failing to publish because an experiment didn't teach us much is not nearly as detrimental to the scientific process as failing to publish because an experiment didn't give the desired result.

Attrition

Sometimes people drop out of an experiment after treatment assignment. Such *attrition* is importantly different from noncompliance. Noncompliance involves people who were supposed to take up the treatment but chose not to. At least we get to observe the outcome for these noncompliers. When people drop out of the experiment, we don't even get to observe their outcome.

Suppose, for example, that Body Vibes make some people feel so young and carefree that they forget to come back for their follow-up meeting where we were planning to measure their skin health. This is bad. If attrition happens at random (i.e., is unrelated to the treatment or the potential outcomes), then we can still obtain an unbiased estimate of the effect of our treatment by comparing the remaining members of the treated and untreated groups. We just lose some statistical power because our sample got smaller. If attrition is nonrandom but unaffected by the treatment assignment, then we can at least estimate the average effect of the treatment for the kind of people that choose to remain in the experiment. This is a genuine effect, but we've kind of changed the question. And, of course, most of the time, if there is attrition, we're left worrying that the attrition is both nonrandom and influenced by the treatment. For instance, maybe people leave the study because Body Vibes work so well that they stop worrying about skin health entirely. In that case, were we to compare the remaining members of the treated and untreated groups, we'd be getting a biased estimate of the effect. (This is the sort of thing that can easily happen in a medical study if the researchers aren't careful.) As with many problems, it's much better if you can anticipate and mitigate attrition at the design stage rather than try to account for it after the fact.

If attrition is unavoidable, what should an analyst do? First, you can test whether the experimental treatment influenced the rate of attrition. If it did, then we know we no longer have an apples-to-apples comparison. And relatedly, you can see whether the treated versus untreated units that remained in your sample differ systematically on other covariates that might be related to the outcome.

If you have reason to think the treatment did affect the kinds of respondents that attrited, what can you do? Do we just have to throw out the experiment? Not necessarily—there is one last resort that doesn't require the analyst to make any assumptions about the nature of attrition. You can try to bound the extent of the bias arising from attrition.

To see how this works, imagine an experiment with a binary outcome (1 = healthy skin, 0 = unhealthy skin). Suppose that 50 percent of the subjects in both our treated and untreated groups appear to have healthy skin, suggesting no effect of Body Vibes, but 5 percent of subjects in each group never showed up to have their skin health measured. We don't know whether attrition was affected by the treatment. But we can ask how bad the bias could be if it was.

The best-case scenario for the hypothesis that Body Vibes are good for skin health would be if all of the people in the treated group who didn't show up had good skin and all of the people in the untreated group who didn't show up had bad skin. In that scenario, 52.5 percent of subjects in the treated group would have good skin health compared to 47.5 percent in the untreated group, implying a positive effect of Body Vibes on skin health of 5 percentage points. Alternatively, in the worst-case scenario for this hypothesis, those numbers would be flipped, and there would be a negative effect of 5 percentage points. We can't be sure that attrition doesn't bias our estimates, but we can say that the bias can't possibly be greater than 5 percentage points.

Interference

Interference occurs when the treatment status of one unit affects the outcome of another unit. This can bias the results of an experiment. To see what we mean, consider the following story we heard from our colleague, Chris Blattman, about a pilot study for an experiment he ran in Liberia.

Blattman was interested in understanding what kinds of interventions might help young men at high risk for engaging in crime or violence in post-conflict settings. In particular, he was trying to evaluate the impact of two kinds of interventions: offering young men small cash grants to start an income-generating business and offering them cognitive behavioral therapy.

One thing you might do, if you were interested in whether either of these two approaches works, is to start an organization offering each of them. You could then compare those who received either (or both) of these interventions to those who didn't, to see if those who received them did better in some important way.

Such an approach, however, would fail to compare apples to apples. It could well be that the young men who self-select into receiving grants or therapy are already different from the average young man in the sample. They might be more ambitious, healthier, smarter, or what have you. Thus, it would be a mistake to attribute the entire difference in performance between those who received the grants or therapy and those who didn't to the causal effect of the intervention.

To address these concerns, Blattman designed a randomized experiment in which he randomly assigned the different interventions to different groups of Liberian young men. Everyone would be given a small fee just for participating in the experiment. Then, some participants would get nothing more (the untreated group), while among the remaining participants, some would get a cash grant of about $200, some would get therapy, and some would get both a grant and therapy.

Blattman's plan was to compare levels of crime and homelessness among the young men assigned to different groups. The idea was that if the young men receiving one of the treatments had better outcomes than the untreated group, this would constitute apples-to-apples evidence that the intervention had a positive impact. So far, so good.

The problems started when the young men in the study found out that about half of them would receive $200 while the others would not. They explained that they did not want to play this lottery. They would prefer to each receive $100, eliminating any risk of getting nothing. Of course, giving them each $100 would ruin the experiment. After all, the purpose was to randomly give some more than others and see whether those who received more actually did better. So Blattman's team dispensed the cash grants as per their experimental protocol—randomly giving only half the participants the $200.

But these young men were one step ahead of the researchers. They seemed to have reached an understanding that they would provide one another with a sort of insurance. As a result of this insurance agreement, the winners of the lottery each gave some of their money to the losers, who had received nothing. This kind of interference biased the estimates that came out of the experiment, since now the carefully constructed untreated group had in fact received some of the treatment and the carefully constructed treated group had given up some of the treatment.

Here we see how hard it can be to design a clean experiment. Sometimes your experimental subjects or another outside force will undo your efforts.

Blattman's failed pilot is a clear example of *interference*. When you design an experiment, you randomly assign a treatment of interest across different units of observation (e.g., individual subjects, households, petri dishes). When you do that, you're assuming that those units of observation are independent from one another. However, if the treatment status of one unit actually affects the outcomes of another unit, that's interference, and that can bias the results of your experiment. In this experiment, the interference concern is that the treatment status of the group that got the cash grants affected the outcomes in the untreated group because the treated subjects actually shared some of the treatment with the untreated subjects.

How do careful analysts deal with interference? Sometimes it's interesting enough that the interference itself becomes the object of investigation. Do the taxes in one state influence economic development in a neighboring state? If a campaign mobilizes a group of supporters, will that subsequently mobilize a group of opponents? If a public health program vaccinates children in one school, will this help protect children in another school? Researchers can sometimes design studies with the goal of estimating these kinds of spillover effects. For example, Blattman could have randomly assigned some friend groups to have one person treated with cash and other friend groups to have nobody treated with cash. Then, he could have tested whether the individuals who weren't given money behaved differently when a friend was given money.

In general, careful analysts need to anticipate interference and design their studies in ways that mitigate these possibilities. This is exactly why researchers do things like running pilot studies. In Blattman's case, when he scaled up the experiment after the problematic pilot, he made sure that it remained a secret which subjects had and had not been assigned cash grants, to reduce the risk of interference.

Natural Experiments

For many interesting and important questions, we'd like to learn about causal relationships; however, an experiment might be infeasible, unethical, unrealistic, or prohibitively expensive. But sometimes the world creates something like experimental randomization for us, even without our intervening to actually run an experiment. We already saw one example of this kind of *natural experiment*, in our discussion of the effect of charter schools on academic outcomes in chapter 9. Although no quantitative analyst has been able to conduct their own experiment where they randomly send some kids to charter schools and others to public schools, many charter schools themselves randomize admissions. The schools didn't randomize for scientific reasons but rather because they were required to by law. The law presumably exists because of concerns about fairness and equal opportunity, not causal inference. But regardless of the motivation, these lotteries create randomization "in the wild" that allows us to estimate the effects of attending charter schools versus regular public schools more credibly than we could by simply comparing the performance of students at the two types of schools and trying to control for all the many potential confounders.

Natural experiments almost always involve some level of noncompliance—for example, not everyone who wins a charter school lottery ultimately attends that charter school, and some people who lose the lottery for one charter school win it for another. Thus, in such settings, we typically either estimate an intent-to-treat effect (i.e., the reduced-form relationship between winning the admissions lottery and academic outcomes) or take an instrumental variables approach to estimate the complier average treatment effect. In this example, the instrument would be winning the lottery, the treatment is attending the charter school, and the outcome is some measure of academic performance (e.g., test scores).

When taking the instrumental variables approach, we need to think seriously about the conditions we described earlier. If there is natural randomization, we can have confidence in exogeneity. That is, we can credibly estimate the effect of winning the admissions lottery on academic performance and on attending the charter school. But we have to think very carefully about the exclusion restriction. That is, are there ways that winning the admissions lottery might affect academic performance other than through its effect on attending a charter school?

It might well be that in the charter schools example, the exclusion restriction is reasonable and that we really can estimate the complier average treatment effect. But let us give you another example where the exclusion restriction is a bit more fraught.

Military Service and Future Earnings

The effect of military service on future earnings is of considerable interest to economists. But, of course, people who serve in the military and do not serve in the military differ in lots of ways that matter for earnings. Hence, a comparison of the earnings of veterans and non-veterans (even controlling for a bunch of stuff) is hopelessly confounded. Such a comparison does not provide a plausibly unbiased estimate of the causal effect.

Fortunately (for social scientists), there is a natural experiment to help. During the Vietnam War, draft-eligible men were randomly assigned draft numbers. People were only actually drafted if their randomly assigned number was sufficiently low. Hence, we have a source of random variation in military service.

Of course, there was not perfect compliance with the draft lottery. For instance, some young men volunteered to serve in the military, despite having a high draft number. (In our earlier terminology, such men are always-takers.) And others, with low draft numbers, left the country or otherwise avoided the draft. (In our earlier terminology, such men are never-takers.) So, if we want to get an estimate of the causal effect of military service on earnings (rather than the reduced-form effect of lottery number on earnings, which seems less interesting), we need to take an instrumental variables approach, which many studies have done. The idea is to use draft number as the instrument, military service as the treatment, and future earnings as the outcome.

In this context, exogeneity is quite plausible. As best we can tell, the government really did assign draft numbers randomly. (Technically, they randomly assigned birthdays, so everyone with the same birthday was in the same boat, but whether one's birthday was selected was random.) So we really can estimate the effect of draft number on military service and on future earnings.

But what about the exclusion restriction? For the exclusion restriction to hold, it needs to be the case that the draft lottery number has no effect on future earnings other than through its effect on military service. How might this be violated?

One possibility concerns how people responded to receiving a low draft number. Such people may have been more likely to engage in various activities that would allow them to avoid the draft. For instance, they may have been more likely to flee the country. Or they may have been more likely to pursue higher education in order to receive a student deferment, which excused them from the draft while they remained in school. Becoming an expatriate or going to college might both directly affect future earnings. As such, these are alternative paths by which the draft number might affect future earnings other than through military service. Because of such violations of the exclusion restriction, it might well be that, even with random assignment of draft numbers, the instrumental variables approach will not allow us to use the draft lottery to credibly estimate the effect of military service on future earnings.

Wrapping Up

There's a reason we call experiments the gold standard for causal inference. By randomly assigning a treatment, we guarantee that the treated and untreated groups have, in expectation, the same potential outcomes, meaning that we can obtain unbiased estimates of a causal relationship.

Even with a randomized experiment, thorny problems can arise. So designing and analyzing experiments requires vigilance and clear thinking. These same thorny problems can rear their heads outside the context of experiments, so we need to continue thinking about them as we move on to other research designs.

Unfortunately for science, the ideal experiment that we'd like to run is often impractical, infeasible, or unethical. What do we do then? The next two chapters discuss special circumstances in which we can still obtain credible estimates of causal relationships even without anything being randomized.

Key Terms

- **Research design:** Approaches to obtaining unbiased estimates of a treatment effect or other estimand.
- **Random assignment:** Deciding which units are assigned to receive treatment in a random fashion (e.g., by flipping a coin or using a random-number generator).
- **Blocked/stratified random assignment:** The process of dividing experimental subjects into different groups (typically groups that you believe have similar potential outcomes) and then randomizing your treatment within each of those groups. This can significantly improve the precision of your estimates. If the probability of treatment varies across blocks or strata, you will have to account for this (e.g., by controlling for block-fixed effects) in order to obtain unbiased estimates.
- **Noncompliance:** When an experimental subject chooses a treatment status other than the one to which it was assigned.
- **Compliers:** Units that take up the treatment status they are assigned.
- **Always-takers:** Units that are always treated, regardless of whether they are assigned to be treated or untreated.

- **Never-takers:** Units that are never treated, regardless of whether they are assigned to be treated or untreated.
- **Defiers:** Units that take up the opposite of the treatment status they are assigned.
- **Intent-to-treat (ITT) or reduced-form effect:** The average effect on the outcome of being assigned to the treated rather than the untreated group. This need not be the average treatment effect because of noncompliance.
- **First-stage effect:** The average effect of being assigned to the treated group on take-up of the treatment. This corresponds to the fraction of compliers.
- **Complier average treatment effect (CATE):** The average treatment effect for the compliers—a special kind of LATE.
- **Instrumental variables (IV):** A set of procedures for estimating the CATE in the presence of noncompliance. The Wald Estimator is a special case of instrumental variables. All IV designs require that we can credibly estimate the effect of the instrument on the treatment and on the outcome (exogeneity), that the instrument affects the treatment (compliers), that the instrument only affects the outcome through its effect on the treatment (exclusion restriction), and that there is not a large number units who take-up treatment if and only if the instrument assigns them to the untreated group (defiers).
- **Exogeneity:** An instrument is exogenous if it is randomly assigned or "as if" randomly assigned such that we can get an unbaised estimate of both the first-stage and reduced-form effects.
- **Exclusion restriction:** An instrument satisfies the exclusion restriction if it affects the outcome only through its effect on the treatment, not through any other channel.
- **Chance imbalance:** The situation where, despite random assignment, the treated and untreated groups differ in important ways because of noise.
- **Statistical power:** The statistical power of a study is technically defined as the probability of rejecting the null hypothesis of no effect if the true effect is of a certain non-zero magnitude. Colloquially, we say that a study has low statistical power if it was unlikely to produce a statistically significant result even if the effect being investigated is large.
- **Attrition:** The situation where experimental subjects drop out of the experiment, such that you do not observe outcomes for those subjects. Attrition is different from noncompliance.
- **Interference:** The situation where the treatment status of one unit affects the outcome of another unit.
- **Natural experiment:** When something was randomized not for research purposes, but careful analysts are nevertheless able to utilize this randomization to answer an interesting causal question.

Exercises

11.1   Suppose a psychology lab attempts to study the phenomenon of behavioral priming. Specifically, they want to know if experimental subjects walk slower when they are exposed to words associated with aging and old age. They recruit subjects to come to their lab and they pay them to complete a word association task. Half the subjects are assigned to an untreated group for which the words have nothing to do with aging, and the other half of the subjects are assigned to a treated group for which many of the words are related to aging and old age.

After the subjects have completed their task, unbeknownst to the subjects, one of the research assistants times how long it takes them to traverse the fifty-foot hallway that leads to the building's exit. The researchers' plan is to test whether the treatment leads to slower walking times.

Below are some facts about the experiment. For each one, think about what implications that fact has for the experiment. Is this a problem for the researchers? If so, what problem is it? What could they have done in their experimental design or data analysis to address the problem?

(a) The subject pool was a wide cross section of society, so some of the subjects were old, some were young, some were athletic, some were clumsy, some were skinny, some were overweight. The treated group over-represented older and less athletic people, compared to the untreated group.

(b) Some of the subjects didn't pay close attention to the word association activity, gave meaningless answers, and just went through it as quickly as possible.

(c) Some of the subjects took a very long time to walk across the hallway because they stopped to talk to a passerby or to check their phone.

(d) Some of the subjects never crossed the hallway at all because there was another exit through the back of the building.

(e) The research assistants who timed the walking speed of the subjects knew the hypothesis of the researchers and they were the same people who administered the treatments.

(f) Some of the subjects talked to one another about the word association task before they exited the building.

11.2   Download "GOTV_Experiment.csv" and the associated "README.txt," which describes the variables in this data set, at press.princeton.edu/thinking-clearly.

We will be analyzing data from a randomized experiment to estimate the effects of get-out-the-vote (GOTV) interventions on voter turnout.

Several factors complicate the analysis of this particular experiment. First, the probability of being randomly assigned to treatment was different for urban and non-urban areas. Second, some people assigned to treatment did not receive the treatment. And third, we are unable to observe turnout for some of the subjects. See the README file for more details.

(a) Calculate the mean value of turnout for people who did and did not receive the treatment, and interpret the implied effect of get-out-the-vote interventions on turnout. Think about the likely biases that arise from the three complications listed above. If you had to guess, would you say that you are likely over- or under-estimating the average effect with this analysis? Explain your answer.

(b) Using the lessons from chapter 10, try to account for the fact that the probability of treatment varied between urban and non-urban places. How did your estimate change? Why?

(c) Using the lessons from this chapter, let's try to account for noncompliance. First, try to estimate the intent-to-treat effect (reduced form) and the compliance rate (first stage). Now divide the former by the latter to estimate the complier average treatment effect.

(d) Think about the attrition problem. What are you implicitly assuming if you just drop the subjects for whom we don't observe their turnout? Let's see how our estimates change under different assumptions. Estimate the complier average treatment effect assuming that none of the subjects who attrited would have voted. What would your estimate be under the worst-case scenario for the effectiveness of GOTV? What about the best-case scenario?

Readings and References

For a thorough guide to conducting experiments, particularly field experiments, we recommend

Alan S. Gerber and Donald P. Green. 2012. *Field Experiments: Design, Analysis, and Interpretation.* W. W. Norton.

The study showing that sickly children in Peru were weaned from breastfeeding later is

Grace S. Marquis, Jean-Pierre Habicht, Claudio Franco, and Robert E. Black. 1997. "Association of Breastfeeding and Stunting in Peruvian Toddlers: An Example of Reverse Causality." *International Journal of Epidemiology* 26(2):349–56.

The randomized experiment on breastfeeding in Belarus is

Michael S. Kramer, Tong Guo, Robert W. Platt, Stanley Shapiro, Jean-Paul Collet, Beverley Chalmers, Ellen Hodnett, Zinaida Sevkovskaya, Irina Dzikovich, and Irina Vanilovich. 2002. "Breastfeeding and Infant Growth: Biology of Bias?" *Pediatrics* 110(2):343–47.

There are many papers on the Vietnam draft lottery. Two of them (one classic, one recent) are

Joshua D. Angrist. 1990. "Lifetime Earnings and the Vietnam Era Draft Lottery: Evidence from Social Security Administrative Records." *American Economic Review* 80(3):313–36.

Joshua D. Angrist and Stacey H. Chen. 2011. "Schooling and the Vietnam-era GI Bill: Evidence from the Draft Lottery." *American Economic Journal: Applied Economics* 3(2):96–118.

If the first exercise question made you wonder whether behavioral priming can actually influence someone's walking speed, we recommend the following study. It turns out that the result depends on whether the timing is conducted by a machine or by a human who knows the hypothesis. In other words, it's easy for researchers to trick themselves into thinking they're detecting something when they know what they're supposed to find.

Stephane Doyen, Olivier Klein, Cora-Lise Pichon, and Axel Cleeremans. 2012. "Behavioral Priming: It's all in the Mind, but Whose Mind?" *PLoS ONE* 7(1):e29081.

CHAPTER 12

Regression Discontinuity Designs

What You'll Learn

- Even when experiments are infeasible, there are still some special situations that allow us to estimate causal effects in an unbiased way.
- One such circumstance is when a treatment of interest changes discontinuously at a known threshold. Here a regression discontinuity design may be appropriate.
- Regression discontinuity designs estimate a *local* average treatment effect for units right around the threshold where treatment changes.

Introduction

In chapter 11, we saw some examples of how clever natural experiments can help us learn about causality, even when we can't run an actual experiment. The idea is to look for ways in which the world creates situations where we can make apples-to-apples comparisons without running an experiment. Sometimes, as with charter schools, the world does this through actual randomization. Other times, you have to be a little more clever.

In this chapter, we'll discuss one special situation that can help us generate credible causal estimates—when a treatment of interest changes discontinuously at a known threshold. In the next chapter we'll consider another such situation—when treatment changes over time for some units of observation but not for others.

In chapter 10, we discussed trying to learn about causal relationships by controlling for confounders. We don't typically have much faith in such approaches because it is so hard to measure all of the confounders out there. And if you can't measure something, you can't control for it. However, there are rare situations where we have a lot of information about the assignment of the treatment that may make this plausible. One example is a randomized experiment, the topic of chapter 11. If we know that treatment was assigned randomly, we know there are no confounders. The focus of this chapter is settings in which treatment is assigned according to some sharp rule. In these situations, we might be able to learn about the effect of the treatment using a regression discontinuity design.

Suppose each unit of observation is associated with a score of some sort, and treatment is determined by that score. Units whose score is on one side of a threshold get the treatment, and units whose score is on the other side of the threshold don't. This sets up a situation where a regression discontinuity design may help you estimate causal effects. Very close to that threshold, units on either side are likely to be similar to one another on average. So a comparison of those two groups (one of whom got treatment and the other didn't) may be very close to apples-to-apples.

Let's be a little more concrete. Suppose that we want to estimate the effect of receiving a merit scholarship to college on future earnings. In general, this is difficult because the kinds of students who receive merit scholarships are probably different in many ways that matter for future earnings—intelligence, ability, ambition, work ethic—from those who do not. And, of course, we can't measure and control for all these differences.

But what if the scholarship was awarded according to a strict scoring rule? A committee generates a score from 0 to 1,000 for every applicant based on GPA, test scores, community service, and extracurricular activities. Everyone with a score of 950 or above gets the scholarship, and everyone below does not. Now, even though nothing is randomized, we might be able to learn about the effect of receiving the scholarship for those applicants who were right around the threshold of 950. How does this work?

Assume that the scholarship committee and the applicants can't precisely manipulate the scores. That is, the students put in effort without knowing exactly where their scores will fall, and the committee honestly evaluates the students also without knowing exactly where the scores will fall. Then, in expectation, the people with scores of 950 are almost identical to those with scores of 949. Nothing is randomized, but there are likely many idiosyncratic factors that could have easily pushed a 949 up to a 950, or vice versa. Had the 949s taken their standardized test on a slightly less stressful day, logged one more hour of community service out of hundreds, gotten one teacher who was a slightly more generous grader in one class, they would have been 950s and won the scholarship. Similarly, had the 950s had one minor, idiosyncratic thing not go their way, they would have been 949s and lost the scholarship. So it seems reasonable to say that, on average, the 949s are essentially the same as the 950s before the scholarship decision is made. And therefore we have something like a natural experiment. The comparison of individuals right around the threshold—some of whom got the scholarship (the 950s) and some of whom did not (the 949s) for essentially random reasons—is apples-to-apples. By comparing the future earnings of these two groups, we can estimate the causal effect of winning a merit scholarship, at least for students with scores close to the threshold.

Here's a more general way to think about this kind of situation. We want to estimate the effect of a binary treatment on some outcome. Treatment assignment is perfectly determined by some third variable (like the score above) that we call the *running variable*. Specifically, if the running variable is above some threshold for a given unit, then that unit receives the treatment ($T = 1$), and if the running variable is below that threshold, that unit does not receive the treatment ($T = 0$). Such a situation might produce data that looks like figure 12.1, with black dots corresponding to treated units and gray dots corresponding to untreated units. In the figure, the threshold is at a value of zero in the running variable.

How can we estimate the effect of the treatment in this kind of situation?

At first glance, it looks like there's not much we can do. The running variable is strongly correlated with the outcome of interest. In the scholarship example, this makes sense because the committee wants to select high-ability people, and, not surprisingly, the criteria they use to create the scores turn out to be highly correlated with future earnings, regardless of whether a student wins the scholarship. The committee uses a

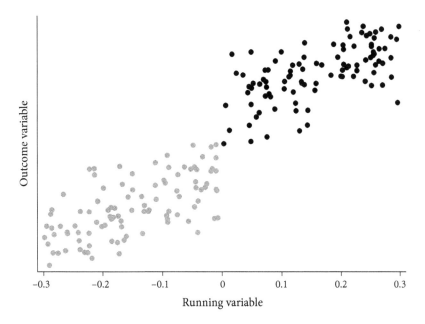

Figure 12.1. Scatter plot with treatment determined by a continuous running variable. Black dots are treated units. Gray dots are untreated units.

cutoff rule, so everyone who receives the scholarship has higher values of the running value than anyone who does not. Clearly, then, if we compare those who do and do not receive treatment, we know that the inputs to the score are confounders. And, because of the cutoff rule, we can't make an apples-to-apples comparison by finding students with the same value of the running variable, some of whom did and some of whom did not receive treatment (i.e., the scholarship). Everyone with the same score has the same treatment status.

But don't give up yet. Let's think more about what we can do here. We can estimate the expected value of the outcome for a given value of the running variable. For units whose score on the running variable is above the threshold, this will tell us the expected outcome with treatment at that value of the running variable. We can estimate this quantity for every value of the running variable all the way down the threshold. Similarly, for units whose score on the running variable is below the threshold, this will tell us the expected outcome without treatment at that value of the running variable. We can estimate this quantity for every value of the running variable all the way up to the threshold. Therefore, right at the threshold, we have estimates of the expected outcome with and without the treatment. The difference between those two values might well be a good estimate of the effect of the treatment, at least for those units with a value of the running variable right at the threshold.

We could estimate this quantity by comparing units on either side of the threshold, all of which have values of the running variable very close to the threshold. This was the idea behind comparing the 949s to the 950s to learn about the effect of merit scholarships. But there are actually somewhat better approaches.

One strategy is to run two regressions of the outcome on the running variable—one for the untreated observations below the threshold and one for the treated observations above the threshold. Then, we can use these two regressions to predict the outcomes

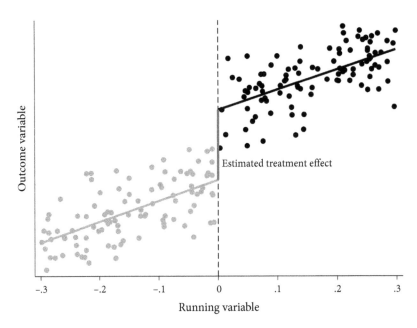

Figure 12.2. The regression discontinuity design estimates the jump in expected outcomes at the threshold, which is the causal effect of the treatment for units at the threshold.

with and without treatment right at the threshold. From these predictions we can estimate the "jump" or "discontinuity" in the outcome as the running variable crosses the threshold. That discontinuity is an estimate of the causal effect of the treatment for units right at the threshold. For this reason, we call this strategy a *regression discontinuity (RD) design*. Figure 12.2 illustrates the idea.

One thing worth emphasizing is the *localness* of the average treatment effect that a regression discontinuity design estimates. It is possible that the average effect of the treatment is different at different values of the running variable, as in figure 12.3. In this figure, both potential outcomes are shown for each unit of observation. For each unit, Y_1 is shown in black, and Y_0 is shown in gray. The actual outcomes that we observe are filled in, and the counterfactual outcomes that we don't observe are hollow. The size of the gap is different at each value of the running variable.

To be more concrete, in our example, the effect of winning a scholarship on future earnings could be different for low- and high-achieving students. The regression discontinuity estimand is the average treatment effect for units with values of the running variable right at the threshold. So, in our example, it estimates the effect of winning a scholarship on the future earnings of students with scores of 950, which might be different from the effect on students with scores of, say, 700. We refer to this estimand as a *local average treatment effect* (LATE). As always, the LATE can differ from the overall average treatment effect in the population. So it is important, when using a regression discontinuity design, to think about whether the quantity estimated is really the one you are interested in.

Regression discontinuity designs are important in a variety of settings. One common application is in estimating the effects of government programs. Many policies change discontinuously at known thresholds. For example, individual-level government benefits are often means-tested, with eligibility determined by whether some continuous

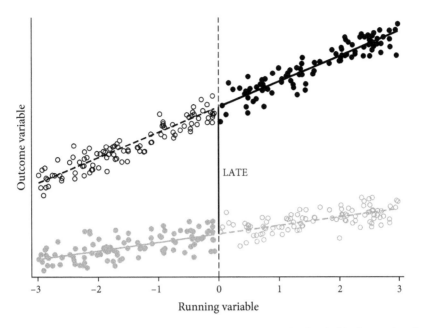

Figure 12.3. A regression discontinuity design estimates the LATE at the threshold. This need not be the overall average treatment effect, as average treatment effects may differ for different values of the running variable

measure of income or poverty is on one or the other side of a threshold. County-level policies are often determined by population thresholds or by the share of residents of a certain type. Regression discontinuity designs provide a straightforward way to estimate the effects of these programs. Furthermore, these designs estimate the effects of the programs for the kinds of people or places about which we care the most—the marginal unit that was just barely eligible or ineligible. So if policy makers are trying to figure out whether they should shrink or expand a particular government program, these regression discontinuity estimates should be highly informative.

How to Implement an RD Design

There are different ways for analysts to go about implementing their own regression discontinuity designs, and there are pros and cons associated with each one.

The simplest approach, as mentioned above, is to just compare the mean outcome for small ranges of the running variable (sometimes called *bins*) on either side of the threshold. For example, we might compare the average earnings for applicants who scored between 950 and 954 to the average earnings for applicants who scored between 945 and 949. For reasons you'll see in a moment, we often call this the *naive* approach.

A clear advantage of the naive approach is its simplicity. What makes it naive is the fact that it is virtually guaranteed to produce biased estimates. Why is this? The running variable is typically correlated with potential outcomes. Why would the committee use the scores to allocate scholarships if they didn't believe the scores corresponded to ability, effort, motivation, or some other factor that is likely correlated with earnings in the future?

Because the running variable is correlated with the potential outcomes of interest, there will always be some baseline difference between the groups just above and just below the threshold. Of course, as the size of the bins being compared (sometimes called the *bandwidth*) shrinks, the bias should shrink, but it will never disappear.

We can already see that one of the important decisions an RD analyst must make is to select a bandwidth. And when they make that decision, they often face a trade-off between reducing bias and improving precision. Smaller bandwidths will generally yield less biased estimates but also less precise estimates because they are using less data.

A potentially less biased alternative to the naive approach is the *local linear* approach. Here, we again select a bandwidth, and for observations within that bandwidth, we run linear regressions of the outcome on the running variable separately on either side of the threshold. We use these estimates to get predicted values of the outcomes with and without treatment right at the threshold, and the differences in those predicted values is our estimate of the effect of the treatment for units at the threshold.

With this approach, we're allowing for the possibility that there is a relationship between the running variable and the outcome, we're allowing that relationship to be different on either side of the threshold, and we're assuming that this relationship is approximately linear (at least for the small window of data that we're analyzing). That is the approach we took in figure 12.2.

To make our lives easier and to obtain an estimate of the standard error, there is a way to implement this local linear approach with a single regression rather than running two separate regressions. First, rescale the running variable so the threshold is zero (i.e., subtract the value of the threshold from the running variable). Second, generate a treatment variable indicating whether an observation is above or below the threshold. Third, generate an interactive variable by multiplying the treatment variable and the rescaled running variable. And lastly, regress the outcome on the treatment, the rescaled running variable, and the interaction of the two for the observations within your bandwidth. The estimated coefficient associated with the treatment provides the estimated discontinuity.

A third common way that people implement RD designs is with polynomial regressions. An analyst might regress the outcome on the treatment, the running variable, and higher-order polynomials (i.e., the running variable to the second power, third power, and so on). This approach accounts for a possible non-linear relationship between the running variable and the outcome. A downside is that data points that are far from the threshold can have a big effect on the estimated discontinuity.

When implementing an RD design, the researcher clearly gets to make a lot of choices, so they have to be careful to avoid the problem of over-comparing and under-reporting. Your particular decisions should depend on your substantive knowledge and beliefs about the relationship between the running variable and the outcome and also how much bias you're willing to accept in exchange for a gain in precision, or vice versa. The best approach is to justify your choices with a combination of theory, substantive knowledge, and data analysis and, perhaps most importantly, show results for different specifications. If your estimates are robust across different bandwidths and specifications, this will lend additional credibility to your results. If your result only holds for one very particular specification, you should be skeptical.

To illustrate how one can explore robustness across bandwidths, figure 12.4 shows an analysis from one of Anthony's papers coauthored with Haritz Garro and Jorg Spenkuch. They hoped to test whether firms benefit from political connections by testing whether a firm's stock price increases when a political candidate to whom the firm

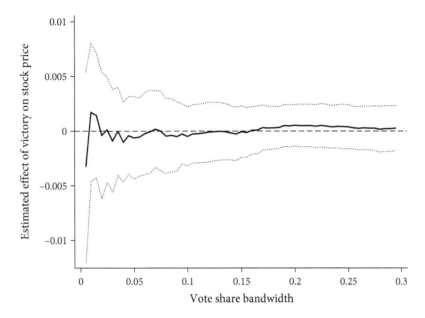

Figure 12.4. Visualizing how an RD estimate (solid) and confidence interval (dotted) depends on the bandwidth.

made a campaign contribution barely wins versus barely loses. So the outcome is a measure of the change in a firm's stock price, the running variable is the vote share of the politically connected candidate, and the treatment is an indicator for whether that candidate won the election.

They use a local linear approach, but they want to make sure that their results are robust to different bandwidths. Figure 12.4 shows the estimated effects along with the upper and lower bounds of the 95 percent confidence interval for sixty different possible bandwidths between 0.5 and 30 percentage points. As we would expect, the confidence intervals are larger and the estimates are more volatile for smaller bandwidths, but the estimates become more precise as the bandwidth increases and more data is included. Fortunately, the estimates are similar for almost all of the bandwidths, which is reassuring. Had the estimate changed meaningfully as the bandwidth increased, that would suggest a trade-off between bias and precision, and we'd have to think further about which estimates we trust more.

Let's think more about how to implement and interpret regression discontinuity designs through an example. The winners and losers of elections are determined solely by vote shares, so if we want to estimate the effects of a certain kind of election result, a regression discontinuity design might be especially useful.

Are Extremists or Moderates More Electable?

Surrounding both the 2016 and 2020 presidential elections, the Democratic party engaged in a heated debate about the electability of extremist versus moderate candidates. In particular, the liberal wing of the party was disappointed by the nominations of Hillary Clinton and Joe Biden, both of whom they perceived as too moderate. The way to win elections, they argued, isn't to appeal to centrist voters. Rather, parties should nominate ideologically pure candidates who can turn out the base. Bernie Sanders, the argument went, was in a better position to defeat Donald Trump in the general election than either of his more moderate rivals. Sure, there might have been some moderates turned off by some of Sanders's policy proposals. But Sanders would have more than made up for those losses by mobilizing progressives who had lukewarm feelings about Clinton and Biden.

How can we assess whether this argument is right? On the one hand, moderate candidates might persuade more people in the middle to support their party. On the other hand, extremists might mobilize the base. So if you want to maximize the chances that your party wins the general election, whom should you support in the primary election? It is, of course, impossible to say with confidence what would have happened if, counterfactually, Sanders had won the 2016 or 2020 Democratic nomination (remember the fundamental problem of causal inference from chapter 3). But maybe we can say more about what happens, on average, when a party nominates a more extreme versus more moderate candidate.

To try to get a handle on this, let's turn to congressional elections, for which we have a lot more data than we do for presidential elections. At first glance, it looks like the advocates of ideologically pure candidates might be onto something. After all, it sure looks like Congress has a lot of ideological purists in it. If moderation is a winning strategy, why are there so many extremists in office?

For starters, we have to make sure we aren't forgetting the lesson of chapter 4: correlation requires variation. The fact that many congresspeople are ideologically extreme does not imply a positive correlation (to say nothing of a causal relationship) between ideological extremism and electoral success. To ascertain the correlation of interest, we need to compare the electoral fortunes of extremists and moderates. Sure, one possible explanation of the large number of extremists in Congress is that extremism really is correlated with winning. But another is that there are just very few moderates running.

Moreover, it may be misleading to think about extremism and moderation on a national scale. Rather, for the purpose of thinking about electoral strategy, we want to know whether a candidate is extreme or moderate relative to the preferences of their particular electorate or constituency. Sanders is surely an extreme liberal relative to the median voter in the United States. But when he's running to represent Vermont in the Senate, perhaps he's only somewhat left of center. Indeed, maybe many congresspeople appear ideologically moderate relative to their constituencies but ideologically extreme relative to the country as a whole. This could happen if the constituencies are themselves constructed to be ideologically extreme compared to the country—some far to the left and others far to the right. But in this case, you wouldn't want to interpret the presence of lots of ideological extremists as evidence that extremism itself is an effective electoral strategy, because the winning congressional candidates would not have been perceived as ideological extremists by the voters that elected them.

Given these concerns, what we really want to know is not the correlation between ideology and electoral success but the effect of nominating an ideologically extreme candidate on electoral fortunes. To find an unbiased estimate of this, we need to compare how parties do in elections when they nominate an extremist versus a moderate, all else equal. On average, is the party better off running an extremist or a moderate candidate?

Of course, a naive comparison of the correlation between electoral outcomes and ideological extremism of candidates isn't apples-to-apples. Presumably, the times, places, and situations where a party nominates a moderate are different from those where a party nominates an extremist for all sorts of reasons that are consequential for electoral outcomes. For instance, most likely, liberal Democrats win primaries in more liberal places where the Democratic Party is stronger, and moderate Democrats win in more conservative places where the party is weaker. So if we found that extremists do better in general elections, that wouldn't tell us that parties are better off when they elect extremists. The causal interpretation of that correlation would obviously be confounded. We could try to control for differences across time and place, but we would always be worried that there are still unobservable baseline differences between places nominating extremists and moderates. We can do a better job using a regression discontinuity design.

Major party congressional candidates are selected in primary elections. And election outcomes are determined by a sharp threshold. Suppose we analyze a large sample of primary elections that pitted one extreme candidate against one moderate candidate. The treatment we are interested in is the nomination of an ideologically extreme candidate. We want to know the effect of that treatment on the party's vote share in the general election. To set up the RD, define the running variable as the vote share of the extreme candidate in the primary. If that vote share is below one-half, the party runs the moderate in the general election; if it exceeds one-half, the party runs the extremist. We can now estimate the effect of running an extremist by implementing an RD design, comparing a party's general election outcome when it just barely nominated an extremist in the primaries versus when it just barely nominated a moderate in the primaries.

Andrew Hall did exactly this in a 2015 study. He estimated a large, negative discontinuity in a party's general election results at the threshold. That is, on average, a party that nominates an ideological extremist instead of a moderate significantly decreases its performance in the general election. Despite the predictions of the Sanders supporters, the evidence suggests that nominating extremists, on average, is a bad electoral strategy.

Hall's design is illustrated in figure 12.5. The two lines represent separate linear regressions on each side of the 50 percent threshold. Each small gray circle corresponds to one observation—a party election. The larger, black circles show the average general election vote share for .02-point bins of the winning margin. The large negative discontinuity right at the threshold is the estimated effect on general election vote share of nominating an extremist instead of a moderate for a race where the primary election was evenly split between a moderate and an extremist.

What explains this result? In a follow-up study, Hall and Dan Thompson investigate further. Using a similar regression discontinuity design, they study the effect of nominating an extremist on voter turnout. Interestingly, contrary to the predictions of the Sanders supporters, there's no evidence that extremist candidates turn out the base. Or, rather, nominating an extremist does appear to turn out the base, but the wrong one. When a party runs an extremist candidate, more people from the *other* party turn out to vote in opposition. Therefore, if we had to guess, these results suggest that if Bernie Sanders had won the Democratic primary in 2016 or 2020, he would have performed worse than Clinton and Biden. He likely would have lost some of the centrist voters that preferred Clinton or Biden over Trump *and* likely would have motivated Republican voters to turn out in greater numbers.

Continuity at the Threshold

In order for the regression discontinuity approach to provide an unbiased estimate of the causal relationship, it has to be the case that treatment status changes sharply at the threshold *and* nothing else that matters for outcomes does. If baseline

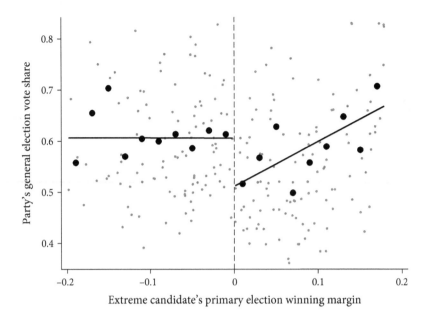

Figure 12.5. The effect of running an extremist on electoral prospects.

characteristics also change discontinuously at the threshold, then any differences in average outcomes right around the threshold could be due to those changes in baseline characteristics rather than treatment. That is, the comparison of treated and untreated units would no longer be apples-to-apples, even right at the threshold, because those two groups would be differentiated by things other than just treatment status. But if average baseline characteristics of the units change continuously (rather than in a discrete jump) as the running variable passes through the threshold, then we can obtain an unbiased estimate of the effect of the treatment for units with a value of the running variable that is right at the threshold because the only thing that will differentiate units just on one or the other side of the threshold, on average, will be their treatment status. We call the requirement that baseline characteristics don't jump at the threshold *continuity at the threshold* (or just *continuity* for short).

Let's see why continuity is crucial. Figure 12.6 illustrates what it looks like if the continuity condition is satisfied. As with figure 12.3, the filled-in dots are data we actually observe. The solid lines plotted through them are the average potential outcome functions (for the relevant value of treatment assignment). The hollow dots are data we don't observe (since we don't ever observe, say, the potential outcome under treatment for a unit with a value of the running value below the cutoff). The dashed lines plotted through them are the average potential outcome functions (again, for the relevant value of treatment assignment). Continuity is satisfied because these average potential outcome functions have no jump. That is, the average potential outcomes under both treatment and no treatment are continuous at the threshold. All that changes at the threshold is that units go from being untreated to treated.

Importantly, if continuity holds, then the gap between the gray and black dots at the threshold is in fact the LATE at that threshold, which is just what we want.

But what if continuity does not hold, so that the potential outcomes look like figure 12.7?

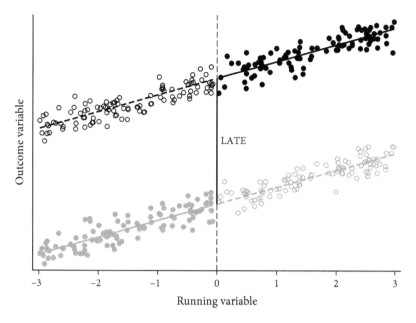

Figure 12.6. A case where average potential outcomes satisfy continuity.

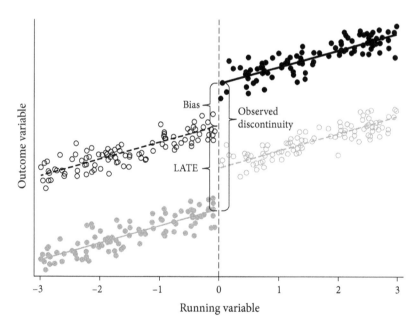

Figure 12.7. A case where average potential outcomes do not satisfy continuity at the threshold.

The true average treatment effect at the threshold is the difference between the filled-in gray dots and the hollow black dots at the threshold. (You could also define it as the difference between the filled-in black dots and the hollow gray dots.) But, right at the threshold, the potential outcomes jump up, even absent a change in treatment. We don't know why, but something besides treatment is changing right at the threshold. As a consequence, not all of the observed gap—that is, the jump between the filled-in gray and the filled-in black dots—is the result of the change in treatment. Some of it is the result of whatever else is changing. As such, that gap is a biased estimate of the LATE—in this case it is a big over-estimate of the true effect of the treatment—since the gap includes both the effect of the treatment change and also the effect of whatever else is changing. Thus, without continuity at the threshold, the RD will give a biased estimate of the local average treatment effect.

When it comes to implementing an RD design, there are many different paths the analyst can take. However, viewed in the correct light, once a researcher has established that plausibility of continuity of potential outcomes at the threshold, their job is clear. Using the sort of techniques we have already discussed (e.g., regression), they simply have to generate unbiased estimates of two things—the average outcome with and without treatment at the threshold.

To think about when an RD design is appropriate, we want to think about when continuity at the threshold is or is not plausible. It is worth noting that the continuity requirement is less demanding than you might have expected for credibly estimating causal relationships. For instance, it does not require that the treatment is assigned randomly (even by nature). In our scholarship case, we were able to use an RD even though, for every single student, treatment assignment was deterministic (i.e., there was no randomness at all). Continuity also does not require that the outcome be unrelated to the running variable. Again, in our scholarship example, the running variable reflects genuine academic merit and, thus, is positively correlated with future earnings outcomes. Finally, it does not require that units have no control over their value of the running variable or that units have no knowledge of the threshold. In our scholarship example, students could do all sorts of things to affect the running variable (e.g., study harder, do more community service).

So what could go wrong such that continuity does not hold?

Suppose that units have extremely precise control over their value of the running variable such that certain types may cluster just above or just below the threshold. This could potentially be a problem. In our scholarship example, we might worry that more privileged or more ambitious students have better information about the scoring system and can do just enough to exceed the threshold. Or we might worry that the committee has reasons to want to grant scholarships to students with certain characteristics (e.g., children of donors, athletes, particular racial or ethnic groups) and manipulates the scores or the threshold a little bit to get the desired result. In both of these cases, individuals just above the threshold would not be comparable to those just below. Instead they would have been *sorted* (by themselves or others) around the threshold by other baseline characteristics that matter for outcomes. If this is the case, regression discontinuity does not provide an unbiased estimate of the causal effect.

Things can go wrong even without sorting around the threshold, simply because things other than treatment status change at the threshold. Here's a pretty interesting real-world example. In France (and many other countries), a mayor's salary depends on the size of a city's population. For instance, by law, mayoral salaries jump when a city has a population of more than 3,500 residents.

This seems like an opportunity to use an RD to learn about the effect of mayoral salary on all sorts of outcomes. For instance, we might want to know whether cities are better governed or elections are more competitive when mayors are paid more. For either of these outcomes, the treatment of interest is mayoral pay. The running variable is population. And we happen to know that, by law, there is a discontinuous jump in the treatment as the running variable crosses the 3,500-resident threshold. Surely cities with 3,400 residents and cities with 3,600 residents are similar on average.

It looks good, no? But there's a problem with continuity. It doesn't come from towns strategically determining their populations to change the mayor's salary. It comes from other policies. You see, mayoral salary is not the only feature of city governance that changes by law at the 3,500-resident threshold. Other things that change include the size of the city council, the number of deputy mayors, the electoral rules, the process for considering a budget, gender-parity requirements for the city council, and so on. So any discontinuity in outcomes at the 3,500-resident threshold does not provide an unbiased estimate of the effect of mayoral salary because other characteristics that might matter for those outcomes also change discontinuously at the threshold.

Clearly, then, before interpreting the results from an RD as an unbiased estimate of a causal relationship, it is important to assess the plausibility of the continuity assumption. There are several ways to do this. The most important is to think substantively. The best way to spot possible violations of continuity is to know a lot of details of the situation, so that you can be alert to the potential for sorting, manipulation, or other things changing at the threshold. In our scholarship example, if you had sat in on a committee meeting or had deep knowledge of the kinds of characteristics the committee was under pressure to make sure were well represented among scholarship recipients, you would be in a better position to assess the plausibility of the continuity assumption than if you had no specific substantive knowledge of the situation. There are also other kinds of analyses one can do to help validate the continuity assumption. For instance, an analyst can look directly at measurable pre-treatment characteristics and see whether they seem to have discrete jumps at the threshold. If many measurable characteristics appear continuous at the threshold, we might be more confident that other, unmeasured baseline characteristics are also continuous. One can also look at the distribution of the running variable itself. If we find bunching—that is, significantly more units whose value of the running variable is just above the threshold than just below, or vice versa—then we might be concerned about some manipulation that violates continuity.

Exactly how bad a violation of the continuity assumption is depends on the details of the problem. If there is just a little sorting, or a small discontinuity in baseline characteristics, the RD is biased, but perhaps only a little bit. And if the researcher has a lot of data and, so, can focus on units only extremely close to the threshold, sorting would have to be extremely precise for it to affect the results. For instance, if we are estimating our scholarship RD using data on students with scores in the 940–949 range and students in the 950–959 range, we might be more concerned about sorting than if we have enough data so that we can consider just students with a score of 949 or 950.

Does Continuity Hold in Election RD Designs?

As we discussed earlier in this chapter, elections are a great setting for RD designs since they have a clear running variable and a sharp threshold for winning. Not surprisingly, the election RD has been used in many studies on the effects of elections on outcomes ranging from campaign donations to drug violence to nominating an extremist versus a moderate candidate. So it is important to think clearly about whether the election RD is in fact a good research design.

Let's remember what needs to be true for the election RD to provide an unbiased estimate of a causal relationship. We need for everything else that matters for the outcome under study to be continuous at the threshold. This guarantees that places where the relevant candidate (e.g., an extremist) just barely won are on average comparable to places where the relevant candidate just barely lost. In any application of the RD approach, including elections, it is always important to ask if this condition is plausible.

And, indeed, some studies have argued that continuity may be violated in some electoral settings. The concerns have to do with manipulation of election results in close elections. For instance, in Hall's study on the effects of nominating an extreme candidate, perhaps the party leadership prefers moderates. If it has ways of intervening (say, by putting pressure on officials responsible for recounts) to nudge close election outcomes, it might do so in favor of moderate candidates. For his study, Hall shows that this does not appear to be the case.

But in another setting, the post-WWII U.S. House of Representatives, some evidence suggests that there may be continuity problems. In the relevant studies, scholars are interested in using the RD to estimate the *incumbency advantage*—How much better does the incumbent party do than the out-party, all else equal? A researcher might compare the probability a Democrat wins an election in situations where a Democrat just barely won or lost the previous election in the hopes of estimating the effect of one election result on subsequent election results. For this to be a valid research design, there must be continuity at the threshold—the probability of the Democrat versus the Republican winning in the next election wouldn't change discontinuously in vote share in the previous election if it weren't for the fact that the previous election result was different. But there is reason to worry this isn't true. In particular, in House elections decided by less than 0.25 percent of the vote, the incumbent party is statistically more likely to win than the challenging party. If this is because parties are able to manipulate close election outcomes, then we might worry that, even very close to the 50 percent threshold, we aren't making an apples-to-apples comparison when we compare future electoral outcomes in places where one party just barely won versus just barely lost. So, what's going on?

Devin Caughey and Jas Sekhon, who wrote a study about this phenomenon, argue that the evidence points to electoral manipulation—incumbents have very precise knowledge of expected vote share and act strategically on or before election day in ways that allow them to win very close elections more than half the time. To believe this, however, you must believe that incumbent candidates can distinguish between situations where they expect their vote percentages to fall between 49.75 and 50.0 versus 50.0 and 50.25. Real-life campaigns appear to have nowhere near this level of precision in their election forecasts. Therefore, strategic campaigning is unlikely to be the explanation. What else could explain the imbalance? Most likely, this is a case of noise producing a false positive, much like Paul the Octopus in chapter 7. When Anthony and four coauthors replicated the same tests that Caughey and Sekhon did, but for twenty different electoral settings across several countries, the postwar U.S. House was the only one for which such an imbalance was present. Thus, we suspect the election RD is in fact a good research design for learning about causal relationships in politics.

Noncompliance and the Fuzzy RD

Thus far, we've talked about using a regression discontinuity design when treatment is completely determined by the running variable and the threshold. When this is the case, we sometimes say we are using a *sharp regression discontinuity design*.

But, just as in experiments, there are sometimes problems of noncompliance in settings that are otherwise suitable for an RD. That is, treatment may be discontinuously affected by which side of the threshold the running variable is on, but not deterministically. In addition to the compliers, there are some never-takers (units with values of the running variable above the threshold but who are untreated) and there are some always-takers (units with values of the running variable below the threshold but who are nonetheless treated).

When there are such noncompliers, we need to combine the regression discontinuity approach with an instrumental variables (IV) approach of the sort we discussed in chapter 11. We do so by using which side of the threshold the running variable is on as an instrument for treatment assignment. This approach is sometimes called a *fuzzy regression discontinuity design*. To see how fuzzy RD works, let's work through an example.

Bombing in Vietnam

A classic question in counterinsurgency is whether violence by counterinsurgents that kills civilians as well as combatants is productive or counterproductive. Melissa Dell and Pablo Querubin shed some quantitative light on this question in the setting of the U.S. bombing strategy during the Vietnam War.

In Vietnam, the United States engaged in a massive bombing campaign in an attempt to suppress the Viet Cong guerilla forces in the north. Dell and Querubin want to evaluate whether such bombing worked.

One comparison they might make to try to answer that question is whether insurgents were more or less active in the parts of Vietnam that experienced more bombing. But if you think clearly, you'll see that such a comparison is not apples-to-apples. One might, for instance, worry that the United States was more likely to bomb locations where the insurgents were already quite active, in which case there would be a reverse causality problem.

In order to better estimate the effect of bombing, Dell and Querubin use a regression discontinuity design. The history underlying their design is quite amazing.

During the Vietnam War, Secretary of Defense Robert McNamara was obsessed with quantification. McNamara had pioneered the use of quantitative operations research during his time as president of Ford Motor Company. And at the Department of Defense, he surrounded himself with a group of "whiz kids" and a large team of computer scientists, economists, and operations researchers, with the goal of providing precise, scientific, quantitative guidance to war planners and the military.

One of these efforts was the Hamlet Evaluation System (HES). This project collected answers to an enormous battery of monthly and quarterly questions about security, politics, and economics. The data were collected by local U.S. and South Vietnamese personnel who obtained information by visiting hamlets. Question answers were entered by punch card into a mainframe computer, and then a complex algorithm converted them into a continuous score, ranging from 1 to 5, that was supposed to characterize hamlet security. These raw scores, however, were never reported out by the mainframe. No human ever saw them. Instead, the computer rounded the scores to the nearest whole number, so that all the analysts or decision makers ever saw was a grade of A, B, C, D, or E. Better letter grades were understood to correspond to greater hamlet security. These grades helped determine which hamlets should be bombed—with bombing being more often targeted at hamlets receiving worse grades.

Dell and Querubin were able to reconstruct the algorithm and, using declassified data, recover the underlying continuous scores. This set them up for a regression discontinuity design.

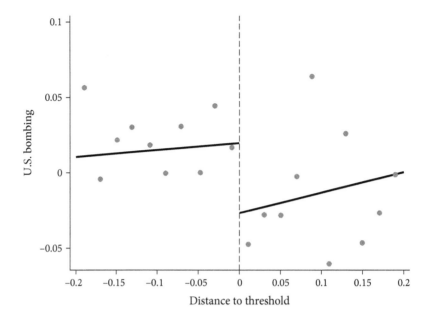

Figure 12.8. Hamlets that just barely received better grades in the Hamlet Evaluation System were bombed less frequently than hamlets that just barely received worse grades.

Think about hamlets with scores in the 1.45–1.55 range. Some of these hamlets ended up with a score just below 1.5 and received an E. Others ended up with a score just above a 1.5 and received a D. But the difference between, say, a 1.49 and a 1.51, on a score created by a complicated (and largely arbitrary) combination of answers to 169 questions is probably pretty arbitrary. So we should expect that the underlying level of Viet Cong activity in these two types of hamlets is the same—that is, we should expect the potential outcomes to be continuous at the threshold.

But treatment—which, here, means being bombed by the United States—changes discontinuously at the threshold. U.S. war planners did not ever see the underlying continuous score. All they saw was the letter grade. And, so, they perceived hamlets that received a D as more secure than hamlets that received an E (and similarly for D vs. C, C vs. B, and B vs. A). As such, they were more likely to bomb the hamlets with lower letter grades.

Figure 12.8 shows that this was the case. The horizontal axis measures the running variable—the distance of the first decimal of a hamlet's score from .5. Hamlets whose value of the running variable is negative (because its score's first decimal was below .5) were rounded down to the nearest letter grade, while those whose value of the running variable is positive were rounded up.

The vertical axis measures the frequency with which a given hamlet was bombed after the scores were tabulated. The gray dots correspond to binned averages of many hamlets with similar values of the running variable. The dark lines correspond to separate regressions on either side of the threshold. The figure shows a discontinuous jump down in the frequency of U.S. bombings at the threshold—hamlets that just barely received better grades were bombed less frequently than hamlets that just barely received worse grades.

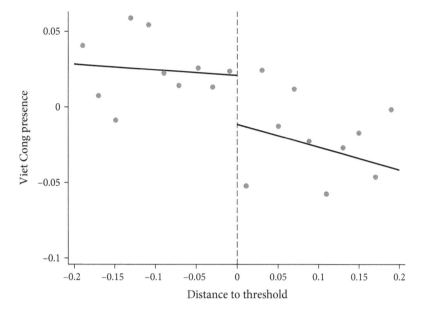

Figure 12.9. Hamlets that experienced more bombing saw more subsequent insurgent activity compared to otherwise similar hamlets that experienced less bombing.

Given this discontinuous change in treatment, it makes sense to use a regression discontinuity design to estimate the effect of bombing on insurgency. Figure 12.9 illustrates the idea. The horizontal axis is the same running variable as above. But now the vertical axis is the outcome of interest—Viet Cong activity in the hamlet following the tabulation of the scores. As the figure shows, indiscriminate bombing appears to have been counter-productive. There is a discontinuous drop in Viet Cong activity at the threshold. This means that hamlets that were bombed more (those to the left of the threshold) experienced more insurgent activity than otherwise similar hamlets that were bombed less.

But notice there is something a little different here from our normal regression discontinuity story. The treatment is not binary (there's a continuum of bombing intensity), and going from a better score to a worse score did not guarantee increased bombing. The security score was only one input to bombing decisions. So it was not the case that treatment went from fully on to fully off at the threshold. That is to say, there was likely noncompliance—hamlets whose treatment status didn't depend on which side of the threshold their score fell.

But we know what to do about noncompliers. As we discussed in chapter 11, we can use an IV approach. Recall, an instrument must satisfy several conditions:

1. **Exogeneity:** The instrument must be randomly assigned or "as if" randomly assigned, allowing us to obtain unbiased estimates of both the first-stage and reduced-form effects.
2. **Exclusion restriction:** All of the reduced-form effect must occur through the treatment. In other words, there is no other pathway for the instrument to influence the outcome except through its effect on the treatment.

3. **Compliers:** There must be some units that receive a different value of the treatment as a result of the instrument.

4. **No defiers:** Whatever the sign of the first-stage effect, there must be no units for whom the instrument affected their treatment value in the opposite direction.

How would we apply an instrumental variables approach here? The idea is to use *which side of the threshold our running variable is on* as the instrument. Let's see that this satisfies the four conditions needed for an instrument.

The whole point of the regression discontinuity design is exogeneity. If potential outcomes are continuous at the threshold, then the RD allows us to obtain an unbiased estimate of both the first stage (the effect of the instrument on bombing, as illustrated in figure 12.8) and the reduced form (the effect of the instrument on Viet Cong activity, as illustrated in figure 12.9).

The exclusion restriction requires that *which side of the threshold the running variable is on* has no effect on Viet Cong activity other than through its effect on bombing. Here there are questions to be asked. For instance, we need to worry about whether these grades were used for any other U.S. military or policy decision making. If so, then the instrument will not satisfy the exclusion restriction.

Dell and Querubin provide two kinds of evidence in support of the plausibility of the exclusion restriction. First, they repeat their RD analysis for lots of other kinds of military operations by both the American and South Vietnamese militaries. They find no evidence of any other kind of military operations changing discontinuously at the threshold. As such, it is unlikely that the effects they find are the result of military actions other than bombing. Second, they review the administrative history of the Hamlet Evaluation System. That review reveals little evidence of the HES scores being used for any other policy decision making. The one exception is a program aimed at driving the Viet Cong out of the least secure hamlets. But that program had ended before the sample period covered by Dell and Querubin's data.

The requirements that there be compliers and no defiers are the most straightforward. It is clear from both the data and the history that the letter grades affected bombing. And it seems unlikely that there were defiers—hamlets that were bombed more because they received a *better* security score. However, unlike in our previous examples, compliance is not so discrete. Different units can change their treatment status in response to the instrument by different amounts.

Given all of this, Dell and Querubin feel justified in employing a fuzzy RD design—using *which side of the threshold a hamlet's security score was on* as an instrument for bombing. In doing so, they are estimating an estimand that is a bit of a mouthful since it reflects the localness of both the RD and the IV. In particular, they are estimating the local average treatment effect of bombing on insurgent activity for hamlets with scores close to the threshold (the LATE from the RD) whose level of bombing is responsive to that score (the CATE from the IV).[1] Doing so, they find that bombing was counterproductive. For such hamlets, going from experiencing no bombing to experiencing the

---

[1] Further complicating matters, each hamlet is not simply either a complier or not. There is potentially a continuum of compliance whereby the instrument increases bombing in some hamlets by a lot, others by a little, and so on. So instead of thinking about a complier average treatment effect, we actually have to think about a weighted average treatment effect, where each hamlet is weighted according to the extent to which bombing responded to the score in that case.

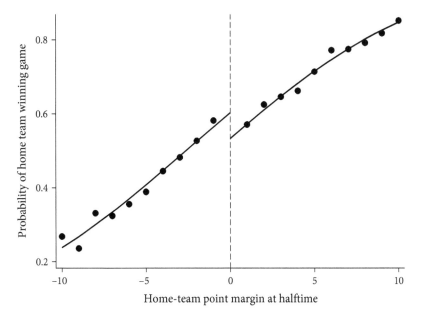

Figure 12.10. The effect of being ahead or behind at half time on winning the game.

average level of bombing increased the probability of Viet Cong activity in the hamlet by 27 percentage points.

Motivation and Success

Let's end with one last, fun example of a regression discontinuity design. Jonah Berger and Devin Pope implement an RD to estimate the effect of psychological motivation on performance. They analyze over eighteen thousand professional basketball games to test whether the motivation of being behind and needing to catch up leads to better performance than the complacency of being ahead and simply needing to hold onto a lead. Their running variable is the point margin of the home team at halftime, and they test whether the probability of ultimately winning a game changes discontinuously as the halftime point margin crosses the threshold of 0, when the home team goes from being just behind to just ahead.

Figure 12.10 shows the results. As we would expect, the point margin at halftime is correlated with the probability of ultimately winning the game. When the home team is 10 points ahead at halftime, they go on to win about 85 percent of the time, but when they're 10 points behind, they only win 25 percent of the time. This makes sense since some teams are better than others—good teams are both more likely to be ahead at the half and more likely to win the game. More interesting, however, is the comparison when the score is almost tied at the half. Presumably, there is very little quality difference, on average, between teams that are ahead or behind by just 1 point at halftime. Yet, the home team is actually more likely to win when they're 1 point behind at halftime than when they're 1 point ahead. Berger and Pope's regression discontinuity shows that being just barely behind increases the probability that the home team wins by 6 percentage points! Maybe those inspirational halftime speeches really do work.

Wrapping Up

When we know that a treatment of interest was determined (at least partly) by a threshold or cutoff, an RD design might allow us to obtain credible estimates of the effect of that treatment at that cutoff.

These situations arise more frequently than you might think. Suppose you're working for a baby food company that asks you to estimate the effect of their television ads. You probably can't convince the marketing department to randomize where they advertise; they want to advertise in places where they are likely to have the biggest effects. But maybe they already decided to air television ads in all media markets where more than 3 percent of households have an infant. This is a perfect opportunity for an RD design. Nothing was randomized, the marketing department did what it wanted to do anyway, but you have an opportunity to learn about the effectiveness of advertising by comparing baby food consumption in places just above and just below that 3 percent threshold.

Another opportunity for us to obtain credible estimates of causal relationships absent any randomization is when treatments change for some units and not others. In these cases a difference-in-differences design may be appropriate, and that's the topic of the next chapter.

Key Terms

- **Running variable:** A variable for which units' treatment status is determined by whether their value of that variable is on one or the other side of some threshold.
- **Regression discontinuity (RD) design:** A research design for estimating a causal effect that estimates the discontinuous jump in an outcome on either side of a threshold that determines treatment assignment.
- **Continuity at the threshold:** The requirement that average potential outcomes do not change discontinuously at the threshold that determines treatment assignment. If continuity at the threshold doesn't hold, then a regression discontinuity design does not provide an unbiased estimate of the local average treatment effect.
- **Sharp RD:** An RD design in which treatment assignment is fully determined by which side of the threshold the running variable is on.
- **Fuzzy RD:** A research design that combines RD and IV. The fuzzy RD is used when treatment assignment is only partially determined by which side of the threshold the running variable is on. The researcher, therefore, uses which side of the threshold the running variable is on as an instrument for treatment assignment. In this setting, continuity at the threshold guarantees that the exogeneity assumption of IV is satisfied. But we still have to worry about the exclusion restriction and the other IV assumptions.

Exercises

12.1   The state of Alaska asks you to estimate the effect of their new automatic voter registration policy on voter turnout. The policy was first implemented in 2017, but they report to you that, unfortunately, they initially didn't have the resources to roll the policy out to everyone in the state. As a result, they initially just applied automatic registration to people who had moved to Alaska within two years of the date of the policy being implemented, but they haven't yet applied it to people who moved to Alaska before then. They're worried that this might be a limitation for your study, and they apologize that they weren't able to implement the policy for everyone, but they're still hoping that you can help. How would you respond, and how might you go about estimating the effect of automatic voter registration in Alaska?

12.2   The U.S. federal government subsidizes college education for students through Pell Grants. An individual is eligible for a Pell Grant if their family income is less than $50,000 per year.

(a) How could you potentially use this information and implement an RD design to estimate the effect of college attendance on future earnings?
(b) Would this be a sharp or a fuzzy RD design?
(c) What data would you want to have at your disposal?
(d) What is the running variable?
(e) What's the treatment?
(f) What's the instrument (if any)?
(g) What's the outcome?
(h) What assumptions would you have to make in order to obtain credible estimates?

12.3   Download "ChicagoCrimeTemperature2018.csv" and the associated "README.txt," which describes the variables in this data set, at press .princeton.edu/thinking-clearly. This is the same data on crime and temperature in Chicago across different days in 2018 that we examined in chapters 2 and 5. Imagine that the Chicago Police Department implemented a policy in 2018 whereby they stopped patrolling on days when the average temperature was going to be below 32 degrees (and suppose they have really good forecasts so they can very accurately predict, at the beginning of the day, the average temperature for that day). Their logic is that it's less pleasant for police officers to be out on the streets when it's cold, and there's less crime on cold days anyway. Use this (fake) information to estimate the effect of policing on crime.

(a) A helpful first step when implementing an RD design is to generate your own running variable where the threshold of interest is at 0. Rescale the temperature such that the threshold is at 0 by generating a new variable called "runningvariable," which is simply the temperature minus 32.
(b) We'll also need to generate our treatment variable. Generate a variable that takes a value of 1 if policing was in place on that day and 0 if it was not.
(c) It's often helpful to look at our data before conducting formal quantitative analyses. Make a scatter plot with crime on the vertical axis and temperature on the horizontal axis. Focus only on days when the temperature was within 10 degrees of the policy threshold, and draw a line at the threshold. Visually, does it look like there is a discontinuity at the threshold?

(d) There are several different ways to formally implement an RD design. The simplest is to focus on a narrow window around the threshold and simply compare the average outcome on either side. Focusing only on days when the temperature was within 1 degree of the threshold, compute the average number of crimes just above and just below, and compute the difference. Notice that you can (if you'd like) do this in one step with a regression.

(e) What concerns would you have with the naive approach above? Think about the trade-offs you face as you're deciding which bandwidth to select. How does your estimate change if you use a bandwidth of 10 degrees instead of 1 degree? Why?

(f) Another strategy is to use the local linear approach. For days that were less than 5 degrees below the threshold, regress crime on the running variable and compute the predicted value at the threshold. (Hint: Because you rescaled your running variable, this should be given by the intercept.) Do the same thing for days that were less than 5 degrees above the threshold. Compare those two predicted values. (Note that this can also be done with a single regression as described in the text.)

(g) What benefits does this local linear approach have over the naive approach?

(h) You might also consider allowing for a non-linear relationship between the running variable and the outcome. Generate new variables corresponding to the running variable squared and the running variable to the third power. Regress crime on policing, the running variable, the running variable squared, and the running variable to the third power. Only include observations within 10 degrees of the threshold. Interpret the estimated coefficient associated with policing.

(i) What are the pros and cons of this polynomial approach relative to the previous approaches?

Readings and References

The study on corporate returns to campaign contributions is

Anthony Fowler, Haritz Garro, and Jorg L. Spenkuch. 2015. "Quid Pro Quo? Corporate Returns to Campaign Contributions." *Journal of Politics* 82(3):844–58.

For a discussion of potential violations of continuity in studies of policy changes at population thresholds see

Andrew C. Eggers, Ronny Freier, Veronica Grembi, and Tommaso Nannicini. 2018. "Regression Discontinuity Designs Based on Population Thresholds: Pitfalls and Solutions." *American Journal of Political Science* 62(1):210–29.

The study on the effects of electing an extremist versus a moderate in a primary election is

Andrew B. Hall. 2015. "What Happens When Extremists Win Primaries?" *American Political Science Review* 109(1):18–42.

The studies on the validity of electoral regression discontinuity designs are

Devin Caughey and Jasjeet S. Sekhon. 2011. "Elections and the Regression Discontinuity Design: Lessons from Close U.S. House Races, 1942–2008." *Political Analysis* 19(4):
385–408.

Andrew C. Eggers, Anthony Fowler, Andrew B. Hall, Jens Hainmueller, and James M. Snyder, Jr. 2015. "On the Validity of the Regression Discontinuity Design for Estimating Electoral Effects: New Evidence from Over 40,000 Close Races." *American Journal of Political Science* 59(1):259–74.

The study on U.S. bombing during the Vietnam War is

Melissa Dell and Pablo Querubin. 2018. "Nation Building through Foreign Intervention: Evidence from Discontinuities in Military Strategies." *Quarterly Journal of Economics* 133(2):701–64.

The study on the effect of being behind at halftime in basketball is

Jonah Berger and Devin Pope. 2011. "Can Losing Lead to Winning?" *Management Science* 57(5):817–27.

CHAPTER 13

Difference-in-Differences Designs

What You'll Learn

- Another situation that potentially allows us to estimate causal effects in an unbiased way is when a treatment changes at different times for different units. Here a difference-in-differences design may be appropriate.
- Difference-in-differences designs effectively control for all confounders that don't vary over time, even if they can't be observed or measured.
- Difference-in-differences designs can often be useful as a gut check, a simple way to probe how convincing the evidence for some causal claim really is.

Introduction

Regression discontinuity isn't the only creative research design that lets us get at causality in the absence of an experiment. When some units change treatment status over time but others don't, we may be able to learn about causal relationships using a strategy called difference-in-differences.

The basic idea is pretty simple. Suppose we want to know the effect of a policy. We can find states (or countries or cities or individuals or whatever the relevant unit of observation is) that switched their policies and measure trends in the outcome of interest before and after the policy change. Of course, we may worry that outcomes are systematically changing over time for other reasons. But we can account for that by comparing the change in outcomes for states that changed policy to the change in outcomes for states that did not change policy. If the trends in outcomes for states that did and did not change policy would have been the same if not for the policy change in some states, then we can use the states that did not change policy as a baseline of comparison, to account for the over-time trends. Our estimate of the causal effect of the policy change, then, will come from any change in outcomes in states that did change policy over and above that baseline trend that we estimated from the states that didn't change policy. This is called a *difference-in-differences design* because we first get the differences (or changes) in outcomes over time for states that did and did not change policy. Then we compare the difference in those differences.

Like the regression discontinuity design, the power of the difference-in-differences approach is that it allows us to estimate causal effects even when we can't randomize the treatment or control for every possible confounder. But nothing is for free.

Difference-in-differences designs come with their own requirements. For regression discontinuity, we needed continuity at the threshold. For difference-in-differences, we need the condition we just described: that the trend in outcomes would have been the same on average across units but for the change in treatment that occurred in some units. This condition is often called *parallel trends*.

Parallel Trends

It's worth making sure we are thinking clearly about what the parallel trends requirement really means. As we've said, difference-in-differences estimates are unbiased so long as the trends in outcomes would have been parallel, on average, in the absence of any changes in treatment. In other words, the parallel trends requirement is really about potential outcomes. For a binary treatment, we can think about each unit's outcome with and without treatment in each of two time periods. To capture this idea, let's think about there being potential outcomes for each unit in each time period. We will refer to the two time periods as period *I* and period *II*. And let's think about our population being divided into two groups: a group that changes from untreated to treated between the two periods ($\mathcal{UT}$) and a group that remains untreated in both periods ($\mathcal{UU}$).

Label the average potential outcome in group $\mathcal{G}$ in period p under treatment status T as

$$\overline{Y}^p_{T,\mathcal{G}}.$$

We observe the outcomes for a sample of the members of each group in each period. Let's start with the group that never changes treatment status ($\mathcal{UU}$). If we just look at the average change in outcome between the two periods, it gives us an estimate of the difference in outcomes in the untreated condition between the two periods:

$$\mathrm{DIFF}_{\mathcal{UU}} = \underbrace{\overline{Y}^{II}_{0,\mathcal{UU}} - \overline{Y}^{I}_{0,\mathcal{UU}}}_{\text{average untreated trend for }\mathcal{UU}} + \mathrm{Noise}_{\mathcal{UU}}$$

The noise comes from the fact that we are looking at a sample.

And analogously for the group that changes treatment status ($\mathcal{UT}$), the average change in outcome between the two periods is

$$\mathrm{DIFF}_{\mathcal{UT}} = \overline{Y}^{II}_{1,\mathcal{UT}} - \overline{Y}^{I}_{0,\mathcal{UT}} + \mathrm{Noise}_{\mathcal{UT}}.$$

The difference-in-differences is, quite literally, the difference between these two differences:

$$\text{Difference-in-Differences} = \mathrm{DIFF}_{\mathcal{UT}} - \mathrm{DIFF}_{\mathcal{UU}}$$

To see where parallel trends comes in, we are going to cleverly rewrite $\mathrm{DIFF}_{\mathcal{UT}}$ by adding and subtracting $\overline{Y}^{II}_{0,\mathcal{UT}}$ from it. You'll recall we did something similar back in chapter 9 in order to understand baseline differences. Just like then, while we know this seems kind of weird, we ask that you trust us for a minute. And, remember, at the very least it should be clear that we aren't doing any harm since, by adding and subtracting the same term, we are really just adding zero. When we do that, we get

$$\text{DIFF}_{\mathcal{UT}} = \overline{Y}^{II}_{1,\mathcal{UT}} - \overline{Y}^{I}_{0,\mathcal{UT}}$$

$$= \underbrace{\left(\overline{Y}^{II}_{1,\mathcal{UT}} - \overline{Y}^{II}_{0,\mathcal{UT}} \right)}_{\text{average treatment effect for } \mathcal{UT} \text{ in } II} + \underbrace{\left(\overline{Y}^{II}_{0,\mathcal{UT}} - \overline{Y}^{I}_{0,\mathcal{UT}} \right)}_{\text{average untreated trend for } \mathcal{UT}} + \text{Noise}_{\mathcal{UT}}.$$

Once again, our algebra trick was actually pretty cool. We can now see that the over-time difference for group $\mathcal{UT}$ is made up of three things, which correspond to our favorite equation. First, there is the average (period II) treatment effect for group $\mathcal{UT}$. In chapter 9 we learned that this was called the ATT, the average treatment effect on the treated units. We can think of this as our estimand. Second, there is the trend in outcomes that would have happened for group $\mathcal{UT}$ even if they had remained untreated. We can think of this as a source of bias that comes from just looking at what happens in the $\mathcal{UT}$ group before and after treatment. And third, there is noise, as always.

With this in hand, we can now rewrite the difference-in-differences in terms of the ATT, the average untreated trends in potential outcomes for both groups, and noise. This will make clear what we are really doing—using the over-time trend in the $\mathcal{UU}$ group to try to eliminate the bias that comes from just looking at DIFF$_{\mathcal{UT}}$:

Difference-in-Differences $= DIFF_{\mathcal{UT}} - DIFF_{\mathcal{UU}}$

$$= \underbrace{\overline{Y}^{II}_{1,\mathcal{UT}} - \overline{Y}^{II}_{0,\mathcal{UT}}}_{ATT} + \underbrace{\overbrace{\overline{Y}^{II}_{0,\mathcal{UT}} - \overline{Y}^{I}_{0,\mathcal{UT}}}^{\text{average untreated trend for } \mathcal{UT}} - \overbrace{\overline{Y}^{II}_{0,\mathcal{UU}} - \overline{Y}^{I}_{0,\mathcal{UU}}}^{\text{average untreated trend for } \mathcal{UU}}}_{\text{difference in average trends}}$$

$$+ \underbrace{\text{Noise}_{\mathcal{UT}} - \text{Noise}_{\mathcal{UU}}}_{\text{Noise}}$$

Now we can see what parallel trends really means in terms of potential outcomes and our favorite equation. The difference-in-differences equals the ATT (estimand) plus the difference between the average untreated trends for group $\mathcal{UT}$ and group $\mathcal{UU}$ (bias) plus noise. So when does the difference-in-differences give us an unbiased estimate of the ATT? When the untreated trend is the same for both groups, so that the difference in average trends equals zero.

This is what parallel trends means. The change in average outcome would have been the same in the treated and untreated groups had everyone remained untreated. When this is the case, by subtracting DIFF$_{\mathcal{UU}}$ from DIFF$_{\mathcal{UT}}$ we eliminate the over-time trend, leaving an unbiased estimate of the average treatment effect (in period II) for units that switched treatment status.

Notice, this notation highlights another subtle point. Difference-in-differences does not quite estimate the ATE. It estimates the average treatment effect for those units who actually change treatment status—that is, the ATT. Whether or not this is a good estimate of the ATE depends on whether treatment effects differ systematically across the units that do and don't switch treatment status. But, in any event, this is a genuine causal effect and, at least for some applications, may in fact be the quantity of interest.

Table 13.1. Fast-food employment in New Jersey and Pennsylvania in 1992.

	January 1992 *NJ and PA* *low minimum wage*	November 1992 *NJ high minimum wage* *PA low minimum wage*
New Jersey	20.44	21.03
Pennsylvania	23.33	21.17

Two Units and Two Periods

So far, we've been a bit abstract. Let's talk about a concrete example from classic work by David Card and Alan Krueger on the effect of the minimum wage on employment. This example is nice because it shows how difference-in-differences works in its most simple form. There are only two units, two periods, and one change in treatment status for one of the units.

Unemployment and the Minimum Wage

Card and Krueger wanted to know whether a higher minimum wage increased unemployment. Their idea was to exploit the fact that New Jersey raised its minimum wage in early 1992, while Pennsylvania, which borders New Jersey, did not. They collected data on the average number of full-time equivalent employees (FTE) per fast-food restaurant (which tend to pay minimum wage) in both New Jersey and Pennsylvania in January 1992 (before New Jersey raised its minimum wage) and in November 1992 (after New Jersey raised its minimum wage). Their data is summarized in table 13.1.

A first comparison we might think to make to learn about the effect of the minimum wage on employment is the difference between the employment levels in New Jersey and in Pennsylvania in November 1992. After all, by November, New Jersey had a higher minimum wage than Pennsylvania. That comparison shows that Pennsylvania fast-food restaurants employed only 0.14 more people, on average, than New Jersey restaurants, suggesting that a higher minimum wage may have almost no impact on employment.

But that comparison is not apples-to-apples, so we cannot interpret the difference as the effect of raising the minimum wage. New Jersey and Pennsylvania might differ in all sorts of ways that matter for employment besides the minimum wage. For instance, perhaps those two states have different levels of economic prosperity, different tax systems, or differently sized fast-food restaurants. And since, in this comparison, the state and the treatment are perfectly correlated, any such difference between New Jersey and Pennsylvania can be thought of as a confounder.

Another comparison we might make is to look at the change in employment in New Jersey between January and November, since the New Jersey minimum wage changed between these two months. This comparison shows an increase in employment of 0.59 employees per restaurant, suggesting that perhaps raising the minimum wage slightly increased employment. This approach has the advantage of comparing one state to itself, so we no longer need to worry about any cross-state differences. But now we have a new concern. Maybe January and November differ in terms of fast-food employment

Table 13.2. Two comparisons that do not unbiasedly estimate the causal effect of minimum wage increase.

	January 1992 *NJ and PA* *low minimum wage*	November 1992 *NJ high minimum wage* *PA low minimum wage*	**Difference** *November—January*
NJ	20.44	21.03	0.59 *effect of high minimum wage* *+ over-time trend* *+ noise*
PA	23.33	21.17	
Difference *NJ − PA*		−0.14 *effect of high minimum wage* *+ differences between states* *+ noise*	

for other reasons—for example, because of seasonality or overall changes to the economy over the course of the year. Any such time trends would be a confounder in this comparison. So this comparison also isn't apples-to-apples.

Table 13.2 shows the two differences we've discussed and lays out, in the terms of our favorite equation, why neither gets us an unbiased estimate of the effect of the minimum wage. The difference between employment in November and January in New Jersey is the sum of the effect of the higher minimum wage (estimand), the over-time trend (bias), and noise. The difference between employment in New Jersey and Pennsylvania in November is the sum of the effect of the higher minimum wage (estimand), differences between the states (bias), and noise. So both differences are biased.

But we can do better. Start by thinking about the comparison between New Jersey and Pennsylvania in November. The problem with that comparison is that it reflects both the effect of the higher minimum wage (the estimand) and any systematic differences between New Jersey and Pennsylvania (the bias), plus, as always, noise. But suppose the differences between New Jersey and Pennsylvania aren't changing over time. Then the difference in employment in New Jersey and Pennsylvania in January, when they both have a lower minimum wage, reflects those same across-state differences, but without the effect of the higher minimum wage that New Jersey adopted later in the year. So we can use that employment difference in January to estimate the underlying differences between the two states. And then, subtracting the January difference from the November difference (i.e., finding the difference-in-differences) will leave us with an unbiased estimate of the effect of the higher minimum wage. (Of course, there is different noise in each comparison, so the noise terms don't just cancel.)

The same procedure works if we start from our comparison of New Jersey in November to New Jersey in January. The problem with that comparison is that it reflects both the effect of the higher minimum wage and any other differences between November and January that matter for employment (plus noise). But suppose those over-time

Table 13.3. Difference-in-differences estimate of the effect of minimum wage on fast-food employment.

	January 1992 NJ and PA low minimum wage	November 1992 NJ high minimum wage PA low minimum wage	Difference November−January
NJ	20.44	21.03	0.59 *effect of high minimum wage + over-time trend + noise*
PA	23.33	21.17	−2.16 *over-time trend + noise*
			Difference-in-Differences
Difference *NJ − PA*	−2.89 *differences between states + noise*	−0.14 *effect of high minimum wage + differences between states + noise*	$0.59 - (-2.16) =$ $-0.14 - (-2.89) = 2.75$ *effect of high minimum wage + noise*

trends are the same in New Jersey and Pennsylvania. Then the difference in employment in Pennsylvania between November and January is an estimate of the over-time trend, without any effect of the minimum wage (since Pennsylvania didn't change its minimum wage in 1992). So subtracting the change in employment in Pennsylvania from the change in employment in New Jersey will also leave us with an unbiased estimate of the effect of the higher minimum wage.

As shown in table 13.3, either way we do this calculation, we find the same answer. Surprisingly, the estimate that this procedure leaves us with is that a higher minimum wage appears to increase employment by 2.75 FTE per restaurant. The key is that the Pennsylvania data suggests that there was a big baseline drop in employment from January to November 1992. So the 0.59 FTE increase in NJ was a misleading under-estimate of the true effect being masked by an over-time trend.

Importantly, by calculating the difference-in-differences, we were able to account for systematic differences between the states and this over-time trend, without ever observing what those differences or trends were. This is the power of the difference-in-differences approach.

Of course, this wasn't magic. As we've said, in order for this approach to be valid, we need the parallel trends condition—that the over-time trend in outcomes (and, thus, confounders) would have been the same across units but for the change in treatment status—to hold. But this is typically a less demanding assumption than assuming we've actually controlled for all possible confounders. For instance, in our example, we're not assuming that New Jersey and Pennsylvania are the same (or that we've directly controlled for any differences) absent any differences in minimum wage. We're also not assuming that there are no time trends. Instead, we're assuming that the trends are parallel: whatever time trends affect employment do so in the same way in both New Jersey and Pennsylvania, at least in expectation.

Difference-in-differences has a lot going for it, and there are a lot of situations where we think this parallel trends condition is quite plausible. This design accounts for all differences between units that don't vary over time that would plague a comparison of the two units in just one time period. It also accounts for all of the time-specific factors that would plague a before-and-after analysis of any one unit. What it does not account for is time-varying differences between units. These are still a problem if they vary in ways that correspond with the treatment. For example, if New Jersey increased its minimum wage because they thought the economy was about to experience a boom relative to neighboring states, then this would be a violation of the parallel trends assumption.

Of course, even if the parallel trends assumption seems conceptually reasonable, just looking at two units is not particularly illuminating. Surely lots of idiosyncratic differences pop up in any two places in any two months, so the noise in the estimate is likely to be large. To do better, we need to extend the intuition we developed in this simple example to situations where we observe more than two units over more than two time periods.

N Units and Two Periods

To start extending our intuition, suppose there are lots of units (e.g., maybe we have data on employment and minimum wage from all fifty states) but still just two time periods. And suppose that some of the units never received the treatment while other units received the treatment in the second but not the first period. We still want to look at changes for units that experience a change in treatment and compare those to changes for units that did not experience a change in treatment. We have three different options for doing so, all of which are algebraically identical and will, thus, provide the same answer:

1. **By hand:** Just as we did in the example above, calculate the average outcome in each period separately for those that never received the treatment and those that got the treatment in the second period and calculate the difference-in-differences by hand.

2. **First differences:** Put the data into a spreadsheet with one row per unit (this is called *wide format*). Calculate the change in the outcome and the change in the treatment for each unit, and regress the former on the latter. The change in treatment will be 0 for the units that never change and 1 for units that do change. So we're just comparing the average change for these two groups.

3. **Fixed effects regression:** Put the data into a spreadsheet with one row per unit period (this is called *long format*). Regress the outcome on the treatment while also including dummy variables for each unit and time period. In this example, we would have a dummy variable that takes a value of 1 if the observation is in period II and 0 if the observation is in period I. We would also have separate dummy variables for each unit. So the dummy variable for unit *i* would takes the value 1 if the observation involved unit *i* and 0 if it involved a different unit (there would be one such dummy variable for each unit). We often call these dummy variables *fixed effects*. For instance, if an analyst says they included *state fixed effects* in a regression, they just mean that they included a separate dummy variable for each state. Including these fixed effects ensures that we're removing all average differences between units and all average differences over

time, and once we've done that, the coefficient associated with the treatment variable is just the difference-in-differences.

Let's look at a fun example with multiple units.

Is Watching TV Bad for Kids?

Matthew Gentzkow and Jesse Shapiro were interested in how watching television as a pre-schooler affects future academic performance. The problem, of course, is that how much television a kid watches is affected by all sorts of factors that also affect future school performance. So a simple comparison of TV watchers to non-TV watchers isn't apples-to-apples. To get at the causal relationship more credibly, they used variation in the timing with which TV originally became available in different locations in the United States. We are going to simplify what they did so you can see their basic idea.

Broadcast television first became available in most U.S. cities between the early 1940s and the early 1950s. Happily, in 1965, there was a major study of American schools (called the Coleman Study) that, among other things, recorded standardized test scores for over three hundred thousand 6th and 9th graders. A 9th grader in 1965 was in pre-school in approximately 1955. A 6th grader in 1965 was in pre-school in approximately 1958. Gentzkow and Shapiro use both the over-time rollout of TV and the Coleman data to learn about the effect of pre-school television watching on test scores.

Let's imagine that we have the Coleman data on test scores for the 6th and 9th graders in two types of towns. Towns in group A first got TV in 1953. So they had TV when both the 6th and 9th graders in the Coleman study were in pre-school. Towns in group B didn't get TV until 1956. So they had TV when the 6th graders were in pre-school but not when the 9th graders were. Overall, then, table 13.4 summarizes the way the observed data look.

If you want to learn about the effect of having access to TV as a pre-schooler on future academic achievement, a first comparison you might think to make is to compare the test scores of the 9th graders in the B towns (who couldn't watch TV in pre-school) to the test scores of the 9th graders in the A towns (who could watch TV in pre-school). You could do that by simply subtracting the average test score of a 9th grader in a B town from the average test score of a 9th grader in an A town.

But we already know lots of reasons why we cannot interpret that as an unbiased estimate of the causal effect of having access to TV in pre-school. These two types of towns might be different in all sorts of ways, besides when broadcast TV showed up, that matter for academic performance. For instance, maybe they have different average quality schools, different industries, or what have you. And since, in this example, the type of town and the treatment are perfectly correlated, any such difference between the towns is a confounder.

Another comparison we might make is to look at the difference in test scores in the B towns between the 9th graders and the 6th graders, since the 6th graders had access to TV in pre-school but the 9th graders did not.

This approach has the advantage of holding fixed the type of town, so we no longer need to worry about systematic cross-town differences. But now we have a new concern. Maybe the 9th-grade and 6th-grade cohorts differ in their test performance for other reasons—for example, because 9th graders are older, or because of cohort-specific differences. Any systematic over-time or cohort differences would be a confounder in this comparison.

Table 13.4. TV and test scores data structure.

	9th Graders in 1965 *pre-school in 1955*	6th Graders in 1965 *pre-school in 1958*
A Towns *TV in 1953*	Avg Test Scores 9A	Avg Test Scores 6A
B Towns *TV in 1956*	Avg Test Scores 9B	Avg Test Scores 6B

Table 13.5. Two comparisons that do not result in unbiased estimates of the effect of TV.

	9th Graders in 1965 *pre-school in 1955*	6th Graders in 1965 *pre-school in 1958*	**Difference**
A Towns *TV in 1953*	Avg Test Scores 9A	Avg Test Scores 6A	
B Towns *TV in 1956*	Avg Test Scores 9B	Avg Test Scores 6B	6B − 9B *effect of TV + cohort differences + noise*
Difference	9A − 9B *effect of TV + town differences + noise*		

Table 13.5 sums up the two ideas we've had thus far and explains why neither gets us a credible estimate of the true effect in terms of our favorite equation.

But, just as with the minimum wage example, we can do better. Start by thinking about the comparison between 9th graders in the two types of towns. The problem with that comparison is that it reflects both the effect of TV exposure and any other systematic differences between the types of towns. But suppose those baseline differences between the types of towns aren't changing over time. Then the difference in academic performance between the 6th graders in the two types of towns, all of whom had access to TV in pre-school, reflects those same cross-town differences, but without the effect of TV. So we can use that difference between the 6th graders to estimate the cross-town differences. And then, subtracting the difference between the 6th graders from the difference between the 9th graders (i.e., calculating the difference-in-differences) will leave us with just the effect of TV exposure in pre-school (plus noise).

The same procedure works if we start from our comparison of 9th graders and 6th graders from the B towns. The problem with that comparison is that it reflects both the effect of exposure to TV in pre-school and any baseline differences between the 6th- and 9th-grade cohorts that matter for academic performance (plus noise). But suppose those over-time or cohort trends are the same in the A towns and B towns. Then the

Table 13.6. How difference-in-differences might give an unbiased estimate of the effect of TV.

	9th Graders in 1965 *pre-school in 1955*	6th Graders in 1965 *pre-school in 1958*	Difference
A Towns *TV in 1953*	Avg Test Scores 9A	Avg Test Scores 6A	6A − 9A *cohort differences* *+ noise*
B Towns *TV in 1956*	Avg Test Scores 9B	Avg Test Scores 6B	6B − 9B *effect of TV* *+ cohort differences* *+ noise*
Difference	9A − 9B *effect of TV* *+ town differences* *+ noise*	6A − 6B *town differences* *+ noise*	**Difference-in-Differences** (6B − 9B) − (6A − 9A) = (9A − 9B) − (6A − 6B) *effect of TV + noise*

difference in academic performance between 6th and 9th graders in A towns is an estimate of the over time or cohort trend without any effect of TV (since both sets of kids had access to TV in pre-school in Town A). So subtracting the difference in test scores in the A towns from the difference in test scores in the B towns will again leave us with an unbiased estimate of the effect of pre-school TV exposure.

As shown in table 13.6, either way we do this calculation, we find the same answer.

For those interested in the answer, Gentzkow and Shapiro find evidence that, during the 1950s, having access to TV in pre-school was actually beneficial for average test scores, especially for kids from poorer families. Of course, this was at a time when kids watched shows like *Howdy Doody*. So you might not want to immediately extrapolate to the present day.

More important, for our purposes, is seeing the power of the difference-in-differences approach. By calculating the difference-in-differences, we were able to account for systematic differences between towns and over time (or cohorts), without ever observing what those differences or trends were.

N Units and *N* Periods

Suppose you have more than two periods and suppose that the treatment is changing at different times for different units. What do you do?

Much of the logic from the above discussion still applies. Of course, option 1 above (calculating the difference-in-differences by hand) no longer works. But you can still use option 2 (first differences) or option 3 (fixed effects). However, first differences and fixed effects are no longer mathematically identical and will not necessarily give you the same answers once you move beyond two periods. What's the difference? With first differences, you're regressing period-to-period changes in the outcome on period-to-period changes in the treatment. With fixed effects, you're regressing the outcome on the treatment while controlling for all fixed characteristics of units and time periods. Both are doing the same basic thing, but they are using slightly different kinds of variation.

Which specification makes more sense depends on the specific context. In general, the fixed effects strategy is more flexible. For instance, it allows you to include additional time-varying control variables in the regression (if necessary), and it also allows you to conduct some helpful diagnostics. Importantly, in both cases, the timing of the effect matters for exactly what you are estimating. In the case of first differences, you are looking for effects that happen immediately after the treatment status changes. If it takes some time for the effect of the treatment to set in, or if the effect size decays or grows over time, you can get misleading estimates. However, complications in the timing of treatment also create complications for interpreting exactly what is being estimated when you use a fixed effects specification. We aren't going to go into these issues in any detail because they are actually the topic of cutting-edge research as of the writing of this book. However, if you go on to do quantitative analysis involving difference-in-differences, you may want to delve more deeply into these questions. We suggest some readings at the end of the chapter.

Even though there can be some complicated technical details, the intuition of difference-in-differences designs should be clear from our examples. And it is an important intuition. If someone shows you that some treatment of interest is correlated with an outcome of interest, you are already skeptical because of what we learned in chapter 9. Difference-in-differences allows you to check whether changes in the treatment are also correlated with changes in the outcome. If they are, then that might be more compelling evidence of a causal relationship. And if they aren't, then the original correlation may have been the result of confounding.

Let's look at an example of a study that uses a fixed effects approach to implementing a difference-in-differences design when there are multiple units changing treatment status at different times.

Contraception and the Gender-Wage Gap

The availability of oral contraceptives, starting in the 1960s, gave women unprecedented control over their reproductive and economic decisions. Understanding the impact of this contraceptive revolution on women's lives is important for understanding the evolution of the modern economy and society.

Of course, if we want to estimate the effects of oral contraception on women's child birth decisions, labor market participation, or wages, we can't simply compare outcomes for women who did and did not use oral contraception. After all, access to health care is affected by things like wealth, education, geography, race, and so on. So such comparisons are sure to be confounded. And no one ran an experiment giving some women access to oral contraceptives while restricting access to others. But this doesn't mean we can't make progress on these causal questions.

In an important paper, Claudia Goldin and Lawrence Katz point out that state policies created a kind of natural experiment. Oral contraceptives first became available in the United States in the late 1950s. However, the legal availability of oral contraceptives to younger women differed across states. In a few states, laws prevented the sale of contraception to unmarried women, and in most states, women under the age of majority needed parental consent before obtaining contraception. Over time, courts and state legislatures gradually removed these restrictions and lowered the age of majority. Helpfully, for the purposes of causal inference, they moved to do so at different times.

This meant that in the earliest moving states of Alaska and Arkansas, an unmarried, childless woman under the age of twenty-one could obtain oral contraception by 1960. In the latest moving state of Missouri, this wasn't possible until 1976. And for the other states, it was somewhere in between. This is important because women under twenty-one make particularly consequential decisions about when to have children, when to get married, whether to pursue higher education, and so on.

In another influential paper, Martha Bailey uses this variation to implement a difference-in-differences design to estimate the effect of early access to oral contraceptives on when women first have children and whether and to what extent they entered the paid labor force.

The basic idea is straightforward. Imagine four groups of women across two states, Kansas (which allowed younger women access to oral contraceptives in 1970) and Iowa (which didn't allow access until 1973). There are women who were aged eighteen to twenty in the late 1960s in both states; neither of these groups had access to oral contraceptives. And there are women who were aged eighteen to twenty in the early 1970s in each state; the women in Kansas had access to oral contraceptives, while the women in Iowa did not. Thus, we can use the changes in outcomes for the women in Iowa as a baseline of comparison for the changes in outcomes for the women in Kansas to try to estimate the effect of early access to oral contraception for women in Kansas.

Bailey can do better than this simple example, since she has data for women from many age cohorts for all fifty states, and different states changed policy at different times. So she makes use of a fixed effects setup—regressing her outcome measures on a dummy variable for whether a given cohort of women had access to oral contraception when they were aged eighteen to twenty, as well as state fixed effects and cohort fixed effects. This allows her to implement a difference-in-differences design with many units changing treatment status at different times.

Since it's not random which states allowed early access to oral contraceptives first, we should think about parallel trends. Is it reasonable to assume that the trends in child-bearing and labor market participation are parallel, on average, across states, and that states did not strategically shift contraceptive rules just as they otherwise expected these outcomes to shift for other reasons? Bailey provides some reasons to think the answer is yes. For instance, she shows that the timing of legal access to contraceptives for younger women is uncorrelated with a wide variety of state characteristics in 1960 that you might expect to influence these outcomes. These include geography, racial composition, average marriage ages, women's education, fertility, poverty, religious composition, unemployment for men or women, wages for men and women, and so on.

Bailey's difference-in-differences results suggest that access to oral contraception at an age when women are making consequential life decisions does in fact have important effects. In particular, she estimates that access to oral contraceptives before age twenty-one reduced the likelihood of becoming a mother before age twenty-two by 14 to 18 percent and increased the likelihood that a woman was participating in the paid labor force in her late twenties by 8 percent. Moreover, women who had access to oral contraception before the age of twenty-one worked about seventy more hours per year in their late twenties. That is, by providing a way to delay and plan childbearing, oral contraception appears to have given women the freedom to pursue longer-term careers and work more.

Useful Diagnostics

As we've said, for difference-in-differences to yield an unbiased estimate of an average treatment effect, we need parallel trends. That is, in the counterfactual world where the treatment did not change, the difference in average outcomes would have stayed the same between the units where the treatment did in fact change and the units where it did not. Since we don't observe that counterfactual world, we can't know if that's true. So a careful analyst always wants to do whatever is possible to probe the plausibility of parallel trends.

One conjecture is that if parallel trends holds, we should see similar trends in outcomes in earlier periods, before any units changed treatment status. We can check these pre-treatment trends (often called *pre-trends*) directly by comparing the trend in outcomes for units that do and do not change treatment status later on. We can also do this in a regression framework by including a *lead treatment* variable—that is, a dummy variable indicating the treatment status in the *next* period. If the trends are indeed parallel prior to the change in treatment, the coefficient on the lead treatment should be zero and the coefficient on the treatment variable should not change when we include that lead treatment variable in the regression.

We can also relax the requirement of parallel trends a bit by allowing for the possibility that different units follow different linear trends over time to see if this changes our results. The specific details for how you implement this are not important for now (you can read about them in a more advanced book). But you can see that there are various strategies for probing a difference-in-differences analysis to see whether parallel trends seem plausible.

Remember that diagnostic tests of this sort are a complement to, not a substitute for, clear thinking. The most important defense of an assumption like parallel trends must be a substantive argument. Why did the treatment change in some units and not in others? Does that reason seem likely to be related to trends in the outcome or independent of trends in the outcome? Can you think of reasons that units might have changed their treatment right as they expected the outcome to change for other reasons? These are critical questions whose answers require deep substantive knowledge of your context, question, and data. Good answers are absolutely essential to assessing how convincing the estimates that come out of a difference-in-differences are.

To get a better sense of how one thinks through questions about parallel trends, let's look at a couple examples.

Do Newspaper Endorsements Affect Voting Decisions?

Newspapers regularly endorse candidates for elected office. Do such endorsements matter?

A study by Jonathan Ladd and Gabriel Lenz attempted to answer that question using a difference-in-differences design with data from the United Kingdom. Their study provides a nice illustration of how to test for parallel pre-trends as a diagnostic for the plausibility of the parallel trends assumption.

During the 1997 general election campaign in the United Kingdom, several newspapers that historcially tended to endorse the Conservative Party unexpectedly endorsed the Labour Party. Ladd and Lenz utilize this rare shift to estimate the effect of newspaper endorsements on vote choice.

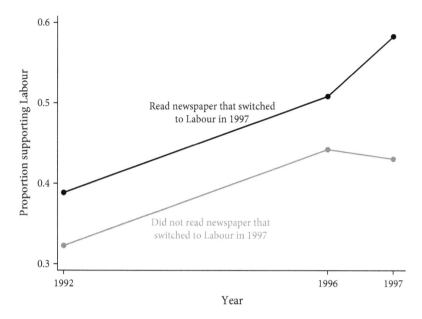

Figure 13.1. Visualizing pre-trends and using difference-in-differences to estimate the effect of newspaper endorsements on vote choices.

Implementing a difference-in-differences design, they compare changes in vote choice for those who regularly read a paper that unexpectedly switched its endorsement to Labour to changes in vote choice for those who did not regularly read one of those papers. Because they had data measuring partisan support of the same British individuals in 1992, 1996, and 1997, they were able to examine the pre-trends to see if they were parallel. If people who did and did not read the papers that switched to Labour between 1996 and 1997 were already trending differently between 1992 and 1996, that would make us worried that the parallel trends assumption is violated (and perhaps we'd worry the newspapers switched because their readers were trending toward Labour). But if these two groups were on similar trends between 1992 and 1996, that would give us more confidence that any resulting difference-in-differences is attributable to the unexpected newspaper endorsement in 1997.

Ladd and Lenz's diagnostics are reassuring, as shown in figure 13.1. People who read a paper that would later switch to endorsing the Labour Party had very similar trends in their level of Labour Party support between 1992 and 1996. But between 1996 and 1997, when the newspapers unexpectedly supported the Labour Party, the voters who read those papers significantly increased their support for the Labour Party relative to those who didn't read those papers. Thus, as long as we don't have reason to believe that other things, besides these surprise endorsements, changed differentially for readers of different newspapers in 1996, we might reasonably interpret the difference-in-differences as an estimate of the causal effect of those endorsements.

Is Obesity Contagious?

Humans are social animals. We live embedded in a complex web of relationships. Increasingly, we are told, our networks define who we are. A growing body of research claims to measure exactly how our thinking, tastes, and behavior are determined by our social networks.

Perhaps the most well-known of this research is authored by Nicholas Christakis and James Fowler. What is striking about Christakis and Fowler's work is that they find that behaviors and characteristics that many of us think of as profoundly personal—smoking, drinking, happiness, obesity—all appear to be network characteristics. Or, to use their more colorful language, "Obesity is contagious."

In a study of the spread of obesity in social networks, published in the *New England Journal of Medicine*, Christakis and Fowler examine the relationship between a change in a person's weight and changes in their friends', family members', or neighbors' weight. They make these comparisons controlling for personal characteristics like age, gender, and education.

What do they find? The chance that a person becomes obese is 57 percent higher if that person has a friend who becomes obese than if that person does not have a friend who becomes obese. Friendship seems to matter more than familial ties when it comes to weight gain. If a person has a brother or sister who becomes obese, that person's chance of becoming obese increases by 40 percent. If a person's spouse becomes obese, that person's chance of becoming obese increases by 37 percent. Having obese neighbors has no effect. On the basis of these findings, the *New York Times* declared in a front-page article, "The way to avoid becoming fat is to avoid having fat friends." Christakis and Fowler didn't love this interpretation. Instead, the *Times* reported, Christakis suggested, "Why not make friends with a thin person…and let the thin person's behavior influence you and your obese friend?"

It seems indisputable that your behavior is affected by those with whom you interact, that their behavior is affected by those with whom they interact, and so on. In this sense, we are entirely with Christakis and Fowler—we are all influenced by our social networks. But these authors, and many other scientists who study network effects, are making a claim stronger than just the commonsensical observation that our interactions affect how we behave. They are claiming to measure and quantify that effect. How do they claim to do so?

Christakis and Fowler's approach is effectively a difference-in-differences design. They test how changes in one person's obesity correspond to changes in another person's obesity. So if we want to think clearly about whether these are credible estimates of a contagion effect, we need to think about whether we find the assumption of parallel trends plausible.

Recall what parallel trends says here. It requires that, in the counterfactual world where there was no change in treatment (i.e., no one's friends became more or less obese), the trend in outcomes (personal obesity) would have been the same on average among people who in fact experienced a change in treatment (i.e., whose friends' obesity changed) and people who did not experience a change in treatment (i.e., whose friends' obesity did not change). If parallel trends holds, then Christakis and Fowler's difference-in-differences yields an unbiased estimate of the effect of your friends' obesity on your obesity. But if the trends are not parallel, then their estimates are biased, since some of the difference-in-differences they are observing and attributing to network effects would have happened even if your friends' obesity hadn't changed.

One concern often raised about studies of network effects is what medical researchers call *homophily*. People with similar characteristics tend to group together. Suppose you find that people whose friends are smokers are more likely to be smokers themselves. Social network researchers might want to interpret this as evidence that having friends who smoke causes you to become more likely to smoke. But, for that conclusion to be warranted, we'd have to be comparing apples to apples. That is, other than how their friends behave, people in the social networks of smokers and people in the social networks of non-smokers would have to be essentially the same. If members of networks of smokers were already more likely to be smokers than members of networks of non-smokers, we'd be comparing apples to oranges.

It seems entirely plausible (indeed likely) that people who are members of networks of smokers are, independent of their friends, already more likely to be the sort of people who smoke because of homophily. Smokers might well meet their friends in bars that allow smoking, in the outside area at work or school where people gather to smoke, or in other smoker-friendly environments. Put differently, it might not be that having friends that smoke causes you to smoke. It might be that being a smoker causes you to have friends that smoke. Because people don't choose their social networks randomly, when we compare people in smoking networks to people in non-smoking networks, we aren't comparing apples to apples.

But homophily, alone, is not enough to create a problem for Christakis and Fowler's difference-in-differences design. That design accounts for fixed characteristics of units, such as the possibility that obese people tend to be friends with each other and smokers tend to hang out together. This is one of the great things about difference-in-differences. Their finding is more compelling than just comparing people with more overweight friends to people with fewer overweight friends. They show that when one person *becomes* obese, their friends are also more likely to *become* obese. For homophily to create a problem, it has to be because of a worry about parallel trends not holding. For instance, if people who are on the path to becoming obese (perhaps because they have similar diets, exercise habits, genetic predispositions, cultural pressures, and so on) are more likely to be friends with each other, that would be a violation of parallel trends. And if parallel trends is violated, difference-in-differences doesn't yield an unbiased estimate of the causal effect.

We can't know whether homophily creates violations of parallel trends. But there is some evidence that points toward the possibility that difference-in-differences is not unbiased here. Ethan Cohen-Cole and Jason Fletcher conducted a study of the spread of two individual characteristics—height and acne—in social networks. Using the same difference-in-differences approach that Christakis and Fowler use to argue for the social contagion of divorce, loneliness, happiness, obesity, and many other things, Cohen-Cole and Fletcher find that both height and acne appear contagious in social networks. Knowing what we do about height and acne, it is pretty hard to believe that their spread is actually caused by social interactions within a network. This is Cohen-Cole and Fletcher's point. Height and acne likely don't spread in a social network. Instead, their apparent social contagion almost surely results from violations of parallel trends, perhaps due to homophily. Having friends with acne doesn't give you acne; people at high risk for acne tend to hang out together. The same may well be true for obesity, divorce, happiness, and so on.

To be clear, we're not saying that we think there are no causal network effects. Indeed, we're certain there are. Furthermore, Christakis and Fowler's study is surely more convincing because they compared changes to changes, rather than simply showing that obese people are more likely to be friends with each other. But there are lots of ways in which parallel trends could be violated. So we must be cautious and think clearly about those possibilities before interpreting the results of a difference-in-differences design as an unbiased estimate of the true causal effect.

Difference-in-Differences as Gut Check

Sometimes difference-in-differences analyses can be useful as a way to probe the credibility of a causal claim. Imagine a scenario in which someone estimates the correlation between a treatment and an outcome, perhaps even controlling for some possible confounders. You, thinking clearly about the lessons of chapter 9, might be skeptical that a causal interpretation of this estimate is warranted. Maybe you can think of a bunch of other confounders that aren't observable and, so, can't be controlled for. Even with such arguments, it can be hard to convince people to take your concerns seriously.

But if the data include multiple observations of the same unit, difference-in-differences can provide a useful gut check.[1] If the treatment really has an effect on the outcome, then we should expect a correlation not just between treatment and outcome but between changes in treatment status and changes in outcome. That is, we should expect the relationship between treatment and outcome to still be there in a difference-in-differences analysis.

Even if you find a relationship in the difference-in-differences, you still might not be sure about the causal interpretation. For that, you'd want to think about parallel trends. But if the relationship disappears in the difference-in-differences, then you have bolstered the case for your skepticism. It would seem that differences between units other than the treatment account for the correlation in the data. To see how difference-in-differences can be used for a gut check, let's look at an example.

The Democratic Peace

At least since the philosopher Immanuel Kant wrote *Perpetual Peace*, theorists have argued that democracy leads to peace—or, in its more contemporary formulation, that democracies will be more reluctant to fight one another than they are to fight autocracies or than autocracies are to fight one another. Some argue that this is because democracies share common norms that prevent them from engaging in violence against one another. Others argue that various features of domestic politics constrain democratic leaders from waging war against other democrats.

Empirical scholars have been similarly fascinated by the relationship between democracy and war. And the finding that country pairs (called *dyads*) where both countries are democratic are less likely to fight wars with one another than are dyads where at least one country is not democratic is one of the most important and discussed empirical findings in the literature on international relations.

Let's think a little about that empirical literature and its findings. A first thing scholars have done to try to assess the democratic peace is to simply look at the correlation between democracy and war. We'll start by replicating that approach. Here's how.

We start with a big data set that has an observation for every dyad in every year. So an observation is a dyad-year. We are going to work with data from 1951–1992 because those are the years one of the most famous papers in this literature works with. For each dyad-year, we have a binary variable that indicates whether that dyad had a militarized interstate dispute (MID) in that year. That is our dependent variable. And for each country we have a measure of how democratic it is. We use the Polity score, which you may recall from chapter 2 is a standard measure of the level of democracy. Higher numbers indicate a more democratic country. For estimating the democratic peace, we

---

[1] It's a gut check because your newly honed clear thinking skills are telling you to always be a bit skeptical.

Table 13.7. The relationship between democratic dyads and war with and without controls and with and without year and dyad fixed effects.

	1	2	3	4
		Dependent Variable = MIDs		
Minimum Level of Democracy in Dyad	−.0082**	−.0066**	.0002	.0005
	(.0016)	(.0016)	(.0017)	(.0017)
Countries Are Contiguous		.0693**	.0002	.0648**
		(.0110)	(.0017)	(.0227)
Log (Capability Ratio)		.0006		.0024
		(.0005)		(.0019)
Minimum 3-Year GDP Growth Rate		−.0001		−.0005**
		(.0002)		(.0002)
Formal Alliance		−.0012		−.0095
		(.0027)		(.0067)
Minimum Trade-GDP Ratio		−.0045**		.0011
		(.0017)		(.0021)
Includes Year Fixed Effects			✓	✓
Includes Dyad Fixed Effects			✓	✓
Observations	93,755	93,755	93,755	93,755
r-squared	.0011	.0289	.2636	.2658

Standard errors are in parentheses. ** indicates statistical significance with $p < .01$.

don't want to know how democratic any one country is. We want to know whether a dyad contains two democracies in a given year. To get at this, we use the lower of the two Polity scores within each dyad. If both countries in a dyad are democratic, then the lower of the two scores will be high. If at least one country in a dyad is not democratic, then the lower of the two scores will be low. We put this variable on a scale from 0 to 1 so we can interpret the coefficients as the estimated effect of going from the lowest to the highest level of democracy. This measure, which we refer to as the *minimal level of democracy in a dyad*, is our treatment variable.

To see the correlation between war and democracy, we regress MIDs on the minimal level of democracy. Figuring out the correct standard errors in this regression is actually a bit tricky, since surely there is correlation between whether, say, France and Germany have a war in a given year and whether England and Germany have a war in that same year. But we aren't going to worry about those issues for the moment.

The first column of table 13.7 shows the results of this regression. We find a statistically significant negative correlation between being a democratic dyad and war. The regression coefficient of −.0082 says that if we compare a dyad where the less democratic country is among the least democratic countries to a dyad where both countries are among the most democratic countries, the probability of there being a war between the two countries in a given year is about eight-tenths of a percentage point lower. Since the overall probability that any given dyad is at war in any given year is only about eight-tenths of a percent to start with, that is an enormous estimated relationship.

Now, we hope that this evidence doesn't convince you there is a causal effect of democracy on war. The lessons about confounders from chapter 9 are still important. And we can think of lots of ways that democracies and autocracies are different that might matter for war.

Scholars are aware of this concern. And the standard approach to addressing it is to try to control for various characteristics of a dyad that correlate with being democratic and with war. For instance, studies commonly control for whether the countries are contiguous, their relative military capabilities, their GDP growth, whether countries are allied, how much countries trade, and so on. Of course, we also shouldn't forget the lessons of chapter 10. Some of these things may be mechanisms by which democracy affects war, rather than confounders, in which case they shouldn't be controlled for. But, to stick close to the literature, in the second column of table 13.7, we control for these variables. As you can see, once we control, the estimated relationship between a democratic dyad and war drops a little bit. But it is still strongly negative and statistically significant.

At this point, many scholars conclude that Kant and other theorists are on to something. There really is a causal effect of being a democratic dyad on going to war. That might be true, but we are certainly entitled to remain skeptical. After all, there are so many features of a dyad that are hard to measure. And any number of them might affect both whether the two countries are democracies and whether they go to war. Indeed, a study by Henry Farber and Joanne Gowa claims that the empirical pattern associated with the democratic peace does not appear in the data prior to World War II precisely because key confounding variables took different values during this earlier period.

Controversies like this are where difference-in-differences can help us. If the theories of the democratic peace are right, then we shouldn't just observe a negative correlation between being a democratic dyad and war. We should observe a change in the likelihood two countries go to war as the dyad becomes more jointly democratic. That is, we should continue to see the correlation we've already observed in a difference-in-differences analysis. If we don't, we have reason to worry about bias—that is, that the estimated correlation reflects the influence of unobserved confounders rather than a true causal effect.

This argument was made in an influential, and controversial, paper by Donald Green, Soo Yeon Kim, and David Yoon. And so, in columns 3 and 4 of table 13.7 we implement a difference-in-differences design for the case of N observations and N time periods. We do so using fixed effect regression, including fixed effects for each dyad and for each year. Column 3 reports the difference-in-differences with no other control variables. Column 4 includes the fixed effects and the controls.

As you can see, once we compare the change in war to the change in whether a dyad is democratic, the correlation disappears. The difference-in-differences finds no meaningful or statistically significant relationship between democracy and war. Our gut check failed. As we've emphasized, this doesn't mean that there is definitely no causal effect. But it does mean that the existing evidence does not make a compelling case for one. By simply checking the difference-in-differences, we come away with a very different picture from the one painted by the simple correlations.

Many scholars who believe in the democratic peace have criticized Green, Kim, and Yoon's argument and the use of difference-in-differences designs to answer questions about international relations. One common critique is that difference-in-differences ignores most of the variation in the treatment variable, making it hard to find evidence of a relationship.

This is true. The regressions in columns 1 and 2 of table 13.7 make use of a lot of variation in democracy to try to detect a relationship between democracy and war—they use variation over time, variation between dyads, and variation within dyads. The regressions in columns 3 and 4 just use the variation within dyads, holding constant differences between dyads and global changes over time. But some of the variation exploited in columns 1 and 2 is probably not very informative about the causal effect of democracy because there are so many other things that are changing over time and that differ between dyads. So yes, difference-in-differences ignores a lot of the variation and attempts to isolate the variation that is most informative for assessing the effect of democracy on war—namely, the within-dyad variation.

It's also worth noting that this critique would have more bite if the difference-in-differences estimates were far less precise than the other estimates. This would indicate that there is a lot less information about the relationship between democracy and peace in the difference-in-difference estimates. But the estimated standard errors on the minimum level of democracy variable in table 13.7 are only slightly larger in columns 3 and 4 than in columns 1 and 2. It's not as if, in doing the difference-in-differences, we threw up our hands and concluded that we just don't know anything about the relationship between democracy and war. The difference-in-differences design allows us to obtain reasonably precise estimates of the effect of democracy. And those estimates are very close to zero. Furthermore, the difference-in-differences estimates are statistically significantly different from the estimates in columns 1 and 2. So imprecision does not account for the disparate results obtained by these two approaches.

Wrapping Up

We've seen that changes in treatment over time can allow us to more credibly estimate the effects of that treatment using a difference-in-differences design. For this to work we need for the parallel trends condition to hold—it has to be that, had it not been for the change in treatment status, the average outcomes for units that did and did not change treatments would have followed the same trend. There are several useful diagnostic tests to help analysts assess whether this assumption is plausible, but there is no substitute for clear thinking and substantive knowledge.

The last four chapters have been dedicated to methods for obtaining more credible estimates of causal relationships. Estimating causal relationships is a difficult and noble task. But often we want to know more. We aren't satisfied just knowing that the treatment did have an effect. We want to know *why*. The next chapter addresses the important challenge of answering such *why* questions using quantitative evidence.

Key Terms

- **Difference-in-differences:** A research design for estimating causal effects when some units change treatment status over time but others do not.
- **Parallel trends:** The condition that average potential outcomes without treatment follow the same trend in the units that do and do not change treatment status. This says that average outcomes would have followed the same trend had it not been for some unit's changing treatment status. If parallel trends

doesn't hold, difference-in-differences does not provide an unbiased estimate of the ATT.

- **First differences:** A statistical procedure for implementing difference-in-differences. It involves regressing the change in outcome for each unit on the change in treatment for each unit.
- **Wide format:** A way to structure a data set in which each unit is observed multiple times, where each row corresponds to a unique unit.
- **Long format:** A way to structure a data set in which each unit is observed multiple times, where there is a row for each unit in each time period.
- **Fixed effects regression:** A statistical procedure for implementing difference-in-differences. It involves regressing the outcome on the treatment while also including dummy variables (*fixed effects*) for each time period and for each unit.
- **Pre-trends:** The trend in average outcomes before any unit changes treatment status. If pre-trends are not parallel, it is harder to make the case that the parallel trends condition is plausible.
- **Lead treatment variable:** A dummy variable indicating that treatment status in a unit will change in the next time period.

Exercises

13.1   For years, the state of Illinois has administered the Illinois State Aptitude Test (ISAT) to third, fifth, and eighth graders. For much of this time, the test was relatively low stakes—not tied to promotion to the next grade, teacher compensation, school resources, and so on. The stakes changed in 2002, when the ISAT became the test that the Chicago Public Schools used to comply with the federal No Child Left Behind law.

Consider two cohorts of students: students who were fifth graders in 2001 and students who were fifth graders in 2002. Both of these groups of students took the ISAT in third grade when it was low stakes. The students who were in fifth grade in 2001 also took the ISAT in fifth grade when it was low stakes. But the students who were in fifth grade in 2002 took their second ISAT when it was high stakes. Make a two-by-two table showing how we could learn about the average effect of high-stakes testing on student test scores using a difference-in-differences design if we had data on the average test scores of these two cohorts of students when they were fifth and third graders.

13.2   The Nike Vaporfly shoe has been controversial in the world of elite long-distance running because some argue that the shoe provides an unfair advantage to those who use it, and it makes previous records obsolete. Suppose you had data from many different marathons that indicated each runner's time and also which shoes each runner wore. How could you estimate the effect of the Nike Vaporfly? You'd want to be sure to account for the fact that marathon times vary from day to day and course to course. You'd also want to account for the fact that some runners are just better and faster than others.

(a)   What analyses would you conduct to separate the effect of shoe technology from other factors, and what assumptions would you have to make?

(b) Do you find those assumptions plausible? Discuss your potential concerns.

(c) Is there anything you can do to address these potential concerns?

(d) Another challenge is that not everyone who starts a marathon finishes it, so you could have attrition in your study. What could you do to address this potential problem?

(e) Could you use the same approach to estimate the effect of a new shoe or glove technology on points scored in professional boxing? Why or why not?

13.3   Suppose we want to estimate the extent to which the policy positions of Democratic and Republican candidates for Congress diverge. In other words, we'd like to know how differently the Democratic and Republican candidate would represent the same set of constituents.

(a) Suppose we measured how conservatively each member of Congress voted on bills and ran a regression of roll-call voting on an indicator for being a Republican. Would this be a satisfying way to estimate divergence? What kinds of bias would you worry about?

(b) Download "CongressionalData.csv" and the associated "README.txt," which describes the variables in this data set, at press.princeton.edu /thinking-clearly. This data set contains information on congressional elections and roll-call voting behavior. Using only the variables available in the provided data set, try to estimate divergence by controlling for confounders. If it helps, you may want to only analyze just one congressional session at a time.

(c) Using the data available, now estimate divergence using a regression discontinuity design. Again, you might find it helpful to focus on just one congressional session at a time.

(d) Finally, estimate divergence using a difference-in-differences design.

(e) Compare and contrast these three different approaches. Which one estimates divergence with the most defensible assumptions? How much do your estimates depend on your design?

13.4   In a study of sex-based discrimination in hiring, Claudia Goldin and Cecilia Rouse study the effect of making auditions for symphony orchestras "blind" by putting candidates behind a screen. The idea is, if the people evaluating the audition can't observe the sex of the person auditioning, they shouldn't be able to discriminate.

It turns out, as Goldin and Rouse document, that different orchestras adopted the practice of using such a screen at different times. Let's think about how we could use that fact to learn about the causal effect of the screens. (We'll talk through a somewhat different empirical approach than the one Goldin and Rouse use.)

(a) Suppose for each orchestra and each year you observed the share of new hires for that orchestra who were women and whether or not that orchestra used a screen in its audition. If you just pooled together all of your data and regressed share of women on using a screen, would you feel comfortable giving the output of that regression a causal interpretation. Why or why not?

(b) Suppose, instead, you wanted to use a difference-in-differences design with this data. What regression would you run?

(c) Describe the assumptions that would have to be true for this to give you an unbiased estimate of a causal effect. (Don't just say "parallel trends"; describe what would have to be true about the world for parallel trends to hold.)

(d) Does this assumption seem plausible to you? What kinds of concerns would you have?

Readings and References

The study on the effect of increasing the minimum wage in New Jersey is

David Card and Alan B. Krueger. 1994. "Minimum Wages and Employment: A Case Study of the Fast-Food Industry in New Jersey and Pennsylvania." *American Economic Review* 84(4):772–93.

The study on television and academic performance is

Matthew Gentzkow and Jesse M. Shapiro. 2008. "Preschool Television Viewing and Adolescent Test Scores: Historical Evidence from the Coleman Study." *Quarterly Journal of Economics* 71(3):279–323.

If you want to learn more about the complications of difference-in-differences when there are N units and N periods, have a look at

Andrew Goodman-Bacon. 2018. "Difference-in-Differences with Variation in Treatment Timing." NBER Working Paper No. 25018.

Kosuke Imai and In Song Kim. 2019. "When Should We Use Unit Fixed Effects Regression Models for Causal Inference with Longitudinal Data?" *American Journal of Political Science* 63(2):467–90.

The two studies on oral contraception that we mentioned are

Claudia Goldin and Lawrence F. Katz. 2002. "The Power of the Pill: Oral Contraceptives and Women's Career and Marriage Decisions." *Journal of Political Economy* 110(4):730–70.

Martha J. Bailey. 2006. "More Power to the Pill: The Impact of Contraceptive Freedom on Women's Life Cycle Labor Supply." *Quarterly Journal of Economics* 121(1): 289–320.

The study of newspaper endorsements in the United Kingdom is

Jonathan McDonald Ladd and Gabriel S. Lenz. 2009. "Exploiting a Rare Communication Shift to Document the Persuasive Power of the News Media." *American Journal of Political Science* 53(2):394–410.

The studies of the contagiousness of obesity and of acne and height are

Nicholas A. Christakis and James H. Fowler. 2007. "The Spread of Obesity in a Large Social Network over 32 Years." *New England Journal of Medicine* 373:370–79.

Ethan Cohen-Cole and Jason Feltcher. 2009. "Detecting Implausible Social Network Effects in Acne, Height, and Headaches: Longitudinal Analysis." *British Medical Journal* 338(7685):28–31.

There is a ton of work on the democratic peace. A Google Scholar search will turn up many interesting theoretical arguments. The papers we mentioned are

Henry S. Farber and Joanne Gowa. 1991. "Common Interests or Common Polities? Reinterpreting the Democratic Peace." *Journal of Politics* 59(2):393–417.

Donald P. Green, Soo Yeon Kim, and David H. Yoon. 2001. "Dirty Pool." *International Organization* 55(2):441–68.

The argument that it was appropriate to include fixed effects in regressions probing the democratic peace was sufficiently controversial at the time that the journal editors invited several other prominent social scientists to comment on the piece in the same issue of the journal.

The study of orchestra auditions discussed in exercise 4 is

Claudia Goldin and Cecilia Rouse. 2000. "Orchestrating Impartiality: The Impact of 'Blind' Auditions on Female Musicians." *American Economic Review* 90(4):715–41.

CHAPTER 14

Assessing Mechanisms

What You'll Learn

- Estimating an average causal effect doesn't tell us why or how that effect arises.
- Learning about the mechanisms underlying a causal relationship is harder than it seems. Generally, we can't just measure potential mechanisms and learn which ones are most important.
- Combining theory, measurement, and clear thinking can help us learn about the mechanisms underlying causal relationships.

Introduction

As we discussed in chapter 3, when we say that a treatment affects an outcome, all we mean is that a change in the treatment changes the outcome. But that effect need not be direct or proximate—the effect of some event on some outcome could be the result of a long chain of relationships. So, in many settings, even once we've credibly estimated a causal relationship, we might remain uncertain why or how the treatment affects the outcome.

For example, suppose we found that attending charter schools rather than regular public schools causes an increase in the likelihood that students go to college. That's an interesting, policy-relevant finding. It tells us that, on average, charter schools are helping students. But it doesn't tell us *how*—that is, it doesn't tell us the mechanisms by which charter schools help students. Maybe the curriculum is more innovative, maybe students benefit from having more motivated peers, maybe discipline is stricter, maybe the facilities are nicer, maybe there are more advanced placement (AP) classes, maybe the students are better prepared for standardized tests, maybe there are more opportunities for after-school enrichment, or maybe the school motivates the students to work harder. People typically think of mechanisms as answers to *how* questions ("How did this effect arise?") or *why* questions ("Why did this happen?").

Randomizing students into charter schools versus public schools, or employing some other compelling research design, allows us to assess the average effect of going to a charter school. But it won't unpack which mechanisms are doing the work. Sometimes, understanding the mechanisms is important. For instance, if we are going to try to build more charter schools, we would like to know which features of existing charter schools are the most important to replicate. Should we make sure that there are nicer facilities,

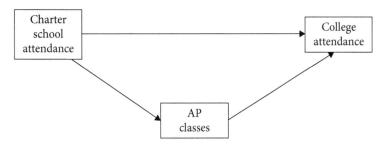

Figure 14.1. AP classes may be one of the mechanisms by which charter schools affect college attendance.

more AP classes, more standardized test prep, or stricter discipline? In this chapter, we consider some of the difficulties in trying to learn not just about effects but also about the mechanisms underlying those effects.

Causal Mediation Analysis

One approach that some researchers take to try to get at causal mechanisms is called *causal mediation analysis*. In causal mediation analysis, the goal is for the data to directly tell us how important a role some mechanism plays in driving a particular effect.

Figure 14.1, which recalls our illustration of mechanisms in figure 9.9, illustrates the idea. Suppose, for instance, that we want to know how much of the effect that attending a charter school has on college admission is due to charter school students taking more AP classes. In our earlier language, attending a charter school is the treatment and college admission is the outcome. We call taking AP classes a *mediator*—a mechanism by which charter schools have their effect on college admission. The idea is that attending charter schools affects taking AP classes and taking AP classes affects college admission. So some of the effect of attending a charter school on college admission runs through the AP class mechanism. We'd like to know how much of the effect is due to AP classes (represented by the arrows from charter schools to AP classes to college attendance) and how much is due to other factors (represented by the arrow directly from charter schools to college attendance).

If you *weren't* thinking clearly, you might be tempted to use the techniques from chapter 10 to try answer this question. You'd start by using an admissions lottery to estimate the effect of attending the charter school on college admission. You can do so by regressing college admission on winning the charter school admissions lottery for the set of students who were entered into the lottery. Then you'd measure the number of AP classes each student took and re-run the regression of college admission on winning the charter school lottery, but controlling for AP classes. The thought is that, if the estimated effect of charter schools shrinks once you control for AP classes, then that portion of the effect that disappeared is attributable to the AP class mechanism since, by controlling for AP classes, you are effectively holding them constant so that they are statistically removed from your estimate of the effect.

This idea might initially sound sensible. We are trying to figure out how much of the effect of charter schools on college admission runs through AP classes. We'd like to compare the effect of charter schools on college admission to the effect of charter schools on college admission *purged of the effect of taking AP classes*. So why won't it work?

The basic problem is that controlling for AP classes is not the same as purging their effect. You can see this just by thinking conceptually. To purge the effect of AP classes from the effect of attending a charter school on college admission, surely we must have a way of estimating the effect of taking AP classes on college admission. But we have described no research design to do so. Let's try to think that through as clearly as we can.

The charter school admissions lottery lets us estimate the effect of charter school attendance on college admission. It also lets us estimate the effect of charter school attendance on taking AP classes. But what lets us estimate the effect of taking AP classes on college admission? We are sure that you can think of lots of confounders for the relationship between how many AP classes a student takes and whether that student is admitted to college. So just regressing college admissions on AP classes surely won't do it.

To see why this is a problem, let's think about an extreme version of what could go wrong. Suppose that charter schools indeed cause students to take more AP classes, but that AP classes have no effect whatsoever on college admissions. (This is, of course, just for the sake of argument.) So, if our controlling strategy works to identify the importance of the mechanism, then we should find no difference between the effect of charter school attendance on college admission, whether or not we control for AP classes (since it is not in fact one of the mechanisms). But suppose taking AP classes happens to be correlated with academic talent (which we don't have a measure of) and that academic talent affects college admissions. Now, when we run the regression of college admissions on charter school attendance and AP classes, we will find that the estimated effect of going to a charter school is indeed lower when we control for AP classes. This is because AP classes are proxying for (i.e., measuring) academic talent. From this statistical result, we will wrongly conclude that allowing students to take AP classes is, therefore, an important mechanism by which charter schools cause college admissions. But, in fact, we've stipulated that AP classes have no effect. Taking AP classes just happens to be correlated with things like talent that are also correlated with getting into college. Our controlling strategy, therefore, was misleading. If we don't think clearly about this type of analysis, we could end up making bad decisions about how to allocate resources or design schools.

A literature delves into what kinds of conditions you would need to have causal mediation analysis work. Without going into the technical details, it boils down to something along the lines of having research designs that allow you to separately estimate the effect of the treatment on the outcome, the effect of the treatment on the mechanism, and the effect of the mechanism on the outcome. If you can estimate these quantities, you can net out the effect of the treatment on the outcome that runs through the mechanism. The key takeaway, of course, is that there is no magical technical or statistical way to identify which mechanisms matter. If we want to learn about mechanisms, just like when we wanted to learn about causal effects, we are going to have to work hard and think clearly.

Intermediate Outcomes

One thing an analyst can do is test for the effect of their treatment on other, perhaps more intermediate outcomes that might provide some hints about mechanisms. Once you have a research design that allows you to estimate the effect of some treatment, it can, in principle, be applied to any downstream outcome that you can measure.

So, to partially assess mechanisms, we can see which intermediate outcomes appear to be affected by the treatment. Returning to our example, we can use the charter school lottery to assess the effect of going to a charter school not just on college admission but also on intermediate outcomes like study habits, extracurricular participation, standardized test scores, taking AP classes, and so on. Of course, this doesn't give us a way to assess the effect of those intermediate outcomes on the final outcome (here, college admissions). For that, we'd need a separate research design. So, for reasons just discussed in the last section, this approach won't tell us exactly how much of an effect is explained by one mechanism or another. But it can allow us to make some progress in thinking about which mechanisms likely do or do not help us understand the effect. For instance, if it turns out that attending a charter school has no effect on taking AP classes, it seems unlikely that AP classes are one of the mechanisms by which charter schools affect college admissions.

One real-world example of using intermediate outcomes comes from research in Liberia by Chris Blattman, Julian Jamison, and Margaret Sheridan.

Cognitive Behavioral Therapy and At-Risk Youths in Liberia

Blattman, Jamison, and Sheridan randomly assigned some Liberian young men who were thought to be at risk for engaging in crime or violence to cognitive behavioral therapy, with the hope of improving economic outcomes and reducing crime and violence. The therapy appears to have worked well, significantly improving both outcomes. That is good news for the therapy program that Blattman, Jamison, and Sheridan were studying. But in addition to knowing that the therapy worked, it would be nice to know *how* or *why* it worked. The treatment lasted as long as eight weeks and included work on a variety of skills, from self-control to personal appearance. Some of the interventions even included monetary compensation. So there are a lot of different features of the treatment that could explain the result. And if you were going to try to transport this evidence elsewhere, you'd want to know which features of this program are important and which ones are incidental.

As we've discussed, there's no way to know with certainty which features of the intervention led to the overall effect. But the authors did measure a number of intermediate outcomes that might help to elucidate the mechanisms and aid practitioners who would like to apply the lessons elsewhere. Interestingly, the authors found little evidence that the therapy affected subjects' self-control skills, such as impulsiveness, perseverance, and conscientiousness. Therefore, they conclude that these self-control skills are unlikely to be an important mechanism through which the therapy reduced violence or improved economic outcomes. By contrast, they did find that their intervention had a large effect on other intermediate outcomes, such as social networks and attitudes toward violence. This suggests that these mechanisms are more likely to explain the success of the treatment and might be more important to replicate in other settings.

To be clear, this study does not show that self-control skills have no effect on economic well-being or violence. They might have very large effects. The research instead shows that the particular intervention under study had little effect on self-control skills and therefore self-control skills are unlikely to explain the large effects of the intervention on economic well-being or violence. Furthermore, if future practitioners were hoping to replicate the success of this behavioral therapy in Liberia, they might learn from this that, for whatever reason, they won't have much success changing self-control skills, so they might be better off focusing more on other factors like social networks and attitudes toward violence, which seem to be the places where this particular approach has the most bite.

Independent Theoretical Predictions

Another way to get at specific mechanisms is to think theoretically and generate independent tests that might help adjudicate between different potential mechanisms. In chapter 7, we discussed how we could use independent theoretical predictions to probe whether some estimated effect was the result of noise (i.e., a false positive). There, we gave the example of re-examining the putative effect of college football games on elections. The idea here is similar. But now, instead of testing whether an observed relationship is genuine or spurious, we want to look for the mechanisms underlying an estimated effect that we believe is genuine.

A study by Sarah Anzia and Chris Berry illustrates how this can work.

Do Voters Discriminate Against Women?

There is much concern about the possibility of discrimination in the electoral process. For example, are voters biased against female candidates? Answering this question compellingly is difficult for obvious reasons. Discriminatory voters may not reveal their prejudices in surveys. And in real elections, there could be factors other than discrimination that could explain why women do better or worse than men.

Some scholars have noticed that in the United States, when female candidates run for office, they perform similarly to male candidates on average. This, they argue, suggests there may be little discrimination by voters. However, Anzia and Berry point out that if there is discrimination, we might expect that only the most qualified women will decide to run for office, which could explain why women do about as well as men even in a world with discrimination. So the fact that women perform as well as men, *when they run*, doesn't necessarily imply that voters aren't discriminating.

Continuing with this line of thinking, Anzia and Berry try to generate theoretical predictions that should hold if there indeed is discrimination against women in elections. One prediction is that if there is discrimination, all else equal, the women who are elected to office should be better at their jobs than the men who get elected. Because of discrimination, they will have to be better in order to get elected. Of course, we don't have perfect measures of job performance. But Anzia and Berry look at several measures of how members of Congress perform, including the number of bills they sponsor and also the amount of federal spending they bring home to their districts. The results are exactly in line with the theoretical prediction. Using a difference-in-differences design, they show that, on average (accounting for differences across districts and time periods to make the comparison as apples-to-apples as possible), women perform better in Congress than men, consistent with the possibility that women have to clear a higher hurdle in order to get elected because of voter discrimination.

Having uncovered an interesting and compelling phenomenon, Anzia and Berry push further still. The evidence is pretty clear that, on average, female members of Congress are more productive than male members of Congress, and discrimination is a potential explanation. But are there other mechanisms that could potentially explain this effect? What if, for example, women are just better at some parts of the job than men, regardless of any selection or discrimination? Or what if women are treated differently once they get to Congress, not because of their ability but because they are viewed as a token minority?

To address these kinds of questions, Anzia and Berry keep thinking. If it's really discrimination that explains this result, are there further theoretical predictions that they can test? One prediction is that the gap in performance between elected women and men should be greater the more discrimination women face. Of course, we don't know for sure which congressional districts discriminate more. But one reasonable hypothesis is that more conservative districts will discriminate against female candidates more than more liberal districts. Therefore, Anzia and Berry test whether the difference in performance in Congress between men and women is greater in more conservative districts, as measured by how the district votes in presidential elections. The answer is yes.

To provide further evidence of their purported mechanism, Anzia and Berry note that one large group of female congressional representatives—those who gained office because they were the widow of a recently deceased member of Congress—likely did not have to overcome the same type of discrimination as other female candidates. As such, we would not expect them to be more qualified on average. And sure enough, Anzia and Berry find that widows do not perform better than male members of Congress and their performance is notably worse than female candidates who were elected independent of their spouses.

The compellingness of the Anzia and Berry study comes not from a single, airtight research design or statistical test demonstrating the presence of discrimination. Rather, they elucidate an interesting and plausible mechanism by generating a theory of discrimination in elections and testing multiple, independent predictions that follow from that theory.

Of course, this still doesn't settle the matter. Other mechanisms might also account for the observed patterns. For instance, a variety of scholars point to evidence that women may under-estimate their abilities or be averse to putting themselves forward as candidates. These mechanisms might also account for female representatives performing better in their jobs, conditional on winning election. So there is still lots of work to do in figuring out which mechanisms are at work. But, in our view, this study provides a model for using a combination of clear thinking and data analysis to try to provide a better understanding of causal mechanisms.

Testing Mechanisms by Design

In some special circumstances, we can design studies in ways that isolate particular mechanisms. Take, for example, a clever study on how social pressure affects voter turnout by Alan Gerber, Don Green, and Christopher Larimer.

Social Pressure and Voting

Gerber, Green, and Larimer mailed postcards to a randomly selected group of registered voters. The postcards informed the recipients which of their neighbors had and had not voted in recent elections. (You may not have known this, but in the United States, whether or not you voted is a matter of public record. Only how you voted is secret.) They also indicated that another, similar postcard would be sent to neighborhood residents after an upcoming election. The implication was that, if the recipient didn't vote in the upcoming election, all their neighbors would find out about it. This unusual (and perhaps invasive) postcard increased voter turnout dramatically; people who received the postcard were 8 percentage points more likely to vote than a control group.

Having seen these experimental results, we might wonder why the postcards had such large effects—that is, we want to know through what mechanisms the post-cards cause increased voter turnout. Was the social aspect of the treatment important? Do people really not want their neighbors to know that they don't vote? Are people mobilized just because the postcard reminded them about the election? Or are people perhaps just trying to impress researchers and so turn out once they know they are being studied?

To learn about the importance of the social mechanism, the researchers designed their experiment to include another randomly assigned postcard. This postcard mimicked every feature of the previously discussed one, with one exception. Instead of containing voter turnout information about all of the recipient's neighbors, it only contained information about members of the recipient's household. Recipients of this type of postcard would no longer worry that all of their neighbors were going to find out if they didn't vote. Now it would just be the people they lived with who would learn about their voting behavior. And those people presumably already had a pretty good guess. The thought is that this small change takes a lot of the social pressure mechanism out of the intervention. And, indeed, this postcard also increased voter turnout, but only by about 5 percentage points relative to a control group.

The clever part of this design is that, by including multiple treatments in the experiment, the authors were able to estimate how much the social aspect of the first postcard matters. In particular, having voter turnout information made public across a whole neighborhood, instead of just within a household, appears to account for 3 percentage points of the overall 8 percentage point effect.

Disentangling Mechanisms

Sometimes, we can do a similar pulling apart of mechanisms even when we don't get to design the study ourselves. To do so, of course, we must have multiple research designs that make it possible to separately estimate the effects of different mechanisms. Let's see an example.

Commodity Price Shocks and Violent Conflict

For decades, scholars have studied economic conditions, violent conflict, and the causal relationships between the two. It's hard to think of a topic where the stakes are higher. We would love to improve economic conditions and reduce violent conflict around the world, but we don't seem to know how to do so.

We already discussed the difficulty of empirically assessing the effect of the economy on conflict in chapter 9. When we observe a strong correlation between conflict and poor economic conditions, it is unclear whether the former causes the latter, the latter causes the former, some confounding factors cause both, or some combination of all these possibilities is at work.

To gain more traction on one part of the problem, many scholars have tried to find research designs that allow us to more credibly estimate the effect of economic conditions on violent conflict. One common strategy involves using commodity price shocks as part of a difference-in-differences design. The basic idea is as follows.

Poppy farming is a major industry in parts of Afghanistan. One might think that Afghan farmers and farm workers making money in the poppy industry would be less willing to go fight because they'd be giving up relatively good economic opportunities. But, clearly, we can't just regress the amount of violence in different parts of Afghanistan against the amount of poppy farming to learn about the relationship between conflict and economic opportunity. Confounders abound. Poppies are the key raw ingredient to heroin, so poppy farming goes along with the drug trade, which might affect violence independently. Moreover, poppies grow in mountainous areas. And the terrain might also affect the amount of violence.

Another thought is that the willingness of poppy farmers and farm workers to fight might go down when the poppy business is particularly good and go up when it is bad. But, again, such an over-time comparison has potential confounders. Perhaps a surge in demand for poppies happens to also coincide with features of the season, U.S. troop deployments, or other factors that also affect violence.

But a difference-in-differences strategy might address both concerns. That is, we'd like to look at differences in violence in poppy-producing places when the poppy business is good versus bad, and we'd like to compare those differences to the same differences in non-poppy-producing places. The idea is that by accounting for any changes in violence over time and accounting for the possibility that the baseline levels of violence differ between poppy- and non-poppy-producing places, we can obtain a more credible estimate of the effect of economic prosperity on violence.

To pull off a strategy like this, of course, we need some measure of when the poppy business is good versus bad. For that, researchers use changes to the world price of poppies (or the world price of heroin). The idea is that, for most commodities, most countries are small players. So the world price of that commodity is unlikely to be strongly influenced by things that are happening in that country. And therefore, perhaps we can use changes in the world price to estimate the effect of local economic prosperity (remember instrumental variables from our discussion of noncompliance in chapter 11).

The idea is a pretty nice one. Using difference-in-differences designs, we can estimate the effects of economic shocks on violence more credibly than we could just by comparing violence levels in rich and poor places, or even over time.

Rather than doing this for just one commodity and one country, scholars have done the painstaking work of measuring how much of each of hundreds of commodities each country produces. From this, they create an index, for each country, of its commodity bundle. They have also collected the world price of each commodity for each year, so they can measure how much the value of each country's commodity bundle changes each year. From this, they can do a giant difference-in-differences analysis to see how violence changes in response to economic shocks the world over.

Interestingly, when scholars did this, they got a bunch of conflicting results. Sometimes it looked like positive economic shocks reduce violence, sometimes they appeared to increase violence, and sometimes they had no detectable effect. These contradictory and inconsistent findings were somewhat disconcerting. Better data and research designs are supposed to provide more, not less, definitive answers.

What is going on? Ernesto Dal Bo and Pedro Dal Bo suggested one possible theoretical explanation. They pointed out that there are at least two mechanisms through which economic conditions might influence conflict, and they pull in opposite directions. On the one hand, good economic conditions create more and better jobs, and workers with those good jobs might be less willing to leave them to fight. In other words, good economic conditions increase the opportunity costs of fighting. If you're unemployed and hungry, then you might join a revolution, but having a good-paying job might be enough to deter that inclination. On the other hand, armed groups often fight over control of economic resources. Good economic conditions mean there is more to fight over. In other words, good economic conditions increase the benefits of predation. If you live in a desolate place with no economic value, what's the point in fighting over it? But if there's money to be made from controlling a booming economy, maybe it's worthwhile to fight. Perhaps the fact that a shock to economic conditions can activate these opposing forces explains the murky results of previous studies.

So where do we go from here? Knowing that there are competing forces is theoretically illuminating, but it's not enough to inform policy. Fortunately, Dal Bo and Dal Bo thought more about conditions under which one force might dominate the other. Their idea was that in labor-intensive industries and economies, the *opportunity cost* mechanism should dominate because economic shocks create more need for labor, higher wages, and better jobs. But in capital-intensive industries and economies, the *predation* mechanism should dominate because better economic conditions create more to fight over without meaningfully increasing wages or employment.

In a 2013 study, Oeindrila Dube and Juan Vargas found a way to empirically test these ideas using the sort of difference-in-differences strategy we've already described. They studied armed conflict in Colombia, and they focused most of their attention on two major industries: coffee and oil. Coffee is relatively labor-intensive, requiring lots of workers to farm and process. Oil is relatively capital-intensive: once an oil well is drilled, oil producers do not need lots of workers on hand. Importantly, some locales in Colombia have coffee-intensive economies, while others have oil-intensive economies. Consistent with theoretical predictions, positive shocks to the world price of coffee appear to reduce conflict in coffee-intensive locales relative to non-coffee-intensive locales. This is evidence in favor of the opportunity costs mechanism. By contrast, positive shocks to the world price of oil appear to increase conflict in oil-intensive locales relative to non-oil-intensive locales. This is evidence in favor of the predation mechanism.

This evidence suggests that economic conditions do indeed influence violent conflict through multiple mechanisms. As such, economic improvements can either mitigate or exacerbate conflict, depending on which mechanism dominates in a given context. This means that if we find no average relationship between economic shocks and conflict world-wide, that doesn't mean economic conditions don't matter for conflict. Rather, the average relationship might be masking multiple off-setting effects that we can only understand if we disentangle the mechanisms. So, perhaps economic aid can mitigate conflict, but only when it corresponds with job opportunities. Economic aid that simply increases the size of the economic pie that warring factions can fight over, but does not provide employment opportunities, will likely make matters worse. This is an important insight that could only have been discovered through the interplay of data, research design, theory, and clear thinking. The data alone wasn't enough. Nor was a good research design. It took all of these tools together.

Wrapping Up

We've accomplished a lot in part 3. We fulfilled one of the central goals of the book—really understanding why correlation need not imply causation. We explored why causal inference is so difficult and delved into the intellectually exciting world of creative research designs that can help us credibly estimate causal effects and uncover mechanisms. This is really important material, and we hope you feel good about what you've learned.

But, on its own, even knowledge of causal effects is not sufficient for making the best use of quantitative information to inform decisions. In part 4 we turn to some final topics that will help us think clearly about the right questions, the right evidence to answer those questions, and the limits of quantification.

Key Terms

- **Mediator:** A feature of the world that is affected by the treatment and affects the outcome.
- **Causal mediation analysis:** Techniques for trying to estimate how much of the effect of a treatment on an outcome is the result of the treatment's effect on a mediator and the mediator's effect on the outcome.

Exercises

14.1 In the 1990s, the U.S. Department of Housing and Urban Development ran a large-scale field experiment called Moving to Opportunity. They randomly selected some households living in high-poverty public housing projects and offered them housing vouchers (i.e., money that could be used to pay rent) if they moved to a low-poverty neighborhood. Other households were given nothing. The goal was to learn whether moving to a low-poverty neighborhood would be beneficial for economic, mental, and physical well-being.

Researchers have examined the data and found that households in the treated condition (receiving a voucher to move to a low-poverty neighbor-hood) experienced better physical health, mental health, and subjective well-being than those in the untreated condition (receiving nothing). There were no significant differences in economic outcomes.

(a) This result is strong evidence that a treatment—receiving a housing voucher that you can use only by moving to a low-poverty neighborhood—causes improved well-being. Does this imply that the treatment works through the mechanism of moving people to a low-poverty neighborhood? Offer at least one other mechanism that might explain the result.

(b) How could you modify or add to the experiment in order to better elicit the effect of moving to a low-poverty neighborhood?

(c) There was actually one additional treatment considered in the exper-iment. Another group of individuals were randomly assigned to receive a housing voucher to move anywhere they liked (not just to a low-poverty neighborhood). In light of this information, what com-parison(s) would you make in order to separate the effect of moving to a low-poverty neighborhood from the potential effects of moving in general or receiving the financial benefit of a voucher?

(d) *Bonus challenge*: Not surprisingly, there was some noncompliance in this experiment—some people who were assigned to the voucher treatment chose not to move. And as you can imagine, the rate of compliance was different between the two treatments: 63 percent of households used the voucher when there was no restriction on where they could move, but only 48 percent used it when it required that they move to a low-poverty neighborhood. Further complicating matters, some of the households in the unrestricted condition moved to low-poverty neighborhoods even though they didn't have to. What would you do if you wanted to estimate the effect of moving to a low-poverty neighborhood in light of these noncompliance issues? (There's no easy answer, but we hope it's illuminating to think through all the complications and appreciate how hard it is to learn about causal mechanisms.)

14.2   There is some compelling evidence that education increases political participation. Let's think about why this might be.

Some people hypothesize this is due, at least in part, to an income or wealth mechanism. Perhaps education increases economic prosperity, wealthy people care more about taxes or economic policy, and therefore they are more likely to vote. Consider the following kinds of evidence that might be brought to bear on this hypothesis about mechanisms. How convincing do you find each, and why?

(a) Suppose, if you run a regression of voter turnout on years of schooling, you get a large coefficient, and if you run another regression of voter turnout on years of schooling and income, the coefficient associated with schooling is notably smaller.

(b) Because of compulsory schooling requirements, people born toward the end of the calendar year tend to get more education (because they are young for their grade and so have to stay in school a year longer before they can drop out). Exploiting this natural experiment and using instrumental variables, labor economists have estimated that schooling significantly increases earnings. Using another natural experiment, researchers have found that winning the lottery increases voter turnout.

(c) Suppose you find that among people who obtain college degrees in engineering, those in higher-paid specialities (e.g., aerospace, chemical, and petroleum) participate in politics more than those in lower-paid specialities (e.g., civil, environmental, and mechanical).

Readings and References

If you are interested in learning more about causal mediation analysis, you could start with these readings:

John G. Bullock, Donald P. Green, and Shang E. Ha. 2010. "Yes, But What's the Mechanism? (Don't Expect an Easy Answer)." *Journal of Personality and Social Psychology* 98(4):550–58.

Kosuke Imai, Luke Keele, Dustin Tingley, and Teppei Yamamoto. 2011. "Unpacking the Black Box of Causality: Learning about Causal Mechanisms from Experimental and Observational Studies." *American Political Science Review* 105(4):765–89.

The study on behavioral therapy in Liberia is

Christopher Blattman, Julian C. Jamison, and Margaret Sheridan. 2017. "Reducing Crime and Violence: Experimental Evidence from Cognitive Behavioral Therapy in Liberia." *American Economic Review* 107(4):1165–1206.

The study on discrimination against women in elections is

Sarah F. Anzia and Christopher R. Berry. 2011. "The Jackie (and Jill) Robinson Effect: Why Do Congresswomen Outperform Congressmen?" *American Journal of Political Science* 55(3):478–93.

The experiment on social pressure and turnout is

Alan S. Gerber, Donald P. Green, and Christopher W. Larimer. 2008. "Social Pressure and Voter Turnout: Evidence from a Large-Scale Field Experiment." *American Political Science Review* 102(1):33–48.

The studies on economic prosperity and conflict are

Ernesto Dal Bo and Pedro Dal Bo. 2011. "Workers, Warriors, and Criminals: Social Conflict in General Equilibrium." *Journal of the European Economic Association* 9(4):646–77.

Oeindrila Dube and Juan F. Vargas. 2013. "Commodity Price Shocks and Civil Conflict: Evidence from Colombia." *Review of Economic Studies* 80:1384–1421.

There is a ton of work on the effects of Moving to Opportunity. For a classic paper, see

Lawrence F. Katz, Jeffrey R. Kling, and Jeffrey B. Liebman. 2001. "Moving to Opportunity in Boston: Early Results of a Randomized Mobility Experiment." *Quarterly Journal of Economics* 116(2):607–54.

PART IV

From Information to Decisions

CHAPTER 15

Turn Statistics into Substance

What You'll Learn

- Statistics are often reported or presented in ways that are misleading or unhelpful for decision making.
- If you think clearly about the question at hand, you can often translate a statistic into a piece of more substantively useful information.
- Quantitative evidence, on its own, can't tell you what to believe. Your beliefs depend on a combination of the new evidence and your prior beliefs. Bayes' rule tells us how to update beliefs in response to new information.
- Quantitative evidence, on its own, can't tell you what to do. For that, you must carefully combine your evidence-based beliefs with your values.

Introduction

Quantitative analysis should provide information that helps us make better decisions. The ideas we've emphasized thus far—how to establish whether a relationship exists, reversion to the mean, the difference between causation and correlation, using tools for estimating causal effects, and so on—are important inputs to that process. But they are not the end point.

Suppose you've estimated that some intervention has a positive effect on some outcome. Does that mean you should do the intervention? You can't know from a quantitative analysis alone. The decision also depends on your beliefs and values and on any trade-offs you might have to consider. To get from evidence to action, you need to translate statistical information into a substantive answer to your question.

People frequently get confused on this point. It's easy to stop thinking clearly once you've got some precise and authoritative-sounding quantitative finding, reaching incorrect conclusions even from correct information. In this chapter, we explore how to avoid such mistakes. The key is to turn statistics into substance, so as to make sure you are asking and answering the question you really care about.

What's the Right Scale?

There is more than one precise and accurate way to represent a piece of quantitative information. But they are not all equally helpful. How the information is presented can have an important effect on its perceived substantive meaning. For instance, changing scales can dramatically alter whether a relationship seems large or small, important or unimportant, a good reason for taking action or not. So it is important, when presented with such information, to think about whether the way that information is presented corresponds with the substantive question you are trying to answer, or whether reframing the relationship some other way might provide a better guide. To see what we mean, consider a couple examples.

Miles-per-Gallon versus Gallons-per-Mile

Suppose you work for the Environmental Protection Agency regulating automobile emissions. Your team brings you two proposed regulations to evaluate. One regulation will result in a 2-miles-per-gallon improvement in the fuel efficiency of small sedans. The other will result in a 2-miles-per-gallon improvement in the fuel efficiency of large SUVs. Suppose there are the same number of these two kinds of automobiles on the road and, on average, each gets driven 10,000 miles per year. The sedans get 30 miles-per-gallon (which the regulation would improve to 32 miles-per-gallon), while the SUVs get 10 miles-per-gallon (which the regulation would improve to 12 miles-per-gallon). The SUV regulation will cost a little bit more to implement. And since the two regulations each offer a 2-miles-per-gallon improvement for the same number of vehicles driven the same number of miles per year, your team recommends regulating the sedans. Does this make sense?

Let's start by remembering the substantive question you want to answer. Your job is to reduce automobile emissions by reducing gas consumption. Does improving fuel economy by 2 miles-per-gallon on sedans and SUVs translate into the same reduction in gas used? Let's turn the statistics into substance to check.

The SUVs get 10 miles-per-gallon, which means that, since the average driver drives 10,000 miles per year, on average SUVs use 1,000 gallons of gas per year ($\frac{10,000}{10}$). If you implement the regulation that improves fuel efficiency to 12 miles-per-gallon, then on average SUVs will use about 833 gallons per year ($\frac{10,000}{12}$). The 2-miles-per-gallon improvement saves 167 gallons of gas per SUV per year.

What about for the sedans? The sedans get 30 miles-per-gallon, which means that, since the average driver drives 10,000 miles per year, on average sedans use about 333 gallons of gas per year ($\frac{10,000}{30}$). A regulation that improves fuel efficiency to 32 miles-per-gallon results in sedans using about 313 gallons of gas per year ($\frac{10,000}{32}$). The 2-miles-per-gallon improvement saves only about 20 gallons of gas per sedan per year.

It wasn't obvious until we translated the statistics into substance, but now we can see that your team's recommendation looks wrong. The same 2-miles-per-gallon improvement in fuel economy has a much larger effect on gas consumption when applied to a gas-guzzling SUV than when applied to an already relatively fuel-efficient sedan. So you should regulate the SUVs unless doing so is much more expensive.

Figure 15.1 shows how much gas a vehicle that drives 10,000 miles a year uses as a function of the miles-per-gallon it gets. As expected, gas consumption decreases as miles-per-gallon increase. Less intuitive, but critical for understanding the results we just showed, is the fact that the slope of this curve is really steep for low values of miles-per-gallon (less efficient cars) and much less steep for high values of miles-per-gallon (more efficient cars). You get a lot more bang for your buck improving miles-per-gallon for inefficient cars than you do for efficient cars. This has interesting implications

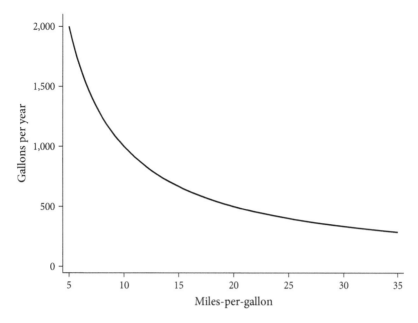

Figure 15.1. Gas consumed by driving 10,000 miles as a function of the miles-per-gallon.

beyond our example. In particular, moving people out of very fuel-inefficient vehicles into somewhat more fuel-efficient vehicles does a lot more to reduce emissions than moving people already in relatively fuel-efficient vehicles into very fuel-efficient vehicles like hybrids.

Returning to our example, there was nothing wrong with the quantitative information your team used to form its recommendations. Yet their recommendation was incorrect. Why? The problem came from the particular metric used to present the quantitative information. Miles-per-gallon is the most commonly reported metric for fuel efficiency in the United States. But it is not a particularly helpful statistic for substantive decision making.

The substantive question we care about is how much gasoline a car burns given how far it is driven. But miles-per-gallon tells you how far a car drives given how much gasoline is burned. That's backward for answering our question. You can do the math, as we did just now, to turn this statistic into substance. But most people won't. In fact, most people won't even notice the distinction. And therefore, consumers and regulators alike may be confused (or tricked) into making bad decisions.

If you wanted to provide more useful information, you would use a more substantively meaningful measure of fuel efficiency, something like gallons-per-hundred-miles, instead of miles-per-gallon. As we just saw, the same 2-miles-per-gallon improvement results in very different improvements in gallons-per-mile, depending on an automobile's baseline fuel efficiency. You'd have had no trouble making the right decision if your team had come to you with two regulations, one of which saved about 8.3 gallons-per-hundred-miles (the SUV regulation) and the other of which saved about 3.1 gallons-per-hundred-miles (the sedan regulation).

Indeed, in a 2008 study, Richard Larrick and Jack Soll show that the way statistics are reported can be quite consequential for important decisions. They quote an automotive expert who seems to think it's not worthwhile to try to make marginal improvements

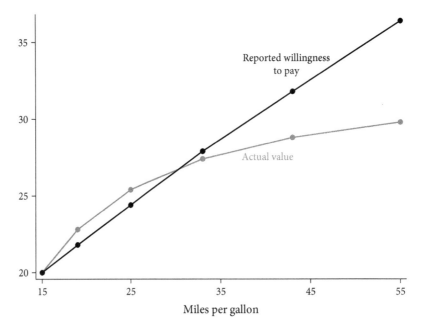

Figure 15.2. Willingness to pay versus the actual value of improvements in fuel efficiency (in thousands of dollars).

in the miles-per-gallon of large SUVs when that's, in fact, where engineers and policy makers would likely get the biggest bang for their buck in terms of mitigating emissions. Furthermore, they show that consumers are often misled by the statistics with which they are presented in ways that could have significant implications for purchasing decisions.

Specifically, Larrick and Soll asked college students to consider how much they would pay for a new car. Respondents were asked to imagine that they drive 10,000 miles per year. They were shown a car that gets 15 miles per gallon and asked to imagine that they value this car at $20,000. They were then shown alternative versions of that car that are reportedly identical to the baseline version in every way except that they get 19, 25, 33, 43, or 55 miles per gallon. How much would respondents be willing to pay for these more efficient cars?

Figure 15.2 shows the results. The black dots are the average willingness to pay (in thousands of dollars) reported by the survey respondents. Reported willingness to pay increases approximately linearly with miles-per-gallon. But it shouldn't! The gray dots in the figure show approximately how the respondents *should* have valued these cars (also in thousands of dollars), assuming that they'll keep the car for ten years and they have a 3 percent discount rate (i.e., a dollar tomorrow is worth ninety-seven cents today). As we saw in figure 15.1, a 1-mile-per-gallon increase in fuel efficiency is a lot more valuable if you're starting at a low level of efficiency than if you're starting at a high level. So the respondents in this study are making a big mistake in how they value these hypothetical cars.

Larrick and Soll go on to show that they can correct this mistake if they present fuel efficiency in terms of gallons-per-hundred-miles rather than miles-per-gallon. In other words, different ways of conveying the same information can be hugely consequential for decision making, so we need to think about the best way to present quantitative information so that decision makers can best translate their preferences into actions.

Percent versus Percentage Point

Often, in evaluating the substantive importance of some effect, we want to know how big the effect is. There are at least two ways the size of an effect might be reported: the percent change in the outcome it induces or the percentage point change in the outcome it induces. The *percentage point change* is the simple numerical difference between two percentages. The *percent change* is the ratio of the percentage point change to the initial value. So, for instance, moving from 20 percent to 22 percent is a 2 percentage point increase (22% − 20%) but a 10 percent increase ($\frac{2}{20}$)—which can lead to very different perceptions of the magnitude of an effect. So it is important to check your intuitions by translating back and forth and thinking clearly about which matters for your question. Here's an example.

The *Wall Street Journal* reported on a medical experiment showing that a new drug reduced the "risk of heart-related death, heart attacks, and other serious cardiac problems by 44%." A 44 percent reduction sounds big. This, coupled with the headline, "Cholesterol Drug Cuts Heart Risk in Healthy Patients," makes it sound very important that people have access to the treatment.

But let's stop to think clearly about the substantive question we are interested in when evaluating a quantitative result like this. To determine whether it is worthwhile to give a particular treatment to a large population, we'd like to know how much the treatment costs and how many people the treatment will save. Knowing that a treatment reduces heart attacks among otherwise healthy people by 44 percent doesn't actually tell you how many people it saves. To determine that, you also need to know how frequent heart attacks are in that population in the first place.

Later in the article we learn that 250 out of the 9,000 people randomly assigned to the control group, which received a placebo pill, had heart attacks over the course of the study. This suggests a baseline heart attack risk of about 2.8 percent ($\frac{250}{9000}$). A 44 percent decrease in heart attacks means going from about 2.8 percent of people having a heart attack to about 1.6 percent having a heart attack. Because heart attacks are so rare in this population, the 44 *percent* reduction in heart attacks translates into about a one *percentage point* reduction—not such a huge difference. Indeed, if the drug is expensive, you might well conclude that the treatment is not worthwhile.

Here, again, we see the value of translating statistics into substance. The article uses statistics that answer one question—Does the drug cause a large percent decrease in heart disease?—to which the answer is yes. But the headline makes it seem as though it is answering a much more important question—Will the drug save a lot of lives?—to which the answer is probably not. By translating the statistics (the percent reduction) into substance (number of heart attacks prevented per 100 people treated), we can easily spot the difference and answer the questions most relevant for decision making.

Visual Presentations of Data

One of the most common ways to present and consume quantitative information is through some sort of graph, figure, or visual display. Indeed, we have displayed data visually throughout this book.

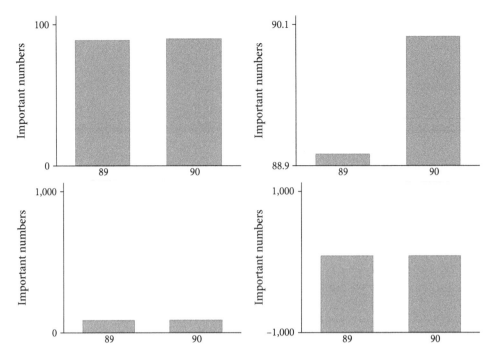

Figure 15.3. Four different ways to show the difference between 89 and 90 with a bar chart.

Displaying data accurately and informatively is part art and part science. So it is worth pausing briefly to reflect on some best practices. There are excellent books dedicated almost entirely to this topic (see the Readings and References section at the end of this chapter), so we won't belabor the discussion. But we want to hit on some essentials.

The most essential of all the essentials is this: no matter how beautiful, data visualizations are not a substitute for clear thinking. It's easy to be fooled by aesthetically pleasing, but misleading, graphics. So as a consumer of quantitative figures, you have to stay focused on thinking clearly about the substance. What are the underlying data and analyses that led to the figure? Are the underlying assumptions sound? Are there other statistics or representations of the data that would be more informative? Do the findings being presented answer the question being asked? Is the scale on which the data is presented appropriate, or was it chosen to hide or exaggerate the substantive magnitude of a relationship? Are there unnecessary, distracting features of the figure that could mislead you?

Choosing the scale on which to present data is one of the most consequential decisions in creating a data visualization. A seemingly innocuous change of scale can transform a graph from one that makes a relationship or finding look enormous to one that makes it look inconsequential, or vice versa.

To see what we mean, have a look at figure 15.3. That figure displays four different bar graphs, each of which is just a comparison of the number 89 to the number 90. But by altering the scale—here, by changing the range of the vertical axis—we change how much we zoom in or zoom out. The result is that we can make 89 and 90 appear to be hugely different from one another or nearly identical. And we can also make both numbers look very large or very small. Therefore, one of the simplest and most important ways to make sure you are thinking clearly about how to interpret a figure is to carefully read the axes and think about what the numbers mean substantively.

Importantly, there isn't a correct scale, separate from the question at hand. You should decide for yourself what constitutes a substantively meaningful difference in your particular context. There are some circumstances in which the differences between 89 and 90 is substantively large. For instance, if you chaperoned 90 school children on a field trip, there's a very big difference between 89 and 90 students returning home safely. Alternatively, it's not likely to be important whether the bus transporting the children home is 89 or 90 seconds late. The right scale for your graph depends on which kind of situation you are in.

If a graph is on a scale so big that you can't see substantively meaningful differences, you should worry that important information is being hidden. If a 1-point difference is substantively important, then a graph on a scale of 88.9 to 90.1 (upper-right panel of figure 15.3) appropriately reflects the important distinction between 89 and 90, while a graph on a scale of 0 to 1,000 (bottom-left panel) obscures that distinction.

And if a graph is on a scale so small that differences you shouldn't care about appear large, you should worry that findings are being exaggerated. For instance, if a 1-point difference is substantively negligible, then a graph on a scale of 88.9 to 90.1 inappropriately makes it look like an important difference, while a graph on the scale of 0 to 100 accurately reflects that the two numbers are essentially the same.

Concerns about the scale of a figure apply far more broadly than just these somewhat silly bar graphs (you could, after all, just report the numbers 89 and 90). By changing the scale of the axes, analysts can make correlations look strong or weak, they can make the slopes of regression lines appear large or small, and they can even make a linear relationship appear non-linear or vice versa (for example, by the choice of whether to show income or log-income). As we've discussed, there are plenty of good and bad reasons to transform a variable or carefully select the scale on which something is presented. An analyst should always think about how to present their data in the most informative way, and a consumer should turn what's being presented into the substance they care about most.

Policy Preferences and the Southern Realignment

Consider an example. In a 2016 book, Christopher Achen and Larry Bartels argue that voters' policy views have little relationship to their political behavior. That behavior, they claim, is driven by non-policy concerns. As one piece of supporting evidence, Achen and Bartels argue that policy views don't explain why white voters in the U.S. South shifted from supporting the Democratic to the Republican party during the so-called Southern realignment that occurred in the second half of the twentieth century. Their evidence for this claim is a visual representation of data, which we have attempted to reproduce as closely as possible in figure 15.4.

The figure separately plots the trend in party identification for white Southerners who opposed and did not oppose integration. The horizontal axis is years. The vertical axis shows the Democratic margin, measured as the percent of people who identify as Democratic minus the percent of people who identify as Republican. So the higher a data point is on the vertical axis, the more Democrats there are compared to Republicans.

The figure clearly shows the Southern realignment. In 1960, Southern whites were overwhelmingly Democrats. But that changed over time, so that by the end of the twentieth century they were overwhelmingly Republicans.

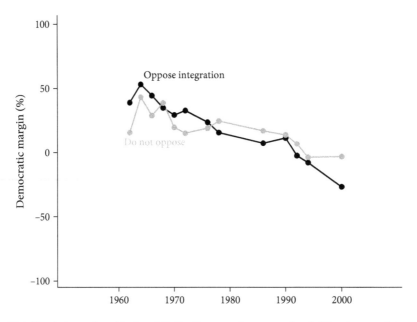

Figure 15.4. Trends in partisanship for white Southerners who opposed and did not oppose integration.

Achen and Bartels argue that the figure also shows that white voters' policy positions on integration do not affect changing party affiliation. That is, they claim these two trends are more or less the same. And this, they argue, suggests that voters' positions on even highly salient policy issues don't influence party affiliation.

What do you notice about figure 15.4? Is it obvious that the trends are more or less the same? First, we might want to look at the scale of the vertical axis. The measure of partisanship—the percent of individuals identifying as Democratic minus the percent of individuals identifying as Republican—in theory could range from −100 to 100. And that's the scale on which the figure is drawn. However, in practice, many people don't identify as either Democratic or Republican, so in almost any large population, we're probably not going to see a Democratic margin anywhere near the theoretical minimum or maximum. Because the range of the axis is so large, isn't it possible that there is a substantively meaningful difference that's difficult to see, much like in the bottom-right panel of figure 15.3?

Also, consider the horizontal axis. The figure only includes data from 1962 through 2000, but the graph is wide enough to include data from 1950 through 2010, leaving a bunch of empty, wasted space. There is no good reason to leave that space blank. But it does compress the data.

How would our substantive conclusions change if we removed some of that wasted space and redrew the same quantitative information on a scale that more accurately reflects the observed range of the data? We can see this in figure 15.5. We have also added linear regression lines, which we believe make it easier to visualize the average trends for the two different groups of voters.

The data visualization in figure 15.5 suggests an importantly different interpretation from the data visualization in figure 15.4. In particular, figure 15.5 shows that the trends in partisanship were actually quite different for people who opposed integration compared to people who did not oppose integration. Those who opposed

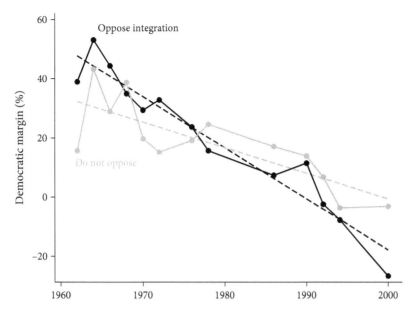

Figure 15.5. Trends in partisanship for white Southerners who opposed and did not oppose integration on a more appropriate scale and with regression lines.

integration were more Democratic in the 1960s than those who did not oppose integration. And they were more Republican by the end of the twentieth century. So their over-time trend was substantially steeper—people opposed to integration switched partisan affiliation at a faster rate than people who did not oppose integration. Perhaps policy views do help explain the shift in party identification during the Southern realignment.

Lest we fall for the trick in the top-right panel of figure 15.3, we'll want to interpret the numbers substantively to make sure what looks like a large difference is substantively meaningful. Most of us probably don't regularly think about percent margins of party identification, so perhaps there are better ways to convey this information. Let's give it some thought.

We see that, from 1962 through 2000, white Southerners who opposed integration went from something like a 48-point margin in favor of the Democratic Party to an 18-point margin in favor of the Republican Party. Those who did not oppose integration also became more Republican, but the change was more modest—from a 32-point Democratic margin to a 1-point Republican margin. So the shift for those who opposed integration was 33 percentage points larger, or twice as big, as the shift for those who did not oppose integration.

But is that a big or small difference? To provide a benchmark, if we look at 2020 data, 33 percentage points is approximately the difference in the Democratic margin between Massachusetts (a solidly blue state) and Idaho (a solidly red state). So we think it's safe to say that two trends that differ by 33 points on this scale are, in fact, meaningfully different, and the visualization in figure 15.4 was obscuring substantively important information.

We've illustrated one set of questions that you would want to ask about figure 15.4 and shown that they matter. But we've only scratched the surface of the questions worth asking as you attempt to turn statistics into substance in this case. For example, why is the right outcome for evaluating political behavior party identification rather than something more politically consequential, like voting behavior? Why start this analysis in 1962, when the Southern realignment is widely viewed as having started earlier? Is a single survey question about views on integration the best way to measure policy preferences in this context?

Some Rules of Thumb for Data Visualization

There is much more to think about in interpreting data visualizations. As we've said, we aren't going to try to provide a comprehensive overview. But here are some key principles that we think are important to keep in mind when creating or consuming graphical depictions of quantitative information.

- Keep it simple. If you don't need multiple colors, don't use colors. If you don't need fancy graphics, don't include them. If a third dimension doesn't add something crucial, use a two-dimensional plot. If you have complicated legends and labels, break things up.
- The focus should be on substance. You're trying to convey information in a transparent and easy- to- absorb manner. Make sure that the design choices you make are ones that advance the goal of conveying the answer to the question at hand.
- If you're just showing some simple numbers (like 89 and 90 or a regression coefficient), perhaps you can do away with the figure altogether and present the numbers in a table. Save figures for situations where a figure would convey more information than a table.
- Show the data. One of the great things about a figure is that you can show far more complicated relationships and far more detail than you might be able to do with a table. If the point of your figure is just to show the intercept and slope from a regression, you might as well just provide a table. But a figure can add a lot if you plot both a regression line and the data underlying the regression, so we can see whether the relationship is or isn't approximately linear. Think about figure 2.5 or 5.8. We learn a lot from the visualizations, relative to just reporting the correlation or regression coefficient, precisely because the underlying data are also displayed.
- When possible, convey uncertainty. Showing your data is a good way to do this. Instead of just showing means, consider showing distributions. If you're plotting estimates, also consider plotting standard errors or confidence intervals as we did in figure 12.4.

From Statistics to Beliefs: Bayes' Rule

The data never speaks for itself. Evidence is always interpreted in light of our existing ideas about how the world works, other related evidence we've seen earlier, and so on. So, in order to make use of quantitative information, it is important that we think clearly about how we should integrate that new information into our existing store of knowledge, so that we can translate statistics into beliefs. A key tool we have for doing so is called Bayes' rule. To get us thinking about Bayes' rule, how it works, and why we need it, let's start with an example.

In 1964 in Los Angeles, an elderly woman named Juanita Brooks was walking down an alley, pulling a basket of groceries with her purse resting on top, when she was pushed to the ground from behind and her purse was stolen. She didn't get a good look at the perpetrator. Around the same time, an eyewitness saw a woman run out of that same alley and enter a yellow car. The witness also didn't get a great look. But he did note that the woman running was white and had a blond ponytail and that the driver of the car was a Black man with a beard and mustache. On the basis of this eyewitness testimony, police later arrested Malcolm and Janet Collins and charged them with the robbery. Malcolm was a Black man with a beard and mustache. Janet was a white woman with a blond ponytail. And they drove a yellow car.

As Jonathan Koehler relates in an article, prosecutors brought in a mathematician to testify regarding the chances that, on the basis of this evidence alone, Malcolm and Janet were guilty of the robbery. The mathematician concluded that there was only about a 1 in 12 million chance that the couple was innocent. Here was the reasoning.

If we just arrested an innocent couple at random, it's very unlikely that the husband would be Black with a beard and mustache, that the wife would be white with a blond ponytail, and that they would drive a yellow car. Why is this?

The argument starts with some quantitative facts. If we just picked a man at random from the population, there's a 10 percent chance that he would be Black, because about 10 percent of the U.S. population is Black. Suppose that 10 percent of all men have beards, so there's also a 10 percent chance that he'd have a beard. Perhaps there's a 20 percent chance that he'd have a mustache. And there's only a 0.5 percent chance that he'd drive a yellow car, given the number of yellow cars on the road.

How do we take these numbers and turn them into an overall probability of a randomly selected innocent couple having this confluence of characteristics? Let's think about an analogy to a deck of cards. What is the probability that a randomly drawn card is the four of hearts? The probability that a randomly drawn card is a four is 1 in 13. And the probability that a randomly drawn card is a heart is 1 in 4. Since being a four and being a heart are independent (i.e., knowing that a card is a four doesn't tell you anything about how likely it is to be a heart and vice versa), the probability of the two characteristics occurring together is simply the product of the probability of each occurring individually. So if we draw a random card from a deck, the probability it is the four of hearts is $\frac{1}{13} \times \frac{1}{4} = \frac{1}{52}$. This makes sense. There are 52 cards in a deck. Only one of them is the four of hearts.

The prosecutor applied the same logic to the Collins couple. He argued that the chances that a randomly selected person would be Black, have a mustache and beard, and drive a yellow car is the product of the probabilities of the individual characteristics: $\frac{1}{10} \times \frac{1}{10} \times \frac{1}{5} \times \frac{1}{200} = \frac{1}{100,000}$. He continued to add characteristics (being married, being an interracial couple, the woman having blond hair, and a ponytail, and so on), eventually arriving at a probability of 1 in 12 million. Indeed, as the prosecutor pointed out, even this was an under-estimate, since the couple had many other characteristics that had not been accounted for, so that the probability of innocence was probably more like 1 in 1 billion! A jury found the Collins couple guilty, and newspapers praised prosecutors for making such a quantitatively rigorous case.

What do you think: Does this example reflect clear thinking? We hope you said no, because indeed, there is so much wrong, it is hard to know where to start. But start we must.

So, first, these characteristics (unlike being a heart and being a four in a deck of playing cards) are not independent of one another. So you can't just multiply the probabilities of each individual characteristic together to get the probability of the confluence of characteristics. For instance, having a beard is positively correlated with having a mustache. As such, the probability of having a beard and a mustache is much higher than the probability of having a beard times the probability of having a mustache. That is, if 1 in 10 men have a beard and 1 in 5 have a mustache, since many of these are the same men, many more than 1 in 50 men have a beard and a mustache. Indeed, the probability is likely much closer to 1 in 10, since almost everyone with a beard also has a mustache. So, if we took into account all the relevant correlations, maybe we wouldn't conclude that the probability that a randomly selected couple fit the eyewitness description was 1 in 12 million. But we would still get a pretty low probability (maybe 1 in a million). That still seems like good evidence on which to convict, no?

No. It really isn't. We haven't even talked about the main thing that's gone wrong in the analysis, which is that it answers the wrong question entirely. If we think clearly about the right question, we reach a very different conclusion.

The jury has to decide whether or not to convict the Collins couple. They don't want to do so if the Collins couple is sufficiently likely to be innocent, and they do want to do so if the Collins couple is sufficiently likely to be guilty. So the right question for the jury is, How likely is the Collins couple to be innocent, given the evidence? The evidence is that the Collins couple matches the eyewitness description. So the right statistic to answer the jury's substantive question is the probability that the Collins couple is innocent given that they match that description. Write this as $Pr(\text{innocent} \mid \text{match})$. This is called a *conditional probability*, since it is the probability of one thing conditional on another. It is read in one of two ways. People either say "the probability they are innocent, conditional on them matching the evidence" or "the probability they are innocent, given that they match the evidence." Either one is fine. The probability they are guilty conditional on them matching the evidence is just $Pr(\text{guilty} \mid \text{match}) = 1 - Pr(\text{innocent} \mid \text{match})$.

The mathematical analysis we've discussed thus far has *not* told us this probability and, so, has not answered the right question. The analysis thus far tells us how likely it is that a randomly selected couple would match the eyewitness description. That is, it tells us $Pr(\text{match} \mid \text{innocent})$, which is read "probability a couple would match the evidence conditional on them being innocent." While this statistic may be useful for answering the jury's question, it is not itself the answer. The jury wants to know $Pr(\text{innocent} \mid \text{match})$. The prosecutor has told them $Pr(\text{match} \mid \text{innocent})$. But the jury (and the press) failed to notice the difference because they weren't thinking clearly.

Let's see why this matters. Suppose we agreed that $Pr(\text{match} \mid \text{innocent})$ is approximately equal to 1 in 1,000,000. We need to figure out $Pr(\text{innocent} \mid \text{match})$. Can we do it?

Table 15.1 will help. It categorizes couples in Los Angeles County according to two characteristics: whether they match the eyewitness description or not and whether they are guilty or not. We know that there is exactly one guilty couple and that couple matches the eyewitness description. So the guilty column is easy to fill in. The innocent column is a little trickier. We've agreed that the prosecutor's analysis, along with a bit of conjecture, suggests that the probability an innocent couple matches the eyewitness description is about 1 in 1,000,000. If we approximate that there were roughly 2 million innocent couples in LA County in 1964, we'll conclude that there were approximately 2 innocent couples who also matched the description. The remaining 1,999,998 couples in LA County fall into the last cell: innocent and don't match.

Table 15.1. LA couples by innocence or guilt and whether or not they match the evidence.

	Innocent	Guilty
Don't Match	1,999,998	0
Match	2	1

So, how likely is a couple to be innocent, given that they match the description—that is, what is Pr(innocent | match)? Well, there are three couples that match the description. Exactly one of them is guilty. So the true probability that a couple is innocent, given that they match the eyewitness description, is not anything like 1 in one million. It is 2 in 3. That means the probability the couple is guilty given that they match the eyewitness description is only 1 in 3. On the basis of the eyewitness evidence, the Collins couple was more likely to be innocent than guilty!

The discrepancy arises not because the mathematician, the prosecutor, and the press looked at incorrect quantitative information, but because they used the quantitative information to answer the wrong question. As the mathematician and prosecutor said, it is very unlikely that a randomly selected innocent couple would match the description of the criminals. But that doesn't mean it is very unlikely that a couple that matches the description of the criminals is innocent. Only one innocent couple in a million matches the description. But two couples out of three who match the description are innocent. If the jury had been able to think more clearly about the quantitative information, we suspect the Collins couple would not have been convicted. Few jurors want to send people to jail on the basis of there being a 1 in 3 chance that they committed a crime.[1]

Bayes' Rule

The analysis we've just done is an example of a general approach to figuring out what we should believe, given some evidence. A mathematical tool called *Bayes' rule* (or, sometimes Bayes' theorem or Bayes' law) gives us the formula for calculating this value. It is named after Thomas Bayes, an eighteenth-century philosopher and statistician.

Bayes' rule tells us the correct formula for how likely a claim is to be true, given the available evidence. It goes like this. Suppose we want to know the probability that a claim C is true, given evidence E. That is, we want to know $\Pr(C \mid E)$. In our example, the claim was that the Collins couple was innocent and the evidence was that they matched the eyewitness decision. Bayes' rule says

$$\Pr(C \mid E) = \frac{\Pr(E \mid C)\,\Pr(C)}{\Pr(E)}.$$

Let's go back to the Collins case to unpack this a bit. We want to know the probability the Collins couple is innocent, conditional on them matching the eyewitness description. In this case, Bayes' rule says

---

[1] Fun fact: Malcolm Collins appealed the guilty verdict on the grounds that the prosecutor had used a faulty mathematical argument to convict him. The California Supreme Court reversed the judgement, arguing for the importance of clear thinking. It wrote, "Mathematics, a veritable sorcerer in our computerized society, while assisting the trier of fact in the search for truth, must not cast a spell over him."

$$\Pr(\text{Innocent} \mid \text{Match}) = \frac{\Pr(\text{Match} \mid \text{Innocent}) \, \Pr(\text{Innocent})}{\Pr(\text{Match})}.$$

We can use table 15.1 to find the values to plug in to see how this works.

What is $\Pr(\text{Match} \mid \text{Innocent})$? It is the probability a couple matches, given that they are innocent. There are 2 million innocent couples. Two of them match. So $\Pr(\text{Match} \mid \text{Innocent}) = \frac{2}{2,000,000}$.

What is $\Pr(\text{Innocent})$? It is the overall probability that a random couple is innocent. There are 2,000,001 couples in LA County. Of them, 2,000,000 are innocent. So $\Pr(\text{Innocent}) = \frac{2,000,000}{2,000,001}$.

Finally, what is $\Pr(\text{Match})$? Again, there are 2,000,001 couples, of which 3 match the eyewitness description. So $\Pr(\text{Match}) = \frac{3}{2,000,001}$.

Putting these together we have

$$\Pr(\text{Innocent} \mid \text{Match}) = \frac{\Pr(\text{Match} \mid \text{Innocent}) \, \Pr(\text{Innocent})}{\Pr(\text{Match})}$$

$$= \frac{\frac{2}{2,000,000} \cdot \frac{2,000,000}{2,000,001}}{\frac{3}{2,000,001}}$$

$$= \frac{2}{3}.$$

Notice, we were able to figure this out earlier without knowing Bayes' rule, just by looking at the table. So there isn't much need to memorize the formula. But it is important to know how to calculate beliefs from evidence and to make sure you are thinking clearly about what question you want to ask and answer. Because it is really easy to convince yourself that $\Pr(\text{Match} \mid \text{Innocent})$ is the same as $\Pr(\text{Innocent} \mid \text{Match})$. But, as we've now seen, they can be really different.

Information, Beliefs, Priors, and Posteriors

Bayes' rule is useful anytime we receive new information and want to update our beliefs about how likely some claim is to be true. Before we get the new information, we have what we call a *prior belief* about the claim—that is, our belief about the probability that the claim is true, without knowing the new evidence. In the formula, this prior belief is represented by $\Pr(C)$—the probability the claim is true, without reference to the evidence. After we incorporate the new information, Bayes' rule gives us what we call a *posterior belief*: $\Pr(C \mid E)$.

In *People v. Collins*, the prior belief is the baseline probability that the Collins couple was innocent, before hearing about the eyewitness testimony. At that point, there was no reason to suspect them more than any other couple living in LA, so the prior belief was very close to 1—something like $\frac{2,000,000}{2,000,001}$, since all but one couple were innocent.

We learned that the Collins couple matches the description of the criminals. In fact, the chances that an innocent couple matches that description was only 1 in 1,000,000, which might make us think that they are almost certainly guilty. But Bayes' rule tells us to hold off before jumping to conclusions. On the one hand, the evidence seems pretty damning. It's extremely unlikely that an innocent couple would match the description. On the other hand, the prior belief pushes in the other direction. It's extremely unlikely that any given couple is guilty. To figure out how likely it is that the Collins couple is guilty, given both of these facts, we have to ask about the relative likelihood of each one. If we ignore either our prior belief or the new evidence, we arrive at the wrong conclusion. Incorporating both, we see that, while the Collins couple is way more likely to be guilty than a randomly selected couple, there's still a good chance that they are innocent.

One way of thinking about the problem with the prosecutor's argument is that he talked only about the new evidence, ignoring the prior. This is a common mistake that people make when they aren't thinking clearly about quantitative evidence.

Abe's Celiac Revisited

Way back in chapter 1, we told you the story of Ethan's son, Abe, being incorrectly diagnosed with celiac disease. In case you don't remember, here are the highlights of the story.

As a little kid, Abe was small for his age, which is an indicator for celiac. His pediatricians administered two blood tests. One came back positive (evidence that he had the disease), the other negative (evidence that he did not have the disease). The doctors concluded that Abe probably had celiac, because the positive test was "over 80 percent accurate."

The test on which Abe came up negative (let's call this Test 1) for celiac disease had quite low false negative and false positive rates, about 5 percent each. We can write this in our new notation. The false negative rate is the probability you get a negative test result given that you have the disease—that is, Pr(Negative on Test 1 | Celiac) = .05. The false positive rate is the probability you get a positive test result given that you don't have the disease—that is, Pr(Positive on Test 1 | No Celiac) = .05.

The test on which Abe came up positive (let's call this Test 2) for celiac disease had a false negative rate of about 20 percent—that is, Pr(Negative on Test 2 | Celiac) = .2. This, we suspect, is where the "80 percent accurate" claim came from. That test has a false positive rate of 50 percent—that is, Pr(Positive on Test 2 | Celiac) = .5.

Prior to the blood tests, a reasonable guess about the probability of Abe having celiac disease, given his small stature, was maybe 1 in 100. That is Ethan's prior: Pr(Celiac) = .01.

Let's ignore Test 1 for a second, and just apply Bayes' rule to Test 2. Imagine a group of 10,000 kids, all of whom were similarly small in stature. Our prior tells us that, of those 10,000 kids, about 100 (1%) will have celiac. Test 2's false negative rate tells us that, of those 100 kids with celiac, about 20 (20%) will nonetheless test negative, while 80 will test positive. And Test 2's false positive rate tells us that, of the 9,900 kids without celiac, about 4,950 (50%) will nonetheless test positive and 4,950 will test negative. Table 15.2 provides a summary.

So what is the probability Abe has celiac, given that he was small in stature and tested positive on Test 2? Well, a total of 4,950 + 80 = 5,030 kids test positive. Of those, 80 have celiac. So the probability that one of these kids has celiac given a positive result on Test 2 is $\frac{80}{5,030}$, or approximately 1.6 percent.

Notice, now that we know Bayes' rule, we could have done this without making the table:

$$\text{Pr(Celiac | Positive on Test 2)} = \frac{\text{Pr(Positive on Test 2 | Celiac) Pr(Celiac)}}{\text{Pr(Positive on Test 2)}}.$$

Table 15.2. Outcomes of a celiac test on 10,000 kids.

	Celiac	No Celiac
Negative on Test 2	20	4,950
Positive on Test 2	80	4,950

We know enough to calculate each of these quantities. Pr(Positive on Test 2 | Celiac) is 1 minus the false negative rate, which is .8. Pr(Celiac) is our prior belief, which is .01.

Calculating Pr(Positive on Test 2) is a bit more involved. Here's how you do it. There are two kinds of people who test positive: kids with celiac who get a correct test result and kids without celiac who get a false positive. One percent of kids have celiac, and of these 80 percent get a positive test result. Ninety-nine percent of kids do not have celiac, and of these 50 percent get a positive test result. So,

$$\Pr(\text{Positive on Test 2}) = \Pr(\text{Celiac}) \Pr(\text{Positive on Test 2} \mid \text{Celiac})$$

$$+ \Pr(\text{No Celiac}) \Pr(\text{Positive on Test 2} \mid \text{No Celiac})$$

$$= .01 \times .8 + .99 \times .5$$

$$= .503.$$

Now we can calculate Ethan's posterior beliefs directly:

$$\Pr(\text{Celiac} \mid \text{Positive on Test 2}) = \frac{\Pr(\text{Positive on Test 2} \mid \text{Celiac}) \Pr(\text{Celiac})}{\Pr(\text{Positive on Test 2})}$$

$$= \frac{.8 \times .01}{.503}$$

$$\approx .016$$

Of course, Abe actually had two tests. What happens if we add in the fact that Abe tested negative on the more accurate Test 1? If we assume that false positives and false negatives on these two tests are independent, then we can just multiply to get the relevant quantities.

$$\Pr(\text{Celiac} \mid \text{Neg on Test 1 \& Pos on Test 2})$$

$$= \frac{\Pr(\text{Neg on Test 1 \& Pos on Test 2} \mid \text{Celiac}) \Pr(\text{Celiac})}{\Pr(\text{Neg on Test 1 \& Pos on Test 2})}$$

What is the probability that a kid with celiac gets a negative result on Test 1 and a positive result on Test 2? Well, Test 1 returns a negative for a kid with celiac (i.e., a false negative) only 5 percent of the time. Test 2 returns a positive for a kid with celiac

80 percent of the time. So, if the false negatives and false positives are independent across the two tests, then

$$\Pr(\text{Neg on Test 1 \& Pos on Test 2} \mid \text{Celiac}) = .8 \times .05$$

$$= .04.$$

The prior belief, $\Pr(\text{Celiac})$, remains the same, 1 percent. And, again, there are two kinds of kids who might get a negative on Test 1 and a positive on Test 2. First, the kid might have celiac (that's true of 1 percent of these kids). That kid would then need to get a false negative on Test 1 but a correct result on Test 2. As we've just seen, the probability of this is $.8 \times .05 = .04$. Second, the kid might not have celiac (that's true of 99% of these kids). That kid would then need to get a correct result on Test 1 and a false positive on Test 2. This happens with probability $.99 \times .5 = .495$. Now we can calculate the overall probability of these two test scores.

$$\Pr(\text{Neg on Test 1 \& Pos on Test 2})$$

$$= \Pr(\text{Celiac}) \Pr(\text{Neg on Test 1 \& Pos on Test 2} \mid \text{Celiac})$$

$$+ \Pr(\text{No Celiac}) \Pr(\text{Neg on Test 1 \& Pos on Test 2} \mid \text{No Celiac})$$

$$= .01 \times .04 + .99 \times .495$$

$$= .49045$$

Plugging all of this into Bayes' rule, we get

$$\Pr(\text{Celiac} \mid \text{Neg on Test 1 \& Pos on Test 2})$$

$$= \frac{\Pr(\text{Neg on Test 1 \& Pos on Test 2} \mid \text{Celiac}) \Pr(\text{Celiac})}{\Pr(\text{Neg on Test 1 \& Pos on Test 2})}$$

$$= \frac{.05 \times .01}{.49045}$$

$$\approx .001$$

The probability that Abe had celiac given the two test results was approximately 1 in 1,000.[2]

Now that you know Bayes' rule, you can see that the doctors were not thinking very clearly about what the evidence really meant.

---

[2] We would have gotten the same answer if we had applied Bayes' rule iteratively. We could have started with the prior belief that Abe had celiac before seeing any evidence, shifted our beliefs according to the evidence from Test 1, treated this posterior belief as our new prior, and then shifted our beliefs again according to the evidence from Test 2. And the order in which we do this doesn't matter. We'd end up with the same beliefs in the end if we started with Test 2 and then went to Test 1. As a bonus exercise, you can try double-checking this yourself to make sure you understand how to apply Bayes' rule.

Finding Terrorists in an Airport

In the years following the terrorist attacks of September 11, 2001, the United States government poured resources into airport security. One of the major new programs was called Screening of Passengers by Observation Techniques (SPOT).

The idea of SPOT was to use behavioral cues to catch potential terrorists before they boarded a plane. Behavior Detection Officers watched people in the security line at airports, looking for indicators that a person was nervous or otherwise suspicious. Different kinds of suspicious behaviors were assigned different numbers of points. If a person exhibited a cluster of suspicious behaviors that rose above some point threshold, that person was targeted for additional questioning, searching, and screening.

By the year 2010, about 5 percent of the Transportation Security Administration's (TSA's) annual budget, hundreds of millions of dollars per year, went to fund the SPOT program. Let's use Bayes' rule to see why this wasn't a very good use of money.

The TSA needs to be able to answer questions like "Given a set of behaviors and characteristics, how likely is it that the person in question is a terrorist?" In other words, the TSA is trying to form a posterior belief about the probability that a traveler is a terrorist, given some evidence gleaned by observing the traveler's behavior. To form such posterior beliefs correctly on the basis of a program like SPOT, the TSA needs to know at least three pieces of information:

1. How likely is a random traveler to be a terrorist?
2. How likely is a terrorist to appear suspicious to a Behavior Detection Officer?
3. How likely is a non-terrorist to appear suspicious to a Behavior Detection Officer?

Unfortunately, according to the General Accountability Office (GAO)—an independent, non-partisan agency that works for Congress and is charged with investigating how the federal government spends taxpayer dollars—the TSA doesn't know the answers to any of these questions. No existing scientific research confirms, much less quantifies, the usefulness of behavioral observation for identifying terrorists. What we do know is that, even according to the TSA's own report intended to show the efficacy of the SPOT program, it seems that no terrorists have ever been caught by it. Indeed, the GAO reports that undocumented immigration status was by far the most common reason for detention of a person identified for additional screening by a Behavior Detection Officer.

So the government doesn't have the data that we need to calculate posterior beliefs on the basis of the evidence collected by the SPOT program. But we can see that this program was never going to work even without hard data. Let's ask how well the program would work in something like the best-case scenario. That is, we'll make up some data, being extremely generous to the SPOT program in all of our assumptions, and see whether the program would be a good idea under these assumptions. If the answer is no even under these generous assumptions, then we can be sure the answer is also no under more realistic assumptions.

First, according to the GAO, there are approximately 2 billion passenger trips through U.S. airports each year. For convenience, let's say there are 2 billion plus 100. Presumably the vast majority of those people are innocent travelers. Very few travelers are trying to hijack planes or engage in other forms of terrorism. Let's be generous to

Table 15.3. How many terrorists and non-terrorists appear suspicious.

	Not Terrorist	**Terrorist**
Not Suspicious	1,980,000,000	1
Suspicious	20,000,000	99

the government and suppose that each year, 100 would-be terrorists are in U.S. airports attempting to hijack airplanes. So that's our prior: $\Pr(\text{Terrorist}) = \frac{100}{2,000,000,100}$.

Second, we need to know how likely these terrorists are to exhibit the suspicious behaviors that the Behavior Detection Officers are looking for. Of course, we have no idea. But all the scientific evidence suggests that these kinds of behavioral cues are quite unreliable. Again, let's be generous and stack the deck in favor of SPOT. Suppose that 99 percent of all terrorists exhibit the behavior that the TSA is looking for—that is, $\Pr(\text{Suspicious} \mid \text{Terrorist}) = .99$. In reality, this number is surely much much lower.

Finally, we need to know how likely innocent travelers are to exhibit the suspicious behavior. As we've already said, these behaviors are unreliable indicators, so at least some innocent people will exhibit them. But we want to be generous to SPOT. So suppose that only 1 percent of innocent people exhibit suspicious behavior, such that $\Pr(\text{Suspicious} \mid \text{Not Terrorist}) = .01$. Again, in reality, this number is surely much much higher. For this exercise, we are assuming SPOT is an incredibly accurate behavioral screening program.

How likely is a person who behaves suspiciously to be a terrorist? Even under these extremely generous assumptions, the answer is not very likely. Table 15.3 shows you the data you'd get based on our assumptions.

Of the 2,000,000,100 passenger trips, 100 involve terrorists. Ninety-nine of them will exhibit suspicious behavior. The remaining 2 billion trips involve innocent travelers. Just 1 percent of them will exhibit suspicious behavior. But this 1 percent amounts to 20 million people! A total of 20,000,099 people act suspiciously. Of them, 99 are terrorists. So the probability that someone is a terrorist given that they acted suspiciously is $\frac{99}{20,000,099}$. That is, approximately .000005—about 1 in 200,000.

We could have similarly calculated this directly from Bayes' rule.

$$\Pr(\text{Terrorist} \mid \text{Suspicious}) = \frac{\Pr(\text{Suspicious} \mid \text{Terrorist}) \Pr(\text{Terrorist})}{\Pr(\text{Suspicious})}$$

$$= \frac{\frac{99}{100} \cdot \frac{100}{2,000,000,100}}{\frac{20,000,099}{2,000,000,100}}$$

$$= \frac{99}{20,000,099}$$

Remember the numbers above come from assumptions that are extremely generous to the government. There is no way that terrorists actually exhibit the behavior the SPOT program looks for 99 percent of the time. And there is no way that innocent people actually exhibit the behavior the SPOT program looks for only 1 percent of the time. So the probability a suspicious person is a terrorist is actually much lower than 1 in 200,000. Indeed, if terrorists exhibit suspicious behavior 75 percent of the time and innocent people 10 percent of the time, the probability of being a terrorist given suspicious behavior becomes about 1 in 37 million:

$$\text{Pr(Terrorist | Suspicious)} = \frac{\text{Pr(Suspicious | Terrorist) Pr(Terrorist)}}{\text{Pr(Suspicious)}}$$

$$= \frac{\frac{75}{100} \cdot \frac{100}{2,000,000,100}}{\frac{200,000,075}{2,000,000,100}}$$

$$= \frac{75}{200,000,075}$$

$$\approx \frac{1}{37,000,000}$$

Remarkably, even with this number, we are still being too generous. According to a study by the National Academy of Sciences, screeners looking for just one facial characteristic (rather than the many things SPOT screeners are looking for) in perfect conditions get their assessment right only about 60 percent of the time. In more realistic conditions, they get their assessment right only about 30 percent of the time. With this level of accuracy and the tiny proportion of people who are terrorists, we think it is safe to say that the over $1 billion allocated to the SPOT program was not money well spent. This is easy to see when we ask the right questions.

Let us end this unpleasant tale with one more distressing tidbit that harkens back to the key lesson from chapter 4, correlation requires variation. The Government Accountability Office is a watchdog organization that is supposed to make sure that government agencies spend money appropriately. After investigating a program it may also provide the relevant government agency with advice about how to improve. This is precisely what the GAO did after evaluating the SPOT program.

One of the areas that the GAO was concerned about was the lack of a scientific basis for the behavioral characteristics that TSA had its SPOT screeners looking for. According to GAO, the TSA had no idea whether terrorists are actually more likely to exhibit the behaviors they are looking for or not. (As we just saw, even if they are, this program is a waste.) And so, here is what the GAO recommended to the TSA to improve accuracy:

> Studying airport video recordings of the behaviors exhibited by persons waiting in line and moving through airport checkpoints and who were later charged with or pleaded guilty to terrorism-related offenses could provide insights about behaviors that may be common among terrorists.

Suppose you watched these videos and found that, for example, all the people who turned out to be terrorists wore sunglasses and looked agitated waiting in the security line. Do you want to start arresting everyone who meets that description? We hope not. As we've known since chapter 4, correlation requires variation. If you want to get better at the (hopeless) task of identifying characteristics that predict whether or not a person is a terrorist, at the very least you must compare the characteristics of terrorists and non-terrorists. You can't just study the terrorists.

Bayes' Rule and Quantitative Analysis

One particularly interesting application of Bayes' rule is thinking about how confident we should be about the truth of some scientific hypothesis, in light of the evidence presented in a scientific study. Of course, we already discussed one approach to this issue in chapter 6. There, we learned that the p-value tells us how likely a given estimate is to have occurred by chance alone. But if you think about it clearly, that doesn't answer the right question. In fact, when an analyst finds a low p-value and concludes that the finding must be true, they've made the same mistake as the mathematician and the prosecutor in *People v. Collins*. They've calculated the probability they would have found a relationship in their data, even if there is no real relationship in the world—that is, Pr(result | relationship not real). But what they really want to know is how likely it is that there is no real relationship, given their result—that is, Pr(relationship not real | result). The probability there *is* a real relationship given the result is just 1 minus this.

Let's use Bayes' rule to think about this a little more clearly. Suppose we collect some data, test for a relationship, and obtain a statistically significant result at the .05 level (i.e., $p < .05$). What's the probability that the estimated relationship reflects a real relationship in the world (as opposed to appearing in the data due to noise)? Bayes' rule tells us.

$$\text{Pr(relationship real | result)} = \frac{\text{Pr(result | relationship real) Pr(relationship real)}}{\text{Pr(result)}}$$

And, like before, we can break down Pr(result) into two components. One way we might have found the result is that the relationship is real and the test correctly identified it. The probability of this is Pr(relationship real) × Pr(result | relationship real). The other way we could have found the result is that the relationship is not real but the test spuriously identifies it as real due to noise. The probability of this is Pr(relationship not real) × Pr(result | relationship not real). So we can write Bayes' rule as follows:

Pr(relationship real | result)

$$= \frac{\text{Pr(result | relationship real) Pr(relationship real)}}{\text{Pr(relationship real) Pr(result | relationship real)} + \text{Pr(relationship not real) Pr(result | relationship not real)}}$$

We know the Pr(result | relationship not real). This is just the significance level used in our hypothesis test. If we would declare a statistically significant result if $p < .05$, then Pr(result | relationship not real) $= .05$.

The other numbers are more complicated. The quantity Pr(relationship real) is our prior belief that a genuine relationship exists, before seeing any of our new evidence. The quantity Pr(result | relationship real)—that is, the probability you find a result in your data given that the relationship really exists in the world—is called the *statistical power* of the test. The statistical power is the answer to the following question: What is the probability we would find a statistically significant result in the data given that the relationship is real? There are ways of estimating the statistical power once we know more details about the data and test. For instance, one might conduct computer simulations to determine how likely it would be to statistically detect an effect of a certain magnitude.

Now we can rewrite the formula for Bayes' rule one more time in terms of these substantively interpretable quantities:

Pr(relationship real | result)

$$= \frac{\text{Pr(result | relationship real) Pr(relationship real)}}{\text{Pr(relationship real) Pr(result | relationship real)} + \text{Pr(relationship not real) Pr(result | relationship not real)}}$$

$$= \frac{\text{Power} \times \text{Prior}}{\text{Power} \times \text{Prior} + \text{Significance} \times (1 - \text{Prior})}$$

Let's put this formula to work to see what it implies about our posterior beliefs in light of new, statistically significant, scientific evidence. Suppose we have a hunch about some causal effect in the world. It's a bit of a long shot. We think there's a 5 percent chance that this effect exists (our prior belief is .05). So we run a randomized experiment. We want to be confident in the answer, so we get a big sample size, such that the statistical power of our test will be .8 (we'll have an 80 percent chance of detecting an effect if one really exists). And following convention, we use a .05 threshold for statistical significance. Now, we can ask, conditional on obtaining a statistically significant result, what should our posterior beliefs be about the probability that the effect is real?

Plugging these numbers into the above equation, we get

$$\text{Pr(effect real | result)} = \frac{.8 \times .05}{.8 \times .05 + .05 \times .95}$$

$$\approx .46.$$

What happened? Even conditional on getting a result that is statistically significant at the 95 percent level, there's still only a 46 percent chance that the effect we believe we are estimating exists at all! The logic is the same as that underlying the conclusion that the Collins couple was more likely to be innocent than guilty even though the probability a random couple matched the description was only 1 in a million. The p-value, just like that 1 in a million, is just one of the numbers we need in order to form our posterior beliefs. If the power is low or our prior beliefs are low, our posterior beliefs are likely to be low as well.

This kind of thinking also helps us to better understand the replication crisis in so many scientific disciplines that we described back in chapters 7 and 8. Remember the ESP study? What was your prior belief about humans having ESP before you saw the results from that study? Probably pretty low, right? So your correct posterior belief that the effect is real, even given the statistically significant evidence, isn't that high. Figure 15.6 gives you a sense of this. The vertical axis is the posterior probability that an observed relationship is real. The horizontal axis is the prior probability that it is real. The curve plots the correct posterior belief as a function of your prior belief, given that a study with statistical power of .8 and a significance threshold of .05 generated statistically significant evidence of the relationship.

Our prior beliefs are hugely important for our posterior beliefs. Indeed, if you have really low priors about ESP, like we do, then it might not even make sense to study ESP, because the results of the study will have virtually no effect on your beliefs.

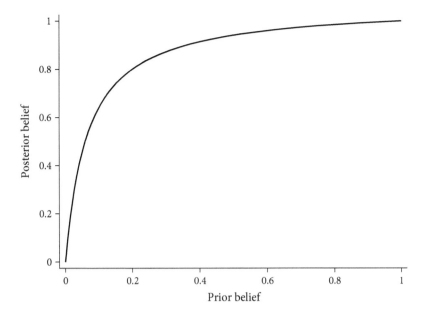

Figure 15.6. Posterior belief that an effect is real given statistically significant evidence, as a function of prior belief.

Figure 15.7 shows how the change in beliefs in response to new evidence relates to the prior. That is, it plots your posterior belief that a real relationship exists minus your prior belief that a real relationship exists, for different values of the prior belief, given that you saw statistically significant evidence in favor of the relationship. As you can see, if your prior belief is already very close to 0 or 1, it is very hard to move your beliefs. The effect of new evidence is largest for moderately surprising results (i.e., results where your prior belief was around .2).

Figure 15.7 also illustrates that two people can (and should) react quite differently to the same piece of information if they have different prior beliefs. Some people might see a piece of evidence about ESP, the consequences of global warming, or Russian interference in American elections and shift their beliefs dramatically, while others might see the same piece of evidence and barely shift their beliefs at all. When we experience this in our day-to-day lives, we often conclude that people who reacted differently than we did are unreasonable or irrational. But Bayes' rule tells us that it is perfectly understandable that different people react differently to the same information if, at the outset, they had different prior beliefs.

Some of this discussion might make you uncomfortable. As data analysts, aren't we supposed to let the data speak without imposing our own prejudices? And where do these priors come from, if not from data? These are tough questions. But there's no way around them. If you want to say something about the probability there is a genuine relationship in the world, given some piece of evidence, you need to have prior beliefs about the likelihood of that relationship. You can't just ignore your priors. Because, as we've seen, Pr(result | relationship not real) and Pr(relationship not real | result) can be very different.

Here's another wrinkle. Most of the time, we're not really interested in the probability that some phenomenon exists or doesn't exist (though we probably are in the ESP

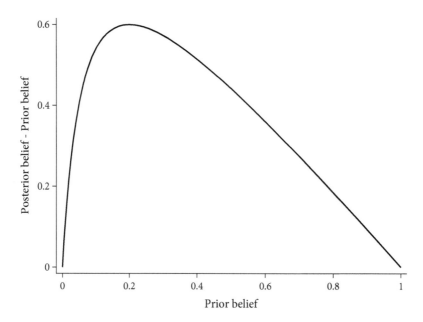

Figure 15.7. How much posterior beliefs change in response to new evidence, as a function of the prior belief.

example). Typically we want to know how substantively important or large an effect or relationship is, not just that it exists. That is, instead of just wanting to know if there is a real effect of, say, campaign strategy on vote share, we want to know the size of the effect of campaign strategy on vote share. How many supporters can a campaign turn out by launching a door-to-door canvassing campaign? Will turnout increase by 0.1, 1, or 10 percentage points? We can also incorporate Bayesian reasoning in such situations, but it's complicated. When thinking about the magnitude of a relationship, your prior belief is not just a single number, as it was when thinking about the probability that a relationship exists. Instead, it is a belief about how likely each possible relationship size is. And when you update your beliefs, you have to update your beliefs about each of these probabilities. Some analysts do this formally, specifying the whole prior distribution of beliefs about all the possible magnitudes and then doing complicated computations to estimate their posteriors. (This is called *Bayesian statistics*.) An alternative approach is to continue using conventional statistics like those described in chapter 6 (called *frequentist statistics*), while still trying to be careful when interpreting the results.

Expected Costs and Benefits

Your beliefs about effects are only one input to a decision. Even once you have made sure that things are on the right scale, you are answering the right question, and you have formed correct posterior beliefs based on the evidence and your prior beliefs, quantitative information still doesn't speak for itself. To use information and evidence to improve decision making, you have to combine your evidence-based beliefs with your values and goals to figure out how to act.

There is a sense in which this is obvious. Suppose a really well-designed series of studies convinces you that a certain kind of school intervention increases the likelihood that students will attend college by 30 percentage points. That's a big effect. But that alone doesn't tell you that the intervention is a good idea. To answer that question, at the very least, you have to know the value of college and how much the intervention costs.

It is easy, in the midst of forming beliefs based on sometimes complicated data analyses, to lose track of thinking about costs, benefits, values, and goals. A giant effect may seem compelling, just on its own. But it is important not to fall into this trap—because what may seem like obvious implications of a piece of evidence may turn out not to be so obvious. Let's see an example.

Screening Frequently or Accurately

As we write this section, a coronavirus pandemic is sweeping across the world. One of the central challenges in confronting the pandemic concerns testing—specifically, identifying infected people quickly enough that they can be isolated before they spread it to too many others.

As we've emphasized several times in this book, in thinking about the efficacy of a test for diagnosing a disease, both the false positive and the false negative rates matter. The lower each is, the more accurate the diagnosis. Not surprisingly, then, regulatory agencies like the Food and Drug Administration (FDA) demand tests that have low false positive and false negative rates, not allowing them on the market if they are too inaccurate on either front.

Much of the time, this is quite sensible. We don't want sick people concluding they are healthy (false negatives) or healthy people concluding they are sick (false positives). And we don't want to undermine testing by having people conclude that they can't trust tests in general.

In the early months of the coronavirus, medical scientists tried a variety of approaches to testing. Several of these had low false positive rates. But the nasal-swab-based polymerase chain reaction (PCR) tests had the additional virtue of low false negative rates. This is because they were able to detect the virus at quite low levels. Because they satisfied the FDA's requirements for low false positive and false negative rates, PCR tests were quickly approved and became the standard testing regimen.

A competing technology, tests that involved putting saliva on a paper strip, had a harder time getting approval. The reason was their higher false negative rate. The paper-strip tests could only detect the virus at higher levels of concentration. So they were more likely to miss someone who was infected, especially in the early days of an infection, when a person's viral load was still relatively low.

For many diseases, the FDA's position might make a lot of sense. If we are testing for celiac disease or cancer, it makes sense to only approve the most accurate tests. But the coronavirus case is, arguably, different in a bunch of ways that are worth thinking through.

In comparing the merits of two diagnostic tests, the false positive and false negative rates are important. But they aren't the only relevant criteria. One should also consider the relative costs of the two tests. And, especially in the case of a highly infectious disease like the coronavirus, one should also consider the speed of the test. It is one thing to wait a week or two for the results of a celiac test. It is another thing to wait a week or two for the results of a coronavirus test, during which time the person in question could spread the disease to many other people.

As it turns out, while the paper-strip tests have higher false negative rates than PCR tests, they are much cheaper, can be administered at home, and can deliver results in under an hour, as compared to the five to ten days people were waiting for PCR results. If we combine these additional pieces of information with the difference in the false negative rates, we might reach a quite different conclusion about whether the FDA did the right thing by delaying approval of the paper-strip tests.

To start to get a sense of the issues, think just about the difference in price. By some estimates, paper-strip tests cost $1–$5, while PCR tests cost $50–$100. So comparing one PCR test to one paper-strip test hardly seems fair. We could do at least ten paper-strip tests for every PCR test.

The main way you get a false negative on a test like this is if your viral load is too low to be detected by the test. The PCR test has a lower false negative rate because it can detect the virus in much lower concentration. But the coronavirus grows very quickly in a person. So scientists suspect it only takes a day or so to go from having the sort of viral load that can be detected by a PCR test to having the sort of viral load that can be detected by a paper-strip test.

If this is right, one way of thinking about the difference between the two tests is as follows. Suppose you can afford N paper-strip tests for each PCR test. So, to keep costs equal, let's imagine we do a paper-strip test every day or a PCR test once every N days. For the sake of argument, let's imagine $N = 10$ and let's ignore delays in getting test results back. You have to choose between taking the PCR test on day 1, 11, 21, and so on and taking a paper-strip test every day. Focus on days 1 through 10. Under the PCR regimen, if you have a low viral load on day 1, you detect the virus with the PCR test on that day, but you don't find out you are infected with the paper-strip test for another day or two. If your viral load is low on day 2, you don't detect you are sick with the PCR test until day 11, but you detect you are sick with the paper-strip test on day 3. The same is true for days 3 through 9. If your viral load is low on day 10, you find out you are sick with either test on day 11. So, all told, the probability you find out you are sick faster with PCR testing is 1 out of 10. The probability you find out you are sick faster with paper-strip testing is 8 out of 10. And the probability you find out you are sick at the same time under either regimen is 1 out of 10.

Of course, there may be other reasons that people get false negatives besides low viral loads. So here's another way to think about the comparison. Suppose, again just for the sake of argument, that both tests had a false positive rate of zero. So we are only worried about the false negative rate. Let p be the false negative rate of the PCR test and q be the false negative rate of the paper-strip test. The probability the PCR misses an infected person is p. How likely are ten paper-strip tests to miss this case? That depends on how correlated false negatives are across tests of the same person. If they are perfectly correlated (which surely isn't true, since a person's viral load is increasing over time), then if you get a false negative once, you will always get a false negative. In this case, the probability that ten paper-strip tests miss the case is the same as the probability that one paper-strip test misses the case, q. If, by contrast, false negatives are completely uncorrelated across cases (which also surely isn't true, since some people have lower viral loads than others and so their cases are harder to detect), then the probability that ten paper-strip tests miss an infected person is q^{10}. So, for instance, if the PCR test had a false negative rate of one-tenth of 1 percent and the paper-strip test had a false negative rate of 20 percent, ten paper-strip tests would be way more likely to catch an infected person than one PCR test ($.001 > .2^{10} \approx .0000001$). The truth, of course, lies somewhere in between.

There are still more factors to consider in evaluating these two approaches to testing. First, as we've already indicated, false negatives are more likely early in a person's infection, when the viral load is low. But this is also when people are less infectious. So, as it becomes more important to correctly diagnose people, the difference between the PCR and paper-strip test goes down.

Second, a test's speed is an incredibly important part of the cost-benefit calculation. The main benefit of testing is to keep people from infecting others once they are infected. The coronavirus grows rapidly in an infected person. So there are huge advantages to administering the test at home and getting results in less than an hour.

For all these reasons, studies that simulate disease spread under a variety of testing regimens find that differences in the frequency and rapidity of testing can be much more important than differences in false negative rates. As such, the FDA's sensible-sounding rule for approving diagnostic tests might not have been so sensible in this case.

One thing you might worry about is that, unlike the PCR tests, perhaps the paper-swab tests did not have false positive rates close to zero. If there are lots of false positives, then daily testing might lead to lots of costly and unnecessary self-quarantining. False positive rates are hard to study, but at least some evidence suggests that they were low, even for the paper-swab tests. But even if false positive rates were non-negligible, the combination of the two technologies suggests a reasonable solution. Paper-swab tests need not be treated as the final answer in order to be highly useful. If everyone did a paper-swab test every day, some people would get false positives. They could be asked to self-quarantine, while being immediately administered a more definitive PCR test. With the load on labs lightened by reduced PCR testing, turnaround times might even speed up. And, as a result, false positives could be corrected relatively quickly, with a minimum of inconvenience.

The point of this discussion is not to provide a definitive answer to this difficult policy problem, on which we are not experts. Rather, it is to illustrate the fact that we have to consider lots of different costs and benefits when we make decisions, and every person or society has to use their personal values to decide how to weigh those different costs and benefits. It's easy to fixate on one particular quantitative statistic like the false negative rate and make decisions accordingly, but that is typically a mistake. We'll return to these themes in the final two chapters.

Wrapping Up

Turning statistics into substance helps us think clearly about what exactly the evidence tells us about the questions we are trying to answer. Keeping those questions forefront in our minds is a key element of thinking clearly about how to use quantitative information. Indeed, we need to do so not only when interpreting the results of an analysis but when choosing how to measure, selecting the samples we study, and deciding which settings our results apply to. Those issues are the topic of chapter 16.

Key Words

- **Percentage point change:** The simple numerical difference between two percentages.
- **Percent change:** A way of measuring the degree of change. It is the difference between the initial value and the new value divided by the original value

(multiplied by 100). Unlike percentage point change, percent change is highly sensitive to the original value.

- **Conditional probability:** The probability of an event conditional on some other information. We write the probability of C conditional on E as $\Pr(C \mid E)$.
- **Prior belief:** Your belief about some thing before learning new evidence.
- **Posterior belief:** Your belief about some thing after incorporating new evidence.
- **Bayes' rule:** A formula for calculating your posterior belief conditional on new evidence and your prior belief. In particular: $\Pr(C \mid E) = \frac{\Pr(E \mid C) \Pr(C)}{\Pr(E)}$. Sometimes called Bayes' theorem or Bayes' law.
- **Statistical power:** The probability of finding a statistically significant result in the data given that the relationship really exists in the world.

Exercises

15.1   A newspaper reports, "Economic growth was 20 percent higher in Country A than in Country B last year."

The typical way that economists measure economic growth is the percent change in GDP from one year to the next. So we'd say economic growth was 3 percent in a particular country and year if the GDP was 3 percent higher at the end of the year than at the beginning.

(a) Suppose GDP growth in Country B was 10 percent. What was GDP growth in Country A?
(b) Suppose GDP growth in Country B was 0.1 percent. What was GDP growth in Country A?
(c) What's an alternative way to write the headline so that you don't misleadingly mask the difference between the scenarios described by (a) and (b)?

15.2   Now consider two other countries C and D. Suppose that growth in Country C is 1 percent while growth in Country D is 0.1 percent.

(a) What is the percent difference in growth? What is the percentage point difference?
(b) Write two headlines, each including a true statistical fact about the two countries. One should make the difference in their economic growth sound like a really big deal. The other should not.
(c) Now suppose that upon a statistical review, growth in Country D turns out to be just 0.001 instead of 0.1 percent. What now is the percent difference in growth between the two countries? What is the percentage point difference? Which of these two statistics better conveys the substantive significance of the shift from 0.1 percent to 0.001 percent? Why?

15.3   During the coronavirus pandemic, governments and private organizations around the world rushed to create diagnostic tests. Those tests varied in their accuracy. Let's think about one of those tests, which was reported to have a 1 percent false positive rate and a 10 percent false negative rate.

We don't know the underlying rate of coronavirus in the asymptomatic population. Suppose the probability an asymptomatic person has coronavirus is some number q—that is, the prior belief any given person is sick is $Pr(sick) = q$.

(a) Using the information above about the false negative rate, what is the probability a person gets a positive result given that they really do have coronavirus (written, $Pr(+ \mid sick)$)? (Hint: You don't need Bayes' rule to answer this question.)

(b) There are two ways to get a positive test result. A person with coronavirus can get a correct test result. And a person who does not have coronavirus can get a false positive. Calculate the overall probability that an asymptomatic person gets a positive test:

$$Pr(+) = Pr(sick) \cdot Pr(+ \mid sick) + Pr(not\ sick) \cdot Pr(+ \mid not\ sick)$$

(Your answer will have q in it because it will depend on the prior belief that an asymptomatic person is sick.)

(c) Now use Bayes' rule to calculate $Pr(sick \mid +)$—the probability that an asymptomatic person tests positive. (Your answer will, again, have q in it.)

(d) We don't actually know q. Let's think about different scenarios.

   i. Calculate $Pr(sick \mid +)$ if $q = .005$ (i.e., if half a percent of the asymptomatic population has coronavirus).
   ii. Calculate $Pr(sick \mid +)$ if $q = .01$ (i.e., if 1 percent of the asymptomatic population has coronavirus).
   iii. Calculate $Pr(sick \mid +)$ if $q = .05$ (i.e., if 5 percent of the asymptomatic population has coronavirus).
   iv. Draw a figure with q on the horizontal axes (going from 0 to 1) that graphs $Pr(sick \mid +)$.

15.4 Discrimination against certain groups in the job market is a major societal and policy concern. Many studies seek to bring quantitative evidence to bear on the extent of such discrimination.

Let's think through a very simple example. Imagine a society with two equally sized and equally qualified groups: the privileged and the unprivileged.

Using the conditional probability notation we developed earlier we will express the probability that a person gets a job given their group membership as $Pr(hired \mid group)$. Similarly, we will express the probability that a person is a member of a particular group given that the person got a job as $Pr(group \mid hired)$.

(a) Suppose you want to know whether, if they both apply for the same job, a member of the privileged group is more likely to be hired than a member of the unprivileged group. So you want to know whether, among those who apply for the job, the following is true:

$$Pr(hired \mid privileged\ \&\ applied) > Pr(hired \mid unprivileged\ \&\ applied)$$

      i. Use Bayes' rule to rewrite Pr(hired | privileged & applied) as a function of three terms, Pr(privileged | hired & applied), Pr(hired | applied), and Pr(privileged | applied).

      ii. Use Bayes' rule to rewrite Pr(hired | unprivileged & applied) as a function of three terms, Pr(unprivileged | hired & applied), Pr(hired | applied), and Pr(unprivileged | applied).

(b) Suppose a study shows that people in a given job are equally likely to be privileged and unprivileged. Express that using our notation. Which two terms from your answer to (a) does that mean you know?

(c) Is the information in (b) sufficient to determine whether, if they both apply for the same job, a member of the privileged group is more likely to be hired than a member of the unprivileged group? Using your answer to part (a), what additional piece of information would you need to know?

(d) Suppose you learned that the same number of members of the two groups applied for the job. Now would you know the answer?

Readings and References

The study on the reporting of fuel-efficiency statistics is

Richard P. Larrick and Jack B. Soll. 2008. "The MPG Illusion." *Science* 320:1593–94.

The *Wall Street Journal* article on a cholesterol drug is

Ron Winslow. "Cholesterol Drug Cuts Heart Risk in Healthy Patients." *Wall Street Journal*, Nov. 10, 2008. https://www.wsj.com/articles/SB122623863454811545.

To learn more about how to create informative data visualizations and how to avoid being fooled by bad graphics, we recommend the following books.

Carl T. Bergstrom and Jevin D. West. 2020. *Calling Bullshit: The Art of Skepticism in a Data-Driven World*. Random House.

Kieran Healy. 2019. *Data Visualization: A Practical Introduction*. Princeton University Press.

Edward R. Tufte. 2001. *The Visual Display of Quantitative Information, 2nd Edition*. Graphics Press.

The figure on partisan trends in the U.S. South is from

Christopher H. Achen and Larry M. Bartels. 2016. *Democracy for Realists: Why Elections Do Not Produce Responsive Government*. Princeton University Press.

The story of the statistical errors made in the trial of the Collins couple is related in

Jonathan J. Koehler. 1995. "One in Millions, Billions, and Trillions: Lessons from People v. Collins (1968) for People v. Simpson (1995)." *Journal of Legal Education* 47(2): 214–23.

For more on the SPOT program have a look at two reports by the General Account-ability Office:

The 2010 report: https://www.gao.gov/assets/310/304510.pdf.

The 2013 report: https://www.gao.gov/assets/660/658923.pdf.

An analysis of testing regimens for coronavirus can be found in

Daniel B. Larremore, Bryan Wilder, Evan Lester, Soraya Shehata, James M. Burke, James A. Hay, Milind Tambe, Michael J. Mina, and Roy Parke. 2020. "Test Sensitivity Is Secondary to Frequency and Turnaround Time for COVID-19 Surveillance." https://www.medrxiv.org/content/10.1101/2020.06.22.20136309v3.

An early blog post on the idea is here:

Alex Tabarrok. "Frequent, Fast, and Cheap Is Better than Sensitive." Marginal Revolution. July 24, 2020. https://marginalrevolution.com/marginalrevolution/2020/07/frequent-fast-and-cheap-is-better-than-sensitive.html.

CHAPTER 16

Measure Your Mission

What You'll Learn

- It is important that you measure outcomes and treatments that correspond to your mission.
- If you measure the outcome in an incomplete way, apparent improvements may be misleading.
- Data always comes from a particular context. When applying the lessons drawn from data to a new context, it is important to think clearly about whether the contexts are sufficiently similar that the lessons will continue to hold.
- Sometimes, there is a relationship in the world that would help you achieve your goal. But once you actually use that relationship to try to do so, the relationship itself disappears, so it is no longer helpful.

Introduction

When you use evidence to inform your decisions, you have some goal in mind. That goal is your mission. Why is it important to measure it?

Suppose you have evidence about a causal relationship; some action affects some outcome in a predictable way. If changing that outcome means you have achieved your goal—that is, if in measuring the outcome you measured your mission—then knowledge of that causal relationship is straightforwardly useful. But what if changing the outcome you measured doesn't necessarily mean you have achieved your goal, or what if it only corresponds to one part of your goal? Then, which action the evidence suggests will further your mission might not be so clear.

The same goes for correlations. Suppose your mission involves trying to predict some outcome, but you've measured a related, though different, outcome. Are you sure that the correlates of the outcome you measured will help you predict the outcome of interest?

In this chapter, we will explore several ways in which things can go wrong when we have good evidence about what might turn out to be the wrong thing. Each of these examples will illustrate the reasons it is important to measure your mission, as best as possible, when trying to use evidence to make better decisions.

Measuring the Wrong Outcome or Treatment

The most straightforward way that you might fail to measure your mission is by measuring an outcome or treatment that doesn't quite correspond to what you are really interested in. Here we consider three ways in which this commonly happens.

Partial Measures

Often our mission is to change some outcome—say, educational achievement, national security, or health—that is hard to measure in its entirety. For instance, we might not have an encompassing measure of overall educational achievement, but perhaps we can measure whether standardized test scores improve. Such partial measures can be helpful. But we have to be careful about interpretation because improving test scores is not our mission. Our mission is improving education.

In many settings, there are good reasons to think that improvements on one dimension might tend to coincide with losses on other dimensions. That is, as we get better at one part of a problem, we might get worse at other parts. A simple reason for this is resource constraints. Suppose your overall mission is to make a local park more beautiful. You have a budget to support your mission. If you spend more resources on trash pickup, you have less money to spend on landscaping. So improving on one dimension means getting worse on another. And if you just have a partial measure of your mission (say, the amount of trash on the ground), then as you spend more money on trash pickup, you might be tempted to conclude you are doing a better job achieving your mission. But, because things are getting worse on the landscaping dimension as a result of devoting more resources to trash pickup, this is misleading.

There are additional reasons, besides limited resources, for a negative correlation across dimensions of a problem. Perhaps the most interesting is *strategic adaptation*—efforts to improve outcomes on some dimension lead people to adjust their behavior to get around those efforts. This too can make partial measurements problematic. Let's see how this plays out in an example.

Metal detectors in airports

Starting in the mid-1960s, hijacking became a serious problem in U.S. civil aviation. Over eighty airplanes were taken by hijackers in 1969 alone. The hijackers included Americans, Croatians, Cubans, Japanese, North Koreans, Palestinians, and many others. Their motivations ranged from simple ransom to nationalist, leftist, and other global political causes. In the early 1970s, in response to this growing threat to air safety, the United States increased airport security. Most importantly, metal detectors were installed in every major U.S. airport in early 1973.

Imagine you were a government official tasked with evaluating the efficacy of these heightened security measures. A natural question you might ask is whether they resulted in a significant decrease in hijackings. Figure 16.1, showing hijackings per quarter from 1968 to 1978, suggests the answer is yes. Prior to 1973 (represented by the dashed, vertical line), there was an average of almost twenty hijackings per quarter. But after 1973, that number drops to fewer than ten per quarter.

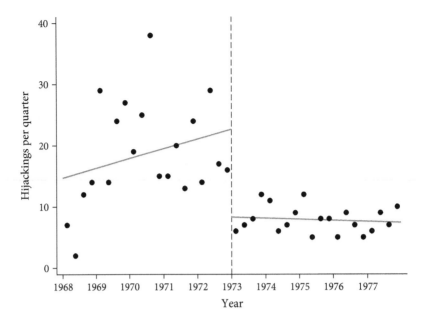

Figure 16.1. Quarterly hijackings 1968–1978 along with separate regression lines for quarters before and after first-quarter 1973. The vertical dashed line indicates when metal detectors were installed in U.S. airports.

Let's think about whether we've measured our mission. One possibility is that the mission is to reduce hijackings. In that case, hijackings are the right outcome to study and this looks like a success. But another possibility is that the mission is to increase security from all terrorist hostage takings, not just hijackings. In that case, hijackings are only a partial measure of the mission because there are lots of other kinds of terrorism.

Moreover, this is just the kind of setting where we might worry that improvements on one dimension of a problem (here, hijackings) tend to coincide with exacerbation of the other dimensions of the problem (here, other kinds of terrorist attacks). The reason is strategic adaptation. As airport security improves, we might worry that terrorists substitute hijacking for other kinds of hostage takings. If this is the case, the apparent reduction in hijackings might be misleading as a measure of how successful increased airport security was in terms of the overall counterterrorism mission.

And, indeed, this appears to be the case. Figure 16.2 shows a finding inspired by the work of Walter Enders and Todd Sandler—after metal detectors were installed in U.S. airports, other kinds of terrorist hostage takings became more frequent. And so, if we have a more encompassing, rather than partial, measure of our mission, we reach somewhat different conclusions.

Of course, this doesn't mean that the metal detector policy was a failure. The substitution from hijackings to other hostage takings does not appear to be one-for-one. Moreover, hijackings might be worse, on average, than other kinds of hostage takings. So this might still be a counterterrorism win. But it is not nearly so dramatic a win as one might have thought looking only at the impact on hijackings rather than a more complete measure of the mission.

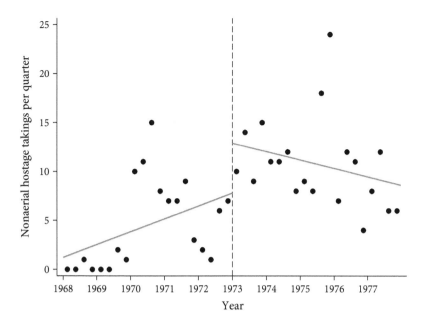

Figure 16.2. Quarterly hostage takings not on airplanes, 1968–1978, along with separate regression lines for quarters before and after first-quarter 1973. The vertical dashed line indicates when metal detectors were installed in U.S. airports.

Intermediate Outcomes

Often, measuring the outcome associated with your mission is difficult, takes a long time, or just doesn't yield enough data. A common solution is to measure intermediate outcomes, steps along the path of the mission, that we hope will be indicative of the longer-term objective.

Suppose you're running a political campaign and you're trying to maximize the probability that your candidate wins. You want to test a few different ads to see which ones are the most effective. You could run the ads in different media markets and see where you do the best on election day. But that won't do much good. You need to know which ad to run before the election happens. So, instead, you have to measure some outcome that will give you some sense of which ad is best while the campaign is ongoing.

One natural option to help you decide on your strategy is opinion polls. Instead of running ads randomly and seeing what happens to vote totals, you could run ads randomly, conduct opinion polls, and see which ad appears to help you in the polls. There's not necessarily anything wrong with doing this. It's a good idea. But you have to keep in mind that you don't care about polls per se. You care about votes. So to the extent that changing poll numbers is indicative of a step along the path to changing votes, learning about this intermediate outcome is informative about your mission. But, for example, it's possible that your ad changes poll numbers by changing which people are willing to respond to the poll or whether people tell the truth to pollsters, without changing people's actual vote choices. If that is the case, impacting the intermediate outcome might not matter at all for the final outcome you care about. So, whenever you use an intermediate outcome instead of a measure of your ultimate mission, you want to think about how sure you are that the intermediate outcome really is a step on the path to your actual goals.

Let's think about an example from medicine, where the impracticality of studying the actual outcome of interest is often particularly acute.

Blood pressure and heart attacks

Suppose the goal of a new drug is to reduce heart attacks. Unfortunately for research purposes (but fortunately for other reasons) heart attacks are rare. So relatively few people in any given sample will have heart attacks during the course of a drug trial. As such, it is very hard to learn directly about whether a drug reduces heart attacks even in a well-designed experiment that randomizes who gets the drug and who doesn't.

So what do medical researchers do? One alternative to waiting twenty years to see whether patients who were assigned the drug are less likely to have heart attacks is to study an intermediate or surrogate outcome, like blood pressure. Since blood pressure predicts heart attacks, the thinking goes, if a drug reduces blood pressure, it is likely to reduce heart attacks.

But we have to be careful. We learned in part 2 that correlation need not imply causation. Playing basketball is correlated with height but experimentally increasing basketball playing does not increase height. Similarly, just because blood pressure and heart attacks are correlated doesn't mean that a drug that reduces blood pressure will reduce heart attacks. For that, you'd have to have compelling evidence that blood pressure has a causal effect on heart attacks.

Now, there are good reasons to believe that blood pressure really does have a causal effect on heart attacks. But for many other intermediate outcomes used in medical studies, the causal linkage may be less clear.

In a 1994 review of the evidence, Thomas Fleming illustrates the point in a discussion of research on cancer. Often, when studying cancer treatments, scientists cannot wait long enough to look at the effect of a treatment on, say, mortality. So, instead, they study the effect on an intermediate outcome. One popular such intermediate outcome is tumor size.

For instance, Fleming describes a medical trial for a drug intended to treat prostate cancer. The researchers determined that if they examined mortality as their outcome, they would need a sample of between 40,000 and 100,000 subjects to detect a reasonably sized effect because death from prostate cancer is rare and slow. Since they could only recruit 18,000 men for their trial, they instead decided to use tumor size, as measured by a prostate biopsy, to assess the effectiveness of the drug.

One problem, as Fleming discusses, is that prostate tumor size is only a very weak proxy for the actual mission, which is presumably not dying from cancer. Thirty percent of men over the age of fifty test positive for prostate tumors. But only 3 percent actually die from prostate cancer. Many prostate tumors grow very slowly. So other things, like heart attacks, get people first. The experiment showed that the drug being tested significantly reduced tumor size. But it is entirely possible that much of the reduction in tumor size was in the kinds of tumors that were never going to harm the subjects in the first place. So we really don't know whether progress on this intermediate outcome contributed much, if anything, to progress on the mission of avoiding death by prostate cancer.

Of course, we don't mean to suggest that studying intermediate outcomes is a bad idea. Indeed, it is often the best that can be done, given other constraints. But in interpreting the finding of a relationship between some action and an intermediate outcome, it is important that we think clearly about what we know about the relationship between the intermediate outcome and our actual mission.

Ill-Defined Missions

Often, your mission may be slightly tricky to pin down. In particular, there is sometimes more than one reasonable way to measure what may seem to be the same mission. But which choice you make can matter a lot. So it is important to think hard about what outcomes and treatments really define your mission.

Suppose you're a college student considering your educational and career choices with the goal of maximizing your future earnings. The first thing you might think to do is study the Forbes list of the richest people in the world and try to follow in their footsteps. One thing you might infer is that the way to maximize your earnings is to drop out of college and start a tech company. This was the strategy taken by Bill Gates, Mark Zuckerberg, and Larry Ellison, three of the eight richest people in the world at the time of this writing. But you won't make that mistake because you learned in chapter 4 that correlation requires variation. To know if dropping out of college and starting a tech company is correlated with success, you can't just study the most successful people.

Suppose you pushed further and tried to get a sense of how many people in the underlying population dropped out of college and started their own tech company. You'd surely find that less than .01 percent of all people dropped out of college and started their own tech company, and yet 37.5 percent of the world's eight richest people did so. So there appears to be a strong correlation. People who drop out of college and start their own tech company are much more likely to end up one of the world's eight richest people than people who stay in college or never start a tech company.

Having identified a correlation, there are still some reasons you might not want to make a rash decision and drop out of college today. First, we might have just inadvertently engaged in something akin to *p*-hacking. We studied a small population of extremely wealthy individuals, we looked for commonalities, and we eventually found something that a few of them have in common. But that might just be a coincidence. Maybe the correlation we observe today won't hold in the future, in which case dropping out and starting a tech company might be a bad idea.

Yet another reason we wouldn't recommend dropping out and starting a tech company is that we're not comparing apples to apples. The kinds of people who drop out of college and start a tech company are likely different from those who don't, and we have little way of knowing whether they would have been equally successful had they not dropped out. That is, following the lessons of chapter 9, this correlation is not an unbiased estimate of the causal relationship.

But even setting all of these reasons aside, there's a fundamental problem with this line of thinking that has to do with correctly measuring your mission. What outcome do you really care about? Is it your expected earnings or is it your probability of becoming a multi-billionaire? To the extent that dropping out of college and starting your own tech company makes you more likely to be one of the richest people in the world, it probably also makes you more likely to be in serious debt. And for all we know, it might significantly reduce your expected earnings, even if it increases your chances of becoming very wealthy. Is that a gamble you're willing to make?

We're not here to tell you what your particular objectives should be. Some people may have a deep desire to become a billionaire, which makes them willing to take significant risks. But we suspect most people are more averse to risk and would rather maximize their expected earnings or perhaps even minimize their chances of being in poverty. Your particular objective should inform the analyses you conduct. If your goal is to maximize expected earnings, it might be a huge mistake to examine the correlates of being on the Forbes list of wealthiest individuals. Instead, you'd want to collect data on earnings to see how various educational and career choices correspond with earnings, on average. We suspect you'd find that graduating from college and perhaps even going to professional school is a better predictor of earnings than dropping out and starting your own company.

This mistake of studying the wrong outcome can be made in the other direction as well. If you're managing a political campaign or coaching a sports team, you don't really care per se about your expected point margin or vote share. What you care about is winning, so you should choose strategies that maximize that objective. For example, if your political candidate is polling badly and there's only a week left in the campaign, you might be willing to gamble on an otherwise ill-advised strategy to give yourself a chance of winning. Maybe you decide to roll out a really aggressive new policy proposal that the voters probably won't like. In expectation, such a strategy reduces your vote total. But there is a small chance the voters will love your wild idea and you will win. If you don't really care about vote share (losing by five points or ten points is still losing) but only care about winning, a strategy that hurts your expected vote share may be optimal.

And, of course, this measurement problem doesn't only apply to outcomes. It also applies to measuring treatments. This is perhaps most clear when the variables we measure are meant to represent abstract concepts. We have to think clearly about what, exactly, we are measuring when we rank some countries as more or less democratic than others or some classes more or less difficult than others. But this concern can also emerge even when we are measuring more concrete quantities in the world. Here's an example.

Climate change and economic productivity

Many people are interested in the long-run effects of climate change on economic growth. Climate change, of course, happens over a long period of time and, thus, is hard to measure and study. But related phenomena, such as weather and temperature, vary frequently. So scholars sometimes use variation in the weather to try to learn about the effects of climate change.

For instance, Marshall Burke, Solomon Hsiang, and Edward Miguel estimate the effect of unexpected temperature fluctuations on GDP growth using a difference-in-differences design. That is, they compare the GDP within a country in years when it is exposed to warmer- versus cooler-than-average temperatures due to naturally occurring atmospheric variation. They find that economic productivity is maximized at an annual average temperature of 13 degrees Celcius and that it declines precipitously as the temperature rises. They conclude that "if future adaptation mimics past adaptation, unmitigated warming is expected to reshape the global economy by reducing average global incomes roughly 23% by 2100."

This is an important study and an important conclusion. But the caveat offered by the authors, "if future adaptation mimics past adaptation," points to a critical measurement issue.

The authors are interested in the effects of *climate change*. But the treatment they measure is *temperature fluctuations*. Climate change happens slowly, giving people and society time to adapt. Temperature fluctuations happen quickly, making adaptation difficult. Moreover, unlike temperature fluctuations, climate change is associated with shifts in weather variability, disease vectors, natural disaster prevalence, and so on. Thus, in important ways, temperature fluctuations do not measure the right treatment. And, in particular, they don't measure the right treatment in ways that are relevant for the question of productivity. In light of these measurement concerns, we probably shouldn't put a lot of faith in that 23 percent estimated effect.

To appreciate the distinction, consider the difference between the effects of a hot day on economic productivity versus the effects of a hot century. We live in Chicago, which can be a pretty cold place. If we were pleasantly surprised by an especially warm day, Anthony might be tempted to leave work early to play golf. But if climate change meant that every day was warmer, he wouldn't quit his job and play golf every day. And if it meant that days were warmer, but storms were more frequent, who knows what would happen to his golf playing. The fact that unexpected hot days decrease productivity does not necessarily tell us the long-run effects of climate change because we haven't measured and studied the right thing.

Do You Have the Right Sample?

Studying the right outcome and the right treatment isn't all there is to measuring your mission. We also need to make sure we have the right sample.

When applying evidence to decision making, we almost always have to take knowledge gleaned in some place and time and try to apply that knowledge to understand what will happen in another place and time. Essentially we are making an analogy between the contexts in which the evidence was generated and the contexts in which we now wish to apply the lessons we learned from that evidence. So we always have to ask whether those contexts are sufficiently similar that such an analogy is valid. Otherwise, we may take actions that are consistent with achieving our mission, but only in a very different context from the one in which we are acting.

External Validity

The basic problem here is that relationships can differ from context to context. We've spent a lot of time so far in this book on what is sometimes called *internal validity*. Internal validity is about credibly estimating the estimand (e.g., Is the estimator unbiased?). But even if you've done everything right with respect to internal validity, you still need to be able to think clearly about whether that relationship is likely to also exist in the context where you hope to apply it. Broadly, this is the problem of *external validity*. External validity is about whether there are good reasons to believe that a relationship estimated on data from one context will hold in some other context. An example will help to illustrate the point.

Malnutrition in India and Bangladesh

In the 1980s, the World Bank implemented the Tamil Nadu Integrated Nutrition Project (TINP) in a region of southern India where malnourishment was endemic. While the project included some resources for supplementary nutrition, the main focus was on helping mothers, the main household decision makers concerning food purchasing and preparation, make better use of the resources already at their disposal. The TINP is viewed as a major success by the World Bank. And, while there is some debate, it is widely credited with making a major difference in reducing malnourishment and malnutrition in Tamil Nadu.

This apparent success inspired the Bangladesh Integrated Nutrition Project (BINP) in the 1990s. By that time, Bangladesh, which borders India to the east, was among the most malnourished countries on earth. Evidence suggests that, in the early 1990s, almost two-thirds of Bangladeshi children under the age of five had growth stunting due to malnourishment.

Because the TINP had been rigorously evaluated and shown to have made a significant and meaningful dent in malnutrition, the BINP was modeled quite directly on the TINP. And so scholars and practitioners alike were surprised when the BINP's impact did not live up to the promise of the TINP. Despite being designed to replicate perhaps the most successful malnutrition intervention in history, rigorous evaluation shows little to no impact of the BINP on malnutrition. What went wrong?

There are, of course, many possible answers. And it is virtually impossible to know for sure why the program failed. But one important factor seems to have been a cultural difference between Tamil Nadu and Bangladesh. As we've mentioned, in Tamil Nadu, mothers are typically the chief decision makers regarding food purchasing and preparation. Thus, it made sense to target mothers for the TINP's nutritional education efforts.

This focus on mothers was exported directly from the TINP to the BINP. But in many households in Bangladesh the father or the mother-in-law (i.e., the father's mother), rather than the mother, has authority over food purchasing or preparation. Because this was not the case in Tamil Nadu, these important decision makers were not targeted by the BINP. Thus, the BINP may have failed, at least in part, because a targeting decision that made perfect sense in one setting was no longer so sensible in another.

This example is particularly interesting to us because it points to the potential for a complementarity between quantitative evidence and qualitative knowledge. Assessing the impact of the TINP required a quantitative approach. But attempting to apply that knowledge to the Bangladeshi context went wrong because of a lack of knowledge about key cultural and institutional differences between Tamil Nadu and Bangladesh. A team that combined both people with expertise in quantitative assessment who could think clearly about the causal effect of the TINP and people with deep qualitative knowledge of the two contexts might have resulted in a better outcome than either alone could hope to achieve.

Selected Samples

A particularly common way for people to end up measuring their mission in the wrong context is by studying selected samples. A *selected sample* is a sample of observations that wasn't drawn at random from the population of interest but rather was selected to be studied because it possessed some set of characteristics. The problem, of course, is that a selected sample may not be representative of the population as a whole. And relationships that hold in that selected sample may not hold in the broader population. If your mission is to predict, understand, or influence the behavior of the broader population, things can really go wrong if you rely on evidence from a selected sample.

College admissions

Here's an example that is near and dear to our hearts. Standardized test scores, for better or worse, have been an important part of the college admissions process for decades. However, in 2018 our own university announced that it would no longer require applicants to submit such scores. (Several other colleges and universities have done likewise.) One (among several) of the rationales for going test-optional was evidence-based. University leaders looked at the students who attended the university and found little correlation between test scores and performance. So, the argument went, maybe test scores aren't very good predictors of college performance.

The mission of a college admissions office is multifaceted. But part of that mission is to identify the most academically talented students from the pool of applicants. To fulfill this mission, the admissions office would like to know whether some characteristic of *applicants* (here, their test scores) is correlated with academic performance in college. But that is not the question the exercise described above addresses. Rather, that analysis asks whether some characteristic of *enrolled students* (namely, their test scores) is correlated with academic performance in college. But the answer to those two questions need not be the same.

The set of enrolled students is a selected sample of the set of applicants. Students were admitted to college based on their test scores and other factors like writing ability, teacher recommendations, grades, community service, and overcoming adversity. The fact that test scores were used in admissions can lead to a fundamentally different correlation between test scores and academic performance in the selected sample of enrolled students and the broader set of applicants.

To see how, think about students with low test scores who were nonetheless admitted to the university. Those students must have had some other characteristics that led the admissions office to overlook their low scores. Maybe they wrote stellar essays, had particularly strong recommendations from teachers, or made great grades in high school. Similarly, students with particularly high test scores were likely to have been admitted even with somewhat weaker performance on these other dimensions. For this reason, in the set of admitted and enrolled students, we might expect a negative correlation between test scores and other markers of academic quality.

Now, it's quite plausible that test scores are a good predictor of college performance among all applicants, but that writing ability, teacher recommendations, and high school grades are also good predictors. Therefore, once we look at the selected sample of enrolled students, we'll find a weak correlation between test scores and performance. But that's because the only people with low scores who got in are people who are really strong on other dimensions. So that weak (or non-existent) correlation in the selected sample of enrolled students does not mean that test scores are a bad predictor of academic performance among applicants.

This issue of studying selected samples is also prevalent outside the context of college admissions. So let's talk through one more example: baseball.

Why can't major league pitchers hit?

Major League Baseball fans know that pitchers tend to be the worst hitters on their teams. In the National League, where pitchers are required to bat, managers will typically have their pitchers hit last in the lineup to minimize their trips to the plate. And if a pitcher is coming out of the game, the manager will always replace them with a pinch hitter. In the 2017 Major League Baseball season, the batting average for the average pitcher was .125. The batting average for the average non-pitcher was .259. This is a massive difference. The American League has a designated hitter rule specifically so that pitchers don't have to bat.

So why are major league pitchers so bad at hitting? If you ask a baseball expert, they'd probably tell you that pitchers spend so much time practicing their pitching that they don't have time to practice their hitting. And there might even be something about great pitchers that makes them weaker hitters. Perhaps the kind of strength, flexibility, or body type that's good for pitching is bad for hitting.

These explanations sound pretty compelling, and they're probably right to some extent. But they also probably are not the whole story. One way to start to see this is to notice that this pattern does not hold for high school baseball.

We collected data on four Chicago-area high school baseball teams from the 2018 season and calculated the batting average for non-pitchers and pitchers (defined as players who pitched more than ten innings in the season). Unlike the pros, among these high school players, the pitchers actually have slightly higher batting averages than the non-pitchers: .322 versus .317.

How can this be? Why is the correlation between pitching and hitting ability slightly positive for high school baseball players but negative for seasoned professionals? It's not as if pitching practice doesn't crowd out batting practice for young pitchers. And you'd think the arguments about physical specialization would apply in high school as well as in the major leagues. So why does the correlation seem to change so dramatically and even flip signs as players age?

Even at the professional level, we can see that there wasn't always a negative correlation between pitching and batting ability. Figure 16.3 shows the batting average for the average pitcher and the average non-pitcher in Major League Baseball from 1871 to 2017. In the nineteenth century, pitchers and other position players had comparable batting averages. But starting in the twentieth century, the pitchers appear to get worse at hitting relative to other players, with the gap gradually increasing over time. And in the modern era, as we already discussed, non-pitchers get approximately twice as many base hits per at bat as do pitchers.

We suspect that the explanations for the changing correlation over time and the difference in correlation between high schoolers and the professionals is one and the same. And it has to do with selected samples.

Start by thinking about the correlation between pitching and batting ability in the entire population. Suppose we just randomly sampled individuals (say, teenagers and older) from the whole world and asked them to play baseball so we could measure their pitching and batting abilities. What do you think we would find? We suspect that we'd find a pretty strong positive correlation. Some people are athletic and have experience playing baseball. They are likely to be good at hitting and pitching. Other people are uncoordinated and inexperienced. They are likely to be bad at hitting and pitching. So, in the population as a whole, you're likely to find exactly the opposite correlation from what you find among professionals.

To see why this is, think about how a person becomes a Major League Baseball player. They almost surely play high school ball. A high school coach is trying to assemble the best team possible. That involves choosing the players, from the set of players available, who offer the best combination of batting and pitching ability. To make your high school team, you have to be pretty good at some combination of hitting and pitching. But you don't have to be amazing—you can be a good hitter (even if you are a bad

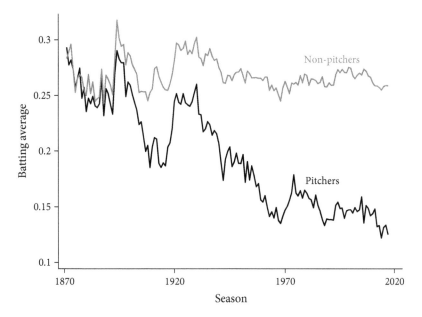

Figure 16.3. The negative correlation between pitching and hitting skill in the major leagues has gotten stronger over time.

pitcher), a good pitcher (even if you are a bad hitter), or an at least passable pitcher and hitter.

For most players, the path to the major leagues runs through the minor leagues. Minor league coaches are also trying to assemble the best team possible. And so, they too need the best combination of hitting and pitching available. So, to make a minor league team, you have to be really, really good at some combination of hitting and pitching. That means being a great hitter (even if you are a bad pitcher), a great pitcher (even if you are a bad hitter), or an at least good pitcher and solid hitter.

Finally, to make the major leagues (at least the National League, where pitchers hit), the test is even more stringent. You've got to be a truly amazing hitter (even if you are a bad pitcher), a truly amazing pitcher (even if you are a bad hitter), or a pretty great pitcher who can also hit.

Below is a simple demonstration (with hypothetical data) of what these ever more stringent selection criteria do to the correlation between hitting and pitching ability in different samples. Suppose (for simplicity) that we can give every potential baseball player a score that separately summarizes their pitching and batting abilities, and teams want to recruit players with the highest possible sum of both pitching and batting ability. How high that sum needs to be is increasing as you move up the ranks of baseball.

In the top-left panel of figure 16.4, we've drawn a scatter plot of some data with a strong positive correlation between pitching (horizontal axis) and batting ability (vertical axis). This is meant to represent the entire population. If we just let everyone on the team (as an entry-level team for kids might do), we'd see a pretty strong positive correlation between pitching ability and batting ability. This seems right to us. Our memory of youth sports is that the kids who were the best at one aspect of the game were often the best at every aspect of the game.

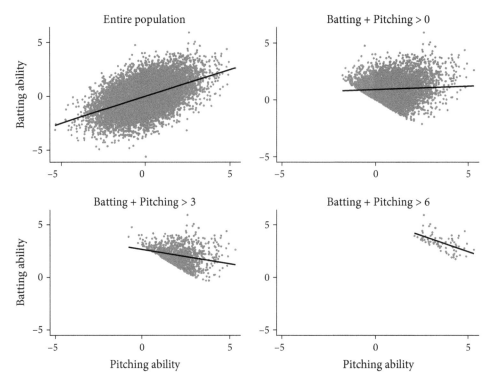

Figure 16.4. Increased selection can turn a positive correlation into a negative correlation.

The upper-right panel of figure 16.4 is meant to represent high school or the major leagues in the nineteenth century. In high school, the coach is only willing to accept players who are above average in the population, which translates into having a sum of batting and pitching ability above 0. Similarly, in the nineteenth century, baseball wasn't that popular, so professional coaches couldn't be so selective. You can make a team like this by being a good batter (say, a 3) and a weak pitcher (say, a −2); a good pitcher (say, a 3) and a weak hitter (say, a −2); or a slightly above-average pitcher and hitter (say .5 on both). But this level of selectivity eliminates people who are bad at both. And so, among the selected sample of high school or nineteenth-century baseball players, there's little correlation between batting and pitching ability.

The panel on the bottom left might represent the minor leagues or the early twentieth century. Selectivity has increased. Players need at least a 3 to make the team. So bad pitchers must be genuinely good hitters, bad hitters must be genuinely good pitchers, and some players can make the team by being solid at both. By eliminating even more players who are only okay at both, this level of selectivity flips the relationship from that in the population—inducing a slight negative correlation between batting and pitching ability.

Finally, the panel on the bottom right might represent the contemporary National League. Here selectivity is very high, since only an elite few can make it. So bad pitchers must be truly great hitters, bad hitters must be truly great pitchers, and for players to make it with a combination of skills, they must be terrific at both. At the highest levels, then, we expect to see a strong negative correlation between pitching and batting ability, even without any difference in time spent practicing or body type.

Figure 16.4 illustrates a fairly general phenomenon. Correlations in selected samples are often quite different from those in the broader population. This is important because we often only have data on selected samples. But we may want to make predictions and inferences about the broader population.

If you're a baseball scout, you have rich data on major league players available to you. You might try to use the data to predict who will become a star player so you can search for those features among high school and college athletes. But if you look for correlations of great performance among major league players, you'll draw misleading inferences. For example, you might find that slow runners are really good power hitters. So should you go find the slowest runners and recruit them to play professional base-ball? Surely not! The reason that slow runners are good power hitters in your selected sample is the same as the reason good pitchers are bad hitters. The only way a slow runner can make it to the major leagues is if they're a great power hitter.

Strategic Adaptation and Changing Relationships

There is another key issue for thinking about measuring your mission. Sometimes, there is a true relationship in the world that would help you achieve your goal. But once you actually use that relationship to try to do so, strategic adaption makes that relationship itself disappear or change, so that it is no longer so helpful. To see how this works, let's look at some examples of this phenomenon throughout history.

The Duty on Lights and Windows

In 1696 King William III of England needed money. Kings, of course, always need money. But this need was particularly pressing. Up until the 1660s, Britain produced coins made of hammered silver. These coins had a serious problem—people shaved or clipped the valuable silver around the edges. As a result, the value of the coins in silver was less than their face value. This widespread practice of coin clipping threatened to undermine the credibility of English currency.

To address the problem, the Crown undertook the great recoinage of 1696, offering to buy back clipped coins in exchange for new, machined coins that could not be clipped.[1] But buying back clipped coins for proper coins was expensive. The Crown essentially had to make up the difference between the face value and the value of the silver. So the Crown needed to raise revenue. But how to do so?

The Crown wanted to tax the wealthy more than the poor. One natural way to achieve this is through an income tax. But the English were opposed to income taxes because assessing income involved an invasion of personal privacy. So the Crown needed to find a way to tax wealth that was more politically palatable. The solution they landed on was a duty on lights and windows, better known as the window tax.

The window tax had the virtue that it could be assessed from outside of a home, thereby limiting any invasion of privacy. In the earliest version of the tax, the Crown established a two shilling base fee for all homes. In addition, homes that had between ten and twenty windows paid an extra four to six shillings and homes that had over twenty windows paid an extra eight to ten shillings. Windows in rooms used for work

---

[1] Fun fact: The new coins couldn't be clipped because they had milled edges, a feature that persists today, even though our coins are not made of precious metals. Milled edges were an innovation created by Isaac Newton in his role as warden of the Royal Mint at the time of the great recoinage.

didn't count. The exact thresholds and fees changed over time (such taxes lasted for well over a century), but you get the basic idea.

The argument for the window tax was an obvious correlation between windows and wealth (of course, they wouldn't have put it in those terms). On average, people whose houses had more windows were wealthier. Thus, by taxing windows, the Crown could raise revenues in ways that put more of the burden on the rich and less on the poor, which was the mission.

But the story doesn't end there. The English, like many others, don't like to pay taxes. And so they strategically adapted. In the short run, windows were boarded up or bricked over to reduce the taxes owed. Over the long run, architecture changed. Larger homes began to include fewer windows and more rooms that could be presented as work rooms. And so, with the passage of time, both the revenue from and the progressivity of the window tax declined.

In this case, the Crown's mission was to raise revenue in a progressive way. To do so, it needed to identify and tax wealthier people without invading their privacy. It noticed a correlation between windows and wealth, which seemed like just what it needed to achieve its mission. But, using that correlation in service of its mission led homeowners to strategically adapt their behavior such that the correlation no longer held (or, at least, held much less strongly), undermining the mission. Thus, in considering some change in behavior or policy in response to some piece of evidence, one must always ask whether the relationship uncovered by the evidence will persist once you change your behavior or policy.

The Shift in Baseball

We know we've already spent a good bit of time on baseball in this chapter. But, if you'll indulge us, we would like to do one more example. It is a pretty good one for illustrating the idea of strategic adaption changing the usefulness of a statistical relationship.

There was a time when defenders in baseball stood in their spot and waited to see if the ball would come their way. To be sure, fielders would adjust their position a bit depending on whether a left-handed or right-handed batter was up. But, for the most part, defensive strategy wasn't too complicated.

That time came to an end with the rise of big data in professional sports. Now teams have detailed spray charts for every batter. These charts provide data on how frequently each batter hits to various parts of the field, whether they hit the ball on the ground or in the air, the angle at which they make contact with the ball, and so on. Using this kind of information, teams can make well-informed forecasts about exactly where a given batter is likely to hit the ball. And armed with such forecasts, teams have started adjusting their defensive setups aggressively, batter by batter.

The most famous version of this change in defensive strategy is called the *shift*. Examining spray charts, teams discovered that when batters (especially power hitters) hit the ball on the ground, it is almost never to the so-called opposite field (for right-handed batters, this is to their right, and for left-handed batters, this is to their left). Rather, if they are going to hit the ball on the ground, they pull the ball (i.e., right-handed batters hit it to their left, and left-handed batters hit it to their right). The shift is the obvious response to this correlation—when facing a right-handed batter, shift the infield way over to the batter's left, and when facing a left-handed batter, shift the infield way over the batter's right. The benefit of such a move is that it makes it much less likely that a ground ball that is pulled will sneak through a hole in the infield for a base hit. The cost of this strategy is that it leaves a big hole in the infield in the opposite field. But since batters find it very hard to hit ground balls to the opposite field, this cost is small.

A few teams started shifting aggressively in the late 2000s. In 2010, the Tampa Bay Rays—led by manager Joe Maddon, an early advocate for evidence-based defense—accounted for 10 percent of all shifts, although they were just one of thirty teams. Maddon consulted spray charts and strategically placed his infielders in locations that were optimal for the particular pattern of ground balls associated with each batter. The Rays and other early adopters had a lot of success. That is, there was a negative correlation between using the shift and runs allowed.

Observing this correlation, all teams started implementing the shift. In 2011, there were only about 2,000 shifts used in total across all Major League Baseball games. By 2014, that number had grown to 13,000. And in 2016, it reached over 28,000.

But something else happened too. At first, the correlation that inspired this surge in shifting held. Teams that shifted allowed fewer runs. But batters noticed that the shift was hurting them. And they strategically adapted to avoid hitting so many ground balls into the shift. Instead, they hit more balls to the opposite side of the field, and they hit more balls in the air—over the shifted infield.

As things stand today, major league teams still use the shift a lot. But, because hitters adapted, the correlation between shifting and runs allowed that drove teams to use the shift in the first place does not hold nearly as strongly as it used to. Setting defensive strategy in response to the correlation led to changes in behavior that undid that correlation. It is perhaps worth noting that Joe Maddon—the early innovator who, as manager of the Rays, helped make the shift so popular—remains a believer in evidence-based defense. He later won a World Series as the manager of the Chicago Cubs, where he employed the shift less than any other manager in Major League Baseball.

The War on Drugs

Before leaving the topic of whether things will change once you act, it is worth pausing to reflect on the overlap between this question and our earlier discussion of the problem of partial measures. That overlap comes from the fact that strategic adaptation can create both phenomena.

Remember what we are concerned about in the case of partial measures. Suppose you have only a partial measure of your mission (like hijackings). You take an action and things appear to improve on that measure. But there might have been strategic adaptation such that getting better on that one dimension of your mission implied getting worse on some other dimension. Hence, improvements on your partial measure may not mean improvements on your overall mission.

Strategic adaptation is again at the root when we worry about whether things will change once you act on some piece of evidence. There is some relationship in the world. You act on that relationship. People adapt to your actions. And, thus, the relationship disappears.

Many examples can fit into both categories, depending on how you think about them. Let us give you one last example to illustrate the point, this time about America's so-called war on drugs.

As we write, most of the illegal drugs in the United States enter the country through Mexico, a country that has been ravaged by a decade-long drug war. But this was not always the case. In the 1970s and early 1980s, very few drugs reached the United States through Mexico. The transshipment route of choice was through the Caribbean and into Florida.

In 1980, the United States government launched a major offensive against the Colombian drug cartels. The Drug Enforcement Administration, Coast Guard, and other agencies deployed thousands of personnel and considerable naval and air power to shut down the Caribbean transshipment route. By the mid-1980s, the flow of drugs into Florida had plummeted.

But that is not the whole story. The reduction in drugs flowing through the Caribbean and into Florida in the 1980s does not reflect a reduction in drugs flowing into the United States during that period. Indeed, drugs continued to enter the United States at increasing rates, as evidenced by the fact that the price of cocaine plummeted fourfold during the course of the 1980s despite soaring demand.

So what happened? The Colombian cartels abandoned the Caribbean and Florida in favor of Mexico. In 1989, one-third of all cocaine in the United States entered through Mexico. Just three years later, that number had increased to one-half. Today, 90 percent of cocaine sold in the United States is smuggled up from Mexico.

This adaptation by the drug organizations has had devastating effects on Mexico. Throughout the 1990s, the Mexican drug trafficking organizations became larger and more powerful. They shifted from being middlemen for the Colombians to having their own suppliers and distribution networks. The drug trade became larger and more important—by the mid-1990s the Mexican drug trade was worth roughly $20 billion, dwarfing Mexico's largest legal commodity, oil, with a value of about $7.5 billion. As this expansion occurred, Mexican drug organizations became more fragmented and more violent. In 2010, the Mexican drug war claimed more than one thousand lives per month. The Mexican government struggled to exert basic control over parts of the country.

One can fruitfully think about this story from both the *partial measures* and the *changing relationship* perspectives.

From the *partial measures* perspective, here's how you'd tell it. The US government had a mission of stopping the drug flow. It noticed that almost all the drugs came up through the Caribbean. So it collected data—drugs flowing through the Caribbean—that was only a partial measure of the overall counter-narcotics mission. Then it took actions that made things improve according to that partial measure. But to conclude that the policy was a success would be a mistake. Because of strategic adaptation, getting better on that partial measure (drugs coming through the Caribbean) goes along with getting worse on other dimensions of the problem (drugs coming through Mexico). Here, the story illustrates the importance of not over-interpreting improvements on a partial measure of your mission.

From the *changing relationship* perspective, we tell the story slightly differently. There was a real correlation in the world—drugs were much more likely to enter the United States through the Caribbean than anywhere else. The government decided to act on the basis of this relationship by targeting its interdiction efforts in the Caribbean and Florida. Drug traffickers strategically adapted their behavior in response to this action, moving transshipment to Mexico. And so, as a consequence of the government's own actions, the correlation that formed the basis of the government's actions ceased to exist.

Both of these perspective are right. Which is more useful depends on the particular question you are trying to answer and the context in which you are trying to answer it.

Wrapping Up

Measuring your mission, like all the other lessons we've discussed, is an essential part of thinking clearly about how to use quantitative information to make better decisions. But, no matter how clearly you think, there are limits to what data and evidence can tell you. In chapter 17 we conclude the book by exploring some of those limits.

Key Words

- **Internal validity:** An estimate is internally valid if it is a credible estimate of the estimand (e.g., the estimator is unbiased).
- **External validity:** An estimate is externally valid if there is good reason to think the relationship will hold in a context other than the one from which the data is drawn.
- **Strategic adaptation:** Changes in behavior that result from an attempt to avoid the effects of a change in someone else's behavior.
- **Selected sample:** A sample of data that wasn't drawn at random from the population of interest but rather was selected to be studied because it possessed some particular set of characteristics.

Exercises

16.1   People who have already contracted COVID-19 and recovered from it are less likely to contract the disease again because of the immunity they have developed. However, a 2020 study published in the *The Lancet* suggests that those rare individuals who do contract the disease twice appear to experience worse symptoms the second time around. Using the thinking principles from this chapter and the fact that, because of limited testing, not all cases of COVID-19 are detected, provide an account of why this phenomenon might occur even if there is no biological mechanism that makes a second case of COVID-19 worse than a first case. Should this make you skeptical of the claim that people tend to experience worse symptoms when they contract the disease a second time?

16.2   Over the past several decades, high-stakes testing has become an increasingly important part of American education policy. The idea of high-stakes testing is to create consequences for students, teachers, or schools associated with performance on standardized tests. The hope is that this will improve educational achievement by creating incentives for better performance. Standardized test scores are, at best, a partial measure of educational achievement. Give an example of why some policy intervention that leads to an improvement in test scores might nonetheless not be leading to an overall improvement in educational outcomes.

16.3   In a required math sequence at the United States Air Force Academy, students take the same exams but are randomly assigned to different sections taught by different instructors. Scott Carrell and James West show that students assigned to an instructor with better teaching evaluations perform better on the course's exams. But they also show that being assigned to a popular instructor *decreases* students' scores in subsequent math classes. What might explain this puzzling pattern? How does it relate to the problem of failing to measure your mission?

16.4   The way high-stakes testing is implemented in primary and secondary education is typically based on thresholds. A student passes the test if they get a score above some minimal cutoff. And a school is deemed to be meeting standards if the number of students passing the test is above some other minimal threshold.

(a) Think of students in three categories: those who will pass the test no matter what, those who will pass the test if and only if they get teacher attention, and those who will not pass the test no matter what. Which students does high-stakes testing of this form incentivize teachers to focus on?

(b) Derek Neal and Diane Whitmore Schanzenbach studied the implementation of high-stakes testing in the Chicago public schools that we discussed in exercise 1 of chapter 13.

But, unlike in that question, the average effect of high-stakes testing isn't quite what they wanted to know about. They wanted to know whether high-stakes testing affected different kids differently.

To get at this, Neal and Schanzenbach used a difference-in-difference-in-differences design. They started by using the third-grade tests to divide students into ten groups (deciles). They then perform a difference-in-differences analysis separately for each of these deciles. This allows them to learn about the difference in the difference-in-differences estimate of the causal effect of high-stakes testing across kids in the different deciles. Their findings are reflected in the figure.

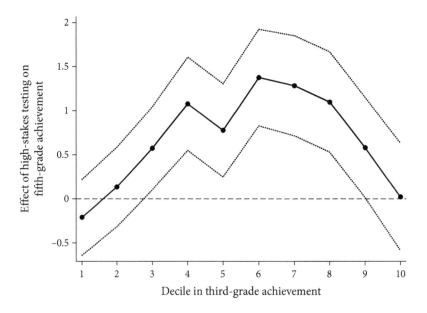

Is this evidence consistent with your answer to part (a) of this exercise? Explain.

(c) In light of this, is a simple difference-in-differences design that uses the percentage of students passing the standardized tests a good way to evaluate whether high-stakes testing achieves its mission? Why or why not?

Readings and References

To read more about hijackings and metal detectors, see

Walter Enders and Todd Sandler. 1993. "The Effectiveness of Anti-Terrorism Policies: A Vector-Autoregression-Intervention Analaysis." *American Political Science Review* 87(4):829–44.

You can learn more about intermediate outcomes in medical research in

Thomas Fleming. 1994. "Surrogate Markets in AIDS and Cancer Trials." *Statistics in Medicine* 13:1423–35.

Thomas R. Fleming and David L. DeMets. 1996. "Surrogate End Points in Clinical Trials: Are We Being Misled?" *Annals of Internal Medicine* 125:605–13.

The study of temperature fluctuations and economic growth is

Marshall Burke, Solomon M. Hsiang, and Edward Miguel. 2015. "Global Non-Linear Effect of Temperature on Economic Production." *Nature* 527(7577):235–39.

For a comparison of the Tamil Nadu and Bangladesh Integrated Nutrition Projects, see

Howard White and Edoardo Masset. 2007. "Assessing Interventions to Improve Child Nutrition: A Theory-Based Impact Evaluation of the Bangladesh Integrated Nutrition Project." *Journal of International Development* 19(5):627–52.

The historical Major League Baseball statistics come from the Baseball Databank at seanlahman.com. The high school baseball statistics are from GameChanger at gc.com.

If you are interested in the history of adaptation to the window tax in England, have a look at

Andrew E. Glantz. 2008. "A Tax on Light and Air: Impact of the Window Duty on Tax Administration and Architecture, 1696–1851." *Penn History Review* 15(2).

Wallace E. Oates and Robert M. Schwab. 2015. "The Window Tax: A Case Study in Excess Burden." *Journal of Economic Perspectives* 29(1):163–80.

On the history of the shift in baseball, you can read

Travis Sawchik. 2017. "We've Reached Peak Shift." FanGraphs. November 9. blogs.fangraphs.com/weve-reached-peak-shift/.

The statistics on drug flows to the United States come from two reports:

United Nations Office on Drugs and Crime. 2010. "The Globalization of Crime: A Transnational Organized Crime Threat Assessment." Chapter 4. https://www.unodc.org/documents/lpo-brazil//noticias/2010/06/TOCTA_Report_2010_low_res.pdf.

Office of National Drug Control Policy. October 2001. "The Price of Illicit Drugs: 1981 through the Second Quarter of 2000." https://obamawhitehouse.archives.gov/sites /default/files/ondcp/policy-and-research/bullet_5.pdf.

The study of math exams and instructor quality in the Air Force Academy discussed in exercise 3 is

Scott E. Carrell and James E. West. 2010. "Does Professor Quality Matter? Evidence from Random Assignment of Students to Professors." *Journal of Political Economy* 118(3):409–32.

The discussion of high-stakes testing and teaching to students on the bubble in exercise 4 is most directly based on

Derek Neal and Diane Whitmore Schanzenbach. 2010. "Left Behind by Design: Proficiency Counts and Test-Based Accountability." *Review of Economics and Statistics* 92(2):263–83.

It also draws on

Bengt Holmstrom and Paul Milgrom. 1991. "Multitask Principal-Agent Analyses: Incentive Contracts, Asset Ownership, and Job Design." *Journal of Law, Economics, and Organization.* 7:24–52.

CHAPTER 17

On the Limits of Quantification

What You'll Learn

- Data and quantitative evidence don't tell us everything we need to know to make decisions.
- Sometimes the relevant evidence is inconclusive or non-existent, but this doesn't necessarily mean the right decision is to do nothing or to stick with the status quo.
- If we're not careful, quantification can have unintended ethical and equity implications.
- The data doesn't tell us what our goals are. Decisions must be made by thinking about both the effects of our actions and also our values.

Introduction

Data and quantitative analysis are full of promise for improving our lives and the world. But they have limits. We've seen many examples of the ways in which we must think clearly to use evidence well. If you mistake correlation for causation, ignore reversion to the mean or the over-comparing/under-reporting problem, try to establish correlation without variation, or pretend the data speak for themselves rather than viewing thinking and data as complements, quantification can lead you astray—resulting in worse, rather than better, decisions. Avoiding these pitfalls is exactly why we've worked so hard together to learn to think clearly about data and evidence.

We want to end by reflecting a bit on some slightly different limits of quantification and evidence-based decision making. These are not limits that come from a lack of clear thinking about some specific piece of quantitative analysis. Rather, they have to do with the realization that, important as evidence is, there is no such thing as a purely evidence-based decision. This is true for at least two reasons.

First, for many critical decisions, credible evidence is limited or even non-existent. But decisions still must be made. Indeed, even the decision not to act is a decision. So, it is important to think clearly about what we do when faced with an absence of evidence.

Second, the right decision can never be identified by evidence alone. Evidence is meant to be a tool used in service of our goals and values. But sometimes it seems like the tail wags the dog—our values become subservient to the dictates of quantification.

This is a dangerous mistake that must be guarded against through vigilance and clear thinking.

Decisions When Evidence Is Limited

There's an old parable that goes something like this. A drunk man is stumbling on the sidewalk looking for his keys under a lamppost. A passerby asks what he's doing, and the man responds, "Looking for my keys." The passerby inquires, "Where did you last see them?" to which the man answers, "I think I dropped them in the park across the street." The passerby reasonably asks the man why he is looking under the lamppost if he dropped his keys in the park across the street, and the man replies, "It's dark over there, I can't possibly find them in the dark! This is where the light is."

Clichéd though it may be, this parable illustrates an important point about quantification. We look where the light is. Not everything can be easily measured or quantified. And so, the analogue of looking where the light is in our data-driven world is narrowing our frame of vision to focus only on those things where quantitative evidence is available.

But such a narrowing poses real risks. First, we might end up simply ignoring crucially important problems because we don't see how to make an evidence-based decision. The fact that quantitative evidence isn't available to answer a question doesn't mean the question is unimportant or safely ignored. Second, the demand for evidence has the potential to create a kind of status quo bias. When someone says, "There's no evidence for that action," they might mean two different things. They could mean that lots of well-powered, well-designed studies have looked and turned up no evidence. But they could also mean that the action has never been studied (or even tried) before, so there is literally no evidence one way or the other. In the former case, it may be reasonable to not take the action. But in the latter case, there is simply no evidence available to guide us. If there are other good reasons to believe acting makes sense, it would be a mistake to let the absence of evidence force you into sticking with the status quo. Let's see some examples of these risks.

Cost-Benefit Analysis and Environmental Regulation

For the U.S. government's Office of Information and Regulatory Affairs (OIRA) within the Office of Management and Budget (OMB), quantitative evidence is the law of the land. A quantitative cost-benefit analysis is required for many new regulatory actions taken by executive agencies, and OIRA can essentially veto such regulations if they are unsatisfied by the evidence.

As we have discussed, not everything can be easily quantified. But, without quantitative evidence, OIRA approval is typically a non-starter. As a result, like the drunk man searching under the lamppost, regulators are forced to focus on those areas where quantification is possible, whether or not those areas are the places most in need of their attention.

Lisa Heinzerling, former head of policy at the Environmental Protection Agency (EPA), describes the bleak terms in which a former EPA staffer put it: "We're constantly asking ourselves not, 'Is this the right thing for environmental protection?' but, 'How can we make this acceptable to OMB?' "

In some sense, of course, requirements to quantify must frustrate regulators. The point of such requirements is to change the kind of regulation we get by changing regulators' behavior. The concern, however, is that these sorts of requirements don't simply prevent the EPA (and other agencies) from creating regulations for which the cure is worse than the disease. They also distort incentives in ways that narrow our field of vision. The mandate to quantify discourages agencies from bothering to work on regulations for which there are good arguments, but for which it is impossible, or too expensive or impractical, to quantify the costs and benefits. For example, in a typical EPA report about the regulation of an environmental contaminant, the regulators might discuss diseases and health conditions that they believe are affected by the contaminant. However, those diseases will only be incorporated into the cost-benefit analysis if we have a way to estimate the effect of the contaminant on disease risk and we have quantitative estimates of the monetary costs of the disease. And if they aren't included in the cost-benefit analysis, they won't have much sway over OIRA's decision making.

A well-known example is the controversy over the EPA's decision to tighten regulations on arsenic in water in the early 2000s. The EPA report making the case for the regulation lists a vast array of diseases that arsenic is believed to increase risk of. These include bladder, kidney, lung, liver, and prostate cancer, as well as a variety of other diseases with cardiovascular, pulmonary, immunological, neurological, and endocrine effects. However, the EPA notes that, because of lack of data, "the quantified benefits" included in their analysis concern only the effects of arsenic on "bladder and lung cancers." The rest of the health benefits of reduced arsenic exposure cannot be quantified. To their credit, the EPA used qualitative information to estimate these broader effects. But because of the demand for quantification, such estimates were easily dismissed in the ensuing controversy.

Floss Your Teeth and Wear a Mask

Two examples slightly closer to home illustrate why there are often good reasons to act, even absent quantitative evidence.

Floss your teeth

For years, Anthony flossed his teeth thoroughly every day because his dentist-spouse told him to do so, and because he believed her when she said that flossing is good for his health. But then, back in 2016, in the name of evidence-based decision making, the *New York Times* published an article entitled "Feeling Guilty about Not Flossing? Maybe There's No Need." It suggested that diligent flossers like Anthony could stop with the nightly flossing hassle.

The article in question cited a meta-analysis of twelve randomized experiments in which researchers compared the effects of brushing and flossing to just brushing. The article reported that the study "found only 'very unreliable' evidence that flossing might reduce plaque." So there you have it. An absence of evidence for flossing.[1]

So why hasn't Anthony stopped flossing? One reason, as discussed in chapter 6, is that failure to reject the null is not proof of the null—that is, absence of evidence is not (conclusive) evidence of absence. Even if we have no statistically significant evidence that flossing reduces plaque, this doesn't mean that flossing has no effect. What if the studies have low statistical power because of small sample sizes or large numbers of

---

[1] The meta-analysis actually does find statistically significant evidence that flossing reduces gingivitis, so the experimental evidence in favor of flossing is perhaps stronger than the article suggests.

noncompliers? Perhaps they wouldn't have detected effects even if flossing does reduce plaque.

Another reason is that researchers haven't studied all of the outcomes of interest. For instance, the authors of the meta-analysis point out that none of the experiments assess longer-term effects, nor do they study a variety of important dental outcomes like tooth decay, tartar, or gum separation.

But even these limitations of the quantitative studies aren't the whole story. As with many decisions, while we lack sufficient quantitative evidence to answer all of our questions about the effects of flossing, there are non-quantitative arguments that are important to consider. Dentists provide compelling biological and mechanistic accounts of why they believe flossing is beneficial. And so, despite what the contrarian data journalists might say, we're pretty comfortable with the decision to floss despite the fact that the quantitative evidence isn't conclusive. There are good reasons to believe that flossing is beneficial, even absent a slam-dunk empirical study.

Wear a mask

At the time of this writing, our society is having a similar debate about the effects of wearing masks in the midst of the COVID-19 global pandemic. Just as with flossing, there are few compelling, high-powered experiments demonstrating that masks and facial coverings reduce virus transmission. There are some observational studies that are subject to the concerns about confounders raised in chapter 9. Some of these studies focus only on selected samples of people who come into health care facilities with symptoms, which, as discussed in chapter 16, also creates problems. As with flossing, when researchers try to conduct a randomized experiment, many of the people assigned to treatment will fail to comply, making it more difficult to assess the effectiveness of wearing masks. And furthermore, we probably need a very large sample size to obtain a reasonably precise estimate of the effect of masks or flossing.

Given the lack of definitive evidence on masks, many people—including Donald Trump and Mike Pence, then president and vice president of the United States—decided to forgo the hassle. Such skeptics sometimes make arguments like "There is no evidence that wearing a mask matters." But as with flossing, there are good theoretical and biological reasons to think that masks are effective. We know that coronavirus and many other viruses are transmitted through respiratory particles, and we have good physical evidence that masks mitigate the flow of some of these particles. Studies also find that people who wear masks are less likely to touch their eyes, nose, and mouth, a second reason why masks likely mitigate transmission.

Of course, we aren't certain that we know the right answer, and we hope further studies will improve our understanding of the effects of wearing masks. But the lack of definitive, quantitative evidence in favor of one decision is not a compelling reason to make a different decision—especially if there is also no clear evidence in favor of that different decision.

Good decision makers use quantitative evidence, but they acknowledge that the quantitative evidence only tells them so much. They don't ignore certain considerations just because we lack good quantitative estimates for those factors. They use the best available theory and data to form their beliefs, and they make the best decision they can, given their goals, values, and those potentially imperfect and uncertain beliefs.

That last sentence pointed to another important thought about evidence-based decision making. No matter how good the data analysis, evidence alone cannot tell you how to act. For that, you need to also think about your goals and values. We end the book with some reflections on the ways in which quantification and those values interact.

Quantification and Values

Quantitative evidence should help us make better decisions that advance our goals and values. But if we aren't careful, matters can get turned around—our goals and values can be shaped by the mandate to quantify, rather than quantitative evidence serving our goals and values.

We are going to think about two ways this can happen. The first is that quantitative tools can sometimes sneak values into our decision making that we don't agree with, without our noticing. The second is that the desire to quantify can push us to embrace values that we might otherwise reject.

How Quantitative Tools Sneak in Values

One risk of quantification, especially in an age when machine learning and algorithmic decision making are increasingly prevalent, is that objectionable values will creep into decisions without our noticing. For instance, an algorithm may exhibit racial or gender bias, even if no data on race or gender were used to create the algorithm. This raises important questions about equity, fairness, and justice that deserve our attention.

Predictive machine learning algorithms get used for all sorts of tasks in the contemporary world. Job placement websites use such algorithms to match job seekers to employers. Banks use them to evaluate credit worthiness. Social media platforms use them to decide what content and advertisements to feed to users. And judges use them to inform criminal sentencing decisions.

How can these algorithms end up yielding ethically troubling results? Machine learning algorithms are, more or less, just fancy ways of using correlations to make predictions. An algorithm that is race- or gender-blind, in the sense of not having access to data on race or gender, could nonetheless end up making predictions that treat people with different racial or gender identities differently. This could happen, for example, if the algorithm has access to data on variables that are correlated with race or if some of the inputs of the algorithm are themselves subject to bias. We already saw an instance of this kind of problem in chapter 2, when we discussed how using the correlation between Yelp reviews and health code violations to target inspections would sneak in racial bias. But let's consider another example.

Algorithms and racial bias in health care

In the United States, large health care providers have special programs designed to coordinate the care of people with complex health needs. Such programs are expensive. So the providers only want to enroll people who are likely to have the greatest care needs. To try to predict who those patients are, they use machine learning algorithms.

There is a strong positive correlation between health care costs and health care needs because sicker patients tend to receive more and more expensive treatment. And health care costs are easier to measure accurately than health care needs. In this study, the algorithm was asked to predict health care costs. In order to do so, in addition to data on health care costs, it was fed data on patients' past insurance claims, medical diagnoses, and medications. Importantly, the algorithm specifically did not receive any information about race.

A simple way to think about how this might work is by analogy to regression. Suppose we had data on lots of patients' health care costs in year t and their insurance claims, diagnoses and procedures, and medications in year $t-1$. We could run the following regression:

$$\text{Costs}_t = \beta_0 + \beta_1 \cdot \text{Insurance Claims}_{t-1} + \beta_2 \cdot \text{Diagnoses and Procedures}_{t-1}$$
$$+ \beta_3 \cdot \text{Medications}_{t-1}$$

Doing so would give us estimated OLS coefficients $\hat{\beta}_0$ through $\hat{\beta}_3$.

When a new patient, i, comes along, we can predict that patient's future health care costs using this algorithm. We feed that new patient's particular values for insurance claims, diagnoses and procedures, and medications into our regression equation to get

$$\text{Predicted Costs}_i = \hat{\beta}_0 + \hat{\beta}_1 \cdot \text{Insurance Claims}_i + \hat{\beta}_2 \cdot \text{Diagnoses and Procedures}_i$$
$$+ \hat{\beta}_3 \cdot \text{Medications}_i$$

This is more or less what a predictive machine learning algorithm is doing, but the algorithm's goal is typically somewhat different than minimizing mean squared error, and it considers more complex functions of the variables than does a linear regression.

A 2019 paper in *Science* describes a health care provider using such predicted values to sort patients. Patients with a score above some high threshold were immediately enrolled in the special program. Patients with a score above a lower threshold were referred to a physician for further screening.

Even though the predictive algorithm was race-blind, it turned out to systematically under-estimate how sick Black patients were relative to White patients. This is illustrated in figure 17.1. Health care needs, as predicted by the algorithm, are on the horizontal axis. A measure of active chronic health conditions, called a *comorbidity score*, is on the vertical axis. This is meant to be a measure of true health care needs. As you can see, for any given level of predicted health care needs, Black patients turn out to be sicker than White patients, on average. Thus, Black patients were systematically less likely to be enrolled in the special program than White patients of similar health.

What might be going on such that this race-blind algorithm is nonetheless giving racially biased predictions? One possibility is an omitted variable. That is, perhaps even conditional on past insurance claims, diagnoses and procedures, and medications, Black patients tend to be sicker than White patients for reasons not observed in the data. This could result in the algorithm systematically under-estimating the health needs of Black patients and over-estimating the health needs of White patients.

In this case, however, it seems something slightly different is going on. The health care provider had the algorithm predict health care costs because costs are easily measured and are highly correlated with health care needs. But this decision proved problematic. A systematic fact about the U.S. health care system is that less money is spent on Black patients on average than is spent on similarly sick White patients.[2]

---

[2] The Readings and References section will point you to a review article documenting the many ways in which there is bias and discrimination against Black patients in U.S. health care.

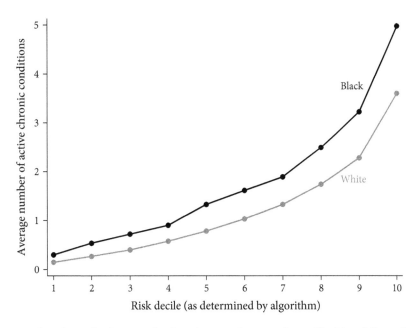

Figure 17.1. The relationship between the algorithmic prediction and actual health is different for Black and White patients.

This means using cost as a proxy for health care needs introduces racial bias into the supposedly race-blind algorithm. The algorithm correctly predicts that health care costs for a Black patient will be lower than for a White patient with similar characteristics (claims, diagnoses and procedures, medications). And that makes it look as though Black patients are healthier than equally sick White patients. Using the same inputs, but reformulating the algorithm to predict a measure of actual health rather than health-care costs, the authors of the *Science* article were able to eliminate the racial bias.

This example demonstrates how using quantitative tools can sneak values into our decision making that we might find objectionable. As the world becomes increasingly quantitative, it takes clear thinking and constant vigilance to make sure that our decisions are informed by data, but that the values driving those decisions are our own.

This brings us to our next topic, the ways in which quantification can shape the values that we think of as our own in potentially troubling ways.

How Quantification Shapes Our Values

Moral and political philosophers describe a rich variety of ethical concerns that one might consider when evaluating the rightness or wrongness of a decision. For instance, there are good and convincing arguments for various rights and duties, such as the right to control one's own body or the duty not to forcibly coerce one's fellow humans. A reasonable person might maintain that good policy or good actions must respect, or even promote, such rights and duties, even if violating them would lead to higher total material well-being in the world. This, for instance, is a position often held by principled opponents of the death penalty or torture or stem-cell research.

There are also good and convincing arguments for having concerns not only with total well-being but with the distribution of well-being. A reasonable person might, for instance, be prepared to accept lower total well-being in society in exchange for greater equality.

But most quantitative policy analysis is rooted in *welfarism,* the view that policies should be evaluated on the basis of their implications for human well-being. Moreover, one welfarist standard predominates over all others: *utilitarianism*—the view that policies should be evaluated on the basis of their implications for the sum total of human well-being, regardless of its distribution. And not just utilitarianism, but what we might call *crass utilitarianism*—one that defines well-being almost entirely in terms of material costs and benefits such as economic prosperity, health, and other factors that are (relatively) easy to quantify by assigning a monetary value.

An ethical position consistent with quantifying consequences is, in principle, quite flexible; it need not be crassly utilitarian. We can put a value on various non-material factors such as rights, duties, responsibility, dignity, or what have you. Moreover, once you know the quantitative effects of a policy on people's well-being, you can introduce all sorts of equity considerations into policy evaluation. We could, for example, after quantifying all the effects, define the best policy as the one that maximizes total well-being, subject to the constraint that everyone is above some minimal threshold.

What crass utilitarianism has going for it over all other normative frameworks—even other forms of welfarism—is that it lends itself easily to quantitative analysis. It is hard to figure out how to quantify the value of rights and duties or how to weigh equity considerations. It is much more straightforward—both conceptually and practically—to quantify material costs and benefits and then just add and subtract to figure out whether a policy or action is good or bad.

Indeed, crass utilitarianism is so easy to work with that it has become a part of the standard assumptions in the background of many quantitative analyses, especially in discussions of public policy. The process of trying to maximize net well-being—ignoring questions of rights, duties, responsibilities, equity, dignity, and so on—is often so ingrained in our practice and thought that we hardly even notice we are doing it. We simply take for granted that a good policy is one that maximizes benefits minus costs.

Notice what this means. The goals and values we pursue are shaped in a deep way by the dictates of quantification. We don't quantify because we are utilitarians. We are utilitarians because we quantify.

What's the problem with allowing a materialist utilitarianism to define our goals? In partial answer, we'd like to tell you a story.

Ethan once attended an academic presentation on the effects of removing children from abusive homes and putting them into foster care. The presenter found that children from abusive homes are, on average, better off in foster care. Moreover, the benefits for the children appear to exceed the costs of providing foster care. Therefore, the researcher concluded that we should remove kids from these abusive homes.

This seems like a great example of data leading to better policy decisions. We can quantify the benefits to children and choose policies that make them better off. We can even show that the benefits to the children exceed the dollar costs to society. So it looks like a clear win. Fantastic.

One of the attendees, someone who has held several senior positions in government, objected. The main critique was that the researcher had not estimated all of the relevant costs and benefits to make a policy recommendation. Specifically, what if the abusive parents derive benefits from keeping their children (and presumably, continuing to abuse them)? If the value to them of keeping the kids is big enough, then might that not reverse the conclusions of the cost-benefit analysis?

Now, you might think that a reasonable response to this line of questioning would be something like, "Well, if one were an unflinching utilitarian that would be right. But there are other values, and personally, I think we ought not give a damn about whether abusive parents want to keep their children. We should focus on what's best for the kids and for the rest of society." But that, in fact, was not the presenter's response. Instead, the presenter conceded the point, acknowledging that he really couldn't say whether or not taking kids out of abusive environments was good policy without knowing how it affected those kids' parents.

Or consider another example. In the early 1990s, the chief economist of the World Bank, Larry Summers—former president of Harvard, President Obama's chief economic advisor, and President Clinton's treasury secretary—circulated a memo written by his staff. It contained the following thought:

> Shouldn't the World Bank be encouraging MORE migration of the dirty industries to the LDCs [Less Developed Countries]?. . . The costs of health impairing pollution depends on the foregone earnings from increased morbidity and mortality. From this point of view a given amount of health impairing pollution should be done in the country with the lowest cost, which will be the country with the lowest wages. I think the economic logic behind dumping a load of toxic waste in the lowest wage country is impeccable and we should face up to that.

That toxic dumping in low-wage countries has "impeccable economic logic" is an interesting assertion. Here are three claims, each of which seems to us correct:

1. It is probably the case that the average willingness to pay for avoiding a little more toxic waste is higher in rich countries than in poor countries.
2. Hence, moving some toxic pollution from rich countries to poor countries will increase net material well-being in the world.
3. If these are the only costs and benefits (e.g., we don't count allowing rich countries not to take responsibility for their own actions as a direct cost) and we are utilitarians, then doing so is good policy.

To call that chain of arguments "economic logic" is troubling, for at least the last step has nothing to do with economics; it has to do with values. And the assumption in the first step that it makes sense to value outcomes based on willingness to pay also builds in potentially troubling normative priorities. We suspect the value of a marginal dollar is lower for richer people. So richer people have a higher willingness to pay than poorer people for the same change in well-being, simply because they value money differently. This means that if we evaluate costs and benefits based on people's willingness to pay, we are implicitly assuming the well-being of the rich is more important than the well-being of the poor.

Despite the ubiquity of these kinds of issues, at times, quantitative analysts seem to lose sight of the fact that making decisions by comparing such measures of material costs and benefits isn't value-free. Michael Greenstone, a prominent energy and environmental economist, makes the issue particularly clear in an argument he offers for using cost-benefit analysis for policy decision making:

> I think once we leave cost benefit analysis, then things start to bleed in often, not always, but often into moral decisions. And the deep problem, from my perspective, about moral-based decision making on a lot of these matters is that your morals aren't my morals, and a third person's morals are different than both of

our morals. And then there's really no bounds on decision making...I have no confidence that what's good for all of society will be the result.

Greenstone is making an important point. By quantifying costs and benefits we put bounds on decision making. Such constraints can be very valuable. But he pushes the argument too far when he suggests that cost-benefit analysis takes subjective moral opinions out of the equation or that there is some objective scientific way to judge what's good for society without first making a set of value judgments that cannot be determined by evidence alone.

Of course, we can think of lots of reasons that, even if it passes a cost-benefit test, shifting toxic waste from rich to poor countries doesn't seem like good policy. Maybe we value fairness, justice, and economic mobility, such that we don't think dumping toxic waste on the poorest countries is a good idea. Maybe we think rich countries should take responsibility for their own actions. Maybe we don't want to live in the kind of world where rich people can simply pay for the right not to be affected by the pollution that is a byproduct of the economic activity from which they benefited. Maybe we think that the fact that poor people are less willing to pay to avoid toxic waste should be interpreted to imply not that their lives are less valuable than rich people's but that money is the wrong way to measure worth. Greenstone's point is right—reasonable people may disagree on all of these moral judgments. But reasonable people may also disagree on whether maximizing benefits net of costs justifies shipping waste from rich to poor countries. We must not let the fact that costs and benefits measured in terms of willingness to pay are relatively straightforward to quantify, while some other values are harder to quantify, fool us into thinking that evaluating things this way is objective science, while everything else is subjective value judgments. It all involves value judgments.

To be clear, we don't mean to suggest that there are no arguments in favor of the views expressed in Summers's memo. Suppose Summers is correct that transferring toxic waste from the rich to the poor will increase net material well-being. Then the rich might be able to more than compensate the poor for taking the toxic waste, leaving both parties better off as a result of a trade. Hence, if we have the technological ability and political will to get the poor to take the toxic waste and to get the rich to pay them for doing so, we might be able to create a win-win situation.

But of course, there are lots of other moral arguments to consider as well. In our view, it should matter how this decision is made. We would think very differently about poor countries agreeing to accept toxic waste in exchange for compensation than we would about an economist in a rich country making the decision and telling the poor country that they're better off. But Summers's memo doesn't even express concern about whether the poor countries will be compensated or agree to this arrangement. The crass utilitarian argument, on its own, appears to suffice. To his credit, in later discussions of the toxic waste memo, Summers expressed a different view. For instance, in a 1998 interview with the *New Yorker* he said, "The basic sentiment that it is good to ship toxic wastes to poor countries is obviously all wrong. Are there real issues about trade-offs between growth and the environment? Sure. But the way the thoughts were expressed wasn't constructive in any sense."

The cases of abused children and toxic dumping are interesting for several reasons. Quantification often pushes us toward crass utilitarianism, which can lead to ruthless and absurd conclusions. But the discipline of quantification also really does teach us something. For many people, the rich dumping their toxic waste onto the poor might not appear to be a policy idea with anything to recommend it. The exercise of quantifying and comparing costs and benefits forces us to see that there is a serious argument to be made for this policy (at least the version of it that involves consent and compensation), even if ultimately some of us come down on the other side.

In both cases, we believe we can (and should) realize some of the benefits of quantification—precision, weighing trade-offs, contestability. But both cases also illustrate a key concern. Rights, dignity, and fairness are hard to quantify. Material costs and benefits are easier. And so, in practice, the desire for quantitative evidence pushes us toward a focus on the kind of highly objectionable, crass, materialist utilitarianism that characterizes these stories. If we are to use quantitative analysis for good, we must strive toward a practice in which data and quantitative tools help us estimate important quantities without distorting the goals and values against which we evaluate our choices.

Think Clearly and Help Others Do So Too

We'd like to conclude by urging you to use the tools and skills you've learned for good. Much of this book was about how thinking clearly can help you spot when someone is intentionally or accidentally misleading you with data. But a cynical reader could turn that noble mission on its head, using these tools as a recipe for misleading others who haven't learned to think as clearly. Unless sales of this book really go through the roof, most people you interact with won't notice if you assert correlation without variation, claim evidence for a causal relationship from a correlation that you know is confounded, or keep making comparisons until you find the conclusion you want and then only report that one. Please don't do that! Think about the larger quest for truth, and take your newfound responsibility as a savvy quantitative thinker seriously. Be transparent about the strengths and weaknesses of the evidence you bring to bear, whether that is evidence you created through your own analysis or read about in someone else's. In so doing, you can help others, as well as yourself, think clearly with data.

But, most importantly, take a moment to appreciate how hard you have worked and how far we have come together. You are now a member of a small but growing group of people in the world who can think clearly about the problem of selecting on the dependent variable, the difference between statistical and substantive significance, reversion to the mean, publication bias, the sources of cosmic habituation, the relationship between correlation and causation, foundational ideas about research design, and so much more. These are fundamental conceptual understandings that will serve you well forever, even if you never run another regression. Because we all now live in a time in which thinking clearly with and about data is absolutely essential for anyone who wants to understand the world and make it a better place.

Exercises

17.1   Your friend Andy has noticed that every time he eats pancakes for breakfast, he does well on his exams. Therefore, he has decided that his diet will, from here on out, consist entirely of pancakes. On the basis of the lessons from the entire book, list at least four things wrong with your friend's reasoning.

17.2   You are the mayor of a major city, and your staff presents you with a plan to provide more amenities to low-income neighborhoods. They tell you that their plan will cost $100 million, but they estimate that it will provide $200 million of economic benefits, so it's a no-brainer. What questions would you want to ask your staff before deciding to proceed with the plan?

17.3   Think of a decision in your life that you've made largely without the help of quantitative evidence (such as Anthony deciding to floss despite there being few compelling, quantitative studies on the topic). What factors led you to make the decision you did? Can you propose a quantitative study that would provide more compelling evidence? What would the evidence have to look like in order for you to change your decision?

Readings and References

You can read the EPA's report on the arsenic regulation, including the long list of non-quantifiable health impacts, in the federal register at https://www.govinfo.gov/content/pkg/FR-2001-01-22/pdf/01-1668.pdf.

The meta-analysis on the effects of flossing is

Dario Sambunjak, Jason W. Nickerson, Tina Poklepovic, Trevor M. Johnson, Pauline Imai, Peter Tugwell, and Helen V. Worthington. 2011. "Flossing for the Management of Periodontal Diseases and Dental Caries in Adults." Cochrane Database of Systemic Reviews, Issue 12. doi.org/10.1002/14651858.CD008829.pub2.

This research team updated the meta-analysis, adding three more experiments on flossing in 2019. See

Helen V. Worthington, Laura MacDonald, Tina Poklepovic Pericic, Dario Sambunjak, Trevor M. Johnson, Pauline Imai, and Janet E. Clarkson. 2019. "Home Use of Interdental Cleaning Devices, in Addition to Toothbrushing, for Preventing and Controlling Periodontal Diseases and Dental Caries." Cochrane Database of Systemic Reviews, Issue 4. doi.org/10.1002/14651858.CD012018.pub2.

For some empirical evidence on mask wearing and the spread of particulates, see

Sima Asadi, Christopher D. Cappa, Santiago Barreda, Anthony S. Wexler, Nicole M. Bouvier, and William D. Ristenparth. 2020. "Efficacy of Masks and Face Coverings in Controlling Outward Aerosol Particle Emission from Expiratory Activities." *Scientific Reports* 10, Article 15665. doi.org/10.1038/s41598-020-72798-7.

For evidence on the relationship between wearing a mask and touching your face, see

Yong-Jian Chen, Gang Qin, Jie Chen, Jian-Liang Xu, Ding-Yun Feng, Xiang-Yuan Wu, and Xing Li. 2020. "Comparison of Face-Touching Behaviors Before and During the Coronavirus Disease 2019 Pandemic." *JAMA Network Open* 3(7).

Tiffany L. Lucas, Rachel Mustain, and Robert E. Goldsby. "Frequency of Face Touching with and without a Mask in Pediatric Hematology/Oncology Health Care Professionals." *Pediatric Blood & Cancer* 67(9).

For a discussion of how race relates to disparate health outcomes in the United States, see

David Cutler, Adriana Lleras-Muney, and Tom Vogl. 2011. "Socioeconomic Status and Health: Dimensions and Mechanisms." *The Oxford Handbook of Health Economics*, Sherry Glied and Peter C. Smith, eds. Oxford University Press.

We referenced this study in our discussion of how quantitative tools can sneak in values:

Ziad Obermeyer, Brian Powers, Christine Vogeli, and Sendhil Mullainathan. 2019. "Dissecting Racial Bias in an Algorithm Used to Manage the Health of Populations." *Science* 366(6464):447–53.

You can find the quotation from Summers and a discussion of the toxic waste memo here:

John Cassid. 1998. "The Triumphalist." *The New Yorker*. July 6.

The quotation from Michael Greenstone is from this podcast:

"The Value of a Life" (episode 1). *Pandemic Economics*. Becker Friedman Institute. April 23, 2020. bfi.uchicago.edu/podcast/pandemic-economics-01.

The discussion of how quantification can shape our moral values draws heavily on

Ethan Bueno de Mesquita. 2019. "The Perils of Quantification." *The Boston Review*. March 11. https://bostonreview.net/forum/economics-after-neoliberalism/ethan -bueno-de-mesquita-perils-quantification.

Index

Note: Page numbers in italic type indicate figures or tables.

www.ingramcontent.com/pod-product-compliance
Ingram Content Group UK Ltd.
Pitfield, Milton Keynes, MK11 3LW, UK
UKHW010650230225
455446UK00009B/105